'*Among the Believers,* published 17 years ago, [was] a brilliantly subtle, cool and despairing assessment of Islam at the moment when it trembled with revolutionary passion. Now Naipaul has revisited these parts, and has written a finer, more profound, yet still bleaker book . . . *Beyond Belief* is the most achieved instance yet of a form refined by Naipaul since his turn away from the novel . . . He is a marvellous impresario of tales'   Sunil Khilnani, *Sunday Telegraph*

'Extraordinary . . . presents a haunting and tragic view of the world. Naipaul, the manager of narrative, leaves no doubt that Islamic fundamentalism results from a failure of intellect. He offers hope, though, through his own example as a man of reason and compassion . . . Nobody is so humble that he has no story. The truth is simple, but only a great writer could have brought it out in this way, so simply' David Pryce-Jones, *Literary Review*

'Fascinating and beautiful . . . a series of profound meditations on societies and individuals in the throes of wrenching change . . . jewel-like individual profiles are set in a filigree-work of acute physical, cultural, historical and psychological detail . . . deeply moving'   Anatol Lieven, *Financial Times*

'Painstaking and meticulous . . . exquisite descriptive skill'   Anita Desai, *The Times*

'No other writer has his moral courage, his willingness to travel to find a subject, to listen and report, without prescription, the opinions of so-called ordinary people . . . In the canon of postwar British fiction, Naipaul is without peer'   Jason Cowley, *The Times*

'Fascinating'   *Mail on Sunday*

A

V. S. Naipaul was born, of Indian ancestry, in Trinidad in 1932. He came to England in 1950. He spent four years at University College, Oxford, and began to write, in London, in 1954. He has pursued no other profession. His works of fiction comprise: *The Mystic Masseur* (1957, John Llewellyn Rhys Memorial Prize), *The Suffrage of Elvira* (1958), *Miguel Street* (1959; Somerset Maugham Award), *A House for Mr Biswas* (1961), *Mr Stone and the Knights Companion* (1963; Hawthornden Prize), *The Mimic Men* (1967; W. H. Smith Award), *A Flag on the Island* (1967), a collection of short stories. In 1971 he was awarded the Booker Prize for *In a Free State*; since then he has published four novels: *Guerrillas* (1975), *A Bend in the River* (1979), *The Enigma of Arrival* (1987) and *A Way in the World* (1994).

In 1960 he began to travel. *The Middle Passage* (1962) records his impressions of colonial society in the West Indies and South America. *An Area of Darkness* (1964), *India: A Wounded Civilization* (1977) and *India: A Million Mutinies Now* (1990) form his acclaimed 'Indian Trilogy'. *The Loss of El Dorado*, a masterly study of New World history, was published in 1969, and a selection of his longer essays, *The Overcrowded Barracoon*, appeared in 1972. *The Return of Eva Perón* (with *The Killings in Trinidad*) (1980) derives from experiences of travel in Argentina, Trinidad and the Congo. *Finding the Centre* (1984) is distinguished by the author's narrative on his emergence as a writer, 'Prologue to an Autobiography'.

In 1981, V. S. Naipaul's *Among the Believers: An Islamic Journey* was published to universal acclaim. In 1995, he returned to Indonesia, Iran, Pakistan and Malaysia. *Beyond Belief* is his account of those travels.

Letters Between A Father and Son, a collection of correspondence between V. S. Naipaul and his family from 1950–57, was published in 1999.

V. S. Naipaul received a Knighthood in the 1990 New Year's Honours' List for services to Literature; in 1993, he was the first recipient of the David Cohen British Literature Prize.

Also by V. S. Naipaul

Non-fiction

India: A Million Mutinies Now
A Turn in the South
Finding the Centre
Among the Believers
The Return of Eva Perón (*with* The Killings in Trinidad)
India: A Wounded Civilization
The Overcrowded Barracoon
The Loss of El Dorado
An Area of Darkness
The Middle Passage
Letters Between A Father and Son

Fiction

A Way in the World
The Enigma of Arrival
A Bend in the River
Guerrillas
In a Free State
The Mimic Men
A Flag on the Island
Mr Stone and the Knights Companion
A House for Mr Biswas
Miguel Street
The Suffrage of Elvira
The Mystic Masseur

BEYOND BELIEF

Islamic Excursions Among the Converted Peoples

V. S. Naipaul

An *Abacus* Book

First published in Great Britain by
Little, Brown and Company 1998
First published by Abacus 1999
Reprinted in 2000, 2001, 2002

A CIP catalogue record for this book
is available from the British Library.

ISBN 0 349 11010 7

Set in Bembo by M Rules
Printed and bound in Great Britain by
Clays Ltd, St Ives plc

Abacus
An imprint of
Time Warner Books UK
Brettenham House
Lancaster Place
London WC2E 7EN

www.TimeWarnerBooks.co.uk

For
Nadira Khannum Alvi

Contents

III PAKISTAN
Dropping off the Map

IV MALAYSIAN POSTSCRIPT
Raising the Coconut Shell

Prologue

THIS IS a book about people. It is not a book of opinion. It is a book of stories. The stories were collected during five months of travel in 1995 in four non-Arab Muslim countries – Indonesia, Iran, Pakistan, Malaysia. So there is a context and a theme.

Islam is in its origins an Arab religion. Everyone not an Arab who is a Muslim is a convert. Islam is not simply a matter of conscience or private belief. It makes imperial demands. A convert's world view alters. His holy places are in Arab lands; his sacred language is Arabic. His idea of history alters. He rejects his own; he becomes, whether he likes it or not, a part of the Arab story. The convert has to turn away from everything that is his. The disturbance for societies is immense, and even after a thousand years can remain unresolved; the turning away has to be done again and again. People develop fantasies about who and what they are; and in the Islam of converted countries there is an element of neurosis and nihilism. These countries can be easily set on the boil.

This book is a follow-up to a book I published seventeen years ago, *Among the Believers*, about a journey to the same four countries. When I started on that journey in 1979 I knew almost nothing about Islam – it is the best way to start on a venture – and that first book was an exploration of the details of the faith and what looked like its capacity for revolution. The theme of conversion was always there; but I didn't see it as clearly as I saw it on this second journey.

Beyond Belief adds to the earlier book, takes the story on. It also moves in a different way. It is less of a travel book; the writer is less present, less of an inquirer. He is in the background, trusting to his instinct, a discoverer of people, a finder-out of stories. These stories, opening out one from the other, make their own pattern and define each country and its promptings; and the four sections of the book make a whole.

I began my writing career as a fiction writer, a manager of narrative; at that time I thought it the highest thing to be. When I was asked – nearly forty years ago – to travel about certain colonial territories in South America and the Caribbean and to write a book, I was delighted to do the travelling – taking small aeroplanes to strange places, going up South American rivers – but then I wasn't sure how to write the book, how to make a pattern of what I was doing. That first time I got away with autobiography and landscape. It was years before I saw that the most important thing about travel, for the writer, was the people he found himself among.

So in these travel books or cultural explorations of mine the writer as traveller steadily retreats; the people of the country come to the front; and I become again what I was at the beginning: a manager of narrative. In the nineteenth century the invented story was used to do things that other literary forms – the poem, the essay – couldn't easily do: to give news about a changing society, to describe mental states. I find it strange that the travel form – in the beginning so far away from my own instincts – should have taken me back there, to looking for the story; though it would have undone the point of the book if the narratives were falsified or forced. There are complexities enough in these stories. They are the point of the book; the reader should not look for 'conclusions'.

It may be asked if different people and different stories in any section of the book would have created or suggested another kind of country. I think not: the train has many coaches, and different classes, but it passes through the same landscape. People are responding to the same political or religious and cultural pressures. The writer has only to listen very carefully and with a clear heart to what people say to him, and ask the next question, and the next.

There is another way of considering the theme of conversion. It can be seen as a kind of crossover from old beliefs, earth religions, the cults of rulers and local deities, to the revealed religions – Christianity and Islam principally – with their larger philosophical and humanitarian and social concerns. Hindus say that Hinduism is less coercive and more 'spiritual'; and they are right. But Gandhi got his social ideas from Christianity.

The crossover from the classical world to Christianity is now history. It is not easy, reading the texts, imaginatively to enter the long disputes and anguishes of that crossover. But in some of the cultures described in this book the crossover to Islam – and sometimes Christianity – is still going on. It is the extra drama in the background, like a cultural big bang, the steady grinding down of the old world.

I

INDONESIA

The Flight of the N-250

1

The Man of the Moment

IMADUDDIN WAS a lecturer in electrical engineering at the Bandung Institute of Technology. He was also an Islamic preacher. So in the 1960s and 1970s he was unusual: a man of science, one of the few in independent Indonesia, and at the same time a dedicated man of the faith. He could draw the student crowds to the Salman mosque in the grounds of the Bandung Institute.

He worried the authorities. And when, on the last day of 1979, I went to Bandung to see him, driving up through the afternoon along the crowded smoky road from coastal Jakarta to the cooler plateau where Bandung was, I found that he was a man more or less on the run. He had not long before finished fourteen months in jail as a political prisoner. He still had his little staff house at the Bandung Institute, but he was not allowed to lecture there. And though he was still being defiant, giving his courses in Islamic 'mental training' to small groups of middle-class young people – holiday groups, really – he was, at the age of forty-eight, getting ready to go abroad.

He was to spend many years abroad. But then his fortunes changed. And this time I found – going back to Indonesia more than fifteen years after that meeting with him in Bandung – that Imaduddin had money and was famous. He had an Islamic Sunday morning television programme. He had a Mercedes and a driver, a reasonable house in a reasonable part of Jakarta, and he was talking of moving to something a little better. The very mixture of science and Islam that had made him suspect to the authorities in the late 1970s now made him desirable, the model of the Indonesian new man, and had taken him up to the heights, had taken him very nearly to the fount of power.

He had become close to Habibie, the minister for research and technology; and Habibie was closer than anyone else in the government to President Suharto, who had ruled for thirty years and was generally presented as the father of the nation.

Habibie was an aeronautical man and his admirers said he was a prodigy. He was a man with a grand idea. It was that Indonesia should under his guidance build, or at any rate design, its own aeroplanes. The idea behind the idea – as I had read in some newspapers – was that such a venture wouldn't only deliver aeroplanes. It would also give many thousands of people a high and varied technological training; out of this would come an Indonesian industrial revolution. Over nineteen years almost a billion and a half dollars – according to the *Wall Street Journal* – had been given to Habibie's aerospace organisation. One kind of aeroplane had been built, the CN235, in collaboration with a Spanish company; it hadn't been commercially successful. But now something more exciting was about to fly, the N-250, a fifty-seat commuter turboprop, wholly designed by Habibie's organisation.

The aircraft's inaugural flight was to be in time for the fiftieth anniversary of Indonesia's independence, on 17 August, for which, for weeks before, the streets of Jakarta and other towns had been strung with the same kind of coloured lights and hung with flags and banners. Against this background of celebration – which was like the state's gift to the people – the *Jakarta Post*, like a lecturer handling the beginners' class, one day took its readers through stage by stage of the N-250's trials: the taxi-ing at the low speed, to check ground manoeuvring; then at medium speed, to check wing and tail and brake systems; and then at high speed, to make sure that the N-250 could fly just above the ground for five or six minutes.

Four days before the inaugural flight a generator shaft (whatever that was) broke down during a medium-speed taxi. A replacement was, however, to hand; and on the appointed day the N-250 flew for an hour at 10,000 feet. The front page of the *Jakarta Post* showed President Suharto applauding and Habibie embracing a smiling Mrs Suharto. Plans were announced for a mid-range jet, the N-2130, for March 2004. It was going to cost two billion dollars. Since this programme stretched far into the future, Habibie's 32-year-old son Ilham, who had done an apprenticeship course at Boeing, was going to be in charge.

Three weeks later, after the climax of the fiftieth-anniversary independence celebrations: a great French-produced firework display, and in an atmosphere of national glory, Habibie proposed that August 10, the day on which the N-250 flew, should be observed as National Technological Reawakening Day. He made the proposal at the Twelfth Islam Unity Conference. Because there was another side to Habibie: he was a devout Muslim and a passionate defender of the faith. He was chairman of a new body, the aggressively named Association of Muslim Intellectuals. And when he told the Islam Unity Conference that mastery of science and technology had to be coupled with stronger faith in Allah, it was accepted that he was speaking with both religious and secular authority.

If it wasn't absolutely certain how the designing and building of aeroplanes with imported components could lead to a general technological or scientific breakthrough; so, too, it wasn't absolutely clear how Islam had been ennobled by the success of the N-250, and the hundreds of millions that had gone to serve one man's particular talent or interest.

But this was precisely where Imaduddin's faith – as scientist and believer – had coincided with Habibie's, where the careers of the two men had crossed, and Imaduddin had been taken up by his new patron to the sky of presidential favour.

Imaduddin, some time after his return from exile, had been one of the principal early movers behind the Association of Muslim Intellectuals. And now he served Habibie in a special way. Habibie, or his ministry, had sent very many students to study abroad. It was Imaduddin's duty – as scientist and preacher – regularly to visit these students at their foreign universities, to remind them of their faith and where their loyalties should lie. In 1979, when he had been on the run, the Islamic mental training courses he had been doing at Bandung hadn't been approved of by the government, nervous of the beginnings of any populist movement it couldn't control. Now – in an extraordinary reversal – these mental training courses of Imaduddin's, or something like them, were being used by the government to win the support of the important new intelligentsia or technocracy that Habibie was creating.

It was out of his new freedom and security, the new closeness to power, which to Imaduddin was only like the proof of the rightness of the faith he had always served, that he told me how, in the bad old days of persecution, he had been picked up one night by the police from his little house at the Bandung Institute of Technology, and taken to jail for fourteen months.

He didn't want to make too much of it now, but he had been provocative, had brought trouble on his own head. He had spoken against some plan of President Suharto, the father of the nation, for a family mausoleum. Gold was to be used in some part of the mausoleum, and Imaduddin spoke now as though it was the use of gold more than anything else that had offended his Islamic puritanism.

So he was expecting trouble, and it came. On 23 May 1978, at a quarter to midnight, someone rang the bell of his little house. He went out and saw three intelligence men in plain clothes. Imaduddin could see a gun on one of them. Many people were being arrested at that time.

One of the men said, 'We come from Jakarta. We would like to take you to Jakarta to get some information.'

'What kind of information?'

'We cannot tell you. You have to come with us immediately.'

Imaduddin said, 'Give me a few minutes.'

And, being Imaduddin, he prayed for a while and washed, while his wife prepared a little prison bag for him. She didn't forget his Koran.

All at once Imaduddin felt that he didn't want to go with the men. He felt that as a Muslim he couldn't trust them. He believed that the intelligence people in Indonesia were under the control of the Catholics. He telephoned the rector of the Bandung Institute. The rector said, 'Let me talk to them.' He talked to them, but the intelligence men insisted that Imaduddin should go with them. The rector began to hurry over to Imaduddin's house, but by the time he got there Imaduddin had been taken away in a taxi.

The intelligence men left the house with Imaduddin about 12.30, forty-five minutes after they had rung the bell. Imaduddin sat at the back of the taxi between two of the men; the third man sat in the front. They got to the Central Intelligence Office in Jakarta at 4.30 in the morning. Imaduddin, with the serenity of the believer, had slept some of the way. It was time for the dawn prayers when they arrived, and they allowed Imaduddin to do the prayer. Then they asked him to wait in a kind of waiting room. They gave him breakfast.

At eight he was taken to an office and he began to be interrogated by a lieutenant-colonel in uniform. There was no hint or threat of abuse or violence. As a lecturer at the Bandung Institute Imaduddin would have been considered of high official rank and had to be handled correctly.

After the lieutenant-colonel there was a man in plain clothes. This man gave his name. Imaduddin recognised it as the name of a state prosecutor.

He asked Imaduddin, 'Are you a Muslim?'

'I'm Muslim.'

'Is that why you think this country is an Islamic state? Do you think so?'

He was an educated man, a lawyer, perhaps five years younger than Imaduddin.

Imaduddin said, 'I don't know what to say. I have never studied law. I am an engineer. You are a lawyer.'

The prosecutor said, 'The government has spent so much money building mosques and many other things for the Muslims. It has built the National Mosque. But still there are Muslims who would like to turn this country into an Islamic state. Are you one of those Muslims?'

'You tell me what you think of this country.'

'It is a secular state. Not a religious state.'

Imaduddin said, 'You are wrong. You are dead wrong.'

'Why? You said that as an engineer you don't know the law.'

'Some things I know. Because I have studied in the States. The United States you can call a secular state. But you have told me that the government here has spent so much money to build things like the National Mosque. What kind of government is that?'

For two hours they argued, saying the same things over and over. Then Imaduddin was taken to the headquarters of the Military Police. There they brought out his file, and from there he was taken with his file to the jail.

The jail had been built for his political enemies by Sukarno, the first president of independent Indonesia; many famous people had been there before Imaduddin. It was a compound of six hectares, with a double wall and barbed wire and other jail apparatus. The buildings were of concrete.

Imaduddin was given a large room, six metres square, with a special Muslim bathroom. There were eight such rooms in the jail. They were for people of rank, and Imaduddin was considered a person of rank.

Imaduddin knew that he was going to spend a long time there. So, with the confidence and briskness of his great belief – and the curious simplicity: he could with equal ease have been an inquisitor or a martyr – he asked for a broom to clean the place up. He thought it was dirty: as a religious man he had certain standards of cleanliness. He even scrubbed the bathroom. Apart from everything else, the bathroom was important for his ritual wash before the five-times-a-day prayers.

He settled into the jail routine. There was a small mosque in the middle of the prison. When he went there for the Friday prayer he met the jail's most famous prisoner: Dr Subandrio, one of the Indonesian old guard, by profession a surgeon, a political associate of Sukarno's, once Sukarno's deputy prime minister, once foreign minister.

Subandrio had been in prison since 1965 for his part in the very serious communist plot to kill the generals and take over the country. The crushing of that plot had altered the political balance of the country. It had brought the army and young Suharto to power; it had led to a bloodletting so widespread that at the end the Indonesian Communist Party, in 1965 one of the largest political groupings in the country, had been all but destroyed. Hundreds of thousands had been sent to labour camps and had later been denied full civic rights. The memory of the 1965 plot had not been allowed to fade; the strange paternalism of military rule under President Suharto, always set against this background of latent communist danger, had been institutionalised.

Subandrio had originally been sentenced to death. But he told Imaduddin that on the day of his execution Queen Elizabeth had made a plea for his life – Subandrio had been the first Indonesian ambassador to Great Britain – and President Suharto had commuted the death sentence to imprisonment for life.

And there, in the jail Sukarno had built for another kind of political person, Subandrio had been all this time, for thirteen years, simply living on, while the world outside changed, and Subandrio and his great adventure became part of the past, and he himself was taken further and further away from the man he had been. He who had once been at the centre of so much now depended for social stimulus on new arrivals at the prison, people like Imaduddin, a kind of human windfall from beyond the high double walls.

The two men met every day. They went to each other's rooms. There was a kind of freedom for prisoners before eight in the morning, and again in the afternoon when the warders went to their own quarters. The two men were not alike. Subandrio was about sixty-five, Imaduddin thought; Imaduddin himself was forty-seven. Imaduddin, describing Subandrio, mentioned the older man's fitness, his small size, his training as a surgeon, his Javanese background. The background was important. The Javanese are known as feudal people with courtly manners and special ways of saying difficult things. Imaduddin was from North Sumatra, blunter in every way, and in the matter of Islam far more puritanical and aggressive than the Javanese.

And Imaddudin would have had no sympathy for Subandrio's pre-1965 politics. He had told me in 1979 that he could not have been a socialist when he was a young man, however generous the socialists were to him, because he was 'already' a Muslim. I believe he meant that all that was humane and attractive about socialism was also in Islam, and there was no need for him to take the secular way and risk his faith.

Thirteen years before, Imaduddin and Subandrio would have been on opposite sides. But the jail was an equaliser. And Subandrio had also changed. He had become a religious man. He said to Imaduddin at their first meeting that he wanted to know more about the Koran, and he asked Imaduddin to help him. This was more than Javanese courtesy or the result of the social starvation of jail life. Subandrio was a true seeker. Imaduddin became his teacher.

They also talked every day about politics. They talked specifically about politics in Javanese culture.

Imaduddin said, 'He learned from me how to read the Koran. I learned from him about Javanese culture.'

'What did you learn?'

'The importance of paternalism. Not in the Western sense, but a mix-up of feudalism, paternalism, and nepotism. You have to know what to say and what not to say. You have to know your position in the society. Your ability sometimes had nothing to do with it.'

Subandrio also got to know Imaduddin's story, and it was easy for him to see where Imaduddin was going wrong. Running together everything he had heard from Subandrio over fourteen months, Imaduddin put these words of political advice in Subandrio's mouth: 'In politics you must not expect honesty and morality right through. Keenness and smartness are not important. In politics the question of winning is the end result. So if you put your idea into the mind of your enemy, and he practises it, you are the winner. Above all, you must remember that you must never confront the Javanese.'

Confrontation: Imaduddin recognised that it had been his own political method. This wasted time in jail was part of the price he was
paying; so were the many years of exile that were to follow. During
those years he never forgot Subandrio's advice; and when his time of
expiation was over, and he had come back to Indonesia, he set himself
to learning the Javanese way of moving in an ordered society, the
Javanese way of saying difficult things. He learned that he shouldn't try
to act on his own. He found a patron, Habibie; he shot up; and as if by
magic people he had thought of as remote and hostile became sources
of bounty and favour.

On the day before the fiftieth anniversary of independence, and six
days after the N-250 made its inaugural flight around Bandung, Dr
Subandrio – now nearly eighty-two – was at last released from jail, after
an unimaginable thirty years, and a full sixteen years after Imaduddin
had been freed.

The announcement had been made three weeks before by President
Suharto. A *Jakarta Post* reporter went to the jail. He found Subandrio
suffering from a hernia and blood pressure. The old man wished now
only not to die in jail, and (a remnant of the fitness Imaduddin had
noticed sixteen years before) he kept himself going – for the little freedom he might yet have, and the little life – with the help of yoga and
long walks in the jail compound.

The reporter asked Subandrio whether he intended to take up politics again when he was released.

Subandrio said, 'It is useless.' His thoughts, he said, were only of the
hereafter.

The reporter asked whether he had an opinion about his release.

He didn't. He didn't want to say anything at all until he was
absolutely out of the jail. He said, 'I'm afraid of a possible slip of the
tongue, because it might backfire on me.'

So now, almost at the very end, taking care to talk only of the
benevolence of God and the generosity of President Suharto, Subandrio
remained mindful of the Javanese advice he had given Imaduddin sixteen years before.

Imaduddin gave un-Islamic and modern-sounding names to his Islamic
ventures. So in Bandung in 1979 he gave 'mental training' courses to
middle-class adolescent groups. One of the modern games he made

them play was to sit in groups of five and attempt to ~~r~~
of variously shaped pieces of paper that had been hande
rate envelopes. The thing could be done only if the g~~r~~
together and exchanged pieces of paper. In this very attra~~c~~
they learned about the need for cooperation, perseverance, kn ~~~~ng
one another, the sense of belonging. And since Imaduddin here was
preaching to the converted — otherwise those adolescents, some of
them from Jakarta, wouldn't have been allowed by their parents to
come to Bandung for those mixed, late-night sessions — everyone knew
that those virtues were Islamic ones; and some of the young people
even had supporting quotations from the Koran.

If that, in 1979, was an aspect of mental training, it was possible for
me, knowing about Imaduddin's current success and glory, to have an
idea what was behind YAASIN, which was the stylish Indonesian
acronym Imaduddin had chosen for the foundation he now ran:
Yayasan Pembina Sari Insan, the Foundation for the Development and
Management of Human Resources. 'Human resources' would have
meant people; their development meant their becoming devout
Muslims; the management of those devout people would have meant
weaning them away from old loyalties, whatever these were, and getting
them to follow the technological-political line of Imaduddin and
Habibie.

The office of the foundation was on the ground floor of a small
block some distance away from the centre of Jakarta. It wasn't easy for
the visitor to find. But Imaduddin was a busy man, with his weekly
television programme and his work for the Association of Muslim
Intellectuals — in a few days, besides, he would be going to the United
States and Canada, and travelling there for two months, visiting twelve
universities to do his mental training work among Indonesian students — and he thought that his office was the best place for us to
meet.

When he came out to the hall to greet me I didn't absolutely recognise him. It wasn't only the effect of the years. His manner had altered.
In Bandung he had seemed to me to have the university lecturer's
manner, not unattractive, the semi-informal, semi-confiding manner of
a man used to going around the seriousness or awkwardness of a subject to win the allegiance of people who were not yet his peers. Now
he was like a man of affairs, without a jacket but quite staid: the green-
striped shirt, the tie, the pen clipped to the shirt pocket, the beige

trousers belted to hold back the firm beginnings of middle-age spread.

In the office, the first open space, to the right as you entered, had a low raised platform, with cheap rumpled rugs; and on the floor were slippers and shoes. This was where Imaduddin's visitors and employees or neighbours faced Mecca and prayed. Two or three people were already there, sitting quietly, waiting for the correct prayer time; in this setting they were a little like office trophies or diplomas, virtue on display.

As we tiptoed past these still people, the woman diplomat who had come with me (and had provided the car for the difficult journey) asked whether we too shouldn't take off our shoes before we went any further. Imaduddin, with something of the preacher's bonhomie, said it wasn't necessary. He spoke as though he knew, out of his experience of the outside world, that this taking off of shoes would be a burden for us, and he was half in sympathy with us; but he spoke at the same time as though what was a burden for us was pure pleasure for him.

After this was the secretary's office, with a flickering computer screen and shelves and files; and after this, at the end of the corridor, was Imaduddin's office, against the outer wall of the building – the sun-struck street and the smoking traffic just outside. It looked like an office where a lot happened. There was a tarnished laptop on the glass-covered desk. On one side of the laptop was a well-handled Koran; on the other side was a pile of shoddily produced paperback books, perhaps a foot high, of similar size and in electric blue covers, which had been published in Egypt and might have been a very long commentary on the Koran: no doubt like meat and drink to Imaduddin.

And it was there, in that atmosphere of mosque and office, that Imaduddin began to tell me of his adventures after 1979, and the changes in his thinking that had led him from persecution in Bandung, where he hadn't been allowed to give his lectures on electrical engineering, to his success here in Jakarta, with his foundation and his ideas about human resources.

Though in 1979 he was in his late forties, he still kept up with two international Muslim student organisations where he had held important positions. These organisations were known, in an impressive modern way, by their initials: IFSO of Kuwait, the International Islamic Federation of Student Organisations, and WAMY of Saudi Arabia, the World Association of Muslim Youth. It was through WAMY that he got a grant from the Faisal Foundation. He didn't use this to go to a

Muslim country, where as a defender of the faith he might have found solace of a sort. He went instead to the heart of the United States, to Iowa State University. Always out there, the United States, an unacknowledged part of the world picture of every kind of modern revolutionary: the country of law and rest, with which at the end of the day a man who had proclaimed himself to be on the other side – in politics, culture, or religion – could make peace and on whose goodwill he could throw himself.

It was at Iowa that Imaduddin made the great break with his past. He found a new subject of study, industrial engineering, and he gave up electrical engineering, which he had taught for seventeen years. He had decided to go into electrical engineering when he was a young man, he said; it was part of the uncertainty of the time; he had the haziest idea how the country could be best developed. Now at Iowa he began to see more clearly.

Imaduddin said, 'I discovered at that time that this country needs human resource development rather than high technology. I realised that the problem of the country was not technology. Technology can be bought if you have the money. But you cannot buy human resources who are dedicated to doing things for their country. You cannot expect Americans to come here to do things for this country. As secretary-general of IFSO I travelled a lot. And one day in 1978, when I was in Saudi Arabia, I saw that they had established a very modern hospital, the King Faisal Hospital, but all the doctors, even the nurses, were non-Arab. The doctors were Americans, the nurses were Filipinos and Indians and Pakistanis. Saudi Arabia can buy Awacs, but the pilots are Americans.'

'You hadn't thought of that before?'

'Not really. But approaching it.'

Though I half knew that the scientific-sounding words Imaduddin was using would have a religious twist, I had also given them a half-scientific interpretation. I thought he was speaking as a scientist and was saying, very broadly, that technology without the supporting science was useless, and I thought he was using Saudi Arabia as an example of technological dependence. But the very next thing he said made me feel I had missed the true line of his argument.

He said, 'When I applied for the scholarship from Saudi Arabia I was thinking of shifting from electrical engineering. I thought there must be something more important than technology.'

I had lost him for a while. He appeared to be saying that in order to develop technology it was necessary to give it up. I cast my mind back over what had been said. He talked on, and it was a little time before I saw that he was not speaking with detachment, laying down the principles of technological advance for Indonesia, but was speaking more personally, of his career, and of the intuitive stages by which he had given up electrical engineering, given up naked technology, and become a full-time preacher and missionary, and how, through this apparent professional surrender, he had reached the heights: the Association of Muslim Intellectuals, Habibie, the splendours of the N-250, and, indirectly, the president himself. In his mind there was no disjointedness or lack of logic. There was only clarity. A country could develop only if its human resources were developed: if the people, that is, became devout and good.

My questions would not always have been to the point. He handled them civilly, but as interruptions; and, like the seasoned politician or preacher, always went back to his main story without losing his way.

He said, 'With the Saudi grant I shifted to industrial engineering. In electrical engineering we study just engineering. No human being is concerned. Except, when you study high voltage, of course you must think of safety. In industrial engineering you combine industrial system and human system, and management. I did this in Iowa. I met a very nice professor who is an expert in human behaviour. I asked this professor to be my major professor, and he very gladly agreed. Starting from this I concentrated my resources on behavioural approach.'

He had no trouble giving up his old subject. 'I am interested in something only when I am learning about it. Once I know everything about it I don't like it any more. It's one of my weaknesses or bad behaviours. An example. Show me any motor or electrical machine. I can tell you about the behaviour of this machine. An induction motor is an induction motor. It doesn't matter where it comes from. I can tell you about it completely. When I get my two babies, each baby has its own individual behaviour. You cannot treat them like machines. Human beings are always enigmatic to me, always interesting.'

Just outside the office wall, the bright light yellowed, turning the dust and smoke into gold: the hot afternoon on the turn, moving now towards dusk, the traffic as hectic as ever, full of event but (like a fountain seen from a distance) constant. Against this, but from within the office, no doubt from the carpeted and rumpled open space at the end of the corridor, hesitant scraping sounds developed into a shy chant.

Imaduddin heard: it showed in his eyes. But, with the same kind of courtesy that had made him tell us earlier that it was not necessary to take off our shoes in the corridor, he appeared not to notice. He didn't interrupt his story.

After four years at Iowa he finished his course in industrial engineering. He received a letter from some friends in Indonesia advising him not to come back just then. He showed the letter to the American immigration people – he had to leave the country as soon as he had graduated – and they gave him an extension. He also showed the letter to his professor. The professor knew that Imaduddin's Saudi grant had stopped with his graduation, and he offered Imaduddin a teaching job. Imaduddin taught at Iowa for two years.

I said, 'People have shown you a lot of kindness.'

I was trying to make a point about people in Iowa, unbelievers. I believe Imaduddin understood. He said with a mischievous smile, 'God loves me very much.'

The chanting from the corridor became more confident. It couldn't be denied now. I could see that Imaduddin wanted to be out there, with the chanters and the prayers. For a while longer, though, he stayed where he was and continued with his story.

In 1986 an Indonesian friend, well placed, in fact a minister in the cabinet, made a plea to the Indonesian government on Imaduddin's behalf. He gave a personal guarantee that Imaduddin would do no harm to the state. It was because of this that, after six years of exile, Imaduddin was allowed to go back home. He went to Bandung. He thought he still had his lecturing job at the Institute of Technology, but when he reported to the dean the dean told him he was dismissed. So – though Imaduddin didn't make the point – it was just as well that he had turned away from electrical engineering.

The chanting now filled the corridor. It was authoritative. It recalled Imaduddin from his narrative of times past. And now he couldn't be held back. He rose with suddenness from his office chair, said in a businesslike way that he would be with us again in a few minutes, and went out towards the chanting.

The room felt bereft. Without the man himself – his curious simplicity and openness, his love of speech, his humour – all his missionary paraphernalia felt oppressive: something being made out of nothing. It was only someone like Imaduddin who could give point and life to the electric-blue Egyptian paperbacks on the glass-topped desk.

When he came back he had lost his restlessness. The prayers, the assuaging of habit, had set him up for the happiest part of his story. This was the part that dealt with the success – still with him – that had come after nearly a decade of jail and exile and being on the run.

The success had followed on his coming to Jakarta, the capital, after the humiliation of Bandung. In Jakarta he was closer than he had been to the sources of power. For the first time he could act on the principles of Javanese statecraft he had heard about from Dr Subandrio eight to nine years before in the jail. They were simple but vital principles: knowing your place in the society and your relationship to authority; knowing what could or couldn't be said; understanding the art of reverence.

He said, 'From 1987 I started to be active in Jakarta life. I learned very fast.'

'What did you learn?'

'The geo-politics of Indonesia. The rules of the game Suharto is playing.'

Still, for all his new tact, he had a nasty stumble. It happened in his second year in Jakarta. He was working in a tentative way on his human resources idea.

'I started collecting some friends to start a new organisation to be called Muslim Intellectuals Association – or something. We met at a small hotel in Yogyakarta. This was in January 1989. Four policemen came and dismissed the meeting. My name was still considered dirty. Suharto was still under the influence of the intelligence people.'

The intelligence people, he was to tell me later, were under the influence of the Catholics, and they were nervous of the Muslim movement. The incident showed him that though the society was completely controlled, it wasn't always easy to read. It would be full of ambushes like this. He saw that it was wrong for him to think – as his Sumatran upbringing and American training encouraged him to think – that he could act on his own. He needed a patron.

'I learned more about the political situation. I read about Professor Habibie. I read cover stories in two magazines. I tried to learn more about him. I asked my friend' – perhaps the minister who had made it possible for Imaduddin to come back to Indonesia – 'to introduce us. I was accepted by Habibie in 1990.'

'What actually happened?'

'I sent a letter by a student to Professor Habibie. Then I went to his office, accompanied by the students, three of whom I had made my "pilots". I met him on 23 August 1990.'

A full year, that is, after the police had broken up the meeting of intellectuals in the Yogyakarta hotel. Habibie agreed to be the chairman of the new body.

'Why did you choose Habibie?'

'Because he is very close to Suharto, and nothing can be done in this country without the approval of the first man. Habibie told me that I had to write a proposal, and that this had to be supported by at least twenty signatures of Ph.D.s all over the country. So I came back and for a fortnight went to work on the computer. I got forty-nine people to sign the letter. They were mostly university people. Habibie showed this letter to Suharto on 2 September 1990, and Suharto gave his approval immediately. He said to Habibie, "This is the first time the Muslim intellectuals have united. I want you to lead these intellectuals to build this country." Of course this letter will become a national document.'

At this point Imaduddin's career took off. 'After coming back from the meeting with Suharto Habibie established a committee to prepare a conference. The Association of Muslim Intellectuals was established by the beginning of December 1990. Suharto committed himself to opening the conference.' And there was a further sign of presidential forgiveness. 'When Suharto through Habibie wanted to find a name for the paper for ICMI, Habibie asked me to find a name. I gave him three choices: *Res Publica*, *Republik*, *Republika*. Suharto chose *Republika*. After that I began to gain my freedom. I can talk anywhere I like. When I came back in 1986 I wasn't allowed to give any public lectures. So things have changed completely in Indonesia. Of course there has been opposition. Non-Islamic, Catholics.'

'Why did Suharto change his mind?'

'I don't know. A puzzle to me. Maybe God changed his mind. In 1991 he went on *haj* to Mecca – the pilgrimage. His name now is Haji Mohamad Suharto. Before that he had no first name. He was just Suharto.' And Imaduddin became a busy man. 'Since 1991 I have been assigned by Habibie. He called me one day and said, "I would like you to do just one thing. Train these people. Make them become devout Muslims."'

'So you've given up engineering?'

'Completely. Since 1991 I have been every year to European countries, United States, Australia, just to meet these students, especially
those getting scholarships from Habibie. I train them to become good
Muslims, good Indonesians. Next week, as I told you, I go to visit
Canada and the United States. I will be there for two months. I will
visit twelve campuses.'

It was possible to see the political – or 'geo-political' – purpose of his
work. The students were already dependent on Habibie and the government. Imaduddin's mental training, taken to the students at their
universities, would bind them even closer.

He said of the students abroad, 'When they become devout Muslims
and good leaders of Indonesia they will not think about revolution but
about accelerated evolution.' It sounded like a slogan, something
worked over, words, to be projected as part of the programme: development, but with minds somehow tethered. 'We have to overcome our
backwardness and become one of the new industrial countries by 2020.'

So, starting from the point that in Indonesia there was something
more important than technology, we had zigzagged back – through the
human resources idea, which was the religious idea – to the need for
technological advance. A special kind of advance, with the mind religiously controlled.

This zigzag had followed the line of Imaduddin's own career, from
his troubles at Bandung to his importance in the Habibie programme.
And in his mind there would have been no disjointedness. The most
important thing in the world was the faith, and his first duty was to
serve it. In 1979 he had had to express his opposition to the government. It was different now. The government served the faith; he could
serve the government. The faith was large; he could fit it to the government's needs. He had not moved to the government; rather, the
government had moved towards him.

'I felt in 1979 that the religion was under threat. The intelligence
group at that time was under the influence of the Catholics, who were
afraid of Islamic development here. They have what is called in psy-
chology projection. They think that because they are a minority they
will be treated like they treated the Muslims in other countries. Now I
have my friends in the cabinet. It's God's will.'

The Javanese way of reverence was now easy for him. He said of
Habibie, his patron, 'He's a genius. He got *summa cum laude* in both
master's and doctorate in Germany, in Aachen. His second and third

degrees were in aeronautical engineering. He's an honest person. He's never missed a prayer. Five times a day, and he also fasts twice a week, Monday and Thursday. Habibie's son is smarter than his father. He went to Munich.' And Imaduddin had also arrived at an awed understanding of President Suharto's position as father of the nation. When Habibie had shown the president Imaduddin's first letter about the Association of Muslim Intellectuals, the president, running his eye down the forty-nine signatures, had stopped at Imaduddin's name and said in a matter-of-fact way, 'He's been in prison.' Habibie reported this to Imaduddin, and Imaduddin was wonderstruck.

He said to me, 'One name. When you think of the hundreds of thousands who have been to jail here—' He left the sentence unfinished.

And now he had a stupendous vision of the future of the faith here.

'I believe what the late Fazel-ur-Rehman told me. He passed away in 1980. He was one of the members of the National Islamic Academy in Pakistan. He was Professor of Islamic Studies at the University of Chicago. I invited him to Iowa to give a lecture.' Interesting, this glimpse of the protected goings and comings of Islamic missionaries in the alien land. 'I met him at the airport. He hugged me and said, "I have read many of your articles and books and I am happy to meet you today. You are Indonesian. I strongly believe that the Malay-speaking Muslims will lead the revival of Islam in the twenty-first century." I picked up his bag and escorted him to the car and asked him why he believed that. He said, "I am serious. You will lead the revival. There are three reasons. First, the Malay-speaking Muslims have become the majority of the Muslim world, and you are the only Muslim people to remain united. We Pakistanis failed to do that. The Arabic world is divided into fifteen states. You have only Sunnis, no Shias. Second, you have a Muslim organisation, Muhammadiyah, with the slogan, Koran and Sunna." Because Fazel-ur-Rehman strongly believed that only the Koran can answer modern questions. "Third, the position of women in Indonesia is just as at the time of the Prophet, according to the true teaching of Islam."'

I asked Imaduddin, 'What are the modern questions that the Koran can solve?'

'Human relations. Sense of equality. Freedom from want, freedom from fear. These are the two things people need, and this is the basic mission of the Prophet Mohammed.'

He had told me in 1979 that he could not be a socialist when he was young because he was 'already' a Muslim. It could have been said then that devoutness did not provide the institutions. But this could not be said now that the faith alone did not bring about freedom from want and fear, because the faith Imaduddin propounded was anchored to Habibie's technological programme, whose glory was expressed in the flight of the N-250.

'Science is something inherent in Islamic teaching. If we are backward it's because we were colonised by the Spanish, the British, the Dutch. Why were men created by God? To make the world prosperous. In order to make the world prosperous we have to master science. The first revelation revealed to the Prophet was "Read."'

It seemed part of what had gone before. But when I got to know a little more of the politics of Indonesia I was to see that this was where Imaduddin was taking the war to the enemy, and making an immense power play on behalf of the government.

In Indonesia we were almost at the limit of the Islamic world. For a thousand years or so until 1400 this had been a cultural and religious part of Greater India: animist, Buddhist, Hindu. Islam had come here not long before Europe. It had not been the towering force it had been in other converted places. For the last two hundred years, in a colonial world, Islam had even been on the defensive, the religion of a subject people. It had not completely possessed the souls of people. It was still a missionary religion. It had been kept alive informally in colonial times, in simple village boarding schools, descended perhaps as an idea from Buddhist monasteries.

To possess or control these schools was to possess power. And I began to feel that Imaduddin and the Association of Muslim Intellectuals – with their stress on science and technology, and their dismissing of old ritual ways – aimed at nothing less. The ambition was stupendous: to complete the Islamic take-over of this part of the world, and to take the islands to their destiny as the leader of Islamic revival in the twenty-first century.

Imaduddin said, 'Formerly they used to read the Koran without understanding the meaning. They were interested only in the correct pronunciation and a certain enchanted melody. We are changing this now. Now I've been given a chance to give lectures through TV.'

Later we went out, past the now empty open space with the rumpled rugs. Imaduddin's wife was there, waiting for him: a gracious and smiling Javanese beauty. It was something in Imaduddin's favour that he had won the love of such a lady. It was she who had packed the jail bag for him seventeen years before, and she reminded me that I had come to their house in Bandung on the last day of 1979.

I went to the bathroom. Ritual ablutions from a little concrete pool had left the place a mess, except for people who would take off their shoes and roll up their trousers.

When I came back there was a tall middle-aged man in a grey suit standing with Imaduddin's wife. As soon as this man saw Imaduddin he went to him and made as if to kiss his right hand. Imaduddin made a deflecting gesture.

The man in the grey suit was in the Indonesian diplomatic service. He had met Imaduddin when Imaduddin had come to Germany to do his mental training courses for students. He looked at Imaduddin with smiling eyes, and said to me in English, 'He is himself. He fears only God.'

And I knew what he meant. And for a while we stood there, all smiling: Imaduddin, his wife, and the man in the grey suit.

Imaduddin told me later that it was the custom of traditional Muslims to kiss the hand of a teacher. The diplomat looked upon Imaduddin as his teacher. Whenever he met Imaduddin he tried to kiss his hand. 'But I never let him.'

2

History

THE MAN whom Imaduddin and the Association of Muslim Intellectuals had in their sights more than anybody else was Mr Wahid.

Mr Wahid didn't care for Habibie's ideas about religion and politics, and he was one of the few men in Indonesia who could say so. He was chairman of the Nahdlatul Ulama, the NU. The NU was a body based on the Islamic village boarding schools of Indonesia, and it was said to have thirty million members. Thirty million people resisting mental training and the Association of Muslim Intellectuals: this made Mr Wahid formidable. And Mr Wahid was no ordinary man. He had a pedigree. In Indonesia, and especially in Java, this mattered. His family had been connected with the village boarding schools of Java for more than a century, since the dark colonial days, when Java had been reduced by the Dutch to a plantation, and these Islamic boarding schools were among the few places to offer privacy and self-respect to people. And Mr Wahid's father had been important in political and religious matters at the time of independence.

The *Jakarta Post*, choosing its words with care, said in one report that Mr Wahid was controversial and enigmatic. There was a story behind the words. Imaduddin believed that it might have been God, no less, who had made President Suharto more of a believing Muslim in these past few years, had sent him on the pilgrimage to Mecca, and had made him a supporter of the technological-political-religious ideas of Habibie. Mr Wahid had other ideas about that. He believed that politics and religion should be kept separate, and he had allowed himself one day to do the unthinkable: he had criticised President Suharto to a foreign journalist. Only someone as strong and independent as Mr Wahid could have survived. He had, remarkably, been re-elected chairman of the NU. But in the eight months since then he had not once been received by President Suharto, and it was now known that Mr Wahid was in the line of fire.

It was no doubt this scent of blood that made people say I should try to see Mr Wahid. One note from a foreign journalist described him as 'a blind old cleric with a following of thirty million'. This gave Mr Wahid a comic-book character and confused him with somebody else in another country. Mr Wahid's eyes were not good, but he wasn't blind; he was only about fifty-two or fifty-three; and he wasn't a cleric.

Sixteen years before, people had been just as anxious for me to see Mr Wahid, but then it was for another reason.

In 1979 Mr Wahid and his *pesantren*, the Islamic boarding-school movement, had been thought to be at the forefront of the modern Muslim movement. The *pesantren* had the additional glory at that time of having been visited by the educationist Ivan Illich and pronounced good examples of the 'deschooling' he favoured. Deschooling wasn't perhaps the best idea to offer village people who had been barely schooled. But because of Illich's admiration the *pesantren* of Indonesia seemed to be yet another example of Asia providing an unexpected light, after the obfuscations of colonialism. And a young businessman of Jakarta, a supporter of Mr Wahid's, arranged for me to visit *pesantrens* near the city of Yogyakarta. One of the *pesantrens* was Mr Wahid's own; it had been established by his family.

There had followed two harrowing days: looking for the correct places first of all, moving along crowded country roads between crowded school compounds: usually quiet and sedate at the entrance, but then all at once – even in the evening – as jumping and thick with competitive life as a packed trout pond at feeding time: mobs of jeering boys and young men, some of them relaxed, in sarongs alone, breaking off from domestic chores to follow me, some of the mob shouting, 'Illich! Illich!'

With that kind of distraction I wasn't sure what I was seeing, and I am sure I missed a lot. But deschooling didn't seem an inappropriate word for what I had seen. I didn't see the value of young villagers assembling in camps to learn village crafts and skills which they were going to pick up anyway. And I was worried by the religious side: the very simple texts, the very large classes, the learning by heart, and the pretence of private study afterwards. In the crowded yards at night I saw boys sitting in the darkness before open books and pretending to read.

It wasn't the kind of place I would have liked to go to myself. I said this to the young Indonesian who had come out with me from Jakarta as my guide and interpreter. He was bright and educated and friendly, always a little bit on my side in all our adventures. Now he dropped all courtesies and became downright irritated. Other people, when they heard what I had said about the *pesantren*, also became irritated.

At the end of the two days I met Mr Wahid in his *pesantren* house. I wrote about our meeting, but it was strange that, until I re-read what I had written, I had no memory of the man or the occasion. It might have been the fatigue of the two days, or it might have been the shortness of our meeting: Mr Wahid, busy as ever on *pesantren* business, was going to Jakarta that evening, and couldn't give me much time. Or – and this is most likely – it might have been because of the very dim light in Mr Wahid's sitting room: it was a great strain to try to see him through the gloom, and I must have given up, been content with his voice, and remained without a picture.

What he said explained much of what I felt about the *pesantren*. Before Islam they would have been Buddhist monasteries, supported by the people of the villages and in return reminding them of the eternal verities. In the early days of Islam here they would have remained spiritual places, Sufi centres. In the Dutch time they would have become Islamic schools. Later they would in addition have tried to become a more modern kind of school. Here, as elsewhere in Indonesia, where Islam was comparatively recent, the various layers of history could still be easily perceived. But – this was my idea, not Mr Wahid's – the *pesantren* ran all the separate ideas together and created the kind of mishmash I had seen.

While we talked there had been some chanting going on outside: an Arabic class. Mr Wahid and I went out at last to have a look. The chanting was coming from the verandah of a very small house at the bottom of the garden. The light was very dim; I could just make out the teacher and his class. The teacher was one of the most learned men in the neighbourhood, Mr Wahid said. The *pesantren* had built the little house for him; the villagers fed him; and he had, in addition, a stipend of five hundred rupiah a month, at that time about eighty cents. So, Islamic though he was, chanting without pause through his lesson in Arabic law, he was descended – as wise man and spiritual lightning-conductor, living off the bounty of the people he served – from the monks of the Buddhist monasteries.

I was immensely excited by his eighty-cents-a-month stipend and, when Mr Wahid called him and he came and stood humbly before us in the great gloom, very small and pious and hunched, with very thick lenses to his glasses, I couldn't get rid of the idea of the eighty cents and wondered how it was given and at what intervals.

Mr Wahid praised him while he stood before us and said he was thirty and knew a lot of the Koran by heart. I said it was marvellous, knowing the Koran by heart. 'Half,' Mr Wahid said. 'Half.' And, considering the hunched man before us who had little else to do, I said with some sternness that it wasn't good enough. He, the eighty-cents man, rounded his shoulders a little more, piously accepting and converting into religious merit whatever rebuke we might have offered him. And I feel that he was ready to round his shoulders a little more and a little more until he might have looked like a man whose head grew beneath his shoulders.

It was he rather than Mr Wahid who survived in my memory of that evening.

The Jakarta businessman who had sent me to the *pesantren* in 1979 was Adi Sasono. He had been a supporter of Mr Wahid then. But now he had moved away from him, and was on the other side, with the Association of Muslim Intellectuals. He had a big job with the Association, and had a big office, with every kind of modern corporate trapping, high up in a big block in central Jakarta.

He wanted me to know, when I went to see him, that in spite of appearances he had remained loyal to his old ideas about village uplift; it was Mr Wahid who had been left behind. Once the *pesantren* schools were all right; now they weren't.

In the last century, in the Dutch time, the *pesantren* gave village people a kind of self-respect, and the *pesantren* heads, who were called *kiyai*, were a kind of informal local leader who could give some protection to village people. Times had changed; in the modern world the old system didn't answer. The *pesantren* was owned by its *kiyai*; headship or ownership rights were passed down from father to son; so that, whatever the virtues of some *kiyai*, there was always the danger of 'élitism' or 'religious feudalism'.

Adi said, 'This traditional method of mobilising people cannot be maintained in the long run. We need a more accountable process and a national collective decision-making.' In 1979 he had joined the *pesantren* movement to promote modern education – to complement traditional religious teaching – and to promote rural development. He thought now that that job was being better done by the Association of Muslim Intellectuals, ICMI in its Indonesian acronym (pronounced 'itch-me'). 'We develop the people to be more independent in making their own decision, especially concerning the challenge of big capital coming to the rural area. The *kiyai* – one man, and a man of privilege – cannot be the guarantee of the people's life. So ICMI is more on the human resource development and the people's economic development.'

Adi had been moving towards it, and now at last it had come: Imaduddin's missionary idea about the development and management of human resources.

There had been nothing from Adi about deschooling and Ivan Illich – that was the modernity and academic line of yesterday. In Adi's current analysis the huts and squawking yards of the *pesantren* were as rustic and limited as they might have appeared to an uncommitted visitor. And a whole new set of approved words or ideas – élitism, religious feudalism, accountability, collective decision-making, the mobilising of people, and, of course, human resources – were used, figuratively, to beat poor old Mr Wahid about the head.

And to beat, too, but only in my own mind, the figure called up from memory: the small, hunched, white-capped and white-clad figure in the sight-baffling gloom of Mr Wahid's backyard or garden, the eighty-cents-a-month man (at present rates of exchange more like a twenty-five-cents man), called from his very dim verandah and his chanting class in Islamic law to stand before us, and meekly with bowed head to accept my rebuke for knowing only half the Koran at the age of thirty, when he had so little to do, and the village had built his narrow little house for him and kept him in such food as met his modest needs: an unlikely successor, in half-converted Indonesia, of the early Islamic Sufis and, before them, the monks of Buddhist times.

*

Islam and Europe had arrived here almost at the same time as competing imperialisms, and between them they had destroyed the long
Buddhist-Hindu past. Islam had moved on here, to this part of Greater
India, after its devastation of India proper, turning the religious-cultural
light of the subcontinent, so far as this region was concerned, into the
light of a dead star. Yet Europe had dominated so quickly here that
Islam itself had begun to feel like a colonised culture. The family history that a cultivated and self-aware man like Mr Wahid carried in his
head – a history that true family memory took back only a century and
a quarter – was at the same time a history of European colonialism and
of the recovery of Islam.

The first time we met on this trip Mr Wahid talked, but only in a
glancing way, of his family history. I was taken with what he said and I
felt I wanted to hear more. I went to see him again.

We met in the main offices of the NU. They were on the ground
floor of a simple, old-fashioned building on a main road, with a cleared
yard at the front for cars. The rooms – not at all like Adi Sasono's –
were like railway waiting rooms, full of that kind of heavy, dark furniture, and with that kind of tarnish.

I wanted to sit on a high, straight-backed chair so that I could write.
All the chairs in Mr Wahid's office were very low. An assistant said that
in another room there were chairs that would serve, but people were
there, talking. Mr Wahid, like a man who had suffered for too long
from these talkers, said they were to be chased away. And they were
chased away with such suddenness that coils of warm, undissipated
cigarette smoke still hung just above the middle air when we went to
the room. The cigarettes were Indonesian clove cigarettes. The smoke
was heavy with clove oil, and there had been so much of it in that room
that after my afternoon there with Mr Wahid the clove smell remained
on my hand and hair for days, resisting baths, like an anaesthetic after an
operation; and it never left my jacket all the time I was in Indonesia.

Nothing had remained in my memory of Mr Wahid from 1979. And
I was surprised now to find that he was only fifty-one or fifty-two; so that
in 1979, when he was already famous and of great authority, he would
not have been forty. He was a short, plump man, perhaps about five feet
three or four inches. As everyone said, his eyes were not good, but his
physique and general appearance suggested someone with other problems
as well, cardiac or respiratory. He was casually dressed, with an open-
necked shirt. He would not have stood out in an Indonesian crowd. As

soon as he began to speak, however, and his English was fluent and good and sensitive, his quality was apparent. He was a man to whom confidence and graces had been passed down over a couple of generations.

Mr Wahid said, 'My grandfather was born in 1869, in east Java, in a sugar plantation area called Jombang. He came of a peasant family who followed a tradition of Sufism. The Sufis in Java had been running *pesantren* for centuries. My ancestors had their *pesantren* for two centuries, for six or seven generations before my grandfather.

'My great-grandfather came from central Java. He studied at a *pesantren* in Jombang, and was taken as a son-in-law by his teacher. This would have been in 1830, at the beginning of sugar planting in the area. That period was also the beginning of steamship travel via the Middle East. This was important for the *haj*, the pilgrimage to Mecca. It became easier. It also led to the emergence of rich new Muslim families growing cash crops. This new rich class could send their children to study in Mecca by the steamship lines. It was a coincidence, but history is often shaped by unconnected developments.

'My great-grandfather was able to send my grandfather to Mecca in the last quarter of the last century. My grandfather went to Mecca perhaps in 1890, when he was twenty-one years old. He stayed there maybe five or six years. Because of the steamship lines you could send money to students. He came back and established his own *pesantren*. This was in 1898.

'The story is that he established that with ten students only. At that time the establishing of a prayer house was considered as a challenge to prevailing values. In the vicinity of the sugar plantations there was an absence of religious life. The sugar factory made people depend on it by providing easy money to gamble, for drinking, for prostitution, all kinds of things frowned on by Islam. In the night in the first few months these ten students had to sleep in the middle of the prayer house. The walls of the prayer house were made of bamboo mats, and spears and all kinds of sharp weapons were thrust in from outside.

'Maybe my grandfather was too strong in his criticism of people. He chose the sugar-cane area quite deliberately. Maybe he had done this with some spiritual insight into the future. The clear wish was there to transform the whole community there, to make them follow the Islamic way of life. In 1947, at the end of his life, my grandfather had a *pesantren* of four thousand students and twenty acres of land. In the beginning he only had four acres. The community now is totally transformed. There is still a sugar mill there, but the whole community has left that old way of life and now follows an Islamic way of life.

'My grandfather had married many times. He married also before he left for Mecca. All his marriages ended in divorce or death of wives. Maybe at the beginning of this century he got this new wife from the nobility. The nobility here means from the line of the kings of Java, ruling in Solo. We share the same family line with the wife of President Suharto. The nobility was already a little bit secularised, westernised. This new wife of my grandfather's was so proud of her noble origin she often said, according to my mother, "I want my children to have a different education. I don't want them to follow the peasant way of life of my husband."

'Because of that she oriented my father and his younger brothers – eleven of them. They were given tutors from outside the area who taught things unknown in the *pesantren* – mathematics and Dutch language, general knowledge. My father even went through a course in typing. People wondered about that, because the Muslim community here still used the Arabic script for the local language. Later, when he went into public life, my father would sit in the back seat of the car and type as he was driven about. At the same time as he did those modern subjects my father had to study in the *pesantren* under his father and his brothers-in-law. And my grandmother invited a sheikh from Al Azhar in Cairo to come and educate my father and his younger brothers for seven years. That was unknown in Java. The Kurds provided very traditional education in Islam. The Egyptians through Al Afghani reformed the whole tradition of religious education in Al Azhar. So my father got the benefits of the two types of education. He was educated like a member of a royal family. That was why my father spoke flawless Arabic and knew Arabic literature very much. He subscribed to the famous periodicals of the Middle East.'

Mr Wahid's father also went to Mecca. He went in 1931, when he was fifteen, and he stayed for two years. It was when he came back – his formal education now complete, though Mr Wahid didn't make the point – that he began to add to the curriculum of his *pesantren*, to make it a little more like the mixed curriculum he had himself gone through. He added geography and modern history. He also added, Mr Wahid said, the idea of the *school*: this meant that students were 'drilled' by the teacher.

'Before, there was nothing like that. It was very polite. No questions.

Everybody just listened to the teacher. With the introduction of the school system in the *pesantren* my father set up a series of incremental changes. There had been changes before of smaller scope but with no less impact. In 1923 my maternal grandfather instituted a new *pesantren* for girls. Now it's so common everywhere.'

The *pesantren* were essentially religious boarding houses. By their nature they could not rise much above the level of the people. The improvements Mr Wahid talked about seemed small: typing, geography, modern history. But perhaps they were not small at the time. Perhaps, as Mr Wahid said, their effect was incremental.

I asked him about the traditional side of *pesantren* teaching. He told me of his experiences of the late 1940s, many years after his father's reforms.

'When I was eight years old, after I completed the reading of the Koran, I was told to memorise this grammar book, *Al Ajrumiyah*. It was about fifteen pages. Every morning I was asked by my teacher to memorise a line or two. I was drilled in that. Later in the evening I had to take this book. A very basic text of religious laws: how to have ablution, how to do the right prayers.'

This was the very thing I had seen in 1979 – thirty years later – in the late evening in the *pesantren*: boys sitting about bamboozling themselves with a simple textbook of religious laws which they would have known by heart, with some boys even sitting in the dark before open books and pretending to read.

Perhaps religious teaching had to come with this repetitiveness, this isolating and beating down and stunning of the mind, this kind of pain. Perhaps out of this there came self-respect of a sort, and even an idea of learning which – in the general cultural depression – might never have otherwise existed. Because out of this religious education, whatever its sham scholarship and piety, and its real pain, there also came a political awakening.

This was the other side of Mr Wahid's family story. It was interwoven with the other story of *pesantren* success and reform.

'In 1908 a local organisation was established in Solo called Sarekat Dagung Islam by a trader who had made the pilgrimage to Mecca. Four years later that organisation was transformed into a national organisation called Sarekat Islam. It was not confined to trade.

'My grandfather had a cousin ten years younger, Wahab Hasbullah. Wahab had been sent to my grandfather to be educated. Wahab went to Mecca afterwards and took a friend, Bisri. After four years in Mecca they heard about Sarekat Islam. Wahab asked to open a Mecca branch of Sarekat. This was in 1913, the year after Sarekat Islam was founded. Bisri didn't go along because he didn't have the permission of my grandfather, who was also his teacher. Bisri became my maternal grandfather. Wahab was my great maternal uncle. When he returned from Mecca, in 1917, he went to Surabaya. In 1919 Sarekat Islam split. A Dutchman influenced two Sarekat Islam members to form the Red Sarekat Islam. In 1924 there was a Saudi congress for the new caliphate for the Muslims. Wahab joined the Surabaya committee.'

In 1926 Sukarno appeared, and national politics were transformed. But Mr Wahid's father and grandfather remained important in the religious movement.

'In 1935 the Dutch, worried by the Japanese threat, made a call for a local militia to defend Indonesia or the empire from the impending Japanese threat. And a congress called by my grandfather debated this point: Is it obligatory for true Muslims to defend a country ruled by non-Muslims? The resounding answer was yes, because the Muslims in Indonesia in 1935 under the Dutch had the liberty to implement the teachings of their religion. This means in my thinking that my grandfather saw Islam as a moral force, not as a political force exercised by the state.'

It was, it might be said, a colonial moral debate, among people who exercised no power, rather like the debate in India when the war came. And, as it happened, the militia in which Mr Wahid's father served was the one set up by the Japanese, who overran Indonesia in 1942.

'The Japanese established two kinds of militias, the Muslim ones and the nationalist ones. My father was the founder of the Hizbullah militia in 1944. The Japanese recruited young people from *pesantren* and religious schools. My father's younger brother was trained and then appointed as battalion commander. With his headquarters situated right there in the *pesantren*, this involved the whole family in national affairs. They discussed the Japanese war, affairs in Germany, the independence movement.

'In 1944–5 the Japanese established a committee to prepare for Indonesian independence. It was chaired by Sukarno. My father was on this committee. He and eight other members of the committee formed the nucleus of the group to draw up the five principles of the new state, the *panchasila*. In that way he became one of the founding fathers of this state. So when the independence war broke out my father was involved directly. First he became a minister and then later he became political adviser to the commander of the armed forces, General Sudirman.

'My father went into hiding when the Dutch unleashed their aggression. I was evacuated to my maternal grandfather's house. And there several times a week my father appeared, hiding in the house, not going out, treating his wounds, which were from diabetes, not from bullets. I had to get frogs to fry, to get oil from, for dressing those wounds. Ten to fifteen frogs a time, two or three times a week. After dressing his wounds he would go back to hiding in the nearby villages.

'When the Dutch yielded sovereignty to our state my father was appointed minister of religious affairs. He held that position for three years. In the Japanese time there had been an office of religious affairs which had been entrusted to my grandfather, but headed by my father as chief executive director. That office was the embryo of the department of religious affairs.'

And, as so often in narratives of this time, if the brutalities of their occupation could be set aside, the intelligence and speed – and the lasting effects – of the Japanese reorganisation of a vast and varied area had to be acknowledged.

Mr Wahid, child though he was, began to live close to national politics.

'My father took me when I was nine years old to this big rally in the Ikada stadium. Sukarno was to be there.' This would have been in 1950. 'The stadium had been built by the Japanese as a sop to us. It was where they now have this national monument.' And it was the park where, before an audience of a million, the French government were to put on their big firework display for the fiftieth anniversary of Indonesian independence. 'Up to sixty thousand people were in the stadium to hear Sukarno. He looked like a giant to me. He made this fiery speech against the imperialists. Asking the public to unite in this fight, this struggle. And the people responded so emotionally. I felt so elated, sensing this movement of people participating in this ecstasy. So I shouted as well. I jumped. My father calmed me down. He said, "Sit down. Don't jump." Maybe he didn't want me to get tired. Otherwise he would have to carry me to the car.'

I wanted to hear more about the physical appearance of Sukarno.

Mr Wahid said, 'The posture was good. The face showed not handsomeness, but steely will, a kind of strength. To be frank with you, his face was rough. Reflecting authority, strength of will. That's why he was charismatic. Especially when he raised his hands and shouted. You could see his eyes then, very alive, as though he was staring the imperialists down. My father being a minister, we were seated not far from him, in the first row. Sukarno stood there, facing us.

'My father died in 1953. He was thirty-nine years old. He had retired from the ministership in 1952 because our organisation had been voted out of the only Islamic party of the time. My father retired from the cabinet and formed the new party, the NU, in 1952. He was very active in establishing branches of the party. In one of those trips I was in the front seat and he was in the back seat, and we had this accident in which my father was seriously injured and one day later died. He fell out of the door and was hit by the spin of the car as it skidded.

'My mother came in the night to Bandung, and a number of dignitaries accompanied his body in a hearse to Jakarta. What I saw impressed me deeply. Along the 180-kilometre route people stood waiting for his body, to bid farewell to him. Thousands of them in the house, in the night. The next morning Sukarno came. And then the body was taken to the airport and flown to Surabaya. In Surabaya we were received by this big throng, tens of thousands of them, crying, bidding their farewell. With my uncle – a major-general – on a motorcycle in front of the hearse, we passed through the crowd, three to four deep on each side of the road for eighty kilometres, to the family cemetery in Jombang.

'Seeing all these people weeping and saying goodbye to him like that, the impression on me was like this: Is there anything greater in life than being loved by so many people? I was a child when Gandhi died. Later in life I saw pictures of Gandhi's funeral. It reminded me of my father's funeral. That sharpens my orientation.'

This was the family story that Mr Wahid told, through much of a warm afternoon, in a room at ground level in his NU headquarters in Jakarta, in the cloying smell of stale clove-cigarette smoke, while the

two-lane traffic roared and fumed outside just beyond the cleared front
yard. The family story – compressed at my request in some places, and
sometimes elsewhere made to jump about – contained, layer by layer,
the history of the country over the last century and a quarter. It was the
story which had dictated the course of Mr Wahid's own life. It was the
story to which he still referred his actions and attitudes.

He had inherited the leadership of his father's party, the NU. In 1984
he had taken the party out of politics.

'We realised how detrimental the direct link had proved between
Islam and politics – as in Pakistan, Iran, Sudan, Saudi Arabia – because
people everywhere then saw Islam as a religion using violence, which
in our thoughts is not so. In our thoughts Islam is a moral force which
works through ethics and morality. This is not my thinking alone, but
the collective decision of the *ulamas* educated by my grandfather. We
had a bitter debate about it in 1983 with a Ph.D. in constitutional law.

'In 1991 the Forum for Democracy was established. This totally
rejects Islamic politics – political Islam as posed by, say, Mr Suharto
and Professor Habibie. The competition between power centres in
our country in the 1990s reflects the need on the president's part for
the widest possible support from the society. Which means from
Islamic movements as well. To get that support, identification of
national politics with Islam is necessary. My grandfather, by the 1935
decision' – the decision of the congress that it was all right for
Muslims to defend a Dutch-ruled Indonesia against the Japanese –
'saw the need to differentiate between the functions of religion and
the functions of politics. Now, the decision of Minister Habibie to
take the route of Islamisation means that he sees politics as an integral
part of Islam. I feel it personally because my father participated in the
writing of the constitution which gives equal status to all citizens.
People should practise Islam out of conscience, not out of fear.
Habibie and his friends create a fear among non-Muslims and non-
practising Muslims to show their identity. This is the first step to
tyranny.'

Mr Wahid was passionate about this point. He came back to it
again and again and always seemed to be waiting for me to take down
his words. I tried to get him to talk in a more direct way of Habibie. I
wanted to get a picture, some conversation, a story. It wasn't easy.

'Habibie came to see me in hospital, and asked me to join ICMI, his
Association of Muslim Intellectuals.'

I liked the detail about the hospital: it seemed to corroborate what I felt about Mr Wahid's health. But I couldn't get more.

'My answer was: "Instead of joining your respectable group, let me stay outside the street-corner intellectuals."'

This was what I noted down. I wasn't sure what it meant, but later I decided that Mr Wahid was speaking with extreme irony from his hospital bed, that Habibie's respectable group and the street-corner intellectuals were the same people. Imaduddin, the preacher, the man on television, whose brainchild ICMI had been, would have been among those street-corner intellectuals, though Mr Wahid hadn't taken his name all afternoon.

Adi Sasono, an old supporter, would also have been in the line of fire. But this became clear only later, after I had been to see them all, and had only my notes to go by.

Adi said, near the end of our meeting in his fine office, 'Mr Wahid travels too much. He is a lecturer and an intellectual rather than a *kiyai*.' A *kiyai*, the head of a village *pesantren*: this would have been Adi's way of twisting Mr Wahid's reputation, and pulling him down a notch or two. 'A *kiyai* usually sits in a certain village in the *pesantren* and village people can come to him to ask questions. He is always with the people.'

Adi was chairman of the board of governors of CIDES, the acronym of an important ICMI 'think-tank' whose full name was the Centre for Information and Development Studies. This explained the splendour of Adi's offices. The elegantly produced, large-format CIDES brochure that Adi gave me carried a foreword by Adi. This was from the first paragraph:

> The birth of the Indonesian Muslim Intellectual Association (ICMI) three years ago established increasingly our nation's collective awareness of the importance of the human resources quality as a major renewable asset for development. This awareness should be manifested in big efforts based on development morality which emphasizes the centrality of human dimension in both the ideas and development practices. This view has also meant that a conscious and active participation of the nation as a whole is a very basic value . . .

Here, remarkably blown up, was Imaduddin's human resources, missionary idea, wrapped and wrapped again in modern-sounding words, corporate and academic. Words used like this were only wrapping. What was in the box was Imaduddin's high idea of the destiny of Malay-speaking Muslims, his wish to complete a process of conversion that Europe had stayed for two or three hundred years, and finally on this far eastern frontier of the faith to raise the flag of Islam.

3

A Convert

HE LIVED near the Heroes' Cemetery, in the Jalan Masjid Baru, the Street of the New Mosque. This was where he wanted me to come and see him, two days after our first meeting, at ten in the morning. I wanted to hear a little more about his past – his ancestry, the Sumatran background – and this was the only time he could manage, because he was flying off any day now to the United States and Canada to do his mental training work.

When he gave me the directions in his foundation office I knew I would have trouble finding the Street of the New Mosque. He wrote something on his card which he said would help the taxi-driver. It didn't help when the time came. The hotel taxi-driver took me for many miles down a wrong road, against the inward-moving morning traffic, partly because he thought it was enough to aim in the general direction of the Heroes' Cemetery, and partly for the pleasure in traffic-choked Jakarta of having a good long fast drive down a clear lane.

In a kind of penance, then, we had to crawl back with the crawl we had ignored on the way out, and after this – asking for directions all the time, ten o'clock coming and going – we had to pick our way between highways. We moved down narrow, half-paved, many-angled lanes, in a constant close play of morning light and shadows, with small new houses in small plots, sometimes with flowering shrubs, food barrows in some of the deeper, shaded angles of the road, occasional patches of wet, dusty heaps of gathered-up leaves, children: the skyscraper wealth of Jakarta, with its global intimations, reduced here to a kind of local small change.

We came at last to the Street of the New Mosque. We turned and twisted until we came to the number on Imaduddin's card. I paid the enormous sum showing on the meter, and the driver left me immediately, as though he was worried that I might change my mind about the money. It was about 10.30.

No one came out of the house. It was a small house, noticeably well kept. At the left a wide gateway led to a big, built-in garage with a sliding door: a tight fit in the narrow plot. To the right was a very narrow strip of lawn, and just beyond that, at ground level, the shiny red tiles of an open porch. I called from there, 'Good morning.' Still no one came out. I went through the open door into the sitting room. It was a low room, cool and dark after the sunlight of the porch. I called again. A serving girl in a brown frock leaned out from the kitchen to the left, beyond the dining area, allowed her eyes to rest on me, with something like fright, and then pulled herself back without a word.

I said to the empty room, 'Mr Imaduddin! Mr Imaduddin!'

Another serving girl came shyly out of the kitchen. She, as though wishing only to see what the other had seen, took one frightened look at me, and she too melted back into some hiding place beyond the kitchen.

I called, 'Mr Imaduddin! Good morning, Mr Imaduddin!'

The house remained silent. He had asked me to come at ten. I was half an hour late, but he should have been still in the house. A large framed piece of Arabic calligraphy on one wall was very much like Imaduddin – foreign travel among the faithful: a gift perhaps, a souvenir – but I began to wonder whether I had come to the right place. I also began to wonder how, without the language and a map, I could make my way back to a main road where taxis plied.

Because of the silence I didn't feel I should call out any more, and then I felt I shouldn't walk too freely about the room. I stood where I was and waited and looked.

The floor was tiled, with beautiful reed mats. The low ceiling, of a composite bagasse-like board, was stained where rain had once leaked through. In the dining area there was a microwave, next to some group photographs. On the pillars of the sitting room there were two or three decorative little flower pieces and, surprisingly, a picture of a sailing ship. About the sitting room were small mementoes of foreign travel, tourist souvenirs, showing a softer side of Imaduddin (or his wife), a side not connected with mental training, if indeed the house was theirs, and if these mementoes had truly tugged at their hearts (and did not, rather, preserve the memory of some pious giver): a number of Japanese things; an Eiffel Tower; above the water-cooler in a corner a Delft china plate with a simple, blurred, romantic view of a winding Dutch road and a farmhouse and a church; against a pillar a dwarf red maple growing out of a white dish, the dish on a silver-fringed doily, the whole thing resting – as if casually – on a slatted magazine stand. The back window of the dark room gave a view of a sunny little rock-walled garden, bounded by the red-tile roof of the neighbouring house: spaces were really small here.

I considered these details one by one, as if committing them to memory, and almost with a separate part of my mind wondered how long I should stay where I was, violating the house, and how when the time came I might get away from the curious trap I appeared to have fallen into.

Suddenly, after ten minutes, or perhaps fifteen minutes, a door to the left opened, and Imaduddin appeared, informal and unexpected in an ankle-length sarong and a dark-green shirt.

He said in a preoccupied way, 'I'm sorry. I have problems.'

I thought they might have been bathroom problems, but then a tall brown-complexioned man came out behind him. The tall man had twinkling eyes and a shiny skin, and was in a sarong as well, but was less informal than Imaduddin. The bottom of his sarong moved elegantly with his slow, stately steps. He had a flat black Muslim cap and a glaucous-blue waistcoat-shirt with a pen clipped to the pocket.

Imaduddin said, 'I am having some massage.'

That explained the shiny skin of the man in the black cap.

The room from which they came out would have been next to the garage and would have overlooked the little lawn and the lane. They would have heard me arrive, and would have heard me call.

Imaduddin said, 'Getting old, you know.'

As though that, and the trouble with his back, for which the masseur came every few days, was explanation enough. And, indeed, there appeared to be some formality about the masseur's visit. Imaduddin's farewell to him, some minutes later, and Imaduddin's wife's farewell, was full of ceremony.

When he had dressed, and was belted and tight and firm in trousers and shirt, familiar again, we settled down to talk at the dining table, between the microwave and the group photographs on one side and the water-cooler and the Dutch china plate on the other side. The serving girls, one in a red frock, one in a brown, had recovered from their fright, and were busy once more about the house and kitchen.

It was astonishing to me, considering their opposed positions now, how much his background was like Mr Wahid's. But Imaduddin was from Sumatra. He was from the Sultanate of Landkat, an area which he said was larger than Holland, on the border of Aceh, which the Dutch had conquered only in 1908, a full century after their conquest of Java. That would have made a difference, would have given Imaduddin the forthright temperament which he recognised in himself as Sumatran.

This was the story I reconstructed. In Landkat – perhaps in the latter part of the last century: Imaduddin gave no dates – there was a muezzin, a man who called the faithful to prayer. The muezzin died before his son was born. The muezzin's widow married again, and when her son by the muezzin was six years old, he was sent by his stepfather to the house of the mufti of the sultan of Landkat. The mufti was a Muslim scholar and the six-year-old boy, following the traditional way, worked in the mufti's house as a servant and was also a student there. The boy was very bright, and the mufti loved him.

Ten years passed. The secretary of the sultan, who was something like the sultan's vizier, and was the second highest man in the land, wanted someone to teach the Koran to his granddaughter. He talked to the sultan; the sultan talked to the mufti; and the mufti sent his servant and student, the old muezzin's son, now aged seventeen or eighteen, to teach the secretary's granddaughter. The boy didn't teach the girl by herself, of course; that would have been improper; he taught her together with some family friends. He was a very good teacher and the secretary's granddaughter fell in love with him. In due course – no date was given, and it didn't occur to me to ask – they married. Their son was Imaduddin; he was born in 1931.

By that time the old muezzin's son, Imaduddin's father, was truly launched in Landkat. In 1918, when travel became safe again after the Great War, the mufti persuaded the sultan to send the young man to Mecca to study Arabic for two years. After that the young man went for four years to Cairo, to the Islamic university of Al Azhar. His education so far had been like that of Mr Wahid's grandfather and father. And the similarity continued even after that: when he came back to Sumatra from Al Azhar in 1924 the old muezzin's son became principal of a well-known school which the sultan had set up.

It was only when the school principal had to educate his own son Imaduddin that the training pattern changed. When he was six Imaduddin was taken away by his father from Malay-language school where he had spent a year; and – oddly, considering his later religious development – sent for five years to a 'Dutch school'. These Dutch schools, Imaduddin said, were usually closed to the children of religious people, because the Dutch were nervous of Muslims being educated. Imaduddin could go to the Dutch school in Landkat only because the school there belonged to the sultan.

In 1942 the Japanese arrived. Their rule was harsh. Local food was commandeered. The school was virtually closed. To survive, Imaduddin and his father had to fish and farm and grow their own rice. Though the Japanese to some extent organised the Indonesians for what was to be their war of independence against the Dutch, there remained with Imaduddin from that time a hatred and a fear of the Japanese.

Little of this fear and hatred had come out in Mr Wahid's account of the Japanese occupation. His family seemed to have dealt with the Japanese at a higher, almost political, level. Mr Wahid's father had founded the Hizbullah militia in 1944; his younger brother had been trained by the Japanese and made a battalion commander; the head-quarters of the Hizbullah were in the Jombang *pesantren* itself. Far away in Sumatra Imaduddin was only a fourteen-year old foot soldier in the same militia.

One day in 1946 he was marching his little militia band on the street when he was stopped by his old teacher from the Dutch school. (On Sunday mornings now, perhaps in preparation for the celebrations of the fiftieth anniversary of independence, little semi-military bands like that one could be seen, in varied and colourful uniforms, on the streets of Jakarta: groups of ten, perhaps, moving in formation on the road, arms swinging from side to side, the leader separate from his group, but swinging his arms with the rest, blowing on his whistle, giving the marchers a beat.) Marching like this with his band one day in 1946, Imaduddin was stopped by his old teacher.

The teacher asked Imaduddin, 'Why are you doing this?'

'Because we want independence.'

'After independence what are you going to do? Do you know?'

'I don't know.'

'How are you going to build this country if you don't have doctors, engineers? You should go back to school and study. I know that a new high school is going to open in a town near here. I want you to join this school.'

Imaduddin did as his old teacher said. He got permission and he enrolled in the new school. It was the big turn in his life. He worked at his secondary-school studies with the intelligence and application which his father had given to religious studies. He was top of his class, top of the school, and finally, in the special circumstances of the independence war against the Dutch, top of the country.

In 1948 the Dutch occupied Landkat. They were after Imaduddin's father (as they were after Mr Wahid's diabetic father in Jombang), and the family fled in five canoes down the Strait of Malacca to Aceh. There must have been some kind of larger family or community support, because Imaduddin was able to continue with his studies, at first in Aceh until the war of independence ended, and after that in the more important town of Medan. In 1953, when he was twenty-two, Imaduddin was admitted to the Bandung Institute of Technology. This meant that, even with the immense upheavals of the Japanese occupation and the war of independence, Imaduddin had been such a good student that he had lost only four years. When he was thirty he became an assistant professor at Bandung; the following year he went to the United States to do a higher degree.

It was a stupendous career for a man born in 1931 in a small town in the Dutch East Indies; and very little of it could have been in the head of the fourteen-year-old boy marching with his little militia band in Landkat in 1946. Yet the new learning that the little boy and then the young man had mastered had always been kept in its place. There seemed never to have been any kind of cultural or spiritual dislocation in Imaduddin. He had always remained the grandson of the sultan's muezzin from the last century, calling the faithful to prayer five times a day; and that man's son, the mufti's favourite, whose higher education had been in Mecca and Al Azhar.

Mr Wahid, with his *pesantren* education and *pesantren* family pieties, had become more internationalist and liberal. Imaduddin had remained committed to the holy war.

Sitting at the dining table – with the two serving girls in frocks flitting about between the sitting room and the little kitchen – he had become restless. After the flight of his family in five canoes down the Strait of Malacca, his story had telescoped and lost detail. His face clouded; he looked as preoccupied as when he had come out of the massage room.

He said, 'How much longer do you want?'

I said half an hour, perhaps an hour.

He said, 'Somebody from Oklahoma wants to be a Muslim. He is going to convert today. He is an electrical engineer. I have met him once or twice. He is going to marry an Indonesian girl. I haven't instructed him, but I have been in touch with the girl's family. He is waiting for me in the mosque. I should have met him there at 11.30.'

It was now a quarter to twelve, more than time to leave. It was during the goodbyes that I heard from Imaduddin or from Mrs Imaduddin, serene and lovely as always, that they were moving to a new house.

We left in the Mercedes. The driver, Mohammad Ali, was already at his station, in the car, and the well-trained serving girls (one in a plain brown frock, one in a red), with very few words having to be said, flitted out from the low dark house into the sunlight of the tiny garden to slide back the heavy garage door and to open the gate, and to wait until Mohammad Ali had manoeuvred the big car out. The car, and the ceremony its size imposed, overpowered the house and the narrow lane. Imaduddin had outgrown this setting.

In no time we had turned into a main road and were driving past the Heroes' Cemetery. Imaduddin was right: his house would have been easy to find if the taxi-driver had taken the right road. But that wouldn't have helped me when I got to the house: the masseur would have been there.

We passed a row of shops with their goods almost out on the road: furniture shops, shops dealing in motor-car wheels. Imaduddin – as though, because he was now close to power, he had to explain what we were seeing – said the shops shouldn't have been there, but it was hard to regulate them.

A minute or two later, as though the unregulated shops might in fact have made him think of evictions, he said, 'The sultan's palace in Landkat was burned down in the war against the Dutch. Not by the Dutch. It was Sukarno's –' He fumbled for the words.

I said, 'Sukarno's scorched-earth policy?'

They were the words he wanted. And again I wondered at the extra-ordinary events Imaduddin – barely a year older than I was – had lived through. Extraordinary events, but he talked of them easily, and did so without affectation: the events appeared hardly to have marked him. 'He is *himself*,' his diplomat disciple had said. And there was a quality of completeness about Imaduddin, a strange innocence that appeared to have protected him right through.

He said he had had Adi Sasono that morning on his religious television programme. They had talked about the importance of the current independence anniversary celebrations and its relation to Islam. It was actually very important, he said. 'Islam is for freedom. It is anti-colonialist.'

Once upon a time the government was nervous of the faith, and Imaduddin was a rebel. Now the government, though unchanged in its ruler and its political forms, said it served the faith, and Imaduddin had no trouble in making the faith serve the government. The faith was capacious; Imaduddin was learned; he didn't violate himself.

The Oklahoman was waiting in the Sunda Kelapa mosque in Menteng. Menteng, though traffic-ridden and polluted, was the diplomatic and fashionable area of Jakarta, and the Sunda Kelapa mosque served the best people.

The name – from the Hindu kingdom that existed here – was on the wall of the mosque in large fanciful letters. The big open courtyard, full of glare, was made of concrete blocks. It was after twelve, and Imaduddin said – as if it was a stroke of luck, an unexpected blessing for being late – that it was time for the midday prayer. He intended to do the prayer and then he would do the conversion. There would be no hardship for the Oklahoman and his party; they would no doubt be doing the prayer too.

If salvation could be compared to a banquet, prayer was for Imaduddin – from the excitement and pleasure with which he went at it – like a tasty preparatory snack taken five times a day, a kind of paradisal fast food, never cloying, always sharpening the appetite. So now, tight and belted, a thick wallet showing in his back pocket, a man completely at home and private in the openness of the main mosque, Imaduddin, after his ablutions, with a slightly tilted walk that made me think of his back and the masseur, padded to the front where the men were lined up, facing the wall, now standing, now squatting, now bowing. Far to the back, thirteen or fourteen women in white head-dresses and long gowns stood in their own line.

Among the men the Oklahoman was noticeable, even from the back, by his greater size, his height and middle girth, and by the flat black Muslim cap he was wearing, like Imaduddin's masseur.

Afterwards, when the prayer was done and people had left the main hall, and the Oklahoman was sitting in the sunlight on the concrete steps, pulling on his socks, Imaduddin went to him and said – with an excess of joviality, perhaps because I was present – 'It's amazing how you've changed. You don't look like an American. You already look like an Indonesian.'

The Oklahoman, straightening a sock over a foot, and looking down at it, said in a voice that didn't carry far, 'Still white.'

After Imaduddin's joviality the words had an ambiguous ring. They might have been defensive, from a zealous convert, or they might have been a way of letting Imaduddin know that he wasn't to go too far. For the first time I saw Imaduddin momentarily uncertain. His smile lasted a little too long before he said, 'Uncooked.' As though carrying on the joviality and the racial game; but then he let the matter drop and left the Oklahoman to his socks and shoes.

The conversion ceremony was to take place in a room downstairs. It was small and low and air-conditioned, with walls faced with grey marble. The marble had disquieting mausoleum suggestions, and the room felt quite cold after the glare and reflected heat of the exposed big courtyard and steps. It was furnished like a lecture room of sorts. For the principals of the ceremony there was a high platform with hardwood benches or forms back and front of an altar-like table, with microphones; for the witnesses, on the floor, there were rows of classroom-style chair-desks.

The bride-to-be – for whose sake the Oklahoman was converting – was the niece of a businessman who was also a well-known poet. Poetry here, for the most part an amateur activity, was much respected, and the people gathering in the marble chamber reflected this mixture of culture and comfortableness. Whispers subsided. The hissing of the air-conditioners, always there, but now suddenly dominant, appeared to act as a fanfare for the ceremony.

When the shufflings were done, Imaduddin, with his glasses hanging down stylishly from his neck, appeared as a central figure on the platform, on the far bench, against the grey marble wall, below an elegant brass plaque with black Arabic lettering. He sat between two men – beginning to chant from the Koran, against the air-conditioner hiss – and faced the Oklahoman and his bride across the table.

They, the couple, had their backs to us, together with their witnesses, one on either side. The bride, Indonesian-small, looked eager and feather-light in a yellow gown and a reddish headdress. The Oklahoman, white-necked below his flat black cap, was broader, stolider. His blue trousers looked American; his green batik shirt – it might have been a gift or a new purchase – did not, on him, suggest frivolity.

When the chanting ended, Imaduddin, smiling at the Oklahoman, said to him in English, 'We welcome you back to Islam. Back to Islam, because in our belief everyone was born as a Muslim, without sin. You have come back to Islam because you have opened your heart to the truth. In everything submitting yourself to the will of God. Islam means submission.'

Then it was time for the Oklahoman to make his declaration. He said first of all that he was speaking in conscience and without duress. He sounded shy. He had no pronounced Southern accent, and for a big man his voice was light, never rising above the hiss of the air-conditioners. This might have been because he had his back to us, and perhaps also because he didn't have Imaduddin's microphone skills. He spoke the words of his convert's declaration first in Arabic – this would have been a further reason for his shyness – and then in English: 'I testify there is no other God than Allah and Mohammed is his last prophet.'

Imaduddin said, with something of his lecturer's jollity, 'Ah.' As though what had just been said hadn't, after all, been so hard. Smiling, and still with his jollity, he said to the Oklahoman, 'You want to change your name?'

The Oklahoman didn't have time to answer. Feminine voices called from the floor in English, 'Yes, yes.' And, 'Better.' And, 'Much better.'

Like an impresario, Imaduddin asked, 'You like the name Mohammad?'

The Oklahoman liked the name.

'And Adam?'

That name was liked, as was Khalid.

'So,' Imaduddin said, 'Mohammad Adam Khalid, you are reborn as a new Adam. I hope you will be happy with the new name.'

The main part of the ceremony was now over. The bride-to-be's family took over. They wanted the change of name and they were happy. Mr Khalid, the Oklahoman – a gentle, small face on his big body – came down from the platform and there was a general kissing and embracing. The women in the gathering, until then demure, became assertive. This part of the ceremony belonged to them. There was a release of pent-up, happy chatter. Cameras flashed, and the food boxes, from a firm of caterers, which had been stacked up all the while on a chest against one wall, were taken around now by girls and offered to everyone.

Imaduddin had appeared to suggest Mr Mohammad Adam Khalid's new names to him one by one, as though each name had required a separate inspiration. But this turned out to be only Imaduddin's preacher's or television style. He said when I asked him about it that Mr Khalid's names had been chosen by Mr Khalid's bride-to-be. So the tremulous, eager girl in yellow and red had known all along what was going to happen to the big man from Oklahoma sitting beside her on the bench.

I learned this, about the names, in Imaduddin's house on Sunday morning. His mental training trip to the United States and Canada had been delayed, and I was able to go and see him again. There was no trouble with taxis this time. He sent the Mercedes and Mohammad Ali to the hotel. He wasn't absolutely sure that Mohammad Ali – as a chauffeur still a little green and shy – would know how or where to pick people up from the hotel. But Mohammad Ali was only five minutes late. The Mercedes smelled of air-fresheners, like a New York taxi; and the gaudily jacketed cassettes might have been of Arab music.

Recognisable and reassuring this time: the small, colourfully uniformed marching groups, arms swinging from side to side; the furniture shops and wheel shops almost encroaching on the highway; the Heroes' Cemetery; the lane, the little house, the big garage with the sliding door, the dark room, the little Eiffel Tower and other mementoes, the small sunlit garden at the back bounded by a rockery against the wall of the neighbouring house with the red-tile roof; the serving girls. One of them, in a red bodice, offered me fruit and fruit juice. Imaduddin wasn't in the room, was perhaps with the masseur again. But Mrs Imaduddin came in to welcome me, padding about on the plain reed mats on the tiled floor, and then she went out again. She came in again a short while later to ask whether I liked the fruit and to say that her husband was 'preparing'. He came out, in his sarong again, from the front room, moving briskly, looking down, not saying much, saving his talk for when he was dressed.

He talked of the conversion of Mr Khalid in a down-to-earth missionary way. He appeared to have no other idea of the wonder of the occasion, no idea of the extraordinary movements of peoples which that conversion could be said to contain. Imaduddin had spent years in the United States. He would have known that there were many states in the American Union. He could have found out that Oklahoma was a comparatively new state, and that it had been created by the overwhelming movement westwards over Indian territory late in the nineteenth century. This would have been at the time of similar expansionist movements in Argentina, Africa, Asia: at the time, in fact, when the Dutch, in their grinding-down way, were waging a long war in Aceh in Sumatra; and when, perhaps, Imaduddin's muezzin grandfather was calling the faithful to prayer in neighbouring Landkat.

The conversion in the Menteng mosque of a young man from Oklahoma was full of historical linkages and ironies. But to see them required another vision of the world. Imaduddin's missionary world-view was simpler. Everyone was born a Muslim, without sin, he had said at the conversion ceremony. What followed from this – though Imaduddin didn't say it – was that everyone in the world outside Islam was in a state of error, and perhaps not quite real until he found his Muslim self.

Imaduddin's father, the mufti's favourite, had had his higher education in Mecca and then at Al Azhar in Cairo, always in a little bubble of Islamic learning, spiritually always insulated from the cataclysms of the time. Imaduddin had travelled far beyond Mecca and Cairo, to the world outside; and he had not gone for religious learning. He had gone for the technical and scientific knowledge that was to be his livelihood, and later for rest and security and asylum after things had become too dangerous for him at home. Yet spiritually Imaduddin lived in the bubble in which his father had lived. Nothing in Imaduddin's world-view acknowledged the implications of the asylum and law and learning he had travelled to find. The outside world seemed to be simply there, neutral territory, something 'found', open to all, to be used as required.

So Imaduddin might in 1980 use his Saudi grant not to go to a Muslim country, but to the United States, to the University of Iowa, benefiting later from a kind of asylum. He might while he was there be given a vision of the high Islamic destiny of the Malay-speaking Muslims by the Pakistani fundamentalist fanatic Fazel-ur-Rehman, himself enjoying, bizarrely, academic freedom at the University of Chicago, and sleeping safe and sound every night, protected by laws, and far away from the mischief he was wishing on his countrymen at home. This kind of freedom and protection was what a Muslim persecuted at home could look for in the neutral world outside Islam, and Imaduddin appeared to see no anomaly. In his world-view – in spite of the mementoes of foreign lands in his cool, low sitting room – nothing seemed owed to the world outside Islam.

He said, with one of the analogies that came to him easily as preacher and scientist, 'The Koran is a value system. It's like a car. A car is a system. If you have only the tyre and the wheel you don't have a car. Islam is a system. You have to have it all. Or you leave it. You cannot be half-way Muslim or third-way Muslim. You become a Muslim wholeheartedly or not at all.'

Nothing therefore affected the faith; every kind of new learning could be made to serve the faith. When he came back from the United States in 1986 with his second degree he could, as he said, use the techniques of power system analysis for his Islamic mental training classes. And now that the faith was the faith of the government, the faith in Indonesia had special political needs.

It had, for example, to deal with Mr Wahid, with his thirty million *pesantren* Muslim followers. And while Adi Sasono lay about Mr Wahid with modern-sounding words like 'élitism' and 'religious feudalism', Imaduddin could use the technological needs of the age (and his own technical training) to beat poor old Mr Wahid – and his 'deschooling' – deeper into the ground. Imaduddin never mentioned Mr Wahid by name to me (just as Mr Wahid, when he had talked to me, had never taken Imaduddin's name). But it was clear who was in Imaduddin's sights when he repeated in his house what he had said in his office, that the whole purpose of the creation was to make the whole earth prosperous.

He said, 'It's written in the Koran. When Adam was created the first knowledge given to him by God is science.'

So when he went to Iowa he was serving the faith. When he came back and attached himself to Habibie and the N-250 he was serving the faith.

He said, 'The politicians will have to understand that – because of that plane – we are gaining our position with science and technology.'

He made politicians – poor Mr Wahid! – sound like people who were not rightful rulers.

It was the perfection of the 'value system' of his Islam. It was curiously circular. It was – adapting his preacher's analogy – like a very smooth and easy treadmill, rather than a car: it kept him busy and went nowhere. Even if you said to him that people in Iowa had been kind to him when he was in need, he was prompted to say nothing about the people. Their kindness was simply another tribute to his faith: God, he said, loved him very much.

Near the end of our talk that Sunday morning I asked him again about his outspokenness in the late 1970s and his troubles then with the government.

He said, expanding on what he had learned in jail in 1978 and 1979 from the former foreign minister, Subandrio, 'Never criticise Suharto. He's a Javanese. Young people shouldn't criticise older people, especially big people.' For Imaduddin – not so young in 1977: forty-six to President Suharto's fifty-six – this went against the grain. 'I was trained in the Dutch way and then in the American way, where criticism is okay. And I was born in Sumatra: I can argue with my father. I had to learn the Javanese way.'

The Sumatran way, which came naturally to Imaduddin, was the forthright, religious way, the fundamentalist way. For Imaduddin it had historically been a source of Sumatran strength.

He had told me earlier, 'The Dutch when they came could conquer Java relatively easily, but they couldn't conquer Aceh and Sulawesi because the people were very religious.'

Mr Wahid had spoken of the new steamship travel that had from the thirties of the nineteenth century made Mecca more accessible for pilgrimage and study. Out of this there had developed, in colonised Java, the new Islamic village schools, like the one run by Mr Wahid's grandfather.

In the independent kingdoms or sultanates of Sumatra, however, the effect of these journeys to Mecca had been more violent. Just as one hundred and fifty or sixty years later colonial students, often the first in their families to travel abroad for university degrees, were to go back home with borrowed ideas of revolution; so these Sumatran students and pilgrims in Mecca, influenced by Wahabi fundamentalism, and a little vain of their new knowledge, were to go back home determined to make the faith in Sumatra equal to the Wahabi faith in Mecca. They were determined to erase local errors, all the customs and ceremonies and earth reverences that carried the taint of the religions that had gone before: animism, Hinduism, Buddhism. There had followed religious wars for much of the century; it was what had drawn the Dutch in, at first to mediate or assist, and then to rule.

This was the missionary faith that Imaduddin had inherited. Java, rather than Sumatra, was rich in the monuments of the pagan past. But nothing outside or before the faith was to be acknowledged, not even a great Buddhist monument like Borobudur, one of the wonders of the world. One of Imaduddin's criticisms of the government in 1979 was that the Indonesian embassy in Canberra looked like a Hindu building. As for Borobudur, that was for the international community to look after.

I asked him about that. He said – like a man whose position now required him to be more statesmanlike – that I had misunderstood. What he had said or meant to say was that money that could be used to feed 'hungry Muslims' shouldn't be used on Borobudur.

In spite of the statesmanlike softening intention, the old Sumatran unforgivingness showed through. For the new fundamentalists of Indonesia the greatest war was to be made on their own past, and everything that linked them to their own earth.

4

A Sacred Place

SOME WEEKS later, near the end of my time in Indonesia, I went to Sumatra. Not to Imaduddin's Sumatra, of Aceh and Landkat in the north; but to the Minangkabau uplands in West Sumatra. I was following up a later interest. In Jakarta I had met a senior civil servant who had spent nearly all her childhood in those uplands. For the whole of one afternoon, in her sunstruck office in a round, modern tower above a roaring avenue, she had talked so lyrically of her land, and with eyes so bright with memory, that the wish had come to me to go and see for myself.

And there I discovered – what I should have known – that this Minangkabau territory had been the scene of the fundamentalist Wahabi wars of the first third of the nineteenth century. It was as though, with or without Imaduddin, religious passion was the inescapable Sumatran theme.

It was a land of high green volcanic mountains, range against range, and broad plains between the mountain ranges. Where there were settlements there were trees and shade. Elsewhere the plains were open, for the rice-fields. Rice was the principal crop. It didn't have a fixed season here. So that on the plains, as if in a kind of pictorial simultaneous narrative, there appeared all the stages of rice-growing. Mud being ploughed or turned over before planting; brilliant tender-green nursery patches of seedlings in a corner of a waterlogged paddy; seedlings planted out in rows; scarecrows (or lengths of plastic fluttering from poles) in full, ripening fields (full except where the rats had been);

groups of reapers and threshers, the reapers with their long curved knives, the threshers beating bundles of cut rice-stalks into baskets with high screens fixed above them – and looking like small sail boats – to catch the threshed grain. And all over the plain small smoking fires of rice straw, giving scale to the very broad and flat land, the thin, brown-white threads of smoke from individual straw fires flattening out at a certain height in the middle sky and joining together in a still bank of smoke.

I had been given no visual ideas by the woman who had spent her childhood here. But I had expected beauty. What I hadn't expected was the antiquity these cultivated plains suggested. It would have taken many generations to achieve the social organisation that those labours of the plain spoke of. I felt that the land went back and back, far beyond the seventh-century beginnings of the Hindu kingdom of Srivijaya with its Sanskrit name, and might have been as old as rice itself. Not many weeks before, in London, I had looked hard at a big Poussin exhibition. And perhaps for that reason I found in these views of mountains and plains something of the landscapes of Poussin: the same pictorial breadth and depth, the same calling up of the idea of the ancient world. And I found in them what William Hazlitt in the early nineteenth century was happy to find in the landscapes of Poussin: the 'eternal forms' – rather than significant form – of the created world, without visual 'accidents'.

On the afternoon of the second day I was taken to Pariangan. It was a big dip in the volcanic land with a hot-water spring. This was where the Minangkabau people were said to have come out of the earth. To see this place was to feel its sacredness; it was not necessary to know anything of its history or its myth. It would always have been a sacred place; it would always have had a power over human imagination. An old stone with an old inscription in an Indian script spoke of that power. It was easy even now to forget the visual accidents – the ordinariness – of the broken masonry ramps that went down from the road to the rough concrete bath sheds, one for men and boys, one for women and girls. It was possible even to ignore the big new red-painted mosque on the far side. The mind stayed with the wonder of the site and the wonder of the water bubbling up hot from the earth for centuries.

Numen inest: the Roman words fitted: the god or spirit of the place was there, more than it was for me at Paphos in Cyprus, where Venus was said to have issued out of the sea. In the time of Tacitus (in the first century) the magic of the – now – unremarkable little cove would have been preserved by the temples and the rites described in the *Histories*, with the mystery underlined by the form in which Venus was worshipped at Paphos – a rock cone sliced off at the top – when elsewhere, far from her birthplace, she already had been invested with her alluring feminine shape.

Visitors to Pariangan, I was told, greeted one another with the word *Sembahyang*: 'Worship the god.' Most of the visitors would have been Muslim, and they would have known with one part of their minds that the salutation was idolatrous. They would have known that the religious intention of the big red mosque was not to honour or claim the sacredness of the place, but to triumph over it. The sacred places of the Muslim faith were connected with the Prophet or his immediate successors. Those places were in another country. There could be no sacred places here. It was part of the law.

My first eighteen years were spent two oceans away, on the other side of the globe, in the New World, on an island in the mouth of one of the great South American rivers. The island had no sacred places; and it was nearly forty years after I had left the island that I identified the lack.

I began to feel when I was quite young that there was an incompleteness, an emptiness, about the place, and that the real world existed somewhere else. I used to feel that the climate had burnt away history and possibility. This feeling might have had to do with the smallness of the island, which we all used to say was only a dot on the map of the world. It might have had to do with the general poverty and the breakdown of the extended family system that had come with us from India. It might have had to do with the wretched condition of India itself; and with the knowledge at the same time that we who were Indian were an immigrant people whose past stopped quite abruptly with a father or grandfather.

Later, years after I had left – knowledge of things never coming all at once, but in layers – I thought that the place was unhallowed because it hadn't been written about. And later still I thought that the agricultural colony, in effect a plantation, honoured neither land nor people. But it was much later, in India, in Bombay, in a crowded industrial area – which was yet full of unexpected holy spots, a rock, a tree – that I understood that, whatever the similarities of climate and vegetation and formal belief and poverty and crowd, the people who lived so intimately with the idea of the sacredness of their earth were different from us.

There would have been sacred places on the island, and in all the other islands to the north. On the tiny island of St Kitts, for example, there were – hidden by sugar-cane fields – rocks with crude pre-Columbian carvings. But the aboriginal people who knew about the sacred places had been destroyed on our island, and instead of them there were – in the plantation colony – people like us, whose sacred places were in other continents.

Too late, then, I remembered with a pang a story I had heard about when I was a child, and later read another version of (in Charles Kingsley's *At Last*, 1871). Every now and then, according to this story, groups of aboriginal Indians in canoes came across the gulf from the continent (where remnants of the tribes still existed), walked to certain places in the woods in the southern hills, performed certain rites or made offerings, and then, with certain fruit they had gathered, went back home across the gulf. This was all that I heard. I wasn't of an age to want to ask more or to find out more; and the unfinished, unexplained story now is like something in a dream, an elusive echo from another kind of consciousness.

Perhaps it is this absence of the sense of sacredness – which is more than the idea of the 'environment' – that is the curse of the New World, and is the curse especially of Argentina and ravaged places like Brazil. And perhaps it is this sense of sacredness – rather than history and the past – that we of the New World travel to the Old to rediscover.

So it is strange to someone of my background that in the converted Muslim countries – Iran, Pakistan, Indonesia – the fundamentalist rage is against the past, against history, and the impossible dream is of the true faith growing out of a spiritual vacancy.

It was Dewi Fortuna Anwar who sent me to Sumatra. She was a pretty young woman of high academic qualifications and more than one person thought that I should meet her. Her responsibilities in Indonesia were quite formidable, and she had two name-cards. She worked for the Indonesian Institute of Sciences. Her special concern there was the Centre for Political and Regional Studies. In Indonesia everything of any importance is known by an acronym or by its initials, and Dewi's centre was known as PPW-LIPI. She was the head of the Regional and International Affairs Division for PPW-LIPI, and in this capacity went to many international conferences. She was also a research executive for CIDES, the Centre for Information and Development Studies (this was connected to ICMI, Imaduddin's and Habibie's Association of Muslim Intellectuals, and Adi Sasono was chairman of the board of directors).

Her hands were really quite full, and at our lunch – arranged by the woman diplomat who had taken me to meet Imaduddin – Dewi had talked formally, and with a certain amount of patriotism, of various important academic-sounding research projects LIPI was engaged in. It was only near the end, perhaps with the coffee, that she began for some reason to talk of Sumatra and her childhood there, the taboos of her clan that she had learned about and still honoured. Everything she said about her Sumatran childhood was new and fresh, and some of it unexpected. It was personal and guileless, after her earlier formal talk of international conferences and research. I wanted to hear more, and we arranged to meet one afternoon in her PPW-LIPI office.

The LIPI building, with its modern round tower, impressive from the highway, turned out to have a bureaucratic tarnish inside, as of a place not personal to anyone. Dewi's office was on the eleventh floor. The waiting room, a segment of the circular floor, was in shape like a piece of a pie that had been cut down and across, with a little arc of external wall like a kind of crust at the side. There were Indonesian wooden puppets on this wall, together with a picture of a temple in multi-coloured, crinkled batik; on another wall there were bows and arrows. Dewi's office was across the corridor. It was on the wrong side of the round tower for an afternoon meeting; the sun was fierce; we needed a blind.

Dewi had an academic background. Her father – who had recently died – was a professor. He had done his higher degrees at Columbia and the School of Oriental and African Studies in London. Her mother was a teacher of history at the university in Sumatra.

When Dewi was a child the family lived in Bandung. She was three and a half – and her father was away, studying in Scotland – when relations from Sumatra came visiting, and one of them said to her, 'But you should see what you have in Sumatra.' This made Dewi passionate to see what she had in Sumatra, and she went back with these relations to what she realised, even as a child, was her ancestral land.

There was a family house in Sumatra, one of the fabulous Minangkabau traditional houses with horn-shaped roofs. But it had been neglected for twenty years and more, and was empty, and there was talk of spirits. Dewi didn't even like going near it. She lived with her mother's maternal uncle. He didn't live in a traditional house.

Dewi said, 'He was an *ulama*.' A Muslim religious teacher. 'In Java they call it a *kiyai*, in West Sumatra they call him an *ulama*. I lived with him for a year. He had a small mosque where he lived. It was called a *surau*, because it was not a public mosque. He had students coming to study with him. He had his youngest wife living with him. This was unusual, but because he was an important man – and his wife was actually one of his students at an earlier time – he didn't go to live with her. Polygamy was quite common in those days, but this was the only wife he cohabited with. Before my time he had one or two wives at the same time. He always returned to his *surau* after being with one of his wives. By the time I was there he had his youngest wife living with him, and she brought me up.'

Dewi spoke in her open, lyrical way. And it was interesting that, with a father studying in Scotland (and probably fending off jokes about Muslims and their shuffling about of four wives), his very young daughter should be discovering and accepting, through an adored and pious older relative, the very same idea, but as an aspect of a beautiful old world.

'When my father came back from Scotland I went back to Bandung. I stayed in Bandung for two years. And when different relatives came from West Sumatra to stay with us in Bandung I decided to ask them to take me back with them. I was five and a half.'

I asked, 'Can you remember why you liked the place so much?'

'It was a very beautiful place. Wide open spaces. And we were some-body. When we are there our family is deferred to. I had no competition. My great-uncle simply doted on me. He was very fierce, but to me he was very loving. My great-uncle's wife was very loving. She used to protect me from my great-uncle's wrath. I was very fortu-nate, because my great-uncle wanted someone to carry on the family name. West Sumatra is a contradiction. It is very Islamic, but it is also matrilineal. And I was the daughter of my mother, who was the last female in the line. For this I was very precious to the family. I was expected to show the flag.

'My great-uncle took it upon himself to educate me. He was an *ulama*, very conservative, all orthodox. But he did not want me to be deprived of modern education. He did not want my mother or my father to blame him for my lack of education. That was why he said he hadn't wanted me to come back to West Sumatra. But in fact I wanted to wear this head covering and to go to the village school – in the religious village school you had to wear a sarong and a headscarf.'

'You thought of the sarong and the scarf as pretty clothes?'

'I didn't think of it like that. I thought it was right. But my great-uncle put his foot down. He said that those village schools taught Islam badly and had a poor modern curriculum. He taught me Islam at home himself – when I went to the normal school. So I learned the Koran, and he read various stories from the *hadith*, the supplementary traditions.

'He would also take me around on a Sunday during the holidays to look at our family land, so that I would know where they are and who worked them. Paddy fields are scattered all over the place. And coconut groves too. Most of the water and the arable paddy fields are at the bottom of the valley; the people at the top of the valley have to walk miles and miles to their paddy fields. My branch of the family tends to control more of the land resources. That is because the women didn't have too many offspring. If a clan becomes very large the land is parcelled out between many people. The land is not alienable, but it has to be divided among the users, the heirs. When an heir dies the land goes back to the nearest female relative.

'So, going round our land, I was being given knowledge of family kinships as well. Because the people who work our land are mostly relatives. And it is important to get to know boundaries. So one acquired a whole picture of village networking.'

From five and a half to fifteen Dewi lived in West Sumatra. Her father visited once, when she was about eight; and her mother visited with some friends two years later. From the age of twelve Dewi went every fasting month holiday to Bandung. So the village was her world.

'Living in the village is a total experience. It wasn't only about going to school or learning the Koran or finding out about your family or knowing about your property. It is about learning the village way of seeing, and their idiosyncratic beliefs, not always rational, and yet very important. You ignore them or discard them at your peril.

'It happens that my family belongs to a clan – Pitapang – which is famous for its various taboos. They are famous in the village. People say, "The Pitapang can't do this. The Pitapang can't do that." A lot of people from other clans do not realise that there are things we cannot do.'

My hearing began to play tricks. I didn't always hear 'Pitapang' when Dewi spoke the word. I sometimes heard 'Peter Pan'.

'There is a belief that the Pitapang is one of the older clans. The Pitapang ancestors probably moved into the area when it was virgin jungle or forest. In the pre-Islamic tradition it was believed that all those forests and springs and rivers were occupied by spirits. Of course, the humans who come to clear the land had to make a compromise with the original spirit inhabitants. So the ancestors had to abide by a code of behaviour. Basically designed to ensure a balance in the environment.'

Though that idea of balance and the 'environment' was a later, borrowed idea, growing out of another kind of knowledge and logic, and did not have the force of the earth reverences Dewi was talking about. She herself seemed to say something like that almost immediately.

'In conducting our everyday lives there are other factors we have to consider. We always have to ask permission when we cut down a big tree, or drain a spring, or build a house. We have to follow certain rituals, ceremonies, to appease the guardian spirits.'

This village idea about the spirits of trees and springs seemed idolatrous and irreligious to her great-uncle, the conservative *ulama*. He already felt that Islam was badly taught in the village religious schools, and had personally taken on the religious instruction of his great-niece.

'My great-uncle basically didn't want to follow these un-Islamic practices. He knew about it and probably believed some of it, but most of the time he believed that making offering to spirits was un-Islamic. The clan, and some of the older people in the village, believed that if a taboo is transgressed by someone of the Pitapang clan, someone in the clan usually suffers the consequences: a child becomes ill, or something unpleasant happens. My great-uncle paid little attention to the taboos. So I was often ill, and his wife and his friends kept saying, "Ah, your great-uncle must have done something again." As happened when they used the rice-granary timbers to build a latrine.'

The rice granary would have been a dependency of a main house,

and it too would have been horn-roofed, a miniature, on stilts, broader
at the top than at the bottom, perhaps with decorated gables, with walls
of variously patterned woven-bamboo panels, and with a ladder rather
than steps. Rice, the staple, the subject of every kind of old reverence
and fertility rite, had always to be treated with respect; to use the
timbers of a rice granary, even an old or derelict one, to build a latrine
was to set two opposed ideas together, and was a serious kind of
desecration.

Dewi said, 'I had been ill for a couple of days. They gave me village
medicine. My *datuk*, my great-uncle, also had knowledge of village
medicines, and had very little faith in doctors; he refused to go to a
doctor. Most of the villagers believed he had the ability to talk to some
of the guardian spirits. So when children became ill a lot of people
came to him for medicine.

'After people asked whether my great-uncle had done "something"
in the past few days, my great-aunt remembered that maybe building
the latrine with the granary timbers wasn't appropriate. So my great-
aunt and a young man took a big axe and went down to the latrine, and
they claimed they saw a creature like a black monkey jumping into the
water when they started cutting the bridging plank to the latrine.'

I asked Dewi, 'What water did the monkey jump into?'

'A fish pond. After that I became well. People claimed that while I
was hallucinating I said all kinds of things.

'There are a lot of things I would hesitate to do, even though I have
moved away. For instance, if I go back to the village I would never dip
a pot straight from the stove into the water. This is considered taboo.
The logical explanation is that the soot might dirty the water.

'And: in fish ponds, to protect the fish, we need to have all kinds of
material put in the water, and the most common is the bamboo with
sharp branches.' Tall bamboos with the branch ends sharpened to
spikes: a hidden obstruction, dreadfully mangling. 'This possibly pro-
tects the fish from poachers. And occasionally, when people drain the
fish ponds, people will take the bamboo out, and careless people will
lean the bamboo against the wall of a house. If a Pitapang does that, it
is considered transgressing a taboo, and we must never do it. I was
taught that if we did that in the evening, the spirits will be angry and
the house will start to shake.

'In the village these taboos are like the equivalent of traffic lights in
the city – things you have to obey.'

Most of these taboos applied only to the Pitapang clan. This was why Dewi believed that the Pitapangs were one of the oldest clans and that at the very beginning, when the rice lands were being developed in the jungle, it was they who had made the early compromises with the guardian spirits of the trees and the springs. These compromises had to be honoured even now.

At the time of Dewi's wedding, for instance, there were strange 'goings-on' (this was Dewi's word) in the ancestral long house. The house, in the traditional Minangkabau style, with a horn-shaped roof, had been neglected for thirty years. Village people used to say that the house had spirits, and Dewi as a child had never liked going there. But custom required that one of the big wedding occasions had to be in Dewi's ancestral house. So the house was opened up, and preparations started for the great feast. Strange things then began to happen. Furniture was moved in inexplicable ways and food disappeared. A cousin of the maternal great-uncle who had brought Dewi up – a cousin, not the *ulama* himself, who would have washed his hands of the whole thing – said, 'Oh, maybe we have forgotten to make offerings to the spirits.' They had forgotten. Since spirits do not live in clearings, but in big trees or springs, meat was thrown into the bush about fifty metres from the ancestral house. That was enough to appease the spirits. There was no trouble after that.

It was believed in the village that in the beginning there were three clans. The Pitapangs were one of the three. The three clans were descended from three cousins; they did not intermarry. It was these three clans who observed the original taboos. And the Pitapangs had an added gift: they were rain-makers.

Dewi said, 'I have noticed in my experience that whenever I have a big party, that during that one day there would be some rain, if only for an hour or half an hour. I got married in April. A dry season. The first day the reception was in my husband's house.'

'He belongs to one of the clans?'

'Different clan, but same village.'

'Arranged marriage?'

'A personal choice. In my husband's house they were having problems with water. My husband's house is on the higher ground, very dependent on rain to fill their water-tank. So they had to be careful with water. During the first day of the wedding it was completely dry. The next day the party was going to be at our ancestral house.' It had not been used for many years and was in bad repair. 'At three in the morning on the big day the rain started to pour, and everybody got wet in the house. The outdoor kitchen was totally flooded. But then in the morning the sun shone beautifully, and everything was nice until eleven o'clock, and the groom came, and the guests. When they were in the house it started to pour again for about an hour. That kind of thing happens at every wedding.

'There was a mistaken belief that when we left the village this kind of Pitapang association with rain would disappear. But such is not the case. An aunt of mine married off her youngest daughter in Jakarta. So, fearing it would rain, she actually took the trouble to go to a medicine man, a *dukun*, in Banten in West Java – which is famous for its medicine. And the *dukun* promised that it wouldn't rain on the great day. And my aunt paid the dukun to make some offerings to prevent the rain on that day. It's quite common here. When they were catering for Singapore National Day they had a *dukun* to ensure it wouldn't rain. At the APEC meeting [one of the international conferences Dewi was connected with] a lot of medicine men were called.

'My mother and I said that we didn't believe that the Banten *dukun* was strong enough to overcome the Pitapang tradition of rain during a family wedding. My uncle, my aunt's husband, came from another part of Sumatra; he didn't believe a word of our Pitapang beliefs. He said, "It is *not* going to rain." So he didn't cover the lawn with an awning. He had all the tables done nicely. They worked all day on it. At three or four on the morning of the wedding the heavens opened, and all the nice tables were ruined. He believed too much in the Banten *dukun*. My mother and I at the time were quite pleased.'

Religious or cultural purity is a fundamentalist fantasy. Perhaps only shut-away tribal communities can have strong and simple ideas of who they are. The rest of us are for the most part culturally mixed, in varying degrees, and everyone lives in his own way with his complexity. Some people manage things instinctively. Some, like Dewi, can be self-aware at the same time. She valued all the many strands of her background. She said, 'My life is rich because my different worlds converge.'

When, after ten years, she left her Sumatran village, it was to go to England, to be with her academic parents. She was fifteen. She had spent very little time with her parents; but she found she had no problems with them. There was no generation problem. The years in the village had made her religious and conservative; she thought that her parents were too liberal, and sometimes she found her mother's skirts too short and tight. In time her political attitudes were to change, but her personal values remained conservative; though, because of the matrilineal traditions of the Minangkabau, this conservatism gave her a degree of self-esteem as a woman that was not strictly Islamic.

In many ways, then, her love of the ways of her village appeared to expose her to the old fundamentalist conflict of the region. It was as though the bloody thirty-year religious war of the last century (which had destroyed the Minangkabau royal family and their palace, and had brought in the Dutch as rulers) had settled nothing. Something like this, or some related theme, must have been in Dewi's mind – there might, perhaps, even have been recent academic seminars or conferences on the 'plural' society: there is no end of these conferences in Indonesia: they are a kind of harmless substitute for a free press – because, without any prompting from me, she went on to make an almost formal statement about the true faith and the old ways.

She said, 'When it comes to relations between men and God one should adhere to the pure form of Islam, not the syncretic form. We cannot be a good Muslim and adhere to polytheistic or animistic beliefs and practices. But when it comes to ordering the relations between man and his neighbours – how we live in society – each grouping has different needs and customs. I do not believe that a universal religion or a national ideology should attempt to eradicate customary practices, as long as those practices do not violate the basic tenets.'

It was a restatement of what she said had been agreed about the relationship between Islam and the *adat*, the traditional ways, after the bitter religious war of the last century.

'Islam was put at the top, the highest body of law, to which the *adat* would be subordinated. The saying is: "The *adat* would lean on the *sharia* [Islamic law], and the *sharia* on the *Kitab*."' The Book, the Koran. 'Practices explicitly violating Islam were to be forbidden – drinking, gambling, cockfighting, marrying more than four wives. But other aspects are considered okay, because there is nothing in the Koran or in the sayings of the Prophet against the matrilineal system.'

Yet, though in Dewi's mind all was clear, the relations between men and God would not always be separate from the relations between men and their neighbours. There would always be ambiguities, even about the position of women, and these ambiguities of the faith in West Sumatra were again awaiting a fundamentalist rage.

I stayed all afternoon in Dewi's office. When I left, LIPI offices were closing, and the bureaucratic round tower, with many of its inmates now apparently running away, seemed more impersonal than ever. On the avenue just in front I waved down a street taxi. Easy enough to do; but the taxi was dilapidated, with open windows and without air-conditioning, and it was the rush hour. Rush-hour traffic in Jakarta was always bad; this was very much worse than usual because some streets in the centre near the presidential palace had been closed off that day in preparation for the celebrations of RI50 – the official shorthand for the fiftieth anniversary of Indonesian independence. For many minutes, in an absolute jam, the hot air quivering with fumes and car-body glitter, I faced the back of a small van:

> *Power up*
> *– Don't be Caught*
> *DEAD Without Jesus*

There were stickers like this on many cars and small vans in Jakarta; there was religious need, the need for consolation beyond what men could give; evangelically, the half-converted country was up for grabs. The young taxi-driver, from Sumatra, sharp-featured, reading me as a man from India, said in English that India was a very good place: it was full of mystics. Between us we didn't have enough of a common language to develop this difficult subject; we let it drop. Sunk in his half-collapsed driver's seat, his knees wide apart, the driver shook his slender khaki-clad legs in nervous irritation and, to pass the time, began teaching me Indonesian. After my long exciting afternoon, the day was dying on the highway in heat ripples and fumes; a migraine built up.

It was under the spell of Dewi's own enchantment that I went to her village when I was in Sumatra. And, of course, everything was smaller than I had imagined: what Dewi had transmitted to me, what had held me in Jakarta, was the enchantment she had felt as a child.

Dewi's mother took time off from the university at Padang to show me around the sacred places. With her was a visiting academic, a family friend, who had done much research on local ways. He told me that he had asked Dewi one day, when she was a child, what she wanted to do when she grew up. She said she wanted to be a Muslim religious teacher, an *ulama*. Only a man could be an *ulama*: the reply spoke not only of Dewi's admiration for her *datuk*, but also of the Minangkabau feminine self-esteem that had come to her at the same time.

The family house we went to was not the house where Dewi stayed as a child. It was the house of Dewi's husband's mother, who was herself a distant relative of Dewi's. It was a modern bungalow. Glass louvres; heavy carved chairs in the Indonesian middle-class style; a big plastic ornament on a side table: a coconut tree with a lot of nuts, simple in outline, and in basic colours; two rows of concrete ventilation blocks at the top of the wall, the lozenge-shaped gap set vertically in the upper row, horizontally in the lower; a *Mahabharat* scene on one wall (an acknowledgement of the Hindu past or the *adat*), and on the facing wall an Arabic scroll. It was modern and middle class and unremarkable.

But perhaps not unremarkable for Dewi's young daughter, who had been sent by Dewi to live in the village, like Dewi at her age; and for whom this house and the rich, sheltering vegetation outside – the coconut, the bamboo, the banana, the rambutan, the sapodilla – might have been acquiring paradisal associations. She had come back from school, the little girl, while we were there; and now, having changed into a fresh frock, was sent off again, with a little book in one hand, and with every sign of content, to her religious class.

Take away the rambutan, and the vegetation might have been the vegetation of the Caribbean. But in the Caribbean the coconut and the bamboo and the banana were old imports, from this part of the world and from the Pacific. And here the sapodilla (the chico of India) was an import from South America. The similarity of vegetation had been arrived at in different ways, and the associations of the vegetation in the two places were quite different. The Caribbean vegetation spoke of the slave plantations and now of the tourist trade. This landscape remained the sacred ground of an ancient clan.

The *surau* or private mosque of Dewi's maternal great-uncle – where, because of his great authority, though contrary to custom, he had lived with his youngest wife — was in a coconut grove that seemed derelict.

Labour was scarce; people preferred going to the towns and the factories; there was hardly anyone to clean the ponds and waterways. In this climate, where things grew fast, chaos quickly came and could look beautiful. Dead coconut branches hung down like giant bird-feathers from the rotting hearts of trees; creepers ran up coconut trunks and brought them down across fern-fringed ponds or water channels; and then the collapsed trunks were skeined with scum, layer upon layer, on which weeds could soon get a footing. The African water hyacinth, a universal tropical parasite in brilliant green and lilac, choked open water into swamp. And in the gloom of the old grove everything, including the sky, could be reflected in what clear water remained.

The *surau* was in ruin; it wasn't going to last much longer. It was unexpectedly small, of wood and corrugated iron. The wood had rotted grey and the darkened corrugated iron had been torn loose in places. Architecturally, though it didn't have the horned roof, it was related to the traditional Minangkabau house; and even in ruin the principal building (there were two plainer dependencies) had its elegance. It had a lower storey with a roofed verandah all around, the roof looking like a corrugated-iron fringe. The smaller upper floor rose out of this fringe, and was topped with a steep pyramidal roof, rising along its slightly curving lines to a tall finial. Much of the architectural energy of the building had gone into this roof. It would have sufficiently expressed the purpose of the *surau*, though it had no overt Islamic sign, no crescent or crescent-and-star. The use of these emblems was comparatively new in Indonesia. Mosques could be like other buildings; though now, with the new Islamic mood, and to Islamise ordinary buildings, there were shops in Java displaying in their front yards silvery sets of domes and crescents in various sizes (in just the same way as other shops displayed furniture or motor-car wheels).

Dewi's ancestral horn-roofed house — again, smaller than the one I had in my imagination — had been repaired and furnished. But I wouldn't have liked to spend a night there. I would have felt imprisoned in the long-house architecture. I would have needed a verandah, or other space around me, or space broken up in another way. This was a kind of house for people who lived outdoors as much as indoors, and to whom outdoors was also home and theirs. It was not a place for strangers.

Near here were the bushes where, during the preparations for Dewi's wedding, meat had been thrown to appease the neglected spirits of forest and springs with whom the clan had entered into a contract, many hundreds of years before, when they had cut down the forest. Just beyond the shade were the rice-fields (bounded now by coconut groves) for which that contract had been entered into: uncleaned in places, with entangling water weeds, and with open, loose-looking patches in the ripening rice where the rats had been. As in so many things here now, the lack of hands showed.

I asked Dewi's mother how old she thought the rice-fields here were. She said that a rice-field's age could be gauged from the depth of the mud. These fields were about a thousand years old. You could sink in this mud up to your armpits. The academic with her said he rather thought they would be two thousand years old. Hard to grasp: this field, a particular kind of crop, going back to the times of Augustus. (And on the winding mountain road between Solok and Padang there was a forest reserve which showed what the primal vegetation might have looked like: dense, old-looking, lustreless, a dark grey-green, without the freshness or lightness of cultivated plants or trees.)

And yet very little was known of this immense history. There were no documents, no texts; there were only inscriptions, and not many of those. Writing itself was one of the things that came from India, with religion. All the Hindu and Buddhist past had been swallowed up. Without writing, without a literature, the past constantly ate itself up. People's memories could go back only to their grandparents or great-grandparents. The passing of time could not be gauged; events a hundred years old would be like events a thousand years old. And all that remained of two thousand years of great social organisation here, of a culture, were the taboos and earth rites Dewi had told me about. I heard about some more now from her mother. For instance, before the rice harvest you went out to the ripe field and cut seven stalks. You hung these up on your house. Only then you could start the full cutting. No one knew why. The original prompting had vanished somewhere down the centuries.

The overthrow of the old religions – religions linked to the earth and animals and the deities of a particular place or tribe – by the revealed religions is one of the haunting themes of history. Even when there are texts, as with the ancient Roman-Christian world, the changeover is hard to follow. There are only indications. It can be seen that the earth religions are limited, offering everything to the gods and very little to men. If these religions can be attractive now, it is principally for modern aesthetic reasons; and even so, it is impossible to imagine a life completely within them. The ideas of the revealed religions – Buddhism (if it can be included), Christianity, Islam – are larger, more human, more related to what men see as their pain, and more related to a moral view of the world. It might also be that the great conversions, of nations or cultures, as in Indonesia, occur when people have no idea of themselves, and have no means of understanding or retrieving their past.

The cruelty of Islamic fundamentalism is that it allows only to one people – the Arabs, the original people of the Prophet – a past, and sacred places, pilgrimages and earth reverences. These sacred Arab places have to be the sacred places of all the converted peoples. Converted peoples have to strip themselves of their past; of converted peoples nothing is required but the purest faith (if such a thing can be arrived at), Islam, submission. It is the most uncompromising kind of imperialism.

5

Kampung

MARIMAN AND Furqan were both CIDES researchers. Mariman was twenty-three, Furqan about the same age; and they would have known that through CIDES they had had a good start in the big city. Mariman, in fact, was already something of a star. Adi Sasono had spoken of him as a kind of CIDES success story, and I had asked to meet him.

So now, at Adi's prompting, Mariman had come to the hotel, with Furqan as his interpreter. Mariman didn't speak English.

We went to the Kintamani, the open pavilion (said to be in the Javanese style) in the gardens of the hotel, between the tennis courts and the big pool. At lunchtime in the Kintamani there was a kind of buffet grill; in the evening there was the same, with a hotel-style local cultural show. The afternoon was a nondescript in-between time, with empty chairs, sunlight angling in from the pool side, the shadows of trees on the other side, and a breeze.

Furqan – whose last name, Alfaruqiy, was as Arabic as his first – was from Sumatra. Mariman was Javanese.

Furqan said, 'We are different. We from Sumatra are travellers, even all over the world. So we don't get homesick. Mariman does. With Javanese people they have a proverb: "Eat or not eat, we have to live together." It means that Javanese people should live in Java. They feel that Java Island is much better than other places. But now with education they can move out.'

And there was another reason why Mariman was homesick, Furqan said: Mariman's parents were divorced. I noted that down as just another background detail. It was only later, when Furqan and Mariman had left, that certain questions about that occurred to me, and it was a cumbersome business to get answers at long range: getting through on the telephone to Furqan at CIDES, putting questions to him, and then waiting for him to give Mariman's responses. So it was only later that I realised that Mariman was one of the seventeen children of his father's two families living in the same village, but separately. And it was only much later, as I travelled, that I realised that the Muslim pattern of multiple marriage and easy divorce was not just a matter of masculine libido: it led to damaged families. It led to a kind of semi-orphaned society. A family abandoned by a father, in order to start a second or a third: it was a story that came up again and again. That was what lay behind Mariman's homesickness. But I didn't think to ask more at the time, and never got to know when Mariman's father divorced his mother and how old Mariman was.

When Mariman was a child in the *kampung* (or village) he looked after sheep and buffaloes for people. He was paid in kind, lambs, young buffaloes. The time came when he had twenty-two sheep. He sold some to go to school. He sold two sheep first of all, one for 42,000 rupiah, twenty dollars, and another for 50,000, twenty-four dollars. He sold them to the cattle broker his father dealt with; his father was a trader in buffaloes.

Why did he want to go to school?

'To deepen his knowledge of Islam.'

This would have been because of his father. Mariman's father had gone to the village *pesantren*. He had a cupboard for keeping books. The cupboard was kept closed, but the books were known to be there. The father was an educated man who could read and write Arabic and even speak it a little.

Furqan said, 'Mariman is unusual in Java because his father trained him in religion. He was educated by his father in praying when he was ten years old. As a trader in buffaloes his father made enough money to go on the pilgrimage. This was in 1985.' Mariman was thirteen then. 'He was very proud that his father went to Mecca. His father came back wearing the white *haji*'s cap. Before that he wore a black cap. He was the first person in the village to go on the *haj*. Now there are three *hajis* in the village.'

Mariman said, as if commenting on Furqan's translation, 'Pilgrimage is the highest duty.'

With this background of books and devoutness, Mariman in 1990, when he was eighteen, was admitted to the Muslim university in Malang, in eastern Java.

To be admitted was one thing. To support himself was another. And though he didn't say, it must have been about this time that his father and mother were divorced. Mariman needed 25,000 rupiah a month, about twelve dollars, for general expenses, and, for food, ten kilos of rice. He went back home to his *kampung* for the rice; and his mother gave the 25,000 rupiah. She ran a little village shop or stall selling vegetables, small street foods for children, and things like soap and sweets.

To save money, he rented a room far from the university; it cost 90,000 a year, about forty-four dollars, or about eighty cents a week. In this room he cooked his own rice; and he bought cooked vegetables from stalls. He seldom ate meat or fish, and he walked to the university. So his living expenses came to less than 10,000 a month, about four dollars eighty, or about sixteen cents a day; and he was able to save 15,000 of the 25,000 rupiah he got every month from his mother. In the third year he was able to buy books.

There was a fascination for me (and for him, and for Furqan) in these tiny sums, on which a man could yet live. It was like a sport in itself, a version of the pleasures of Lilliput. (There was something similar, too, in the memoirs of his very early days, by William Chambers, the nineteenth-century Scottish publisher.)

When he was twenty-one, in 1993, Mariman began to write. Extraordinary for someone who had begun life as a herdsman; but the ambition, that idea of possibility, would surely have come to him from his now absent father, an educated man, with books in a locked chest. Mariman wrote articles on economic matters and they were published in *Pelita*, a Jakarta daily. For every published article he was paid 50,000 rupiah, nearly ten dollars. This high payment shattered his delicate balancing of tiny sums, made him a new man. He began to feel he had a future. He felt this more strongly when the Muhammadiya University in Malang invited him to be a lecturer. He asked his mother and his father. They were small people, but they knew about buying and selling. His mother did that every day, with her little stall, and his father dealt in buffaloes. They said the salary was too low, and Mariman turned the university down. He decided then to leave the *kampung* and come to Jakarta.

Jakarta was at the other end of the long island of Java. The fare was

50,000 rupiah. One article in *Pelita* settled that. He had clothes. And he had lodging: his mother's sister agreed to take him in. She had a house with three small rooms in a slum in south Jakarta. Mariman was a little bit frightened to be in Jakarta, because for the first time in his life he had no close family within reach. But he didn't mind about the conditions. They had to pump water for the bathroom and the kitchen. He lived like that, in the small house in south Jakarta, for seven months, from November 1994 to the end of June 1995 – that was just six weeks ago, but already (a day is very long for a young man) that life felt far away, and Mariman felt he couldn't go back to living in those conditions. And though he didn't say, it was no doubt during that time that he became a CIDES researcher.

I asked Furqan, 'He misses the village?'

'Yes. He misses his mother. He would like the village or *kampung* atmosphere in Jakarta, but he can't get it.'

'What does he mean by the *kampung* atmosphere?'

'The respect for older people, praying together in the mosque. But he's not frightened of Jakarta now. He tries to make the *kampung* atmosphere in his neighbourhood. And he has a girlfriend. He plans to get married as soon as possible.'

But Mariman had hardly begun to make his way.

I asked Furqan, 'Does he feel his life has changed so completely in the last seven months?'

'He feels he has made a big jump intellectually. But he has become a consumer.'

Already, that piety, that bit of tutored wisdom. I asked, 'What does he mean by that?'

'He is influenced by the consumerism of the big city.'

'He is wearing a nice shirt and a nice colourful tie. Is that what he means by consumerism?'

The shirt was carefully chosen: white, with button-down collar, the shirt and the broad striped tie sitting flat on his almost flat chest. There was a pen clipped to the pocket. He wore belted beige trousers; the belt emphasised his narrow waist. And he wore gold-rimmed glasses. Everything represented expenditure, thought; he perhaps had never dressed so carefully in his life.

Furqan said, 'When he was young he wore very simple clothes and could still feel confident.'

I felt that there was a tremulousness about Mariman. He was aware of the clothes he wore, and perhaps they made him nervous. Perhaps they made him worry about pride and the vanity of transient things, and awakened in him, almost in a religious way, some Javanese-Muslim idea about luck and success bringing the greater danger of a fall.

Furqan said, 'Now he feels proud to wear nice clothes, but he doesn't think that's all to do.'

I asked to see Mariman's CIDES card. It was the standard CIDES name-card (Furqan had one, and Dewi Fortuna Anwar), with the CIDES lettering big in the bottom left-hand corner. Mariman's name was printed in small underlined letters in the top right-hand corner:

Mariman Darto
Researcher

It was part of the change that had come to him, but he wasn't letting it go to his head. He wasn't forgetting his *kampung*.

Furqan said, 'There is no one like him in his *kampung* now. But he can talk with them. And many of the people are proud of him, because he is still humble, although he lives in Jakarta. He goes back twice a year. If there is an event in the *kampung* he will go back. He fulfils all the prayer obligations. He feels that prayers are important, especially when he feels he is very distant from his mother and his father. Because of his religious feeling he is special in his village. Some of his friends have lost confidence as men and have begun to drink in the city. Most of these people are of low education. His religion makes him feel different from his friends.'

'What does he think will happen in the village?'

'He has an ambition through education to alter the village and the disparities. Nowadays his *kampung* is changing because of him, his prestige.'

In this, as in his education, he was an extension of his father, the buffalo-dealer, who had been the first man in the village to go on the pilgrimage to Mecca.

I asked, 'Are people following him in the religious way?'

Furqan said, 'Many of his friends feel that the key of his success is his education and not his religion.'

I was struck by the frankness: I felt that Mariman was still his own man.

Furqan added, 'But after education they go back to religion.'

'Is there a difference between education and religion in his own mind?'

'There is. But with education he can also show the performance of a religious person.'

'What does that mean?'

'He can be a better religious person.'

'So he shares Professor Habibie's ideas about religion and technology?'

'He's read in a magazine that Habibie fasts twice a week, on Monday and Thursday. So Habibie can combine success and religious spirit.'

'Religious spirit is necessary for success?'

The answer was roundabout, but perhaps Furqan hadn't understood the question. 'Many people in the village fast two times a week, but when they went to high school they stopped fasting and became bad people. They even gave up Ramadan fasting. So he, Mariman, made an innovation.'

'Became bad people? In what way?'

'Working hard in the factories, they feel they are not strong enough to fast.'

Our talk had become circular. It might have been that the third person, the interpreter, was a constraint; or it might have been that we had really come to the end of what was arresting and original in Mariman's story.

'Is he still studying hard?'

'He is still studying hard.'

'What would he like to be?'

'An expert in economy.'

'He sees Islam as a continuing source of strength to people?'

'He is sure that Islam can be a source of spirit in the future. So he is trying to make education for people in the *kampung*. This is the concept he is trying to propagate in the *kampung*.'

I said, 'A modern *kiyai*?' A *pesantren* head.

He understood the word, and he began to laugh. In English he said, 'Thank you, thank you.'

Later I remembered something I didn't ask. I telephoned Adi Sasono on his mobile phone, and he, busy as he was, passed on the question.

'What about the sheep he didn't sell? He had twenty-two, and he sold two to go to school.'

Two days later, on a noisy CIDES line, Furqan said, 'He gave them to his brother. But he doesn't want his brother to continue in that way of life.'

The new wealth was great, and to the government's credit it had gone down far. A big new middle class had been created, and the new housing developments outside Jakarta for this middle class were so many and so vast, and so sudden, that some country roads seemed for long stretches to be like film sets, with old *kampung* streets – a general effect of low buildings, pitched corrugated-iron roofs and fruit trees – kept whole in front of the hard new tree-less lines of ochre-coloured concrete and glass and red-tile roofs going up at the back. So that two kinds of life seemed to be going on at the same time in the same place, extending the idea that had come to me on the first day, of history here existing in layers, of having speeded up to such an extent in the last fifty years – the Japanese occupation, the war against the Dutch, the events of 1965, and now the immense manifest wealth – that most people, whether in the new developments or the *kampung*-style road, were only two or three generations away from *kampung* or agricultural simplicity.

In anthologies of Indonesian writing I looked at while I was there this nearness to the village came over as an unworked-out feeling of loss. It expressed itself in simple tales. It is possible to create a composite tale. The old peasant gets off the bus in the city; he has a gift perhaps for a relative, once known as a village person, but now a famous general or an important civil servant. The peasant, gaping at the city sights, might be jostled and insulted by people in the street crowd. Various memories play in the peasant's head as he approaches the presence. The peasant, getting nearer and nearer, is staggered by the trappings of power. The general or the civil servant is welcoming or cold – it depends on the politics or sentimental inclination of the writer; but at the end the peasant knows that the past is finished.

Sustained great writing, rather than polemic, can only come out of societies that offer true human possibility; and in Indonesia we have, instead, a pastoral people who have lost their history; who have been involved in prodigious, often tragic, events, but are without the means – the education, the language, and above all the freedom – to reflect on them.

Abstractions: consider this from an editorial in the *Indonesia Times*.

Materialism is still pervading the Indonesian society. Some of the
religious leaders in Indonesia view the emergence of people with
low moral character as the result of indiscriminate adoption of
Western values . . . The best way to cope with increasing materialism and individualism is to intensify built-in control in tandem
with instilling moral teachings. The development of religious ethics
should be intensified in order to counter materialism . . .

And so on, that single idea (rather like Mariman's) repeated over
nine paragraphs.

Abstractions: the theme of the RI50 celebrations, as given in the
Jakarta Post, reporting or summarising a speech by Emil Salim, executive chairman of the celebrations committee. It begins like the
programme of a Beethoven symphony. 'Under the theme of
"Expressing Reverence and Gratitude for Independence by Enhancing
the Roots of Our Republic's Populace", the planned celebrations fall
into three categories.' The first category will include programmes to
reflect the five tenets of the state ideology: belief in God, national
unity, consensus through deliberation, humanism, social justice. To
deal with the God tenet, the Indonesian Ulamas Council will be urging
Muslims to 'perform a bow of thanks following the Friday prayers'. The
humanism and social justice tenet (or tenets) will be dealt with in the
Indonesian way: with a national seminar on human rights. No seminar
for the democratic principles tenet, though: the French business community of Jakarta will deal with that by putting on a laser show. A
sailing extravaganza will make a statement about national unity. Then
there is social solidarity; that can't be left out. It isn't certain where it fits
into the – now – almost Buddhist complexity of the five tenets and the
three categories; but it will be handled in this way: Emil Salim will be
calling on businessmen to 'give something back to the community by
decreasing their profit margins to benefit the public in a giant sale. And
this discount shouldn't be on used or defect goods either.'

A simple people involved in great events. And on an occasion like
RI50 many words have to be used, but few will have meaning; since
the reality, which all understand, needs no words. With religion, the
consoler, as recommended in the editorial in the *Indonesia Times*,
adding to the simplicity – as, thirty years before, in a poorer, darker
time, communism did.

★

I talked to Goenawan Mohamad about the abstractions of language. Goenawan was a universal man of letters, in the Indonesian way, a practitioner of all the forms; but he was best known as an essayist, admired not only for his independent thinking and knowledge and elegant mind, but also for his use of the Indonesian language.

He was born in 1940 in a small fishing *kampung*. In 1946 his father was killed in the Dutch war (but Goenawan bore no grudge). His mother, who couldn't read and write, brought the children up. Such money as she made came from dealing in eggs. She bought the eggs in central Java and sold them in Jakarta. Goenawan's orphaned background was like Mariman's (though for different reasons, and in a much more unsettled time); and, as with Mariman, there would have been more to the family than poverty and struggle. Goenawan's family was clearly uncommon. Both of Goenawan's sisters became teachers; a brother became a doctor; and Goenawan worked through, as journalist and writer, to being very much his own man.

He stayed away from the communists in the 1950s and early 1960s, as he was staying away now from the religious people. This independence would have been more than a political or personality quirk. It would have been related to Goenawan's quality and self-respect as a writer. Good or valuable writing is more than a technical skill; it depends on a certain moral wholeness in the writer. The writer who lines up with any big public cause like communism or Islam, with its pronounced taboos, has very soon to falsify. The writer who lies is betraying his calling; only the second-rate do that. In a country like Indonesia the true tragedy, the lasting corruption, of the lost post-war generations, communist once upon a time, and now fundamentalist, is that kind of second-rateness.

Goenawan said, 'I don't think educated Indonesians speak any language which can be used to express and develop their thinking. In Sukarno's time the language was steered into a totalitarian use, and in Suharto's time it has been bureaucratised. I wrote poetry in the 1960s, and I discovered that all the language had big abstract connotations – nation, people, revolution, socialism, justice. I was so lonely. When I was sitting in the old gallery I saw birds, sparrows. I had forgotten this thing, the small, transient thing. Everything fits into this. Even some adopted liberal ideas. Like free market. They are dead, not derived from experience, the soil, the street.'

The surviving local traditions were not strong enough to deal with these borrowed ideas. 'People have moved very fast. There is no *city* life. People have the brain, the fear, the trauma, the attitude of their past. They will go back trying to find a community. That is why religion is important – the number of young people going to the mosque, the church! The old local traditions – not Islamic or Christian – have been eroded.

'My brother-in-law was getting married into a Javanese family. They wanted a wedding done in the Javanese fashion. But he didn't know anything about it. So what did he do? He hired a consultant. There are a number of these wedding consultants. They're making a lot of money now. They remain – the old traditions – like a beautiful memory.

'My wife has an uncle, half-educated. He spoke Dutch. A military officer in the old days, just after the revolution, in the 1950s. He read English. He read Dutch. But what he presented as his thinking was a confused mumbo-jumbo. Like: three or four or five years ago we had this total eclipse of the sun, and people went to see it at Borobudur.' The seventh-century Buddhist pyramid. 'Borobudur under a total solar eclipse. And this uncle – I call him my uncle – told me that people went to Borobudur to find a book there which has the secret of life. Can you believe it? There are many like that.

'This uncle was not exactly prepared. He never did any critical thinking about people. Democracy is not about voting. It is about debate, the quality of intellectual life. The narrowing of the mind is not orchestrated by Habibie or anybody else, but by this new influx of students coming from provincial backgrounds who want some certainty in this confusing time. The regime offers no ideas. So there's no debate. Ideas fall into their own boxes, and remain there, undeveloped.'

6

Below the Lava

I WENT TO the old royal city of Yogyakarta in the south of Java to see Linus. Linus was a poet whom I had met in 1979. He was twenty-seven or twenty-eight then; and though (as I understood) he hadn't yet published anything important, people knew about him. The culture and spirit of old Java were said to be his inspirations, and he lived in a village not far from Yogya.

One of Linus's older encouragers was Umar Kayam, an academic and writer and a tremendous attender at seminars and conferences; and it was Umar Kayam (not a pen name: Umar had been given the name by his father) who took me one day to Linus's village. We went to Linus's house and met Linus's mother and others; and then for the rest of the morning Linus walked about the village with us and introduced us to people.

Linus was deferential with Umar, who was about twenty years his senior, and I had the impression that Linus was just about making a start as a poet. It wasn't absolutely like that. I learned now from people in Jakarta that at the time of that meeting Linus had in typescript a very long narrative poem, *Pariyem's Confession*. And I was also to learn now, from Linus himself, that Umar, who had been reading the poem as it was written, had been worried about the length. At one stage he had said, 'Enough. It's quite long enough already. It's getting like an old nineteenth-century Javanese poem.' Like many other writers looking for encouragement, Linus had preferred to follow his own heart and had written on. A year or so after our meeting in his village he had published his poem. It had had a great success; it had sold twenty thousand copies; it was still Linus's best-known work.

Now, in an English-language anthology, *Menagerie*, I read a translation of a section of the poem that would have been on both Linus's and Umar's minds as we had walked through the village. The poem – which had a village heroine, and a village setting perhaps like the one we were in – was elegiac about the ways and private calendar of old Java. Even the good and painstaking translation (by Jennifer Lindsay) showed – away from the inevitable erotic passages – how very hard it was for Linus's elegiac sense, and all the cultural particularities it implied, to be understood outside its setting. Only Javanese words could describe certain Javanese things, and only those words could unlock Javanese sentiments.

> My father was in a *ketoprak* troupe in Tempel
> he used to come home once a week
> And the *gamelan* was lively
> loud, fast
> Playing in a *slendro-sanga* mode
> A sign that the *gara-gara* had begun
> And the moon was leaning to the west
> a sign that it would soon be daybreak

A different climate, a different use of the hours, different associations of music and theatre and time and landscape: all this was to be extracted from a description of something as well known as the Javanese shadow play. There would certainly have been more intricate reaches of sentiment and belief and ritual which were beyond translation, where only Javanese could speak to Javanese. And it was perhaps for a similar reason that in West Sumatra a rice culture as rich and complete and organised as this – and without the need of record – had, after a thousand or two thousand years, left no trace apart from the taboos and the clan names. Once the old world was lost its ways of feeling could not be reconstructed.

In 1979 Java had given me – perhaps too romantically – the feeling that it was of itself alone, still a complete civilisation. Linus's village had contributed to that pastoral idea; and over the years fantasy had elaborated on the details: the rice-fields coming up to the houses, the village vegetation where everything had a purpose, the shrines of the rice goddess, Linus's elegant mother. In my memory she had remained as she had been that morning, returning in her finery from an expedition to the town, a woman of a high civilisation, exchanging long courtesies with Umar Kayam, in the old language of the court (as Umar said), talking with her head thrown back, complaining in a well-modulated torrent of speech about Linus's idleness, refusing to take the business of his poetry seriously, since in her mind (as part of the perfection of her world) all poetry had already been written, and new poetry was an absurdity.

It was that pastoral morning that I wished to experience again. And then I learned that Linus had recently been in trouble with the Muslims of Yogya. They had objected to something in a column he had written and had wanted his blood. Linus signed his name *Linus Suryadi AG*, and the AG was not a local decoration, as it appeared to be, but an abbreviation of Agustinus, which was Linus's way of announcing that he was Roman Catholic. I would have known that about Linus in 1979 but wouldn't have been able to give it its proper value or understood its context: the competition between the two great revealed religions for the soul of the half-converted, colonised country that had lost touch with its own beliefs, its own wholeness.

The Linus affair had created a stir; the army had had to offer Linus its protection. Matters had settled down now. But I knew that the earth had moved in Eden.

Linus had no telephone. But he said in his letter, after I wrote to him, that there were two Yogya friends with telephones who would take a message. I telephoned one of the friends; and when I arrived at the Meliá hotel there was a message from Linus, a computer print-out, saying that he would come for me after nine the next morning. That 'after' was ominous. He came at two in the afternoon.

He was in a light-blue denim suit. At forty-four he was broader and sturdier than he was in my memory, and not as tall: hard to find in him the slender young man in khaki trousers and white shirt who had listened carefully in the house when his mother or Umar talked, and had, deferentially, when we began to walk, offered us his village and its ways and its people.

He had come on a motorbike (that no doubt explained the denim suit), and he had had some trouble with it. He said that the message the hotel had stylishly printed out for me hadn't come from him, but from his younger brother. He would not have known that I was in town if he hadn't, purely by chance, met this brother in the street a short while before.

We took a hotel car to go to his village. With Linus's recent trouble in my mind, I thought as we drove through the town that I saw signs of the new Muslim aggressiveness: in the new Muslim school, with the girls in white headdresses that emphasised their Mongoloid appearance, denied them individuality, and made them, when they were in groups, look like little shoals of blanched big-headed tadpoles; in the many shops dealing in building goods or materials that displayed silver-coloured or tinny domes topped with the star-and-crescent in their front yards; and in the very big sign above a building saying in English in plain red letters: MOSLEM FOOD. Linus told me later that the use of the English words meant perhaps that the food had come from Arab or non-Indonesian countries.

Outside the town the road hardly changed. Village ran into village, and for stretches the road was closely built up on both sides. The fields, the pure country, would have been at the back. But more and more, even on the main road, there were country patches; and, as I saw it, the well-worked, over-peopled country scenery of Java revived in my memory. Every scrap of land was used. The little bunded fields of rice or tobacco or peppers or maize never stopped, and the boundaries of the fields were marked by banana trees and cassava plants with their knotty stalks and purple young scalloped leaves.

In the pastoral in my memory Linus's family house stood in the shade of trees at the very edge of fields. It wasn't like that: the house, which was low, with concrete walls coming right down to the ground, stood quite exposed beside the main road, which was like a road through a country town rather than a village. For some miles – adding to the town effect – this road had been decorated for RI50 with red-and-white Indonesian flags, and with simpler coloured flags (like upright banana fronds) on bamboo poles, leaning towards the road to make what looked like a series of broken Gothic arches: gaiety for which, according to Linus, the Jakarta government didn't pay, but the local community.

The village of my pastoral hadn't been lost. My memory had con-flated this village, with Linus's house, with another village, off the main road, where Umar and I had been taken on our walk to see a big, traditional Javanese house owned by one of Linus's many relations.

The front yard of Linus's house was flat and hard and bare. It was like that so that paddy could be spread on it to dry, Linus said; or a bamboo tent put up for some festival. On two sides of the bare yard were useful trees or plants: coffee, coconuts, the South American chico or sapodilla, a guava tree (the guava another South American import, known to some as the Brazilian weed), everything growing well in the volcanic soil. On a third side of the bare yard, and for the beauty alone, was an irregular little patch of manila grass, tight and springy like a deep pile on a rich carpet, bordered with hydrangea and tall zinnias, beside a superseded amenity: a broken, tainted-looking pond.

We entered the front room. It was as wide as the house. The floor was of very smooth concrete, the ceiling of matting, now darkened. The left-hand side of the room was screened off; there were low dusty armchairs on the right. Against the screen there was a small oilcloth-covered table with two kitchen chairs. On the inside of the front wall, shielded from the glare, there was a photograph of Prince Charles with a printed copy of a letter he had written about Indonesia (in connection with an Indonesian Performing Arts Festival held in London); and Linus's certificates or diplomas from universities abroad for attendance at special courses: the very small change of diplomatic benevolence on which, in countries like Indonesia, people like Linus depend, for excitement, travel, refreshment.

A very small old woman in a dun-coloured blouse and sarong came out from the inner room, to be introduced, as courtesy demanded. This was Linus's mother, shrunken and dimmed by age. The woman I had had in my head from sixteen years before was in her finery and had just come back from her shopping, her hair carefully combed and flat and tight, her high-cheekboned face warm and brown and tilted upwards, her eyes bright with courtesy towards Umar and complaint about Linus. The dun-coloured blouse and sarong of this small woman, not erect, matched and killed her complexion. They might have been her working clothes. It was now past mid-afternoon, and in a little while, when it would be cooler (a different way of arranging time here), she would be going out to the rice-field. In 1979 I had not associated her with that kind of labour.

She spoke little, and not loudly, and didn't stay long with us. Then, as on a cue, someone else began to come out of the inner room. I heard words oddly distorted by rage and tears, building up to a deep scraping sound; and even before I could see who was so out of control, almost about to scream, I knew she was Linus's handicapped sister. I had forgotten her, edited this shadow in Linus's life out of my pastoral memory. But now it was as though I had never really forgotten, had only filed it far away, and at this very moment it came back to me: the silent young woman of uncoordinated movements who had come out dragging her slippered feet from a dark side room and then sat on a chair in the corner frankly considering us, the guests, new people, sitting before the platefuls of steaming corn cobs, village hospitality, the farmer's plenty: her eyes angry, tearful, yet looking for attention, her twisted mouth hanging open and wet with dribble. She seemed young, in her teens, but she was twenty-five. When we left the house Umar Kayam told me that this sister of Linus's had had a wrong injection when she was a child; it had damaged her nervous system.

The woman who came raging into the front room of Linus's house was now forty-one. She wasn't interested in Linus, but in me. She seemed to rage and rage at me, attempting to speak, but no words coming out, crying between attempts, the spittle running down her lips and unhinged mouth, making what looked like old-fashioned elocutionist's gestures. Linus held his head slightly to one side and let her rage. He listened; he knew what she was trying to say. His eyes were full of pain and tenderness.

When she had finished, and had left the room, he told me what had happened. There had been a Christian house-blessing service in the house of an older brother; it had been combined with a celebration of the fiftieth anniversary of Indonesian independence. The priest offered communion at the end, but he didn't know how to offer the wine and the wafer to Linus's sister, and so he passed her by. She had returned in a frenzy. She complained to everyone who came to the house. When things like this happened to her, Linus said, they had terrific problems with her for three days afterwards.

Even without the mother and the sister, I would have felt that a light had gone out of the house. And it came out – indirectly, and not as a statement of tragedy – that Linus's father had died two years before, and the family were now very poor. Linus's father had been the village leader. In Java, where everything was highly organised, this was an official post. (People said the Japanese were responsible for this military-style organisation of Java, but the Japanese occupation had lasted only three and a half years. Perhaps the serf labour of the old Javanese kingdoms and the later Dutch agricultural colony had always required high organisation.) Linus's father had become village leader because of his family connections. A village leader was given one and a half hectares of land while he held his post; but the rule was that when a leader died the land was given back to the government after a thousand days.

This was why Linus's mother was now poor and the house was so gloomy; and why these days, Linus said, his mother railed against her grandfather. This grandfather, after having one family with three children (including Linus's mother), had taken a second wife and had had two more children. The first family had as a result been impoverished. And then at the end the grandfather had divided his property unequally.

Just the day before, Linus said, when his mother had been railing against her grandfather, he had had to be firm with her. 'No tears, please. Don't think like that. Think instead of your children who have gone to the university. Better we look at the future.'

In fact, it was because of the Christian preaching against polygamy, and the suffering it had brought in their own lives, that Linus's father and mother – as recently as 1938 – had converted to Christianity. They had not been Muslims before, but Javanists, with a mixed local religion made up of survivals of Hinduism, Buddhism and animism. They had both attended Christian schools; they had learned about Christianity there. The Christianity they had adopted had not meant a break with the past.

'Here even when we became Christians we continued with our old customs. Taking flowers to the cemetery, praying to the spirits of our ancestors. When someone dies even today in our Christian community we have mixed rituals. The ceremonies three days after the death, seven days, forty days, a hundred days, one year, two years, a thousand days.' Because of his father these death ceremonies would have been on Linus's mind.

Linus said, 'Christianity is important because it teaches you to love somebody as you love yourself. It means teaching us to become tender persons, not wild or aggressive persons. In Javanism also we have the concept of restraint. It is easy therefore for Javanese people to embrace Christ's teaching.'

High up on the inner concrete wall, above the central doorway, out of which Linus's mother and sister had come from the room at the

back, there was a big brown cross. It was above a grotesque leather
puppet. It was the standardised puppet figure of the clown, Semar,
from the shadow play, a character, Linus said, from one or the other of
the two Javanised Hindu epics, the *Ramayana* or the *Mahabharata*: 'a god
turned into a man, always supporting the good people'.

In 1979 there had been a leather puppet there, but I didn't remember Semar. I remembered another figure. I couldn't say what it was, and
I didn't ask Linus about it. It was only while working on this chapter
that I checked, and found that in 1979 the mascot figure on that wall,
the associate divinity of the house, above the horizontal ventilation slits
and below the cross, was the Black Krishna. Not the playful Krishna of
India, stealing the housewife's freshly churned butter and hiding the
clothes of the milkmaids while they swam in the river; but the Black
Krishna of Java, a figure of wisdom. That Krishna would have been a
sufficient protector of a man starting out as a poet. Now, in a time of
deeper grief and need, Semar – the man-god who helped the good –
was a more appropriate divinity.

Linus had pinned the figure there – through the upper body, leaving
the jointed arms and legs free to move.

He said, 'I try to understand my culture. The kind of myth that stays
in my culture.'

And for Linus much of the myth of his culture was kept alive in the
wayang kulit, the shadow theatre. His love of the *wayang* was like reverence. It might have been something he had got from his father, who, in
addition to his official duties as village leader, taught Javanese dance, and
put on a dance show every independence day. Before he started going
to school Linus looked at the *wayang* every day: every day there was a
puppet play going on in the village. Even when he began to go to
school he went to the *wayang* almost every day. When he came back
from school he would have food and a shower, and at about eight or
nine he would go to a night performance. The older *dalangs* – the pup-
peteers, the story-tellers – did the show through the night up to five in
the morning. The younger *dalangs* did the day-time performances,
which started at about ten or eleven.

'People would sometimes fall asleep and then wake up again. It's not
like a Western performance. The *dalangs* were invited for wedding parties, or circumcision ceremonies, or at certain Javanese ceremonies to
celebrate the washing of the streets, the cleaning of the village; and
ceremonies connected with the rice goddess.'

So, as in the section of *Pariyem's Confession* I had read, the *wayang* – allied to different uses of day and night, different patterns of living, and very old local rituals – could release emotions that were not easy for the outsider to enter. This old world of feeling was dear to Linus, and it was something he felt was now being lost. People (and even Linus's mother) watched more television. And the village was poorer, and *dalangs* were more expensive. In the old days a family could sell four hundred kilos of rice and invite a *dalang*. Nowadays the minimum fee, even for a local village *dalang*, was a million rupiah, about 425 dollars. The more cultivated court *dalangs* of Yogyakarta and Solok could ask for twice or four times that amount.

So Linus lived with the idea of decay, a precious world in dissolution. His recent trouble with the young Muslims of Yogyakarta was like part of the new uncertainty.

'I write a short cultural essay for the local paper. I was in charge this year of the Javanese and Indonesian literature section of the Yogya art festival. In one of my columns I tried to present the Javanese music that still lives in our society but is not popular today. In the *gamelan* there is an instrument called the sitar, and a group called *sitaran*. As far as I know, people use this *sitaran* group at weddings and circumcision ceremonies. I tried to understand the custom of circumcision. I know from the Old Testament that the prophet Musa introduced this custom, and Musa is Jewish. Jewish in Indonesian is "Jahudi", and circumcision is *jahudi-sasi*. I wanted to make a historical–cultural point. To make for a better festival. I wasn't touching the Muslim custom only, because Christians here also practise circumcision. Today it's not only a religious thing, but a health precaution.

'I went to the paper, the office, on Thursday afternoon, two days after, to get my money for the article. Seventy-five thousand rupiah.' About thirty-five dollars. 'And the journalists told me that some young Muslims had just brought some leaflets to the newspaper. The leaflet said, "Hang Linus. Linus mocks Muslims." They were trying to stir up the students.'

I said, 'Weren't you expecting something like that?'

'I was surprised. I thought that if someone doesn't agree he would write in the newspaper against what I had written. Maybe they have a

crisis of identity as a young generation. They are young people who
have not finished in the university.

'I came home, and in the morning some soldiers came here with a
captain and said, "Linus, what did you do? Did you mock the
Muslims?" I said, "No." The captain had a copy of the article. He said
he didn't see any reference to Muslims. Then he said, "And now we
will all go to Yogya. And follow me, please." We went, to the fourth
level of the local command.'

It was Linus's way of expressing the seriousness with which the army
took the affair. On a pink paper napkin – we were sitting facing each
other at the kitchen table next to the dividing screen, close to a wall
shelf with mementoes and ornaments – he made a rough chart to
explain the structure of the local army command.

This interest in the army structure took me aback. But it wasn't really
surprising. Linus's family, and there were many branches, was of some
local importance – another reason for his mother's pain at what had
happened to her house. Linus's father had been a senior village official;
his mother's father (the polygamist's son) had been a secretary of the
local government, and Linus himself had wanted, for all the years of his
childhood – even when he was going night and day to the village
wayang – to be a general when he grew up. Linus spoke of the
Indonesian army with something like love; it was still for him the
defender of the state.

'In Yogya I saw a lieutenant-colonel in his office. He said that if I
didn't feel safe in my house I was to stay in the mess at the army bar-
racks. I told him I had to stay with my mother, who was a widow. And
for a week he sent one or two persons to sleep here at night.'

And though Linus said that the new Muslim aggressiveness was being
encouraged only by a few people, there was with him a clear irritation
with this aggressiveness, as at something that went contrary to the way
of Java. In 1979 the village mosque had been a plain wooden hall, like
the Christian church. Now the mosque was of concrete, and though it
didn't have a dome – like those silvery ones stacked together like a
cumbersome kind of bauble in the front yards of some shops – it had
loudspeakers on the roof; and Linus didn't think that in old Arabia there
would have been loudspeakers on mosques. Some women had begun
to be muffled up and veiled, and Linus thought it was strange in a tropical country to see people wearing clothes like that.

But most upsetting to Linus was the change in the function of the village *koum*. The *koum* had been special, with special duties. He was Muslim, but he carried over many of the old Javanist ways. He was the man who was called in to wash and bury the dead. He was also the man who on certain ritual occasions informally led the community in prayer. It was possible to see in the *koum* an old outcast Hindu figure, with the burial duties of the untouchable. And – just as the early Christians used the crucifixion and the cross, the centuries-old Roman punishment of everyday criminals, as the most moving symbol of human pain and redemption – so it was possible here to see how the early Muslims, looking for converts, might have used this outcast to do a karate throw on the long-established faith: the washer and burier of the dead was to lead the community of the new faith in prayer: the untouchable, at one bound, scaled the caste pyramid and became the equivalent of a priest.

I had met the old *koum* in 1979, a small, strong, wiry old man, with a laughing voice and bright eyes, and hair flattened by his hat; and with memories of the wars. He had died the next year, Linus told me.

'He loved to look at the puppet play, which is the mixture of Hinduism and Javanese culture. His son has taken over, but he is seldom asked to lead the community in prayer. Because of the changing orientation of the Muslims themselves, they have fewer rituals – commemorating the dead in the Javanese way, sharing food in the *kenduri*, ritual food. They used that custom only when the old *koum* died.

'When my father died we asked the son of the *koum* to pray with us. The Christian leader led the prayers, and the *koum* and others, non-Catholics, were asked to pray for my father in their own way. This is the way of tolerance and equilibrium in relations in the village.'

So Linus's thoughts constantly went back to that death in his house, and, almost as a parallel theme, the loss of equilibrium in his world.

Without any change in his expression or in his tone, he said, 'Six or seven feet below us here are many Hindu temples or Buddha temples or Hindu-Buddha temples, buried by eruptions of Merapi a thousand years ago and also two thousand and fifty years ago.' Merapi, the active volcano of the region, creator of the lava that enriched the soil, and showed as black boulders in the beds of streams. 'This creates a job for people who want to study about Java culture and religion, because behind these phenomena we can catch the spirit of Javanese people today.'

The vegetation of Java was a composite of the trees and flowers of the Old World and the New. It was like the vegetation of Trinidad and Venezuela and some of the islands. I was even to see one day – on the busy road from Yogyakarta to Prambanam, with the half-restored towers of the great tenth-century Hindu temple complex – a giant *immortelle* tree bare of leaves and in full, lava-fed flower: red-and-yellow bird-shaped flowers ceaselessly falling on the road, as I had seen them fall in Trinidad in cocoa woods: the *immortelle* a Central American import, used there as a shade tree for cacao. It was hard to shake off old associations; but I was to feel with Linus, as I had felt in West Sumatra, that there were different things in this soil, other emanations.

Linus's mother was at a funeral when Linus brought me back the next morning. And after some time Linus's sister appeared in the back room. She sat almost formally in a straight-backed chair before the television. I could see her from where I sat with Linus at the table next to the dividing screen. She paid me no attention. She looked rested; she was calm. She had complained about the priest the day before, and had nothing more to say to me.

Linus said, 'My sister cooks. If my mother cooks, and she doesn't like it, she will cook for herself. But she doesn't know how to judge things. She will use too much rice, for instance. She can cook vegetables, too. Fried eggs. She will buy these things for herself.' He spoke with pleasure and pride and delicacy. 'She feels very much that people shouldn't treat her differently. We suffered a lot during my big sister's wedding party. "Why am I not married?" she said. We said nothing. We can do nothing for her. We shook our heads to say, "No, we cannot do anything."' And, reliving the moment, he shook his head slowly, and the pain showed in his eyes. 'But she will cry. She will use new clothes and complain about it to new people.'

'How does your mother manage?'

'My mother says often to others: "I don't know why God gave a gift of an invalid daughter."' Invalid: it was the word Linus used for his sister: he allowed nothing stronger. 'My mother has a big trouble with her. Sometimes she will attack my mother. We went this season after the rice-fields had been harvested and bought a lot of rice, to sell later. My sister will tell my mother, "Don't sell it." Maybe she thought the rice shouldn't be sold. We had to tell her that the rice had to be sold to buy other things.'

His face was grave; his tenderness touched it with beauty.

I asked, 'Have you written about her?'

'I have tried to write a poem about this sister. But the time hasn't come yet. I have only written poems about another sister, number eight, who died in 1983.'

He went through the doorway below the cross and Semar to get the book. The display shelves on the dividing screen had simple Hindu images among its Christian pieces and its simpler ornaments and keepsakes. The sister was still calm, watching the television.

The booklet he brought out had a white lotus on a green leaf on the cover. The dedication was to the sister who had died. All the poems in the booklet were written in six weeks in 1987, four years after the sister's death. There was one poem which Linus particularly liked; and in an anthology of Indonesian poetry which he gave me there was this rendering (by John McGlynn) of the last stanza of that poem:

> From the earth to earth return
> From shadows to shadows return
> like heat lightning in swiftness rising
> your soul rises and leaves your body
> *Asal bumi balik bumi*
> *Asal bayang balik bayang*
> *Bagaikan tatit kumedap* – lap –
> *Atman oncat dari badan*

The feeling could not be denied. In the second line there was an indirect, moving reference to the *wayang*, Linus's obsession; and I thought that the last two lines recalled the death of Dido in *The Aeneid* ('The warmth all failed, and the life was taken up to the winds'): . . . *omnis et una / Dilapsus calor atque in ventos vita recessit.*

In the house this poem was like a private possession of Linus's. His mother hadn't read a line he had written. She had encouraged him, or not objected, when he wanted to have an army career. He had gone far; he had got a place at the Indonesian Military Academy at Sukabumi. But then after two weeks – and after a childhood and adolescence dreaming of being a general – he had decided that the military life was not for him, and he had left the academy. It was after that that the poetry vocation had come to him, which his mother had never stopped thinking of as absurd.

And Linus had been discovering that the poetic and literary life was hard. After his great beginner's success with *Pariyem's Confession* things had slowed up for him. A four-volume anthology of Indonesian poetry – a great labour, and a famous work that had sold three thousand copies – had earned him only five hundred dollars; and he could get no more than two hundred dollars for a book of articles. And articles and anthologies made enemies; poets didn't like being criticised or left out. Linus said, 'People are jealous of me. Jealousy was behind those young Muslim agitators.'

As hard as anything else was the writer's need to go on, to go beyond the first impulse, the impulse that had committed him to the career, to dredge up material that when he began he didn't know about. Now, however, things had begun to move for Linus again. He was just about getting started on a new book, something that might turn out to be bigger than *Pariyem's Confession*. The new book was going to 'reflect' Javanese history.

Linus was a Catholic, the son of converts. To some extent, then, in the religious divide of Java, the competition between the two revealed religions, his side was chosen for him. For him all the mingled emanations of the past, below the lava, the Hinduism and Buddhism and animism that together made for the 'restraint' of Javanism, ran naturally into Christianity with its message of love and charity.

He said, 'It is easy for Javanese people to embrace Christ's teaching. And maybe Javanism has some spirit of Buddhism. Siddharta taught people love.' Siddharta, the Buddha.

With no change of tone, he said, 'I think the spirit of Siddharta often comes to teach us, to teach wisdom in living. He comes to a small group of my friends. When we collect together, in the night usually, the spirit of Siddharta will come sometimes to teach us, and we will ask him about our problems. Sometimes he writes on the palm of my friend Landung, a poet and translator. I can't read it, but my other friend, a woman – she works as a palace guide in Yogya – she can read it. Landung will feel somebody writing on his palm: *tuk*, *tuk*, *tuk*, like that. And at the last the person writing will write his name: *Sincerely, Siddharta*. And my woman friend can read what Siddharta has written.'

I asked, 'Can you remember any message?'

'I remember. It was: "I don't teach about *devas*, the many gods of Hinduism. I don't teach about reincarnation. You could arrive at nirvana even if you live in this world."'

'What year was that?'

'This was in 1993, about.' The year, perhaps, when his father died.

'When did Landung discover this gift?'

'Maybe around 1990. Once Landung told me he didn't believe he had this gift of receiving messages from God or Siddharta or the true spirit in this way. That night Siddharta came and said, "When you receive a gift from God, don't throw it away."'

'When do you have your meetings?'

'A spontaneous feeling in all of us. But sometimes we can't collect together all of us. Sometimes Landung feels there is a message in his palm—'

'Even when he is working?'

'Yes. He will stop it, saying, "Wait, wait, wait. I am busy today. Maybe tonight." And then we take it to the lady to read.'

'Are the messages short?'

'Sometimes short, sometimes long. If Siddharta comes, it means he wants us to think and discuss his teaching.'

'Do you get messages in a moment of crisis?'

'He told us about Jesus Christ. He is coming in a mystery. We cannot predict.'

'Does he give more practical advice?'

'When I was sick, Siddharta told Landung through the palm that I had to try to look for a certain kind of leaf, something in the village. Then you must steep it in hot water and drink the mixture. It worked.'

'Does your mother know?'

It was as with Linus's poetry. 'I never told her. Her narrow experience in the spirit world will be surprised. She will not believe my explanation.'

The most important revelation they had had from Siddharta was that he was a prophet – which meant (though Linus didn't say so) that Siddharta, the Buddha, was in the line of prophets that (according to the Muslims) ended with Mohammed: which meant that this Indian-Javanese figure had connections with the two competing revealed religions of Indonesia.

What Siddharta said through Landung's palm was, 'When I meditated for fifty-four years in a small lake, suddenly I received a voice:

"Look at the bright star in the sky." In that sky I saw a man in blue clothes, very bright, and he brought a bucket, and inside the bucket was a baby, and the man in the bright blue clothes introduced himself as Adam, and the baby introduced itself as Jesus. Then I saw writing in the sky: *This is the man I promised you.*' Siddharta told Landung, 'I don't know who gave me the direction to look at the sky.' When Linus heard this he said directly to Siddharta through the woman friend who was translating, 'It was John the Baptist.' And Siddharta answered, 'A long time I have wondered about that person. It's only today that I've got to know his name.' So Linus began to feel that he was in touch with Siddharta.

I asked Linus, 'When did this mystical group start?'

'It just happened. In the early 1990s.'

We were sitting at the oilcloth-covered table, next to the dividing screen and the wall shelf with the ornaments and images. I had a partial view of the dark inner room. Linus's sister had some time before left her chair before the television. Now Linus's mother appeared, small, her footsteps almost without sound. She had come back from the village funeral and was in her home clothes, which might also have been her working clothes; later, when the sun was lower, she would be going to her rice-field to plant out seedlings. Now she sat in the chair before the television set – the blue light flickering on her face, the sound turned down low – and watched a Latin-American *tele-novela* or soap, very slow, in bright, unnatural colours. It was something she followed, Linus said; and it was strange to think of this low commercial form (so particular to the yearnings of Latin America) leaping the hemisphere, leaping cultures, to speak directly to this sorrowing old woman in her shut-in Javanese world.

While her husband, the village leader, lived, the broad-fronted house on the main road had been one of the six important houses in the village. Now, without him who had been its light and centre, with the tarnished sofa set low on the concrete floor, the darkening ceiling matting, and with Linus's mementoes – in a corner, on a wall – of a festival of the performing arts in London from five years before, it was as though dust had metaphorically settled on people and things.

But the house had treasure: in Linus's bedroom was his collection of antique krises, local daggers, of serpentine shape, with leaf upon leaf of various metals. These krises, always personal to their owners, had spiritual significance, Linus said. The handle and the hilt, or the blade and the sheath, had an obvious sexual symbolism: the spirit came from the *lingam* and *yoni* emblems of Javanese Hinduism. He had about sixty of these krises. He had been collecting them since 1982 (the year before his sister had died, the sister whose death he had written poems about, in a six-week burst in 1987). The krises were mainly from the thirteenth and fourteenth and fifteenth centuries. Some, he said, were of the sixth and seventh centuries. I thought he meant the sixteenth and seventeenth centuries, but he insisted.

The krises were in his bedroom, and we went to see them when his mother (unwittingly like a dragon guarding mystic treasure) had done with her *tele-novela*, and had gone to her work in the rice-field. It was dark in the bedroom, and the darkness was like part of the privacy of the rooms at the back of the house. The krises were in an old brown wardrobe. The ones with scabbards stood against the corners of the tall compartment. The naked ones lay flat and hidden on a top shelf. They were fearful things, their blades jagged and sharp, different leaves or layers of metal showing, some of them seemingly rusted. They encouraged thoughts of Linus's invalid sister (perhaps now resting in her own dark room) and her three-day rages; and then they set the teeth on edge.

It occurred to me that Linus had over the years spent a fair sum on these krises. But he didn't answer when I asked. He said that he was guided in these and other spiritual matters by a wise man of sixty-five, also a Javanist-Christian, in the next village. Krises gave off vibrations of energy; it was possible for this reason to be led to them by 'pendulum study'. Knowledge about them also came to him in dreams.

When he saw that I couldn't follow, he said, 'All the animals in this world have a magic power, and some of them a very strong one. When this animal dies this magic doesn't die, but comes out and stays in the sky.'

'Where in the sky?'

'I don't know at what level of the sky. And when the kris-maker makes a kris he will fast and pray, and the blessing of the god of the animals' magic power will come down in the process of the making.'

Linus also, again with the help of his adviser, had a collection of magic stones. These stones could be found anywhere; he had even found one in the United States. In the pattern of the colours in a stone could be seen – as I understood – the souls or magic of animals.

He said, with a giggle, 'Sometimes you can see a beautiful woman.'

*

The village was closely built up. Neighbours pressed on one side of Linus's yard, beyond the broken pond and the flower patch. Between the yard and the small plot of *salak* fruit trees that belonged to Linus's family there were two sets of neighbours. A sharecropping family, a widow and two of her five children, lived in a poor hut seemingly patched together with old bits and pieces. After that there was a more established farming family, with a well-used but more traditional house, with a separate kitchen and washing-up place at the back, and with their own yard. Chickens – black and tall and slender: the chickens of Java – scratched in the dust. In a pen at the end of the shady yard two white bullocks rested after the labours of the day, skin loose over bone, oddly frail-looking and small for their ploughing duties in the deep volcanic mud of the rice-fields. Bullocks were smelly, Linus said, but not as smelly as buffaloes. And, not far away, in a corner of a yard shaded by young bamboo, we saw two black buffaloes, their skin dulled with dirt and muck, tethered to stout, tall poles and resting on a spread of dried grass.

The main village road was a narrow, twisting dirt lane, now showing broom marks, now with damp patches: everyone had to clean the lane in front of his yard, and did so in his own way. There were house plots and fruit or garden plots. These plots were not big, and sometimes they had walls of beautifully cut and fitted lava blocks. Lava, like bamboo, was a local material; people handled it well. The village was full of shade. There was no feeling of openness. People didn't want openness in a village.

With the volcanic soil and the damp heat everything grew fast, here and in the open rice-fields. You couldn't forget the lava of Mount Merapi: Linus's obsession with the worlds buried underfoot was understandable. Part of the bounty of Merapi and the volcanic soil was the distinctive *salak* fruit of the region. Home-made boards on the main road advertised *Salak Pondoh*. The small orchard plot that Linus's family had was of young *salak* trees – like palm trees, but with thorny trunks, and with intricate spider webs on the thorns. Someone else had a plot of mature *salak* trees protected by an old lava-block wall made higher with wire and matting. Where there was so little space, where neighbours (and outsiders) always pressed, the products of the earth were precious.

But it was no longer a purely agricultural village. The five principal houses belonged to people who did other work, town work, and sometimes quite unusual work. The man just across the main road was a government officer of the third grade: he was Linus's uncle through his step-grandmother (perhaps the second wife who had been indirectly responsible for the impoverishing of Linus's mother). There was a compiler of an Indonesian dictionary; then another uncle of Linus's who was a sculptor, a maker of official statues; an aunt, who was a Javanist and a mystic with a huge following, Linus said, and who sometimes lived in the city; and there was a retired Muslim high-school teacher who had done the pilgrimage to Mecca. A factory worker kept a nice house, beautifully painted, and with Japanese bonsai trees and other plants outside, quite unprotected; but this was 'only for show', Linus said, meaning that the man wasn't as well off as the others. And there was another relation of Linus – living next to the plain wooden building that was the Catholic chapel – who was a PE instructor in Yogya and travelled to work every day.

The village had changed, and Linus's family circumstances had changed. But old village commitments, old loyalties, had to be honoured; they were helping to impoverish Linus's mother even more.

The neighbour who was a sharecropper was a widow and very poor. She had five children. Two worked as servants in Jakarta. The eldest and the youngest lived with her, working as labourers in the rice-fields and elsewhere. The fifth child was a mason.

Linus said, 'The mason came three months ago and asked to buy some little piece of land from us, to make a small house for himself.' The poor and cramped *kampung* hut in which the family lived was on land that belonged to the sculptor. 'The mason said, "If you don't give us land, where would we go?" And then my mother reminded us that when my father was a child, the woman who took care of my father was the grandmother of this family. "So we have to remember this history of your father." So we will sell the land, a hundred square metres. We have a thousand square metres of garden. This relationship with our neighbour is more human. We've made a written agreement. That is new: until now everything was oral.'

They had three pieces of rice land, in all about an acre. It would have been worked cooperatively. This explained the crowded, busy little rice-fields on the other side of the main road, far down the dirt road behind the good houses and the flags and decorations for the independence anniversary celebrations, RI50. As soon as the car began to go down that road, I recognised the land as the land I had seen in 1979 with Linus and Umar Kayam: it was what I had carried away in my head as Linus's village and turned over the years to a pastoral vision of a complete civilisation. I had seen it in 1979 on a morning in December. Now, in August, on a late afternoon, it was dustier and harsher, the Java of straw hats and many hands, fertility eating up itself.

For every eight kilos reaped, Linus said, a helper received one kilo in payment; if the helper was a member of the family he received half of what he reaped. And this village was full of Linus's relations.

There were other obligations. 'When there are weddings in the village we have to make a gift of ten thousand rupiah.' Something under five dollars. 'This is the custom of the village people. After my father's death, of course we don't have many invitations, but we still receive some. One hundred kilos of rice will fetch forty-five thousand rupiah. From our land we get from twenty to twenty-five quintals. That is, two thousand to two thousand five hundred kilos.' Five hundred dollars' worth, at the higher figure.

Linus said later – without prompting from me, and as though it was something he had had to think about – 'I could become a rice-farmer if I decide, but I think it will be hard for me to spend all my energies in the rice-fields.'

And too many things had changed. The village life had changed. There was no longer the music, the night-long shadow theatre with the well-known characters and stories. Even the rice had changed. 'The old traditional rice was full of savour and taste.' He made a gesture, taking his fingers to his nose. 'The new Filipino rice – you can't eat it in the evening if you cook it in the morning.'

Somewhere in those fields his mother was working. Somewhere in the house his invalid sister was living out her day.

We began to drive back to Yogya.

He said, 'The village is in crisis. The urban process is happening here too. They already divide the rice-fields for their children, and the fields become very narrow. Many young-generation Javanese do not have rice-field. They look for a job in the city. My mother is the last generation to live and work in the village. The young generation who stay in the village and work in the rice-fields usually are not educated. The educated people who work in the towns and live in the villages become commuters.'

And rice work was now a torment; the cycle had speeded up too much. The old rice took four and a half months to ripen. The new rice ripened in three months.

'Now after sunset the farmer is tired and only wants to look at TV. In the village there are no longer enough *gamelan* instruments. They don't have enough money to buy. Their money goes to educate their children and on health.'

He telephoned me at the hotel late that evening. It was something I had asked him to do, so that we could have a last talk before I went back to Jakarta.

He said there was something he had forgotten to tell me. He had had an important message from Siddharta not long before. It was one of those messages tapped out – *tuk, tuk, tuk* – on his friend Landung's palm, and read later by the lady from the mystic circle. Life on earth was only a process, Siddharta had said. The true process, the true life, began after death. 'Process': that was the best Linus could do: the word used by Siddharta was hard to translate. I felt that the word might have been a Javanese word, like those Linus was well known for using in his poetry, words that limited his appeal, but which he used for their accuracy and their emotional charge.

When I got back to Jakarta I found a letter which Linus had sent me more than two weeks before but which I had not had. It was a letter which (partly because of the language) I would not have understood without having met him. It was about the stresses with which he lived, and also about his spiritual teacher, a man of sixty-five in the next village, a Javanese-Christian-Reformist mystic. It gave a further twist to what he had told me.

His dream of Siddharta and death worked on me during the night, and in the morning I awakened to a clear knowledge – almost as to something about myself – of the pain Linus lived with, family pain, pain as a writer, pain for all the things of Java and his village which he saw being washed away. I saw at the same time that – unlike Mariman Darto, the young Muslim, who had found a kind of support outside his village with CIDES, however illusory that support might be – Linus could live nowhere else but in his village and in his house. It was the only place where he could find all the things and relationships that gave savour and point to his life.

7

Oh Mama! Oh Papa!

LUKMAN UMAR was born in 1933 into a poor farming family in Padang in West Sumatra. He was the last of six children. Life, already hard, became much harder with the Japanese occupation in 1942. More than fifty years later Lukman remembered how in 1943 he and other boys of his age had been made to carry stones from the river for the airport the Japanese were building at Tabing, a few miles north of Padang.

Some years later – perhaps after the end of the war, though exactly when wasn't clear – Lukman's father left his family to go and open a piece of forest and turn it, in the immemorial way of Sumatra, into a rice-field. The father didn't return; and though nothing was said directly, it is likely that he had started another family. A second marriage, a second family: in Indonesia, as in other Islamic countries, it was a familiar story. The adventure had religious sanction, but the consequences never ended for the two families. It made for a society of half-orphans, in a chain of deprivation and rage: an abandoned child often became an abandoning parent.

Lukman's mother, when she was left alone, earned a livelihood by making and selling Indonesian sweetmeats. Lukman helped with the baking and the serving; he also, in the mornings, hawked the sweetmeats about the village before he went off to his school. He could have gone to the Dutch school – he had passed the entrance examination: a teacher in the primary school had made him go in for that – but his mother didn't want him to go to the Dutch school. She wanted him to go to the Muslim school. At the Muslim school half his time was spent on religion, half on general subjects.

In 1955, when he was twenty-two (and – just to give a context and a reference – about two years after Imaduddin from North Sumatra had got to the Institute of Technology in Bandung), Lukman Umar went to Jakarta. The family – and this would have meant various branches of the extended family – didn't want him to leave Padang. In Minangkabau custom a husband is bought by a wife, not a wife by a husband; and though Lukman Umar didn't say, it is possible that the family was hoping to get something from his marriage. His mother, however, wanted Lukman to go to Jakarta to carry on with his studies. She pawned her land certificates to get the money for the fare; she had inherited a little land and rice-field from her parents.

In Jakarta Lukman Umar stayed with a relation. For a month, making use of his talent as a hawker, he sold peanuts. With the money he made he went to Yogyakarta. He stayed in very cheap rooms, costing a hundred to a hundred and twenty-five rupiah a month, something under a dollar; and he moved many times. He wrote the entrance examination for the Muhammadiya University, the Indonesian Islamic university, and did so well that he was offered a scholarship.

At the university he saw a business opportunity: he saw that students needed lecture notes. With the help of some of the university lecturers he began to publish their lecture notes. That led him to the selling of books and paper, handling goods on consignment. From that a maga-zine agency and book-distribution business grew. In this way, without capital, he was launched. He called his agency Ananda Agency (*ananda* meaning 'beloved son'), and it was dedicated to his mother. The busi-ness grew very fast. He was able soon, with the help of God, as he saw it, to lease a house which he also used as his office; later he built a house for himself. It was just as well that his business grew like this: there were twenty-five people of his mother's family in Padang that he was now looking after.

He became a publisher in his own right. In 1973 – his publishing ambition now reflecting economic and educational changes in Indonesia – he began to work on a fortnightly magazine for women. It was to be called *Kartini*, after the short-lived Javanese princess – born in 1880, and dead in childbirth in 1904 – who, in the discouraging cir-cumstances of colonial Java, spoke up for the rights and education of women. The first issue of *Kartini* was published towards the end of 1974, and was an immediate success.

Lukman Umar thought it was Allah's blessing. But it was also his publisher's instinct, his flair, his truth to his own emotions. Just as politicians and writers have their own way of dealing with the demons of their early life, so Lukman Umar found in *Kartini* the perfect way of transmuting and sublimating the pain of his early life. It was a magazine pitched at the lower middle class – no one had done anything like this for them before – and it was known for its emotionalism. The combination had made *Kartini* the most popular magazine in Indonesia, with a circulation of 160,000; it was now published three times a month. The emotionalism was not artificial, the work of consultants; the publisher had only to look inwards, into his own heart, to know what would find readers.

One of the famous features of *Kartini* was its agony page. It was called, in English, 'Oh Mama! Oh Papa!' The idea must have been Lukman Umar's, because when I met him he said, through an interpreter, that for him the English words stood for a cry from the heart. The originality of the feature was that it just gave the story. There was no aunt to comment or to give advice; readers did that. The device was simple and trouble-saving, but the effect was powerful. Private trouble wasn't being idly exhibited; it was given importance – the 'emotional' title of the feature ensured that – and it was shared with a community; there was no wise person above it all.

More subtle (and more Indonesian) was the feature called '*Setetes Embun*', 'One Drop of Dew'. The words were mysterious, but Dita, the woman journalist who translated bits of *Kartini* for me, said in a matter-of-fact way that the language was symbolic and would be understood as such. Dew might stand for tears or for beauty or for kindness; every reader would interpret the words in her own way.

The 'One Drop of Dew' story we looked at was called 'In the Fierce Heat of the Sun'. The narrator is a girl who is the last of seven children and is very spoilt. She can stand no hardship; she is frightened whenever she has to leave the house and go somewhere; she doesn't like making any decision.

I said to Dita, 'Isn't this girl overdoing things?'

Dita said very seriously, 'This is a person without confidence. I know many people like this.' A friend of Dita's, from an over-protective family, was like the girl in the story; she wanted other people to make every kind of decision for her.

In the story the narrator is especially tormented by the heat of the day. It is one of the reasons why she is afraid of doing anything or going anywhere. She is worried about getting too tired. She gets a headache when she goes out into the sun; she can even become sick. To go anywhere in the city means running out in the sun to get a scooter taxi. When she does get one it is crowded, and people jostle her. Sometimes, when she's going far away, she has to take three different scooter taxis, and then she feels she is the unluckiest person in the world.

She goes (braving everything) to spend time at her sister's. The first day, in the afternoon, when the sun is really hot, she sees an old man working in the garden, cutting the grass with a long curved knife – she is such a town girl, and so sheltered, that (somewhat unbelievably) she has never seen people cutting rice, and doesn't know that the old man is using a common reaping knife. So, like a child, she looks on with fascination at the old man, so wrinkled, running with sweat, but working on steadily with his long knife in the afternoon sun. She asks her sister about the old man. The sister says he works as a gardener for a big company in the mornings; then he comes to work for her. One day the girl takes the old gardener his lunch. She talks to him. She learns that he is sixty years old, and is living alone in the city, in one poor room; the wife and four teenage children for whom he is working are far away in the village.

I said to Dita, 'Didn't she see people like the old man before?'

Dita said, in her judicious, un-blaming way, 'It's rather impossible. You see them, for example, from a bus – you see people working on the road or sweeping the road. We know that their homes are far away, and they are working here for their families. I don't know why the narrator didn't notice that before.'

Now the narrator is tormented by the thought of the old man, who not only has to work hard in the sun every day, but also has to live alone, away from his family.

Dita said, commenting, 'Family is everything for us.'

The narrator sees what a small thing the heat is, and how wrong she was to complain. It is the resolution of the story, the moral, the one touch of dew in that issue of *Kartini*, to balance the cry of pain on other pages.

I had thought that Dita was held by the story. But at the end she let it go very easily, and said, 'It's a very simple story. *Femina* maybe would have been more interested in why the girl is so indecisive, and so frightened of going out. Here the girl says it's only because of the sun.'

Femina was the rival, middle-class magazine. Lukman Umar, with professional severity, had not taken its name. But at *Femina* he was never far from their thoughts. They said, though, that they were the very first women's magazine in Indonesia. They had started a year or two before *Kartini*, and Lukman Umar had been one of the early distributors. And they too had a success story to tell. Their first issue – after six to eight months of planning – had sold 15,000 copies at 250 rupiah, then worth about twenty-five cents; the second issue had sold 25,000, the third 35,000. When sales reached 50,000, the competition, *Kartini*, appeared. And Lukman Umar had shown his flair: he had not tried to imitate the successful middle-class paper; he had followed his instincts and created his own, an extraordinary mixture of the sensational, the religious, the emotional. Now, twenty years later, the current was running his way.

Mrs Mirta, elegant, slender, at ease in many languages, was one of the two founder editors of *Femina*, and also the daughter of the scholarly founder of the press that owned the magazine.

She said, 'I should tell you that for quite a lot of people *Femina* is so Westernised.' Though that wasn't how she had thought of it. 'What I was trying to give when we started was a more pragmatic way of looking into things. Giving people alternatives. An outlook that is more open, and not based on traditionalism.'

Things were now more clouded; traditionalism and pragmatism had different associations. The changes that had come to the limited colonial society after twenty years of independence, the opening out of everyone's world, had made a woman's magazine possible, and had appeared to show a clear way ahead. But now religion, the stresses of the half-converted country, and the great new wealth, had given an unexpectedly backward twist to things.

Mrs Mirta, describing the potential audience of her magazine, said, 'They are simple people with money. They are not *nouveau-riche*, though some are. The set-up of Jakarta society still has the same values. Their intellectual scope is the same.' It was easier for Lukman Umar to speak to that audience. He was a graduate of the Muslim university, and he knew his audience well enough to publish a successful religious magazine. 'He's more Indonesian, more familiar with the roots of the people. So he's got more readers. His way is not pragmatic, but more emotional.'

In *Femina* the agony page was called '*Dari Hati ke Hati*', 'From Heart to Heart', and was a serious advice feature. 'Oh Mama! Oh Papa!' was the corresponding feature in *Kartini*. It offered no editorial advice; and Mrs Mirta said the stories it played up were 'more sensational, not discreet', on the lines of 'My mother-in-law suppresses me.' (It wasn't clear why that complaint was indiscreet, but I didn't ask; and the moment passed. Perhaps Mrs Mirta, with her own high standards of behaviour, thought that domestic complaint, when it became a wallow, not really requiring help, was unacceptable.)

She turned the pages of a recent issue of *Kartini*. 'Here is a film star who goes on the *haj*.'

The pilgrimage to Mecca: such an important religious obligation wasn't something I had associated with this kind of journalistic treatment: a photo feature: glamour, dark glasses, travel, companions, fashion, the lightest and whitest clothes for very hot weather, religion at the end: a version of the *Canterbury Tales*. Had it always been like that? I asked Mrs Mirta whether this kind of pilgrimage feature was something *Femina* would do. She said yes; it depended on the actor. And I thought much later, considering my Indonesian notes, that this might have been another area where Lukman Umar, with his greater religious security, might have been first.

'But,' Mrs Mirta said, 'we won't do this.' She showed a feature about a condemned prisoner, with pictures of his execution and his coffin afterwards. 'We won't do that.'

Later she again appeared to be meeting Lukman Umar half-way. 'Our magazine is mostly known for its cooking and career advice. When we started people said, "You are presenting dreams." I thought dreams were important: life shouldn't be drab. But now everything has become flashy because everything is flashy. It's the Western commercial aspect that's being stressed.' Commercial, as against cultural. 'We have to rely on advertising now. We didn't have advertising when we started. The whole Indonesian economic system hadn't been set up.'

In spite of everything that was said, or could be said on both sides, about pragmatism and emotionalism or Westernisation and traditionalism, the difference between the two magazines might have been no more than the difference between two generations, at a time when history in Indonesia was moving fast.

Mrs Mirta's father, the founder of the press that owned *Femina*, was born in Sumatra in 1908. This was at the zenith of the colonial time: just five years after the Dutch had completed their conquest of Sumatra, and four years after the death of the historical Kartini, the Javanese princess who – like Josephus with the Romans after Masada in the first century, or like Garcilaso, the half-Inca, with the Spaniards in the sixteenth century – had sought to make her peace with the Dutch as if with the forces of history. To any Indonesian born at that time it must have seemed that colonial rule was the future. Yet Lukman Umar, born only twenty-five years later, was to see as a child, with the Japanese occupation, the sudden overthrow and rooting out of colonial Dutch rule.

Mrs Mirta's father, born into a 'strong' Muslim family (as they told me at *Femina*), but making his way in a colonial world, declared himself a 'universal humanist'. When that world began to break up, Lukman Umar's mother, very poor, but with her own sense of the fitness of things, wanted her son to go to a Muslim school and not a Dutch one. Both men had an early life of struggle, but the stresses and possibilities were of different eras. Lukman Umar, the son of a poor farmer, had stories to tell of being made by the Japanese to carry stones for an airport at Tabing, of hawking his mother's sweetmeats in Padang, and selling peanuts in Jakarta. At *Femina* I heard that Mrs Mirta's father, the son of a high government official in Sumatra, lived as a child in a *kampung* close to a forest and walked to school through this forest, which was full of tigers.

This child, when he grew up, went to colonial Jakarta, worked in the government publishing house, became a writer and scholar, and married a Sumatran lady of the nobility. With the Japanese occupation his world changed; all its colonial assumptions blew away. He became head of a commission for the modernisation of the Indonesian language – the Japanese showing themselves as more than occupiers, showing themselves as the most ruthless and intelligent de-colonisers.

So while Lukman Umar and his eleven-year old friends in Sumatra were doing forced labour, Mrs Mirta's father, in his mid-thirties, was working for the Japanese at an altogether different level, bringing the Indonesian language up to date, and doing it so well that the Dutch language, the language of power for two centuries, was in a few years almost completely eradicated. A pre-Dutch, pre-colonial past was stressed by Sukarno; and the visitor to Jakarta today sees more Sanskrit than Dutch in the names on big buildings. It might be said that Mrs Mirta's father in those years of the Japanese occupation was doing work that would in thirty years or so make both *Femina* and *Kartini* possible.

Later, with independence, when Mrs Mirta's father had established his press, there was trouble with President Sukarno. In 1963 the press was seized, and other family assets in Jakarta. Then the press was given back. There was a story at *Femina* about how this happened. Mrs Mirta's brother, who had been running the press, had married into a family of the Javanese nobility. Sukarno knew this family; a son had been killed during the war against the Dutch. When Sukarno saw the mother one day he said, 'What can I do for you?' She said, 'Just give the printing plant back to my son-in-law, so that we can buy milk for the little child who is my granddaughter.' So the plant was given back.

It was Mrs Mirta's brother who in 1972 thought of an Indonesian magazine for women. The family press, which had become the first in Indonesia to print colour, was doing magazine covers for other people; and the idea came to him that he should be doing his own magazine. He talked to his sister, and she talked to a friend, Widarti, when they met at the shopping centre.

Widarti was a lecturer in Indonesian literature. Her work didn't give her time to read new books or consider new things, and she had grown to feel that she was giving her students stale knowledge. Widarti's husband, Goenawan Mohamad, was editing a very successful weekly news magazine. So Widarti was feeling very much left out of things, and was receptive to the idea of the magazine for women.

Widarti's background was like Mrs Mirta's. Widarti had gone to one of the best Dutch schools in Jakarta. The only Indonesians admitted were the children of the nobility, or the very rich, or civil servants; so in a class of twenty-five there might be only five Indonesians – as the school photographs would show. Widarti qualified because her grandfather had worked for the government.

She and Mrs Mirta decided, during the months they spent thinking about the new magazine, that they should treat their readers as friends and equals. They should share the knowledge that privilege had put in their way, but they should not talk down. They should get the trust of their readers; they should avoid gossip and sensation. But Widarti and Mrs Mirta couldn't deny their background; and their knowledge of the world was one of the strengths of the magazine.

Widarti, explaining the success of *Femina*, said at our first meeting,
'We have better taste. We know how to dress in Western style better
than the other papers. When we have a fashion page everything has to
be fitting. Even for house decorations we know that less is more beautiful. We understand we live in tropical countries, so we don't need
thick Persian rugs or thick draperies. The other magazines imitate the
Western papers 100 per cent, or they add something which is
improper.'

I asked for an example of something improper.

'In the middle-class Jakarta house they have this sofa that's not the
simple sofa. They add the intricate wood carving, and they gild it. It's
too much. And they have these chandeliers. They become this status
symbol. Our rivals don't know. You see, Mirta and I have the same
background and are open to Western civilisation, Western households.
We travel. For us it's not entering another world.'

Always, though, there was the wish not to talk down, not to appear
to be 'telling' people. They managed this even on their advice page,
'*Dari Hati ke Hati*', 'From Heart to Heart'. There were two 'aunts' on
the page. They dealt with the same problems, and they often disagreed:
so it was up to the reader to judge. One aunt was a man of forty, a
physician. The other was a lady of seventy who had been with the feature since it started. She was the wife of a high police official, was a
feminist (but in the Indonesian way, Widarti said), and did much social
work. Her work on '*Dari Hati ke Hati*' had made her a star; she was
invited all the time to seminars. Religion, though, had now begun to
soften her copy, making her at times a little too ready to leave the solu-
tion of readers' problems to Allah. She lived in a fine 'complex' on the
outskirts of Jakarta; she sent in her copy by fax; it was part of her style.

Dita, the journalist, told me of a problem that had recently divided
the aunts of '*Dari Hati ke Hati*'. Should a widow of twenty-three marry
a bachelor student who wants to wait until he graduates? Or should she
marry a widower of thirty-five who has a child and wants to marry her
now? The woman says the widow should wait for the bachelor; the
man says the widow should marry the widower. The question is like
something from the shadow theatre, with no single correct answer,
and it is perfect for '*Dari Hati ke Hati*': every person will respond
according to his own character and circumstances and experience. (The
woman writer here will know – better than a man – that it is not always
easy for a new wife to live with someone else's child.)

Mrs Mirta said the feature had value because most people in Indonesia were afraid to assert themselves. They needed advice and stiffening. A recurring problem was the difficulty of living with in-laws, which people in Jakarta had to do, often for years, because they didn't have the money to move out. She gave a rough, abbreviated translation of one letter.

'I have been married less than a year. I work in a big company, while my husband has his own business. My eldest sister doesn't like my husband. She didn't want to lend a hand for the marriage, and it's still like that now. One day the unavoidable happened. My sister had a big quarrel with my husband. My sister is very afraid of her own husband. I also don't have a good relationship with him. My sister leaves her children at our place every day, and she only goes back to her house after her husband comes home from the office. Because my husband can't get along with her, he won't come home as long as she is in the house – and she is in the house every day. I don't know what to do. I wish we could move to our own place, but our savings have been used to renovate my parents' house. I have tried to talk to my parents about my sister, but they told me that all children are welcome in the parents' house at any time.'

The woman half of '*Dari Hati ke Hati*' says the situation is bad. The unhappy couple should leave the house, get a room somewhere. Get some money; even sell some jewellery; move. Otherwise things will get worse. Get out of the house for six months, breathe fresher air; and perhaps then the husband's anger against the sister will subside. 'If you love your husband, and are willing to sacrifice your jewellery for him, maybe it will turn into a blessing from Allah, something not material. And pray. And perhaps Allah will lessen the friction between your husband and you.'

Mrs Mirta, with something like resignation overlaying old affection, said of her veteran columnist, 'That's where she is nowadays.'

The male half of '*Dari Hati ke Hati*' was altogether tougher. 'I would like to know what really happened between your husband and your sister. Why is it so mysterious? Something must have happened. Otherwise they wouldn't hate each other so much. You have to find out, and you are the only person to be the mediator.' Once the true cause of conflict was out in the open, everybody had to be cool and rational. 'And you should leave your pride behind. If your husband is still dependent on your parents, he'd better be more careful.' Though the husband would do better to rent a house, if he worked harder and earned a little more.

But there were levels of desperation and raw distress below this – distress set off or sublimated, on the faces of poor young girls, by the black or brown *hijab* or Muslim head cover, as though that simple form of self-suppression was the only way open to them of dealing with instincts and needs that couldn't be satisfied. And, thinking about the success of a magazine like *Woman's Era* in India, I wondered whether there wasn't a great need here as well for a magazine for women just emerging.

Widarti said that it was true, but she couldn't do it, and no one at the press could do it; they didn't live in that 'mode'. If they tried, they would be talking down, and that would be hurtful and bad. The only thing would be for her to find someone educated from that social level; but that would be hard, because it would be asking someone to 'go back'.

'It's my opinion that you can't go back. All over the islands there is a sort of parable about a son who travels and gets rich and educated, and when he comes back to the village he feels alienated, gets everybody angry. And the mother says something, and the boy turns to stone. This story occurs all over the islands. The moral is that you as a child must never hurt your parents' feelings.' Widarti didn't apply this story to herself; but I felt it cast a light on her own – almost religious – dread of talking down.

They couldn't reach out to the other world, but that other world was now coming to them. When *Femina* was started no girl on the staff wore the Muslim headdress; now there were five or six who did, and neither Mrs Mirta nor Widarti felt she could say, 'This is something I don't want to see you wearing.' From the late 1980s certain Muslim groups started to become critical of women's magazines like *Femina*.

Widarti said, 'In former times there was no preaching in the mosque or on television. Only in Ramadan. But in the late eighties, early nineties, this Muslim thing is not only in Ramadan, but more and more all the time. In the beginning these religious lectures were only once a week, Sunday for the Christians, Friday for the Muslims. Now it's every day for the Muslims, early-morning lectures.'

Those early-morning lectures on television were Imaduddin's. In this new, well-lighted office it was strange, even a little jarring, to be reminded of him and his mental training. It was like being reminded of another world: it was a tribute to his new power.

'In front of our office is a mosque, and the loudspeaker becomes louder and louder. And I can see my staff becoming more and more religious. They go now to the mosque for prayers three times a day, and we can't do anything. This morning we had a discussion about our chief cook in our test kitchen. After her *haj* she changed her dress. A Muslim wardrobe now, the veil, the long blouse, the scarf to cover herself up even in front of the flames. We are thinking about her safety. Because her clothes are of polyester material, very easy to catch fire. But she refused to change.' She was about thirty, the chief cook, with two children. Before the pilgrimage to Mecca she wore Western clothes.

An angry group of students had recently come to the office. 'They were critical of a lady wearing a white bathing suit. They asked me to write an open letter of apology. There were about twenty-five to thirty of them, in their twenties. Some girls among them wearing purdah, some girls wearing jeans. Maybe – this is a guess – they like it, seeing the girls in the swimsuits, but they know it's forbidden by religion. Their anger is they are forbidden, and we are not. We have the liberty they don't have.'

But Lukman Umar didn't have to talk down to attract the women outside the *Femina* pale. That world outside was his own. He just opened his heart and looked inwards, and knew what would speak directly to those women.

He was a small, slender man with the complexion of the *langsat*-fruit – the colour of the water chestnut or pale adobe – which is the complexion most admired by Indonesians. He received me in his office, which was quite dark – and, almost as if by design, the opposite of the airy, blond-and-white open plan of the *Femina* building. We sat formally with three of his senior managers at a very big, dark-coloured table, the centre of which had been laid out with his firm's publishing catalogues. A Christian lady on his staff was also there, to do the interpreting for him. The arrangements were too formal for anything beyond formality. And something was wrong with the air-conditioning unit that afternoon; it was blowing out warm air.

He was in a dark-blue, short-sleeved safari suit. His eyes were watchful, his expression neutral, buttoned up; perhaps he was not well that afternoon. But there was such an atmosphere around him, in that office, it was hard to forget that the executives worked for him, that the building was his, and that the whole publishing enterprise had been created by him out of nothing.

I wanted to hear from him about his past; but I soon felt that what was coming out had come out many times before, and that in that too-formal setting there was no way of going any further. I felt that the executives knew the stories: the stations of his ascent: the Japanese occupation, his father going away, his mother selling little snacks, pawn-ing her land-titles to pay for her son's fare to Jakarta, his publishing of the lecture notes at the Muslim university in Yogyakarta. There was a vast submerged experience, but these were its visible points, always able to awaken emotion, as they were doing even now, in the dark, crowded office, emotion running in a line from his mother and his childhood to his magazines and their readers. Though we couldn't talk long about the past, because time was short, a little less than an hour to get through everything. If I wanted to know more I was to send in written ques-tions to the Christian lady.

What was more on his mind was a recent business success. He had been granted a licence by the government to export labour. I had read two days before in the *Jakarta Post* that thirty-four of these new labour-export licences had been granted, so that now in Indonesia there were eighty-six of these licences altogether. There had been objections to the new licences from some of the older exporters; they said the labour-export market was saturated. There had also been stern words from the minister of manpower. The government, he said, didn't want to hear any more stories of Indonesian workers being abused by foreign employers. There had been recent reports of a maidservant being tor-tured: the government didn't want to hear anything like that. Labour exporters should 'properly manage the way they dispatch Indonesian workers abroad'.

I said to Lukman Umar that I found it strange that he, a publisher, should have gone into labour-exporting. There were disagreeable pos-sibilities, and I would have thought that echoes from his own childhood would have made the business too painful for him.

He said, in his interpreter's translation, that there was really no strange-ness. He had been moved by the situation of people who couldn't get jobs. He was acting on their behalf, and it wasn't easy. The labour they were competing with came from India and Bangladesh, and in those countries the governments were organising the labour-export business.

On my last day in Indonesia I got faxed replies from Lukman Umar's office to questions I had sent in. His mother, he said, had never stopped living in the village in Sumatra. Her land and rice-field, which she had inherited from her ancestors (the title deeds of which she had pawned in 1955 to pay for Lukman Umar's fare to Jakarta), she had passed on to Lukman Umar's three brothers and sisters; they still lived in the village and needed the land for their livelihood. His mother had come some-times to stay with Lukman Umar in Jakarta after he was married, but she had never stayed longer than two months. She died at the age of 102. He had built a 'cemetery' for her, her mother and her brother in Padang. He gave the full address of the cemetery: it was important to him.

If the figures were right, his mother was forty-six when he was born. It was as though all his life had been a making-good to her of her abandonment by his father, who had left to open a piece of forest to make a rice-field and to start a second family. And perhaps, apart from its business side, the labour-export licence mattered. It closed a circle: it gave Lukman Umar the ability now to manage the lives of people who were as needy as he and his mother had been.

8

Ghosts

WE AGREED later that I was to call him Budi (a common Indonesian name, descended no doubt from the Buddha); but he was at first only a voice in the darkness. It was just after nightfall, and he was in the back seat of the Meliá hotel minibus which was taking us from the Yogyakarta airport to the hotel. He spoke English well. He said he had come to Yogya only for the night. A friend was getting married that evening. She was the daughter of the fried-chicken queen of Indonesia, and the party after the ceremony would go on in the hall of the local university until four in the morning. A little sleep, then, and he would be flying back to Jakarta. He was in computers, and had worked for a big international company for thirteen years.

Through the traffic and the lights of the little town he told his story, content to talk to the back of my head, not minding that I didn't turn round. It was early evening, and the regulation strings of coloured lights, very dim, for RI50, masked the shapes of buildings and obscured the life of the streets.

He had his own company now and his partner was the close relative of a very important man. Through this partner big government contracts came their way. They employed thirty people and they were planning to become one of the leaders in software; they weren't leaving it all to the Indians and the Filipinos. The partner had access to the president and other important people; in Indonesia you needed a partner like that. The partner's family wasn't as grand as the family of the great minister Habibie, the builder of the aeroplane, and connected with much else besides; but it was big enough.

When – to get an idea how things looked from this corner – I asked about the Habibies, his voice changed. They were people whose cup overflowed. They were on a higher level altogether, impossibly blessed, beyond emulation. Habibie's brother was the ambassador to London; there were three sisters who were powerful in business; and there were all the nephews, energetic and prospering in many fields. The ideal in Indonesia was so to order one's affairs that one could extend protection to the seventh generation afterwards: if anyone (always after the president) could be said to have done that, it was the Habibies.

I said I found it strange that I hadn't heard of the Habibies until I had come to Indonesia, and yet they were such a dominant family.

He said, 'Please don't use that word. You must have read some of the speeches of our president. Nobody has to be too dominant in Indonesia.'

Was he speaking ironically? I wasn't sure. Irony comes with the English language, enters the simplest texts; but English was for him a foreign language, something to be used with strangers, and might have been quite sterilised, without tone.

He told me, when I asked, how success had come to him. He had had the good luck, he said, to fail the entrance examination for the Bandung Institute of Technology, ITB. (And again what sounded like irony might have been said quite straight.) He had wanted, like so many other young people, to go to ITB and do electrical engineering. This was how Imaduddin's career had begun (after the Japanese occupation and the Dutch war); and many people, in more settled times, had wanted to do the same thing: as though, because ITB had been the first institute of its kind in Indonesia, that career pattern had been stamped out for later generations.

He had failed the ITB entrance twice, in successive years; he was in despair; and then his uncle had suggested, quite simply, that he should forget electrical engineering and do something else. He had joined a private college for information technology. He had known nothing about computers when he joined, but then everything had come together for him. And religion had helped him. In fact, his business had started doing very well – they had got some very big government contracts – after he had gone on the *haj*.

I knew now that he had been speaking dead straight all along. Though this idea of religion and the pilgrimage, in someone so jaunty

with success, as I judged him to be, was as unexpected as the photo feature in *Kartini* about the stylish pilgrimage of the stylish actor. It was his
partner, a very religious man, like so many successful business people in
Indonesia, Muslim and Christian, Indonesian and Chinese, who had
made Budi take religion seriously.

The partner had a young religious teacher who had suddenly come
up, and was known to many successful and important people. The
partner introduced Budi to this teacher, and it was this teacher who had
made Budi go to Mecca. He had told Budi that when he saw the
Qaaba in Mecca he wasn't simply to ask forgiveness for his bad ways: he
was consciously to throw aside his bad ways for ever. This was what he
had done. And now, with his growing success in the computer field, he
wasn't letting go. In fact, he was now more religious than his partner.
He was praying five times a day. He didn't eat beef in hotels or restaurants because the meat there came from Australia, usually, and the
animals wouldn't have been slaughtered in the Muslim way. His partner
didn't mind about the meat.

All this was said in the darkness to the back of my head, as we drove
through the dim illuminations of the town. And it was only in the glass
and marble and bright lights of the lobby of the over-decorated new
Meliá – waterfalls and fountains playing noisily in the rock garden of
the patio, a Chinese woman half-hidden in the mezzanine singing (as if
to herself and her woman pianist) popular old operetta songs, a *gamelan*
orchestra with a middle-aged woman singer (with her hair tightly
combed back and one cheek round over her tobacco chew) waiting in
their corner downstairs to start up – it was only there that I was able to
see Budi properly.

He was a little above average height, strongly built, perhaps getting
heavy below the batik shirt. He had friendly brown eyes and his cheeks
were round and pale; he had a moustache and a full head of straight
black hair. Though his openness with a stranger was a mystery (but perhaps not: a stranger could be expected to go away), he was as jaunty
with money and success as I had imagined him to be. He appeared to
exemplify what Imaduddin taught, and what Habibie had committed
the country to: the congruence of Islam and technology. With the
rich wedding he had made a long journey to attend, the celebrations of
people who, as he had told me, were of simple background, he seemed
to be living out in himself the excitements of wealth and all that was
new in the country.

But everything he had said to me, every impression I had of him, was to be modified in many ways over our subsequent meetings. He was not as jaunty as I had thought. The wedding celebrations in the university hall went on till four without him; he did not stay long. He had not mastered the new society; he was one of its orphans or half-orphans. Everything I had seen of him represented a series of little triumphs: the greeting of the stranger, talking in English, the correctness in the Meliá lobby. He was desperately ambitious, and he had almost no protection; he could be crushed quite easily. He lived with the knowledge of his danger; and in his head he carried pictures of old humiliation.

My base in Jakarta was the Borobudur hotel, and Budi, as it happened, was working in a room there that week. His firm and a firm in Europe were partners on a big project, and two men from the European firm were in Jakarta (and in the Borobudur) to have discussions with him. The final project, Budi said, was going to cost sixty million dollars; the report alone – on which they had begun to work – was going to cost six million. On Friday, the sabbath, and after the midday prayers at the big, modernist Istiqlal mosque in front of the hotel (mightily amplified quavering calls to prayer five times a day), Budi came for a late lunch. We sat next to the glass wall overlooking the mature hotel gardens – big shade trees, tennis courts open and covered, the big swimming pool, the barbecue pavilion, the perimeter jogging track.

He was willing to talk, but he was not always easy to follow. He stored experience in separate segments or, so to speak, files. When, staying with the analogy (appropriate for a computer man), he took out a file he handled it like a file: he started with the present and moved backwards. When he ran together two or three files the time sequence became confusing. All the connections would have been clear to him, but he couldn't present them in a clear narrative. It might only have been that he hadn't been asked to do so before. So he appeared to me over our many meetings to be always adding to, and altering, what he had said before. A narrative came out at the end, however; and even at that Borobudur lunch there were the scattered bones of the same story.

When he was in his mid-thirties Budi's father, worked on by some profound feeling that he should be his own man, gave up a very good job with a foreign oil company in Indonesia (he was the highest-placed Indonesian in the company), and went into business on his own. His extraordinary idea – extraordinary in an oil man – was that he should design and manufacture furniture. He went bankrupt. This was in the town of Surabaya in East Java. The family had to sell their big house; there was often, literally, nothing to eat at lunchtime; and Budi had to cycle ten miles to school. After seventeen years that bankruptcy was still close to Budi, something he was reminded of every day: the cycling which he had had to do out of necessity he now did as a sport. In a corner of his office he kept, oiled and clean, and almost like a sacred object, an extravagantly equipped and expensive mountain bike which he had imported from the United States.

I felt there was a mystery or an embarrassment about Budi's father. He might have been born in a second marriage. I thought Budi said something like that at our first lunch. I was waiting for him to say a little more, but he didn't; and I didn't ask. What he did say was that he wasn't close to his father's family, and hadn't ever met his father's father. He was a head judge in a town in North Sumatra; this meant he was of good family. Budi's mother – the wife of the head judge's son – wasn't of such good family. Her father was a civil servant in the Dutch time, with the rank of major; civil service people had ranks like military ranks. Her mother came of a farming family and still sometimes went to the fields. But the post-independence society of Indonesia was socially dynamic. Budi's mother's younger brother – the uncle who was to be so important in Budi's life – became a lawyer and a university professor.

The mystery or embarrassment that had marked Budi's father seemed also to have marked his children. There were seven of them, and four had, socially speaking, vanished. There remained a brother who was a doctor; a sister who had married a man in the oil business in Kalimantan (formerly Borneo) and was rich, Budi said; and there was Budi.

He knew that his family had fallen. He carried that knowledge like a cross. He said, 'My big family may be middle class, but my own family is low.' And: 'I really come from a simple family, really.' And: 'Not many people have backgrounds like mine. The common background is: during the Dutch time the family live in a poor situation economically; after independence the second generation live in an improved situation; and then in the third generation they live in a wealthy situation. My case is exceptional. My father's family were very powerful, but in the third generation we were poorer than in the second.'

That was why for Budi the failure, two years running, to get into ITB was like part of the family calamity.

Twice a year, following old custom, Budi's uncle, the lawyer, came to visit his elder sister in Surabaya. He found on one visit that Budi, then aged twenty, had no job and no university place. He took Budi back to Jakarta with him. There Budi joined an information technology college, and discovered that, though there was nothing in his background to explain it, he had a gift for computers. He lived with his uncle for four years.

'My life changed after that. I know how to dress well, and behave well.'

'Didn't you know that before?'

'If I stayed in Surabaya I would never have the chance to visit a hotel. I would never have the manners of entry in a hotel dining room. And, maybe, I cannot speak English and I don't know how to talk to people.'

'Do people here worry about that?'

'Lots of Indonesians worry about that.'

After the college he joined a computer company, a very famous one. He joined at the lowest level, but soon he began to rise and get awards; soon he began to travel for the company. Soon, through colleagues in the company, he got to know very important people outside. He discovered that the worlds of business and computers and political power in Indonesia ran into one another, were almost one and the same; the circle of power was really very small. He also discovered at this time that, in spite of his uncle, he was still paying for his father's failure, and was a man without a family, without a group. He had left his uncle's house and was living in a rented house with two servants, a couple. He was lonely. He had no social life to speak of. His very success – and the famous and powerful people he had got to know – made him aware of his own isolation. He could find no girlfriend matching his new situation. So, in a roundabout way, success began to turn his thoughts to religion.

'When I was getting awards from the computer company I began to think, for the first time, that I am something, I am special. When they moved me up to marketing I thought I was also special. But then I saw many other people who were better than me. And I began to think that in the world nothing can be said to be the best, because after the best you see, there will always be something better. So, based on that belief, I felt I needed God. In the Koran school you read again and again that God is the highest, but you don't feel it in your heart.'

'How old were you at this time?'

'About twenty-nine. Not very successful, just improved, compared with common people. I felt this about God every day. Whatever I think I think alone. I don't even have a close friend in the company with whom I can talk about religion. For about four or five years I lived in a very contradictory situation. On one side I need God and religion very badly, but at the same time I am doing bad things that the religion forbids. I drink liquors. I drink beer. And I do other bad things, bad in a Muslim way. It always worried me, right after the act. But not drinking: drinking I consider minor. I know that the punishment for a little pleasure in the world is paid for by many years in hell.'

'Did you always believe in hell?'

'I always believed in hell. And everyone here believes in heaven and hell, or life after death, whatever their religion. I know that my sin was too big, that whatever I did I was going to hell. I know that my life was not balanced between good things and bad things.'

And then, at this moment of worry and doubt, came a business development. A colleague in the computer firm introduced him to the man who was going to be his partner. The colleague was the childhood friend of the partner: it was the world of connections from which Budi felt himself excluded. Just a few weeks after they had been introduced, the man who was to be Budi's partner said, 'Why don't we do a business together?' He needed Budi because, though well connected and rich and knowing about all the contracts that were waiting to be picked up, he didn't have Budi's computer talents. In the technological age talent like Budi's was a kind of leveller.

Budi made a quick decision. He decided to leave the computer company right away. After ten years with them, after all the awards and travel and first-class hotels, he gave them a day's notice.

When he told his father, the old man, remembering the penniless-ness he had tumbled into with his wretched furniture business, said, 'Be careful.' His mother, beaten down by that pennilessness, and her own memories of her mother going out to work in the fields, said nothing.

I asked Budi what he thought was the source of his computer gift.

'I do not know. Maybe it was my destiny. In my business lots of people fail because in the first place you need innovation. It's actually like dreaming. For example, like in a hotel here, while I'm eating I'm thinking of automating the process – ordering the menu, perhaps. I saw that in Europe. The waiter comes with a computer, pushes a few buttons according to your instructions, and a few minutes later another waiter brings the order through. Automatically you get the bill from the waiter who took your order. So I'm sitting here, eating and talking to you, and also thinking how to create the software for that. I am also thinking you could apply that kind of concurrent engineering to many other business sectors. My mind is working like that all the time. I could apply that to railway wagons, or stock in a warehouse.'

It was not long before the partner introduced Budi to the religious teacher.

'The first time I met him he was in a very simple house which was also a mosque. It was his own house, in Bandung. My partner took me. He was going a week later to Mecca, and so we asked the teacher for his blessing and advice for my partner on the pilgrimage. The first time I saw him I don't believe him. He is very young. Then, after I discovered how deep his knowledge is, I never underestimate young people any more. He spoke to about ten people in his house. They sat on the carpet. A simple carpet. He said the secret of life is: Let God decide what's good for you. He didn't mean that we should give up, but that whatever we did we should do to the very best. You have to assist your destiny, but you can't go beyond it.

'The first meeting lasted one hour. I thought he was very interesting, but I wasn't converted yet. Several months later my partner offered me a proposal to invest several thousand rupiah to build a mosque that would be coordinated by the teacher. My partner said that everyone should pay for two square metres. I hadn't seen the teacher since our first meeting. My partner invited me to the opening of the mosque while it was still under construction. I met the teacher again. I saw how the simple house had been converted into a beautiful mosque.

'Altogether I met him about thirty times. I don't learn the details of the religion from him. I needed someone to do other things: how to balance between living in the world and the afterlife, only very heavy things. People appeared to think that he had a supernatural power, but I don't believe that. I saw the evidence – the little house becoming the big mosque – but I don't believe it. I believed more in his teaching: Let God decide what's good for you.'

The teacher had been seven times to Mecca. He had never paid. Someone always paid for him. And something like that happened to Budi, after the teacher said he should go to Mecca. He didn't have the money, but when he told his partner the partner paid.

On Saturday we went to Bandung to see the teacher. We went there by a CN-235, which was an earlier and smaller plane built (with Spanish collaboration) by Habibie's aerospace organisation. In the first-class waiting room at the domestic airport the chairs were carved and gilded; I imagined they were like the chairs Widarti Goenawan said *Femina* didn't like.

It was a short hop to Bandung, but the little CN-235 was very late. The day which had appeared so long, so full of promise, began to shrink. Nerves began to go. And then the plane itself, which was really very small, was very warm while we waited on the asphalt; the panelling was like rough carpenter's work; and it was so noisy and trembly when we took off that I wondered why, since many of its vital components would have been imported, such a plane had been made at all.

Budi said, 'I am proud that it flies. Don't ask me about its economic viability and so on.'

And Bandung came up so quickly now that at the end, after all the strain, I felt something like that too.

Budi had said that his partner was working at Bandung that Saturday and would meet us at the airport. He wasn't there. We saw him later, quite by chance, in a new four-wheel drive packed with his family. This was on one of the now crowded avenues of the Dutch-built hill station, where colonial-style administrative buildings and small residences were being altered and extended for commercial use, and where shade trees had grown old, scant-leaved, with swollen trunks (whitewashed at the base) making pavements uneven.

The partner stopped readily for us, but he was unabashed. He said simply he had forgotten to meet us. The moment passed; Budi appeared not to have noticed; but I felt that in his too-quick friendliness for me, a visitor, possibly without credentials, he had overreached himself, asking his partner, an important man, to meet us at the airport. The partner was friendly but un-noticing with me. He was short and stocky and blunt-featured; he would have passed in an Indonesian crowd. He was a year or two younger than Budi, and Budi said he was already worth thirty million dollars. His family in the four-wheel drive was elegant, with a maid for the children; his wife was pale, with sharper features, and an almost Indian beauty.

We began to drive up and up, to where the teacher was, on the edge of the town. We passed the old landscaped grounds of the Institute of Technology, still Dutch-looking: built in 1918, famous as Sukarno's old school in the 1920s, and ever since then the focus of so much Indonesian ambition. The Salman mosque on the campus was where Imaduddin had reigned as preacher in the 1970s; it couldn't be missed. Partly because of Imaduddin it had outgrown the colonial Dutch intention; and, as if in deliberate contrast with the colonial restraint of the setting, it was now a big concrete building in very bright colours. On one shady road we passed a brisk line of matriculates in white clothes, and with a kind of comic hat. Budi, whose dream at one time had been to be a matriculate like that, didn't know the origin of the clothes; and perhaps they might have been a transplanted Dutch tradition.

As we drove away from the Institute and the Dutch town, Budi added to what he had said about the teacher. The supernatural power that some had attributed to him had blessed him with further great success. He had a supermarket now; a car-hire business; a garment factory; a bank; a computer-rental service. These things attached themselves to him, grew around him. He remained as he had started: a teacher. A foundation set up by disciples looked after the business side. All this had been achieved in three years. It was the success in which others – and Budi now as well – saw the divine hand.

When we arrived there was a further surprise: a further adjustment: the words used by Budi for the business ventures of the teacher or his foundation were too grand. We were now far from the colonial town, in a simple country village, with informal houses and yards and gardens on both sides of a narrow asphalted lane. And the computer-rental service was a little stall; the supermarket was a kind of country shop; and the big mosque (atop the shop) was not very big. All the buildings of the commune were modest. They were, in fact, in spite of all the new concrete and paint and clay roof-tiles, the higgledy-piggledy buildings of a *kampung*, spontaneously assembled here into a *pesantren*, a religious boarding school; though here the pupils were also disciples of the teacher, and dedicated to his service.

The *pesantren* had the village road cleaned every day; and though there might be unavoidable drifts of dust against the broken edges of the lump-laid asphalt on the road, every fifty metres or so there was a pole fixed with a coloured plastic bucket for rubbish, so that there might be no rubbish on the road. The buckets were rather small. But, just as the old-fashioned beggar's matches were not meant to be actually sold, so I felt the coloured small buckets were more like a heraldic device, an emblem of service and piety, and not meant to be stuffed with real refuse or anything very dirty.

The teacher's house – his current house, not the original house, which had been rebuilt as a mosque and shop – was in a short lane off the main village road. The lane, between two of the houses of the commune, led to a courtyard. The teacher's house was on one side of this courtyard. It was of one story, raised a few feet off the ground, and the walls – which would have been of concrete, Budi said – were decorated with woven-bamboo panels in a striking dark-brown and beige diamond pattern.

Just as we got to the courtyard the teacher came out to the verandah of his house. And he made an impression: he was leading a plump, blind boy in a long blue tunic. He was very small, perhaps not taller than the boy, and a good deal thinner. There were farewells; the blind boy was handed over to someone else and led down the two steps to the courtyard. One audience was over.

We took off our shoes and went up to the verandah. In Jakarta Budi had told me that the teacher was 'skinny'. But that didn't suggest the overall fineness of the small man: the pared-down face, the thin moustache, the wispy beard, the small lively eyes, which were now assessing us. He had an unexpectedly full, well-defined mouth, with the merest tuft of hair below the centre of the lower lip. His skin was a smooth clear brown, and he was dressed in white or off-white, in a kind of Arab dress which he had established as his religious costume and which Budi had told me about: a turban of some quilted material, with a long tail, and a long tunic over a dark-blue sarong. In spite of his dress, and vocation, and the blind boy, it wasn't a solemn house. It was a family house, as we could hear and partly see, with playful children, and busy women happy to be connected with the teacher.

He sat down with us on the green nylon carpet, which was hairy, not fixed to the floor, and not flat. The verandah rail – bamboo uprights between timber cross-pieces – was very low; the teacher could lean on it. As he did now, in an abrupt moment of abstraction: leaning on the rail and looking away from us and down at the little pool just below, with running water and a rockery of nicely cut lava blocks – an unexpected touch of elegance in the courtyard.

Helpers in white caps, young men, *pesantren* students, were beginning to unroll cheap machine-made rugs – various colours, floral patterns – on the concrete courtyard for the afternoon sermon. No doubt it was from this verandah, as from a pulpit or a ruler's dais, that the teacher spoke. Budi had told me that the teacher's sermons drew crowds of a thousand; now, with his own growing excitement (prayer time was getting near, and Budi offered all the five prayers), he said two thousand. Everybody couldn't fit here, but for the overflow crowd, in the road, and even in some of the neighbouring houses, there was closed-circuit television.

Budi said, 'He's high-tech.'

But the teacher didn't want Budi to interpret. He wanted to talk to me on his own, and in English; and that made things difficult, especially as he wasn't sure what I had come for. I wanted to hear about the beginning of his ministry or vocation. I don't believe he understood that. He wanted to stay in the present, to talk about the commune that had grown up around him, and the various gifts of his disciples, part of the favour of God – and I felt that the pond and rockery below the verandah at which he looked from time to time, so finely made, so separate from the setting, might have been one of those special gifts.

When I pressed him about the first preaching, he talked generalities. 'Many people don't have nice life. They have money but no happiness. Their soul is floating.' When the language let him down he tried to make up for that with an intensity of voice and expression and gesture, bunching up his thin fingers. Once or twice I had a sight, quite affecting, of his small bare feet below his sarong.

I thought I should try a smaller question. I asked about his father. He said his father was a soldier; he left the army with the rank of lieutenant-colonel; all his service had been in Java. 'I thought of joining the army. Macho. Like my friends.' He laughed. 'Now I am in the army of Allah. My friends are in the green beret of the army. Now I am in the white beret or turban of Allah.'

I tried again. Budi had told me that the teacher had been an ITB dropout, and before seeing the light had lived a 'naughty' life. So now I asked the teacher about his education, and found that Budi had got it wrong. He had tried to create the teacher too much in his own image. The teacher wasn't a dropout at all; he thought of himself as versatile and successful. He had studied many subjects, administration, electronics, and he had taken a degree in electronic engineering at ITB. 'God gave me success in most of the things I did. Writing. As a speechmaker. I was elected commander of the student battalion. But after all the successes I felt empty. I was twenty-four or twenty-five. I tried to find what is the most important thing in life.'

I wanted to hear about that.

'I was the eldest of four children. The third child of the family died from multiple sclerosis. I carried him on my back to school. But in spite of his pain he was always happy. Happier than the doctors, happier than us. Something is important in him. What is the secret?'

There was a new visitor, a big young woman in an off-white Muslim headcover and a long black gown. She was round-faced, without make-up, with something like old pain at the back of the smiling eyes. This was Hani. She worked in IPTN, Habibie's aircraft organisation, and was famous for being the only woman worker there in full Muslim clothes. The teacher welcomed her and introduced her, explaining that in Islam she was not allowed to touch men.

She squatted before us on her knees and heels, her thighs spreading wide below her gown. She said she had worked in France for eight years. She had studied in Poitiers.

Budi said, 'She's a high-tech lady.'

She said, modestly, that she was working on only a 'little part' of the aeroplane for Habibie. But when she came here, to the *pesantren*, she did what she could to meet the needs of the people. What did she actually do? She said she made garments for Muslims. It was a way of saying she made clothes; she was finding pious words for something quite simple.

From the inner room of the teacher's house women helpers brought out plates of bright yellow cakes and some sort of red liquid in china cups. The cups sat unsteadily on the hairy, rumpled carpet.

Hani said she came back to Indonesia because she had a contract with IPTN. She had had a scholarship from Habibie. Fifty people were sent every year, and the scholarships were mainly in the aeronautical business.

I asked the teacher to finish the story about his brother.

'He died and said, "We cannot work together in the world, but we will work together in the afterlife."'

Hani, squatting in her way, smiling, her gown spreading about her, looking quite big and upright beside the teacher, said of him, 'When I came back from France and went to work at IPTN, and heard him for the first time, I began to cry.'

'Do you remember what he said?'

'He said our work here was temporary. If we worked hard we would have a good afterlife. He gave me the courage to wake up and work harder. He never says the same thing twice. God works in his mouth.'

And at last – prayer time now, Budi gone, chanting coming from somewhere, a sound system for the afternoon sermon squawking and booming as it was being set up, a green-veiled woman or girl sweeping the porch of the house on the other side of the courtyard, thin *pesantren* cats walking about, slack bellies swinging – at last, as if led on to it by Hani's words, the teacher told me about the first preaching. He spoke in a mixture of English and Indonesian; Hani translated the Indonesian.

It was when he was twenty-five; it would have been after the death of his brother. It was in his father's house. He simply began to talk to people. At the first preaching there were ten. Then he left his father's house (he didn't say where it was) and came here and rented a room in a house which had now become the *pesantren* mosque. When he had forty people listening to him he began to worry. He thought, 'Why are those people listening to me?' He lost some friends. For three years it was difficult for him – though he didn't say how. All his friends left him, except for one. He didn't mind.

'I know Allah watch me all the time. I know Allah listens to me. So I cannot lie. It is enough for me. I just liked to talk about good things. And some people said it is nice, very beautiful. I didn't feel it was beautiful. It is very difficult for me to talk about these things. I just opened my heart. I talk from my heart, not the brain.'

This no doubt was what Hani meant when she said God worked in his mouth.

I felt that, if I had the time, and if I could get the teacher to answer a lot of small questions, there might have been more to learn about his mission; but not much more, and nothing that would alter what had been said. This was as far as one could go without the language, and without faith, and the needs of faith.

I asked about the blind boy.

'I give the blind boy a place to stay here with other students. But now he is working for a government hospital. He stayed here for about three years.' What did he do? 'There is an orphanage here. Only four of the children here are my own. I take care of the orphans here.' How many? 'About six or ten.'

Strange imprecision; but it might only have been a trick of speech. We had heard the children in the house; and now some of them, one or two with white caps, boys, not girls, were rolling about in the court-yard on the rugs where in a short while the faithful were to sit.

Budi had come back; it was time to leave. The watchfulness had gone out of the teacher's eyes; our meeting had gone well. He went down to the courtyard and the lane with us. He was happy to pose for photographs: long turban tail hanging down, a pen clipped to the pocket of his tunic, his delicate feet showing below his sarong. He called to the children (white caps for the boys, white headdresses for the girls), their nurse (in a saffron sarong and black headdress), Hani: he wanted them to pose too. At the end everyone was laughing.

As we left we saw, two or three houses up the road, food being fer-ried in from a car by white-capped *pesantren* students. The food would have been a gift from a follower, like so much else we had seen: like the green carpet in the verandah, the china cups for the red drink (and per-haps the drink itself), the woven-bamboo panels on the house wall, the pool and rockery in the courtyard: everyone giving according to his means. It was as Budi had said: the faith of his followers had caused the *pesantren* and all its enterprises to grow. And since his success proved his divine favour, his success, and the number of his followers, grew.

He didn't offer simple faith. He would have offered versions of the 'very heavy things' he had offered Budi: guidance spiritual and worldly ('Let God decide what's best for you'), together with the path to abso-lution. He offered solidity and reassurance to everyone according to his need; and the needs of the important were great. At least one relation of Habibie's was a follower, Budi said. He even suggested that the great Habibie himself was in touch with the teacher. But Budi, as I had grown to understand, liked to feel that he was in the thick of things now; and this might have been one of his over-excited stories.

The whole matter, of the teacher's *pesantren* and the teacher's mission, had been taken out of the teacher's hands. He remained only the teacher, as he was now, standing and smiling among the children, saying goodbye.

We took the train back to Jakarta. The Dutch-built railway station was

well kept – Java was not like India – though a Dunkin Donuts stall, in
its international livery, was like an oddity. In the executive class coach,
which was air-conditioned, there was a noticeable taint of spicy food on
everything. An attendant turned on the video screen high up in one
corner; the film was *The Little Buddha*, which Budi had seen. In the
fading light the train ran slowly over gorges in the forested hills outside
Bandung: gorge after gorge, bridge after bridge, the track winding all
the time, so that sometimes, looking ahead, looking back, you could
see two or even three white-painted bridges, the curving metal sup-
ports, very broad, showing up in the dusk like decorative swags against
the dark green of forest. The little terraced rice-fields, irregular patterns
of bund and water on the steep hillsides, caught the fading light and
were like leaded stained glass, dark or gold or red, sometimes with
seedlings planted out in rows.

Budi said that the rice-growers didn't see the beauty we saw. Often
they had to walk for hours up and down hills to get to a main road.
When we passed a village he showed what he meant. In those villages
a thousand rupiah, fifty cents, was a lot of money. (A thousand 'roops'
was what he said, 'roops' for rupiah being part of the curious jauntiness
of his speech.) An ear of maize fetched no more than fifty 'roops'
there, two and a half cents; so that for a great labour, not least that of
carrying the crop to market, a farmer might get only five dollars. A
little later he showed the forested land where he said a relation of
Habibie was going to build nine hundred houses for IPTN people; the
aircraft business had its ramifications.

He said he knew it was strange that he, who was now on the other
side, should be talking like this about the poor. But he quarrelled every
day with his partner over some new piece of corruption he saw or
thought he saw. He couldn't help it; though he knew he depended on
the partner (and his ways) to get the big jobs that came their way. It was
something he had also taxed the teacher with: that he accepted corrupt
men as his followers.

What had the teacher said?

He said he knew the stories about people. But he couldn't go by
that; he could judge people only by what he saw of them. Which was
as good an answer as the one he had given when Budi had asked about
his half-Arab clothes. Yes, the teacher had said, they were extravagant,
but they were meant to be: they made him conscious of himself, so that
while he wore those clothes he couldn't do anything bad.

Budi said, 'I left you for some time with him, after Hani came. I went to pray. It was the time of day. While I was praying I discovered I had lost my wallet. The actual loss wasn't important. But it was going to be troublesome. Telling the cards people. The ID card was going to cause problems; to get a new one would take months. So just after praying I had these worries. And I thought, "If I lose them it is God's will. It means that more things will come to me." And then I went out to you and the teacher and saw the wallet on the carpet beside you.'

So for Budi this visit to the teacher had yet again had some element of religious experience: loss, panic, resignation, faith, immense relief, new faith. But, Budi being Budi, the religious moment also contained a practical lesson. 'Never keep your wallet in your side pocket. It will slip out some time. Always keep it in the back pocket.'

The sky became dark. There was no longer a view outside. The fluorescent light of the coach was faint; the windows threw back reflections. The enclosed dim light, the motion, the noise of the wheels – and *The Little Buddha* on the video screen, going on all the time – led Budi into deeper, personal talk.

He told me about the uncle, his mother's younger brother, who had loved him and done so much for him. This was the uncle who had rescued him from his poverty and despair in Surabaya, had brought him to Jakarta and set him on his feet, and shown him the world. Budi had lived with this uncle, who was a lawyer and university professor, for four years. But then there had been a quarrel. Budi, when he had first talked to me of this uncle, had left out the quarrel. But the quarrel had marked him, and partly explained his present solitude.

The uncle had had a pre-university Dutch education in Indonesia; and though he was a good Muslim, and said his prayers four times a day, he had never lost his admiration for the culture of the Netherlands; he went there every other year. Budi was able to list – as though he had done it many times before – all the things he had learned from this uncle. He had learned to go to restaurants; he and his uncle went three times a week. He had learned to drive (his uncle sometimes lent Budi his car); to do photography; to buy books other than schoolbooks; to go to the Koranic school; to dress well, to wear Marks and Spencer blazers and Bally shoes, for instance, never sneakers or jeans; and, curiously, to paint a house.

After four years there was the quarrel. It had to do with girls, with Budi staying out late, sometimes with the car, and lying about the girls. It didn't have to do with any particular girl; it was an objection to Budi's way of life at that time. Budi did a strange thing when the quarrel blew up. He took the girlfriend of the moment away from her family and put her in the house of another girlfriend. After two days the girl's family went to the police. The police came to Budi's uncle to ask about Budi. The uncle dealt with them and asked Budi afterwards, 'Do you know where this girl is?' Budi said, 'Of course.' The uncle said sternly but without anger, 'If you aren't careful you're going to get into trouble.' And Budi, though he didn't say, might then have given his uncle some pledge.

One evening some time later the girl telephoned the house. Budi's uncle answered. Budi had feared that this would happen. And now the uncle was truly enraged. He said to Budi, 'Don't you realise you are nothing? Look what happened to your father. That's a good example for you. He's not living in a house. He's living in a bird's nest.' ('And it's still true,' Budi said, telling the story. 'I can take you to the house.') The uncle gave his ultimatum: Budi had to leave the girl or leave the house.

Budi said he would leave the house. His aunt pleaded with him. She even got into Budi's bed and held him and asked him to go and apologise to his uncle. But he left the next day.

Budi told me, 'There was one more reason for leaving. My family is very, very poor. I live in a very wealthy environment. Very often I am thinking about my family. Every time I spend money on myself I remember that amount of money will be useful to them if I can send it to them. I am wearing Bally shoes, eating in those fine restaurants, buying expensive books, and sometimes they can't even find things for lunch.'

He went to stay in the house of a college friend. A younger brother of the friend was made to give up his room to Budi. That first week, through another college friend, Budi got a small job as a clerk, and earned thirty thousand rupiah, about fifteen dollars. At the end of the second week he found a place, as a simple computer operator, with a big computer company. He was to stay, and succeed, in this company for ten years. So, in this quick and unexpected way, he had started on his true career. It was what his uncle had been training him for; but now his uncle wasn't there; and there was no one as close or as concerned or as informed to whom Budi could take this kind of news about himself. He began to feel his solitude.

There was a further sourness for Budi, with the friend from the

computer school in whose family house he had gone to stay. The
friend wanted Budi to do his homework; then he got Budi to write an
examination for him; then he began to ask Budi for money. Budi
couldn't complain to anyone in the house; and when at last he left the
house he created a bad impression all round.

He sent a third of what he was earning to his father and mother in
Surabaya, assuaging some of that old pain. Four years after he had left
his uncle's house Budi's mother began to press him to make it up with
his uncle. She said to Budi, 'You are younger. Your uncle can't apologise to you. You must apologise to him.' At last he agreed. She came
from Surabaya to Jakarta for the festival at the end of the Muslim fasting month, and she took him to his uncle's house. They went early in
the morning and they stayed in the house all day; but the uncle never
came out of his room to greet them. The following year, for the same
festival, Budi's mother came again and took Budi to the house. This
time the uncle came out of his room. But the relationship had been
broken. It couldn't be the same again.

It appeared to be the pattern of Budi's life: the friend, the rescuer,
always turning, as in a legend, into an enemy. And – remembering the
offhand partner with his elegant family in the four-wheel drive in
Bandung – I wondered whether that pattern wasn't going to repeat
now, with the business associates Budi had found among the enor-
mously wealthy people of the Indonesian boom. I put the point to him.

He said, repeating some of my words, 'There is a possibility now that
friends become enemies. If you hear bad things and say nothing, some
day you will blow up, like my uncle.'

He was vulnerable. He had no protector. And I discovered now
that, with all the luxurious tastes in clothes and shoes and imported
dark glasses which his uncle had trained him in, tastes which he still
had, he didn't have a house or an apartment. He lived in rooms in
friends' houses, rotating the houses; and there was a place in his office
where he could sleep. He said he couldn't afford a house. I told him
about the thousands of houses I had seen in the big new satellite cities
of Jakarta. He said only corrupt people like policemen and accountants
could afford to pay the 20 per cent deposit on a forty-thousand–dollar
house; when you lived in those places you knew you were among
crooks. But then he said he didn't want a house in a satellite city
because he would have to have a servant in it all day to look after it,
and that would be a burden for him. A little later he appeared to say

that he wouldn't be able to endure the solitude of having a house of his own.

He was tormented by his solitude. His destitute parents in Surabaya had not been able to do much for him socially. And since he had not gone to a university he had been cut off from a whole generation of his peers. The girls he might have married had married other people. Even when he was rising in the computer company he hadn't been able to find girlfriends among his colleagues because he didn't have their kind of background or confidence. Before the Bandung teacher had made him go on the pilgrimage to Mecca he had had lots of sex, but without 'environment' – his computer word for a suitable social life. Now, after his vow, even the sex had gone.

He had hundreds of friends. But loneliness, he said mysteriously, had no direct relationship with happiness; and the loneliness he suffered from was 'not knowing what to do'. He got on with his parents, but they thought Budi far above them; and there was no real conversation with them, as there had been with his uncle.

'My father doesn't regret about the bankruptcy. He never regrets. He likes to wear very old shirts, even when I buy him new ones. He is very Indonesian that way. He has no desire for luxury. He is happy with the bird's nest. I told him what my uncle said, and he laughed. He said, "So you ran away from the house because he said that?" I said, "It was humiliating." He said, "But it's true. The house is like a bird's nest."'

At the new Japanese-built railway terminus in Jakarta, which was far finer and more attractive than anything in India, with its clean open areas and its tempting food stalls, Budi bargained hard and for some minutes with the taxi-drivers. I offered to pay, but he wanted to bargain. He beat one man down to a price which I thought very low. When we were in the taxi he said he intended to double the agreed payment, to show his appreciation of the courtesy of the man.

Something of the mystery and oddity of his father had passed on to him. His fear of solitude had committed him to living as he did, in the houses of friends and in his office; and this style of life was ensuring his solitude.

His office was a large room in a modern block in central Jakarta. This room was divided by partitions into smaller spaces. In the principal area there were five executive chairs. A cupboard attached to this area was where Budi slept when he was not staying with friends. The cupboard had a bunk-bed and clothes-rails, and since there was no air-conditioning he slept with the cupboard door open. In drawers in the executive office area were those of his clothes that were not on hangers. The clothes were as expensive as his uncle had taught him clothes should be; and on shelves close to the cupboard there were books – meant for night-time reading – like those his uncle had taught him to buy, among them the Koran in Indonesian and English, a number of religious books, and a set of Heinemann Asia business-management books which he had bought after our day at Bandung.

In a small space outside the executive area was his expensive American mountain bike with shock-absorbers back and front: cycling, in Surabaya an aspect of his great need, converted now to sport and luxury. At the side or back of the area for employees, as packed as a classroom, was a green-carpeted mosque recess with a prayer rug at an angle to indicate the direction of Mecca.

I was reminded – though the scale here was smaller – of Imaduddin's office. It turned out that Budi followed Imaduddin's religious programmes on television (remembering especially an interview Imaduddin had done with a murderer who had turned to Islam in jail). And when I sat through one of Budi's regular staff-training sessions I thought he had adapted some of Imaduddin's mental training exercises; though both might have had an American corporate origin.

A friend of Budi's, a man of twenty-five, an ITB graduate, working in his family's telecommunications business, had recently visited the office. He was an expert in martial arts. He was also known for his ability to see spirits and to divine people's illnesses and auras. He saw that Budi's partner had a kidney problem, and he saw that Budi suffered from sinusitis. When Budi, impressed, took him to his sleeping cupboard the seer said, 'In that sleeping room there is the spirit of a very old woman. But she's not bothering you. So just let her stay there.'

I asked Budi, 'What is this old lady like? Did he see her?'

'I asked him what you asked me. And he said, "The old lady is of transparent material. Like what is in the movie *Casper, the Friendly Ghost*." In an Egyptian book I've read it's stated differently. The spirits in that book can imitate themselves in the form of human beings. Can also transform into an animal.'

I said, 'I didn't know you were interested in these things.'
'I've always been interested in these things.'

At our last meeting Budi had gifts for me, books – his uncle's style still with him. They were books about the first nine teachers or spreaders of Islam in Indonesia, and they were given to remind me of our visit to the teacher in Bandung. They were books for children; but Budi thought them suitable, because they contained the folk stories about those teachers.

Budi translated the story of Kali Jaga for me. Kali Jaga's reputation was that he was the teacher who had fitted the old Hindu epic of the *Mahabharata* to the story of Islam for the puppet theatre. In that way he took Islam to the people and taught them to worship God and not stone.

Kali Jaga's father was a minister or regional ruler in the Majapahit empire, the last Hindu empire in Java. The father's domain was in the north of Java, where there was already some Islamic influence. Though he was himself a believer, he didn't want his son to teach Islam; he didn't want to antagonise the Hindu ruler of the empire. When Kali Jaga grew up he became unhappy about the gap between the rich and poor in his father's domain. He began to steal rice and other food from the state warehouses and gave it to the poor. His father caught him one day and asked him to leave his domain. Kali Jaga became a robber in the forest, robbing for the poor.

One day he saw an old man walking in the forest with a stick with a gold handle. Kali Jaga went and seized the stick from the old man, and the old man said, 'What do you want? Do you want gold? If you want gold, look at those trees.' Suddenly the trees the old man pointed to turned to gold. Kali Jaga ran to the trees to get the gold, and the old man went on his way. When the old man disappeared the gold on the trees turned to leaves again, and Kali Jaga realised that the old man was a powerful man.

In fact, the old man was Sunnan Bonang, one of the nine teachers, a man of great power; he could fly and call up water at will. Kali Jaga ran after the old man and begged the old man to accept him as a student. The old man said, 'I'm busy. But if you really want to be my student, take this stick of mine and sit here beside the river and wait until I come back.'

The teacher went away. He forgot Kali Jaga for many years. When one day he passed that way again he found Kali Jaga sitting beside the river, with long hair and beard and whiskers and nails, and still with the teacher's stick. Vines had grown over him. So the old man gave Kali Jaga much knowledge and power, and told him to go out and start preaching Islam to the people. Kali Jaga found it hard to preach to the people, who were Hindus. So he stuck as much as he could to Hindu stories and ceremonies, but changed the words. Instead of the Hindu mantras he recited the Koran.

Budi said, 'This preaching was in Tuban, about two hundred kilometres from Surabaya. A big city today, with a harbour.'

'Do you have a date?'

'I don't know.'

'A century?'

'I would relate this to the fall of the Majapahit empire. This book is meant for children. They don't put the year and so on.'

The fall of Majapahit is put at 1478. Fourteen years, that is, before the fall of Granada, the last Muslim kingdom in Spain, and fourteen years before the discovery of the New World. So while Islam was arrested in the west, in the east it was spreading over the cultural-religious remains of Greater India. India had been ravaged by centuries of Muslim invasions; its light, in places like Indonesia, had been put out.

The figure of Kali Jaga, covered by vines, but loyal to his duty, is a magical and simplified version of the Hindu-Jain saint, Gomateshwara, meditating on the infinite. The most spectacular rendering of the vine-wrapped Gomateshwara is a 57-foot free-standing nude statue at Sravana Belgola in the Southern Indian state of Karnataka. It dates from the tenth century and still looks new. At the statue's feet, disturbingly, as if in a further testing of the saint, real rats run about. It was strange to find him in this fifteenth-century Javanese story, sitting on a river bank with a quite different purpose.

Budi's world, still at a time of crossover between faiths, was more full of ghosts than he knew.

II
IRAN
The Justice of Ali

1

The Foundation of the Oppressed

IN JAKARTA the new wealth could at times feel oppressive. It was changing landscape and lives too fast, or so it seemed: the past was too close.
Every weekend, from the disorganised new city created by the new
wealth, rich people, rich Chinese especially, looked to get away, for rest,
cleanliness, cool air, order. They went, with their families and maids, to
the new five-star hotels; these were now the city's weekend sanctuaries.
In 1979 some Jakarta Chinese had used city hotels in that way, but they
had done so mainly during the important holidays. Now the new
money, the new luck, made every weekend festive; and on Sunday
mornings, in the Borobudur hotel, the rich folk, Chinese and others,
from the Bethany Successful Families, one of the new American evan-
gelical faiths, met and sang hymns and clapped hands in one of the
larger public rooms, praying for the luck to last. It felt like luck, this
wealth that could bless even the uneducated, because the technologies
and the factories that produced it had been imported whole. For that
reason, too, it felt like plunder, something that had to end. In the
authoritarian state, where luck and licences came only to the obedient,
every idea of development – including 'technology' – went with that
idea of plunder. Even the rich could be made anxious. So on Sunday
mornings they met in the sanctuary of the hotel and sang hymns and
clapped hands with sabbath abandon; on the rear window of their cars
there were stickers, BETHANY SUCCESSFUL FAMILIES, like a
fixed prayer to ward off the evil eye.

I often felt in Jakarta that it was a version, less elegant perhaps, of what Iran might have been like before the revolution: so grand and overwhelming that it seemed wrong to see the sham or to imagine the great city collapsed or decayed.

But the Tehran I went to in August 1979, six months after the revolution, had been like that imagined city: like a modern metropolis, the creation of untold wealth, whose life had been miraculously suspended: the international advertisements still up, but the goods not always there (and Kentucky Fried Chicken angrily re-lettered to Our Fried Chicken, with the face of the Southern colonel smudged and redrawn); the cranes arrested on a dozen unfinished towers; the bad meals in empty restaurants, the rubbery sturgeon in brown sauce in the almost empty but still impeccably laid-out dining room of the hotel still called the Royal Tehran Hilton on its crockery and bills and menus, where the sullen black-tied waiters whispered and grumbled together, like people who knew their talents and style were no longer needed. Premonitions of decay there; but, outside, the excitement of the immense crowds at Friday prayers at Tehran University (crowds so great that their footsteps roared like the sea, and dust could be seen to rise above them as they walked), with the famous preachers shown live on television; and the Revolutionary Guards, in the guerrilla gear that was now like an attribute of the faith, driving round very fast in open small trucks to proclaim their possession of the city.

I was staying this time at the Hyatt. It wasn't absolutely the Hyatt now: it was the Azadi Grand Hotel (ex-Hyatt). '*Azadi*' meant freedom. All the five-star hotels of Iran had been taken over by the state and re-named and handed over to the Foundation of the Oppressed (the name mocking the Shah's Pahlavi Foundation). But people still spoke of the Hyatt. It was on the outskirts of the city, in north Tehran, up in the mountains.

The polished marble floor of the big lobby was reassuring, and there were people at the desk even at three o'clock in the morning. But the piece of carpet in the lift was dirty and stained and didn't absolutely fit. The gilt of the lift doors, part of the original Hyatt glamour, had been torn away or worn away in places, and could be seen now to be only a laminate, like the laminate that covers a credit card. The hotel porters were all in open-necked shirts; this was one of the badges of the revolution. The collars had sagged into irregular folds below the jacket lapels, and looked at this dead time like a kind of grubby low ruff. Many of the porters were unshaven; this was Islamic. Some were shiny-faced and dirty. This was a form of social defiance: the two styles of revolution, the political and the religious, running together. And when later I came down again, to look for a hotel safe box, the porters were sitting unabashed and sullen and unhelpful on the upholstered chairs in the central part of the lobby, like a little conclave of the oppressed in whose name hotels like the Hyatt had been taken over.

Later, in daylight, there was reassurance of a sort. A waiter brought up coffee. And then two women came to do the room. Their ankle-length gowns, of a glaucous-blue colour (perhaps to hide the dirt), and their black headdress, like black hoods, made them look like monks of a service order. But they were friendly; they even had some words of English. Nothing there to prepare me for the man who brought up my lunchtime omelette. He was surly from start to finish, looked at me with absolute hatred, and never said a word. Still some revolutionary rage, I thought; and when in the late afternoon I went down to the lobby I saw something I had missed in the semi-stupor of arrival that morning: a big sign on the atrium wall above the lobby: DOWN WITH USA. It had been there (and in the lobbies of all the five-star hotels) since the revolution.

Below this sign people were having tea and coffee and cakes, middle-class-looking people, with many women among them. On the mezzanine floor there must have been a party of some sort for children: young women of elegant bearing and with elegant shoes (elegance overcoming the long gowns and the black headdress) were going up the winding staircase to the mezzanine with little girls in brightly coloured dresses; suggesting a society more open than one would have thought from the announcement by the Lufthansa steward on our arrival that women should keep their heads covered.

But the man to whom I said that – coming to take me to a perfor-mance of *The Conference of the Birds*, Sufi rhythms, Sufi dancing, in the Versailles-style open-air theatre below the chenar trees in the grounds of the Shah's palace – the man to whom I said that about the people in the lobby of the Hyatt said that the true middle class of Iran, the class that had taken a century, and incalculable wealth, to produce had been destroyed or scattered. What I had seen in the lobby of the Hyatt were the sad beginnings of a new middle class.

★

Things unfolded. The traffic was as I remembered, driving still a power game at every intersection, some games won, some lost, cars bashed up either way. Every day the fumes built up into a darkening bank; you looked down on it from the mountains of north Tehran; from the city centre it hid the mountains.

The bookshop in the Hyatt had a good, educated selection of new and old English books, old paperbacks, pre-revolutionary stock, somehow still there. Unlikely titles had been censored, and sometimes in unlikely detail: a small black girl, sitting outside her Southern hovel, in a grainy photograph in a school edition of *Black Boy*, had had her shins scratched over by the black marker.

Outside the café area of the Hyatt lobby there was a framed poster of a woman with her head covered. Mehrdad, the university student who was my guide and interpreter, read the caption for me: 'This is the picture of an innocent woman.' The poster was in many public places in Tehran.

And there was the war, the eight-year war with Iraq. It was the inescapable theme. It was close, but it was also like something mythical, like something that had occurred a hundred years ago. Mehrdad, when he first talked about it, used strange language. He said, 'It is a war that was lost.' When I asked what it meant to him he said, 'Nothing.' He didn't mean that; it was his way of speaking of an almost inexpressible pain.

Mehrdad's sister was in her early thirties. She was educated and not bad looking, but there was no husband for her: there was a shortage of men because of the war. She had a job in a publishing house. In that she was lucky; many young women didn't have that opportunity of leaving the house; it wasn't easy in revolutionary Iran for unmarried women to have a social life or even to move about. When Mehrdad's sister left the office she came home and stayed home. She stayed in her room much of the time. She was moody, Mehrdad said; she had become heavy, and had rages and often cried; their mother didn't know what to do for her.

Mehrdad's father worked in a bank before the revolution. After the revolution the banks were nationalised, and he had lost his job. He had managed to build up a little haberdashery business; that was how he had kept his family. Mehrdad – going back a long way now, going back to when he was eight: the revolution was all that many young people knew – Mehrdad remembered that at the beginning of the revolution the cry was the communist one of '*Nun, Kar, Azadi*', 'Bread, Work,

Freedom'. Within a year it had changed to 'Bread, Work, and an Islamic Republic'.

There were religious rules now about every kind of public behaviour, and there were green-uniformed Revolutionary Guards – their beards and guerrilla gear now the sign of authority, and not young rebellion – to enforce the rules. Mehrdad took me late one afternoon to a pleasure park not far from the Hyatt. Young men and women went to the park to look at one another; the Guards also walked there, to catch them out. The girls, in small groups, were in black gowns and chadors. They were easy to see; black now, in this park, the quite startling colour of female sexuality, making signals from afar. Mehrdad, thinking no doubt of his sister immured at home, said that the girls, some of them already women, were older than they should have been, because men were scarce after the war.

On either side of very wide steps in one part of the park there were busts, remarkably alike, of the great men of Islamic Iran: the Islamic revolution producing here a kind of Soviet art in a park for the people.

Just as, in the old communist countries, the news in the neutered papers was principally of other communist countries, so the news in the English-language *Tehran Times* was of the Muslim world. In between there were local items: the trial of three terrorists of the Mujahidin Khalq Organisation; a shortage of spare parts in the oil industry because of the United States trade embargo; the currency going down.

There was censorship, of course; there was no secret about that. There was an especial cruelty about book censorship. Every book had to be submitted to the censors, not in typescript, but in its printed and finished form, and after the full print run. It made for a passionate and searching self-censorship. However much you wanted to be in the clear, though, you couldn't always be sure that you were. Was music all right? There were different opinions. Was chess all right, or was it a form of gambling? After much uncertainty and argument, the Imam Khomeini had said it was all right; and that had become the law.

The lifts with the peeling gilt doors had never been in good shape. They broke down from time to time, and sometimes, after mending, the sequence of their grating journeys up and down the shaft became disordered. The air-conditioning in my room failed. '*Kharab*,' the man downstairs said. 'Bad.' And that was all. I was prepared to stick it out, but when Mehrdad heard he got the hotel to give me a room at the back, out of the afternoon sun, and with a view of the mountains to the north.

Khomeini's shrine and its adjunct, the Martyrs' Cemetery (the martyrs of the war with Iraq), were in the desert south of Tehran, off the road to the holy city of Qum. Both Mehrdad and the driver thought that we should get there before the heat of the day, and we left Tehran while it was still dark.

Abruptly in the darkness, and from far away in the flat desert, a low, wide spread of lights appeared: the blue and gold lights of the shrine, and the lights of the stretch of the highway leading up to it. Slowly then, like an optical illusion being undone, details began to show through the lights and against the pre-dawn sky: the very high dome, of a curious bronze colour, and the four minarets like telecommunication towers, each with a coronet of yellow lights, and above that a kind of spire topped by the symbol for Allah, and above that again a blue light, as though the designers (like the designers of the Albert Memorial in London) wanted to go on and on.

The parking area was very big. Oleanders grew between the lanes, and there were many old vans and cars in the parking places. The desert light quickened from minute to minute, and more and more people could be seen: whole families asleep or lying on the pavement beside their cars or vans, country people with sunburnt faces, in dark clothes and with ragged-looking bedding, and with their goods in plastic bundles.

A sign-board said, unnecessarily, 'Holy Shrine'. And beyond that was clutter: a number of low sheds for receiving offerings; a Lost and Found shed; a tea shed that offered free tea and sugar and said in a sign that it welcomed gifts of tea and sugar and cups. All this ancillary construction was basic, everyday, even casual, as though piety was well enough served by the big dome and the four minarets with the coronets of lights: all done, Mehrdad told me, in four months, so great was the need for the shrine to the Imam.

In the flat land and below the high sky people looked small. They looked small in the mausoleum too. Their unshod feet made almost no sound. They looked through the bars at the tomb of the Imam; every kind of vow and hope was in that looking. That was what they had come to find. What was outside was incidental.

In front of the mausoleum was a big courtyard paved with concrete slabs, and in the middle of this was a pool for ablutions. The half-finished dust-coloured concrete structures at the side of the courtyard were going to be hostels. Everywhere there was concrete, rough concrete spreading over the desert. The concrete platforms at the side of the main building were already crumbly. The paving slabs of the courtyard in its extension here were broken in places, or abraded down to the aggregate, and finally at the outer edge worn back to simple earth, with puddles of water here and there, and patches of loose gravel.

Mehrdad said, 'They clean it only for the anniversaries.'

The recesses in the brick wall around the mausoleum, traditional sleeping places for pilgrims, were screened, some of them, with blankets and sheets hung on lines. The dawn breeze caused the sheets to lift above the recesses, exposing the families with their blankets and bedding and goods. People without the privacy of screens were already up and about. Many of them were poor-looking village people. Some of them were saying their prayers. The chadors of the black-clad women flapped in the breeze and made the women seem taller than they were. Seen from close to, many were very small and thin, and some were starved-looking. They would have come from far: old village distress, not yet reached by any idea of reform.

Orange-coloured drums were stencilled with the Persian for 'garbage'. Scattered about the main courtyard, and looking like a kind of post-box, were fancifully shaped blue-and-yellow alms boxes. The box said at the top, in Mehrdad's translation, *Alms make you richer*. On two sides were stylised hands, one holding or receiving, one giving. The hands were coloured yellow and the giving hand was stencilled in red *Begin your day with a gift, with alms*. The business or collecting bit of the box was coloured blue; the message there was *To give alms is to protect yourself against seventy kinds of illness*. The whole thing rested on a yellow pillar about three or four feet high. The concrete paving slab of the courtyard had been dug through for the pillar and then mortared up again; so the alms boxes looked like somebody's afterthought.

The alms from the boxes were for the 'Helping Komiteh of Imam Khomeini'; this *komiteh,* or revolutionary committee, had been set up in the first year of the revolution. There was a joke in Tehran about those *komiteh* alms boxes, Mehrdad said. A rustic Turk (an Iranian Turk: many jokes are made about the community) went and gave his alms and almost immediately was run over by a pilgrim bus.

Mehrdad said, 'For the Turk it was like a telephone booth that didn't work.'

There were also suggestion boxes in the courtyard, unexpected in a shrine, but perhaps they, too, had been put up by the *komiteh*; and the idea behind them might have been only that all public places had to have suggestion boxes. These were like little bird-houses on pillars. The pillars, like the pillars for the alms boxes, had been set in holes dug through the concrete and roughly mortared in again; so that they too looked like an afterthought.

The sun began to come up. It was time to leave for the Martyrs' Cemetery. The three-branched metal lamp standards at the entrance to the concrete courtyard were damaged already. I had missed them on the way in. The dome-shaped tops of the lamps, looking like a kind of high ecclesiastical hat, had been done in aluminium. The plinths, too, were damaged.

It had all been run up very quickly, as Mehrdad had said. Perhaps it was how shrines had always begun, to meet an immediate need, to absorb some overwhelming public emotion or grief. Perhaps this shrine, or its ancillary buildings, would be built over and over as long as there was the need. I felt that for most of the people who had come there would always be the need; the world would always be outside their control.

On the pavements now, beside the cars and the vans in their parking places, and among the oleanders, families were sitting round a formal spread of the flat bread and white cheese they had brought. Some of them had samovars.

In 1979 there were revolutionary posters and graffiti everywhere. The graphic art of the revolution was high, like the passions. There was almost none of that now; instead, there were the signs and exhortations of authority. **DO NOT THINK THAT THOSE WHO ARE SLAIN IN THE CAUSE OF ALLAH ARE DEAD. THEY ARE ALIVE AND PROVIDED FOR BY ALLAH**: this was the English sign on the left-hand side of the board above the main gateway to the Martyrs' Cemetery.

The avenue at the entrance was wide and well kept and watched over by soldiers in ceremonial uniform. That avenue led to other great avenues between plantings of pines and elms. The graves were there, below the trees, and among shrubs. Aluminium picture-holders, stand-ing on two poles, like sign-boards, were close to one another. They were of varying sizes. At the top of each holder was a glass case with a photograph of the dead man; and these photographs were disturbing, because the men were all young and were like the young men you could still see on the streets. The Revolutionary Guards I had seen in Tehran in 1979, driving around with guns, as if only to show them-selves, had seemed to me theatrical. They might have been that, but they also were as ready to die as they said; and they had died by the ten thousand in the war.

The most famous martyr of the war was thirteen years old. He had strapped a bomb to himself and thrown himself below an enemy tank. Khomeini had spoken of his sacrifice in one of his speeches. A small handwritten sign, decoratively done, as if in celebration – the script in black, shaded with red – was nailed to a pine tree to point people to where the grave was.

The young martyr's brother had also died in the war, and they had been buried together. The plaque on the headstone had the logo of the Revolutionary Guards: like a gun. In the main section of the glass case there were framed photographs of the brothers, with artificial flowers on lace on either side. On a shelf below there was a mirror and a lace doily again, and more artificial flowers. Mehrdad told me that a mirror and lace were traditional gifts for a bridegroom. Khomeini's famous tribute, in his famous literary style, was also there, done in white or silver on black: 'I am not the leader. The leader is that boy of thirteen who, with his little heart which was worth more than a hundred pens [his faith, that is, was more valuable than any amount of writing], threw himself with a bomb under the tank and destroyed the tank, and drank the martyr's glass and died.' This happened two months after the war began; no one knew at the time that the war would go on for eight years.

The simple headstones, easy to recognise, had been provided by the government. Families had paid for the more ornamented ones. One very simple stone was seen again and again. It said, in beautiful Persian script, *Unknown Martyr*.

Mehrdad said, 'There are thousands here. Families who don't know where their son is come and say their prayers over one of these stones.'

Below the pines and the elms everything was close together, the lines of headstones and picture-holders, the spindly shrubs that grew in the sand, and the flags, hemmed in by the shrubs and trees and not able to flutter, and like part of the vegetable growth.

Mehrdad said, as we picked our way through, 'You can see the flags everywhere. The flags of Iran.' He meant the flag of the Islamic Republic: green, white and red, with the emblem of Allah in the middle of the white, and, just below the white, a Koranic line in a script looking like a Greek-key pattern. He said, pointing to one, and then another, 'Losing their colour. Losing its meaning.'

Mehrdad had done his military service in the army. What appeared to be irony in his words was a form of pain. The army and the flag mattered to him; and these flags, never moving, never meant to catch a breeze, put up by the families of martyrs, were coated with the dust of the desert.

Pink oleanders grew among the shrubs. They were like the oleanders that grew between the parking lanes at Khomeini's shrine. The crowds were there, at the shrine. There was hardly an attendance here. The few people who were about were mostly cemetery workers. The public came, Mehrdad said, on certain special days.

The desert dust, kicked up by motorcars or by cleaning vehicles, had ravaged the aluminium picture-holders at the edge of the avenues. Some of them were absolutely empty now; sometimes the photographs had decayed or collapsed within the frame. It might have seemed impossible at one time, but no one from the families came any more, Mehrdad said. The mourners might themselves have died. Personal memorials last only as long as grief.

Around one corner, above neglected gravestones and picture-holders, there was a sign-board, still new-looking, with a saying of Khomeini's: **MARTYRS LOOK TOWARD ALLAH – THEY THINK OF NOTHING ELSE. THEY SEE ALLAH. THEY ARE CONCENTRATED ON ALLAH**.

We went to the blood fountain. It used to be famous. When it was set up, early on during the war, it spouted purple-dyed water, and it was intended to stimulate ideas of blood and sacrifice and redemption. The fountain didn't play now; the basin was empty. There had been too much real blood.

2

Mr Jaffrey's Round Trip

I WENT looking for people from the past. One of them was Mr Parvez. He was the founder and editor of the English-language *Tehran Times* (with the motto 'May Truth Prevail', of which he was proud); and in August 1979 he had seemed to me to be on the crest.

His paper had well-appointed offices in central Tehran, and a staff of twenty, some of them foreigners, young English-speaking travellers pleased to be picking up a few rials for their English. The paper was doing so well that Mr Parvez and his fellow directors were planning to expand it from eight pages to twelve in the new year. There was still enough revolutionary excitement in Tehran, and foreign coming and going, for Mr Parvez to feel, like the hotel and restaurant people, that after the upheavals of the revolution, and the temporary stalling of the economy, things would pick up again, and the liberated country would soon once more be the boom country it had been at the time of the Shah.

Mr Parvez looked Indian rather than Iranian. When I asked him he said he was an Iranian of Indian origin. I thought this was a neat way of putting something complicated, and I assumed he was an Indian Shia who had migrated to Iran as to the Shia heartland.

He was a gentle man. He thought that, like many other visitors, I had come to see him to ask for a little job, and he must have been on the point of offering me one, because with a sudden tormented shyness, looking down at the proofs on his table, not looking at me, he asked in a roundabout way, as though he couldn't bear to put the question directly, what my 'terms' were. When he understood that I simply wanted to talk about the situation in Iran, he sent me to Mr Jaffrey, who was in the reporters' room.

Mr Jaffrey was a middle-aged man with flashing eyes and a wide, mobile mouth. He radiated energy. He had broken off from the copy on the high standard typewriter in front of him, and was eating a dish of fried eggs which the office messenger had just fetched for him. He was going at the eggs (it was Ramadan, but he wasn't fasting) with zest; and I felt he had been going at the copy on his typewriter with a similar kind of attack.

Mr Jaffrey, too, was an Indian. He was a Shia from Lucknow. He had left India in 1948, the year after independence, because he had been told 'rather bluntly' that as a Muslim he wasn't going to get far in the Indian air force. He went to Pakistan. There after ten years he had begun to feel unhappy as a Shia. So he had gone to Iran, where nearly everyone was Shia. But – religious ease ever receding, in this communal quest of Mr Jaffrey's – Iran under the Shah was a tyranny, and the great wealth when it came had led to corruption and sodomy and general wickedness.

Still, he had stuck it out. Then had come the revolution. Religion had made the revolution, had given it its overwhelming power. That, at last, was something good, something of which Mr Jaffrey could approve. But already, in less than six months, the revolution had gone bad. The ayatollahs hadn't gone back to their religious centres, as Mr Jaffrey thought they should; they hadn't handed over to the politicians and the administrators. Khomeini, Mr Jaffrey said, had usurped the authority of the Shah, and the country was now in the hands of 'fanatics'.

This no doubt was the kind of cantankerous copy that was on Mr Jaffrey's typewriter while he ate his eggs and talked: I felt he was talking out and amplifying, and making more intemperate, what he was in the process of writing. And perhaps, after a lifetime of rejecting things, the cantankerous or protest mode was what brought out the best in him as a journalist.

All his life Mr Jaffrey had had a dream of the *jamé towhidi*, the society of believers. This was a dream of re-creating things as they had been in the earliest days of Islam, when the Prophet ruled, and the spiritual and secular were one, and everything that was done by the as yet small community could be said to be serving the faith.

It was like a dream of the ancient city-state, and in the modern

world it was a dangerous fantasy. At its simplest it was a wish for security; it also contained an idea of exclusivity. Both these ideas in varying
proportions had made Mr Jaffrey reject India for Muslim Pakistan, and
then made him reject Pakistan for Shia Iran. In another way it was a
dream of a society ethnically cleansed (to use the words of a later time).
Such a prompting had led to the partition of the Indian subcontinent
and the creation of Pakistan; and yet the Muslim state that had been
achieved, at such cost in human life and suffering, hadn't been able to
hold Mr Jaffrey and his dream.

In Iran now Ayatollah Khomeini ruled politically and spiritually by
almost universal consent. Such a figure wasn't going to come soon
again; and it was hard to imagine a country in a higher state of religious
excitement. (Going by an item in the *Tehran Times*, there was even an
Islamic way of washing carpets now.) Iran under the Ayatollah should
have been very close to Mr Jaffrey's dream of the *jamé towhidi*, the society of believers, the oneness of government and faith.

But it was just at this point that Mr Jaffrey's Indian–British education
and experience came into play, ideas of democracy and law and institutions, the separation of church and state, ideas that made him sit at his
typewriter in the reporters' room and rap out peppery calls for the
mullahs to get back to the mosques and the ayatollahs to get back to
Qum.

Mr Jaffrey's dream of the *jamé towhidi* was to him so pure and sweet
that he hadn't begun to go into its contradictions. He loved his faith; he
had travelled from country to country because of it; he felt it entitled
him to judge the faith of others. And it was just there, in fact, in his fabulous dream of an impossible, antique completeness, in his awareness of
his own piety, which was like pride, his constant rejection of the
impure, that the tyranny of the religious state began. Other people had
their own ideas; they, too, felt they could judge the faith of others. Mr
Jaffrey was suffering now from the 'fanatics'. But in his own way he was
like them.

Six months later, when I went back to Tehran, it was winter, bitter
weather, and that office was empty. A big bound folder, with file copies
of the paper, had been cracked open and the file copies had fanned out
on one of the desks. Mr Jaffrey's typewriter was there, empty, harmless.

The American embassy had been seized some weeks before by one

Iranian group and the staff held hostage. This had killed business and economic life at one blow. The eight pages of the *Tehran Times* had shrunk to four, a single folded sheet. The staff of twenty had become two, Mr Parvez and one other person. Mr Parvez was losing three hundred dollars with every issue he brought out. And yet he felt he had to keep on, because he thought that if he stopped publishing for even one day, the paper would cease being a going concern, and the fortune he had invested would be lost. He was tremulous with nerves. He could hardly bring himself to speak of his great fear: which was that the American hostages would be killed.

I asked after Mr Jaffrey. 'Is it hard for him?'

'It is hard for everybody.'

Outside the embassy it was like a fair: tents, stalls, books, food, hot drinks. The pavement outside the high walls was roped off. The gates were guarded. The students who had taken over the embassy called themselves, in careful language that seemed intended to conceal who they were, 'Muslim Students Following the Line of Ayatollah Khomeini'. They were in guerrilla garb; they had pitched low khaki tents. They were perfectly safe here outside the embassy in North Tehran. They were only playing at war.

The real war was to come sooner than they thought, and was to last eight years.

Now, fifteen years later, I went looking, but without much hope, for Mr Parvez and Mr Jaffrey. The *Tehrān Times* still existed; occasionally it was on the desk of the Hyatt. But it had lost the motto, 'May Truth Prevail', of which Mr Parvez was proud; and typographically it was a little dilapidated and uncertain. In spirit it was like the Hyatt. Mr Parvez would never have allowed that dilapidation; he was a professional; he knew how to bring out a paper. His name, in fact, wasn't on the masthead.

But he had survived. He had lost the *Tehran Times*, but he was working on another English-language paper, *Iran News*. The offices were in a small building in Vanak Square in central Tehran. They were finer than the offices of Mr Parvez's old *Tehran Times*. *Iran News* was up to date in every way. To enter the reception area was to feel that, in spite of their long isolation, and financial stringency, and in spite of the pretentious revolutionary shabbiness of places like the Hyatt, Iranians at a certain level could still do things with a style that was like a carryover from the – now glittering – time of the Shah.

There was nothing in Mr Parvez's face to speak of the stresses he must have lived through; and only a slight puffiness around the eyes, as though he had overslept, spoke of age. I wasn't sure that he remembered me. Both our meetings had been brief; and the first time he was preoccupied and shy, and the second time he was tormented. Still, no doubt or hesitation showed, and he led me to the top of the building, where we were to have lunch and where, he said, it would be easier to talk.

It was a spacious, well-lighted attic room. On the floor, almost in the middle, newspaper sheets had been spread at an angle to make the equivalent of a prayer rug aligned towards Mecca. At the head of this spread of newspaper was a cake of earth from some holy place: Shias when they pray touch their foreheads against such cakes of earth.

Mr Parvez gave a little start when he saw what was on the floor. He must have reserved the room for our lunch. But he quickly recovered. 'Ah,' he said, with a touch of weariness, picking his way around the newspaper sheets, 'these Shias.'

And now it was for me to be surprised, by this weariness and distance, because I had always thought that Mr Parvez was an Indian Shia, and that it was his Shia passion that had drawn him to Iran from Bhopal and India, and his early life there as a poet in Urdu, the Persianised language of Indian Muslims. But Mr Parvez had lived through a lot. He had lived through the Shah's time, and then he had survived fifteen years and more of the revolution, at heaven knows what cost; and certainties, if they had existed, might have dissolved.

We sat at white plastic chairs (of a stacking kind) at a white plastic table, with the newspaper prayer rug at our back. The table was decorated with a very bold pattern of bamboo leaves. Messengers brought up lunch, setting down the dishes in a no-nonsense way, as though that was part of their own style: rough, meaty, messy, oily food, which Mr Parvez went at with the kind of relish Mr Jaffrey had taken to the dish of fried eggs on that Ramadan afternoon sixteen years before. Eating a little of this and then a mouthful of that, enjoying his food, Mr Parvez told me about Mr Jaffrey.

The end had come for Mr Jaffrey not long after my second visit to the *Tehran Times*, in February 1980, when I had found Mr Parvez in a

desolate office, full of nerves about the seizing of the US embassy and
the kidnapping of the staff by 'Muslim Students Following the Line of
Ayatollah Khomeini'.

The students were going through the embassy records and almost
every day were making 'revelations' about more people. They had even
made 'revelations' about the *Tehran Times*.

One evening a student came to the *Tehran Times* office and asked Mr
Parvez for Mr Jaffrey. The student didn't give his name, but he was from
the group holding the embassy and the hostages. Mr Parvez said that
Mr Jaffrey would be in the office the next day at eleven. The student
went away.

Mr Parvez was concerned. He knew that Mr Jaffrey was a stringer for
the Voice of America radio. What he didn't know at the time was that Mr
Jaffrey's money from the Voice of America came directly from the US
embassy. The receipts Mr Jaffrey had given (or signed) never said what the
money was for. They said only, 'Received from the US embassy'.

Mr Jaffrey was an old man. He had a heart problem and other ail-
ments. Mr Parvez telephoned him at his house.

Mr Jaffrey said, 'I am coming to the office.'

When he came, Mr Parvez said, 'Is there anything wrong? Did you
have any contact with the embassy?'

Mr Jaffrey said, 'No. Except for the Voice of America. I used to send
some stories. I used to get money through the US embassy.'

I asked Mr Parvez, 'Do you know how much he got?'

'I think three hundred dollars a month. It was good money at that
time. Seven *toumans*, seventy rials, made a dollar.'

It would have been even better money now: four thousand rials
made a dollar.

Mr Parvez said, 'I advised him to go to the embassy and talk to the
students there and explain. I said they looked very nice. He promised
me he would go to the embassy.'

The next day Mr Jaffrey didn't come to the office. Mr Parvez telephoned his house. Mr Jaffrey wasn't there. Mr Parvez was greatly upset.
He tried to tell himself that Mr Jaffrey's telephone was probably out of
order. He sent his driver to the house. After an hour or so the driver
came back and said, 'The house is locked.' The driver had talked to a
neighbour and the neighbour had said that during the night Mr Jaffrey
had dumped some household things in the boot of his car. Mr Jaffrey
had a big American car, a Chevrolet, an old one.

Mr Parvez got in touch with Mr Jaffrey's friends. He couldn't believe that Mr Jaffrey was a spy. He also began to think that Mr Jaffrey might have been arrested. He got in touch with the security people. They said they didn't know about Mr Jaffrey.

In the afternoon the student from the embassy came again and asked for Mr Jaffrey. He became angry when Mr Parvez said he didn't know where Mr Jaffrey was.

The student said, 'Why did you tell me he was going to be here at eleven o'clock?'

Mr Parvez said, 'Look. He was a nice man, an old man. I know there was nothing wrong.'

The student became very angry, and Mr Parvez learned later that that student and some others broke into Mr Jaffrey's house and took away some things.

The next day Mr Parvez got a telephone call from Pakistan. It was from Mr Jaffrey. He said, 'I am here with my Chevrolet.'

Mr Parvez asked him, 'How did you manage that?'

Mr Jaffrey said, 'I had to pay some money to the border guards. On both sides. Iranian and Pakistani.'

'You made a mistake. You are a clean man. You shouldn't have gone.'

'No, no. I am an old man, and I am sick.'

Mr Parvez, eating in the attic room of *Iran News*, sitting at the white plastic table with the big bamboo-leaf pattern, recounting the events of fifteen years before, said, 'Fortunately he had a son and a daughter already in Pakistan. Then he started work there, in Islamabad. And then in 1990, I think, I received another call from Pakistan, from his son, to inform me that he had expired.'

That was how it had ended for Mr Jaffrey, that dream, so sweet in Lucknow in India in 1948, of the *jamé towhidi*, the pure society of believers, which seemed worth leaving home for.

Mr Parvez said, in a kind of final tribute, 'He was very fond of playing bridge. At that time there were *so* many people here who played bridge.'

The time Mr Parvez spoke of was the Shah's time. The playing of cards was now deemed un-Islamic and banned.

At the time of Mr Jaffrey's flight Mr Parvez (according to what he had told me in 1980) was losing three hundred dollars with every new issue of the *Tehran Times*. He felt nevertheless that he absolutely had to go on, and somehow he was doing so. But revolution was revolution; disorder had its own momentum; there were no happier times just around the corner.

Just a few months after Mr Jaffrey's flight – and after the pretend war outside the American embassy, and the pretend battledress of the 'Muslim Students Following the Line of Ayatollah Khomeini' – the real war came: the eight-year war with Iraq, a war so terrible that the Iranian newspapers now referred to it in certain emblematic ways: 'the imposed war', 'the Iraqi-imposed war', 'the sacred defence', 'the eight-year sacred defence'.

On a long front to the west, a great bloodletting. And, very soon after, a revolutionary bloodletting at home as well: the revolution beginning to cut down some of its makers.

Mr Parvez said, 'After 1982 all the good leaders began to be assassinated. The top people. The assassinations were by different groups. Then comparatively second-grade people began to come up. Only Beheshti was left. And then he was killed. He had his own ideas about the Islamic republic. They were very clear. He wanted relations with all countries except Israel and South Africa. And he wanted to end the war.' After his death, and the death of some others, the opposition began to be 'wiped out'.

Mr Parvez said, 'Now they want to control your way of sitting here' – he tapped the white plastic table with the bamboo-leaf pattern – 'and your way of talking. It has to be Islamic.'

Beheshti was the ayatollah who was, or had become, Mr Parvez's patron (though Mr Parvez didn't use the word); and I felt it was Beheshti who had helped to keep the paper going during the difficult months of the hostage crisis.

'As long as Dr Beheshti was alive nobody could touch me. He was supporting me. Please mention Beheshti. He was martyred in 1981. With a bomb. He was addressing a meeting of economic experts of the Islamic Republic Party. That party was later closed down.'

Mr Parvez's regard and tenderness for Beheshti, fourteen years after his death, showed in the use of the word 'martyred'. And he had reason to mourn Beheshti, because a few months later the paper was taken over by the authorities.

Mr Parvez had started the *Tehran Times* in 1979, after the revolution. '*Tehran* "May Truth Prevail" *Times*,' he said, speaking the title and the splicing motto as it had appeared on the front page. Sitting in the attic room of *Iran News*, having lunch, with the newspaper prayer-rug and the cake of holy earth at our back, Mr Parvez's eyes brightened at the sweet memory; and he spoke the title and the motto again.

'That title was registered. They have changed it now. They just came one day to the office and asked me to sign this blank paper. I signed it. The person who came is now an important ambassador. Now he is a good friend of mine. But at that time I didn't know him.'

After a few days this man said to Mr Parvez, 'It's better you take out your name from the newspaper. It's better for you. You have never been a revolutionary. You have been working with a newspaper that was close to the Shah.' And it was true that Mr Parvez had been associated with an English-language paper in the time of the Shah.

One day Mr Parvez asked the new people in his office, 'Is it possible that I have some compensation? Whatever I've earned here I have invested in the *Tehran Times*.'

Somebody in the accounts department said, 'Don't ask about money.'

Mr Parvez said, 'Why? I have no house. I have a son in America. I have to send him money. Look, the time when I was a journalist before the revolution, there was no journalist here. Either they fled from here, or they were in prison, or they were executed.'

The man from accounts didn't take that as Mr Parvez was expecting. He said, 'Thank God that you are still alive and working.'

Mr Parvez remained with the paper as editor. There was always a mullah in the office now. It helped that the mullah was a nice man, an open-minded man, as Mr Parvez thought. The mullah would say, 'Be moderate. Not extremist.' That was all. If he hadn't been so nice, Mr Parvez wouldn't have stayed. And, in fact, the authorities treated Mr Parvez with regard. On official occasions he would be introduced as 'the father of English-language journalism in Iran'. Once he was even taken to meet Ayatollah Khomeini and Mr Rafsanjani, the prime minister.

'They introduced me in a very refined way,' Mr Parvez said. 'Very respectably.' These forms mattered very much in Iran.

And Mr Parvez was used to censorship. In the Shah's time, until 1975, four years before the revolution, there used to be an intelligence man from Savak, the Shah's secret police, in the office of the *Tehran Journal*, which was the name of Mr Parvez's paper at that time. The Savak man would come at three in the morning with an

English-speaking team, and they would go through everything, even the advertisements. In its reports of anti-government demonstrations or marches the *Tehran Journal* wasn't allowed to use the words 'student' or 'youth'. 'Hooligans' was the word that had to be used. In 1975 this day-to-day censorship of the newspaper pages stopped. But the government still controlled; the top people in the newspapers were told what to do.

There was no formal censorship now, Mr Parvez said; there was only self-censorship. Journalists now knew how far they could go. In the Shah's time they didn't. Nowadays they could go surprisingly far.

'We have criticised presidents, ministers, etc. But we know that if we even try to hurt or destroy the basic system, we would not be spared.'

'Basic system?' The words were new to me.

'That's the institution of leadership and obedience.'

That, too, was new to me. Mr Parvez leaned to his left and took up a copy of that day's *Iran News*. He marked two items and said, 'These two stories would explain.'

The first story, 'Ayatollah Kani Underscores Importance of Ulama', was from the paper's 'political desk'. The *ulama* are the clerics, the religious teachers, the men in turbans and gowns. '. . . Ayatollah Mohammad Reza Mahdavi Kani urged the Ulama on Monday that they should remain active as politicians and executive officials and never think of abandoning these vital duties . . . Speaking on the occasion of the start of the new academic year at Imam Sadeq (AS) University, Ayatollah Kani . . .'

The second story was more important: 'Obedience to Leader Only Way for the Left Wing to Survive'. Though it was presented only as an interview with a 'left-wing' deputy, it was an explicit restatement of the principle of leadership and obedience. The writer first defined the Leader: 'The highest authority in the Islamic Republic is the Leader – or alternatively the Leadership Council – who exercises the supreme political and religious powers and, indeed, is a manifestation of the integration of politics with religion, according to Article 5 of the Constitution of Iran.' And this was how the left-wing deputy defined his obedience: 'The Left Wing believes in total obedience to the Leader without any terms or conditions, execution of government orders, implementation of pure Mohammadan Islam (*Islam-e Nab*) as the late

Imam [Khomeini] wished, creation of social justice, implementation of the Article 49 of the Constitution . . .'

The writer then quoted from Article 49: 'The government has the responsibility to confiscate all wealth accumulated through usury, usurpation, bribery, embezzlement, theft, gambling, misuse of endowment, misuse of government contracts and transactions, the sale of cultivated land and other resources subject to public ownership, the operation of centers of corruption . . .'

In spite of the punitive, religious tone, the aims of Article 49 might be said to be an aspect of the regulatory business of responsible government everywhere and in all times. What made it Islamic was 'the integration of politics and religion', a kind of institutional short-cut, since the integration was enshrined in the figure of the Leader, to whom absolute obedience was due. Islam meant 'submission', and in an Islamic republic, such as the people of Iran had passionately wanted and had voted for in a referendum, everyone had to submit. It could be said that the Shah also required people to submit; but the Shah ran a secular and corrupt tyranny; whereas now, in return for their surrender of everything, the people were made a gift of the almost unbearable beauty of 'pure Mohammadan Islam, *Islam-e Nab*', which the Imam Khomeini had wished for them.

It was like a version of Mr Jaffrey's *jamé towhidi*. Poor Mr Jaffrey had had only the sweet dream. It had ruled his whole life: the dream of being a Muslim among Muslims alone, a Shia among Shias, living in a restored antique world, when the Prophet ruled and the little community obeyed, and everything served the pure faith. Only the dream; and then, like a man who had never truly wanted what he had made so much trouble about, he had objected at the first sign of religious rule, Khomeini's Imamate, and he had finally run away in his Chevrolet, before this very bold realisation of his dream, with the Leader and the Leadership Council standing in for the Prophet.

This 'basic system' – of a leadership mysteriously evolving, and the people obeying – explained the official photographs of the three top men that appeared in many places. It explained the sometimes enormous painted portraits on the side of buildings, linking the present spiritual leader to the Imam Khomeini, and making a simple call for obedience.

Mr Parvez said, 'I never thought it would be like that in 1979. I thought that the régime of the Shah would go, and we would have a Western-style democratic government, as we had in India. I have never been Islamic as such.' His paper gave another impression in 1979. 'That has made it difficult. My background was not religious at all. I voted in 1980 in the referendum. I voted for the Islamic Republic. It was a yes-or-no referendum. The people gave 85 per cent for the Islamic Republic, without knowing what the Islamic Republic would be.'

Mr Parvez was attracted to Khomeini because he spoke about the oppressed and the third-world countries. He especially remembered Khomeini's famous speech in the cemetery when he returned from exile. Many promises were made in this speech: kerosene brought to houses, free electricity, free water.

'He promised employment, saying he would take away employment from the Americans. In the Shah's time about one or two million people were unemployed or half-employed. Today there are ten million unemployed. But I will tell you one thing. The Imam was very sincere. He wanted to have good relations with all the third world. But he could not implement his plan. Because of the war.'

And then the cemetery had other associations.

As for himself and his own future, Mr Parvez was trying to get the *Tehran Times* back. He was taking his case to court.

'But financially I will always be in trouble. Hostage crisis – if it hadn't been there, my paper wouldn't have been in trouble. The businessmen and foreign companies left, and there were no ads.'

So many things had happened in the world. So many things had happened to me. He endlessly relived the hostage crisis. It was strange to think of him – if the metaphor wasn't too unsuitable – as nailed to that cross now as he had been fifteen years before. He had gone through a great deal; he would have done many things to survive. It would have been unfair to go too far into the uncertainties I had noticed in his narrative.

They want to control your way of sitting and your way of talking, Mr Parvez said. And Tehran at night, in some of its main roads, was like an occupied city, or like a city in a state of insurrection, with Revolutionary Guards and, sometimes, the more feared Basiji volunteers at roadblocks. They were not looking – on these almost personal night hunts – for terrorists so much as for women whose hair was not completely covered. And not so much for weapons as for alcohol or compact discs or cassettes (music was suspect, and women singers were banned).

The people of Tehran could spot these roadblocks before the visitor did. One night, when we passed some people who had been picked up, the lady driving us said it was all a matter of knowing how to talk to the Guards. Once, when she was stopped, she had said, as though really wishing to know, 'What is wrong with my *hijab* [headdress], my son?' And the young man, of simple background, not feeling himself rebuffed or challenged by the lady, but thinking he was being treated correctly, had let her go. Such were the ways of obedience and survival that people had learned here.

But parallel with this was a feeling that this kind of humiliation couldn't go on. Though all the capacity for revolution or even protest had been eradicated after forty years of hope and let-down, and people were now simply weary, after all the bloodletting – first of protesters in the Shah's time, and then of the Shah's people after the revolution, and the communists, together with the terrible slaughter of the war – there was a feeling now, with that weariness, that something had to snap in Iran. And, almost as part of wishing for that breaking point, stories were being told now that Khomeini had really been foisted on the Iranian people by the great powers; and that certain important mullahs were making their approaches to people to ask for their goodwill when things changed, and the Islamic Republic was abandoned.

From my new room in the Hyatt I had a view of the mountains to the north. On sunny days light and cloud shadows constantly modelled and remodelled the ridges and the dips of the bare, beige-coloured mountains. On cloudy days the further hills faded in colour, range by range; and the low hills in the foreground seemed to come forward, defined by the paleness behind, and became brown or tawny or gold. The cropped or sun-beaten vegetation sometimes appeared very soft. The green of trees going up the hills stopped abruptly. The lower hills seemed levelled for further building.

3

The Great War

SIMPLE BLACK-AND-WHITE posters on roadside metal poles in central Tehran announced the third seminar on Ayatollah Khomeini's thoughts on defence. The posters were quite plain, with nothing of the graphic fury of revolutionary days; in spirit they were like the unplaying fountain of blood in the Martyrs' Cemetery. An item in *Iran News* from the Iranian News Agency said more. The seminar was being arranged by a high cleric, Hojjatoleslam Qaemi, who was the head of the Ideological and Political Department at Defence and Armed Forces Logistics Ministry. The religious people were in everything now, and their political titles could be as resonant as their religious titles. Five hundred 'personalities' were going to be at the seminar and – the department dealt in figures – fourteen papers were going to be presented, out of the 130 that had been sent in. 'A photo show of the eight-year-long sacred defence (1980–88) and an exhibition of the documents of the imposed war are to be set up on the sidelines of the seminar.'

Arash, who was going to talk to Mehrdad and me about his war experiences, didn't know about the seminar. Like so much else in government, it was happening very far away.

Arash was twenty-seven. He had been at the front for the last four years of the war. For the first two years, when he was sixteen and seventeen, he had been a volunteer; after that he had been a conscript. Now he was a taxi-driver, like the officer who used to be his best friend. And Mehrdad wanted me to catch the special words Arash used for taxi-driver, and the way he spoke them. The former officer, like

Arash, was not a driver for an agency, which would have given him a certain standing; he drove his personal car back and forth along certain fixed routes, picking up fares, using his car like a bus, and he almost certainly had no taxi licence.

Arash said, 'This war didn't have anything for me. Let's see whether my memories of it have something for others.'

We went to a café in North Tehran, a middle-class place, glass-walled, on a busy *chenar*-lined avenue. The *chenar* is the Iranian plane tree, loved for its beauty there and in Kashmir (where its shade is even said to be medicinal), and it is often naturalistically rendered in Persian and Mogul painting.

It was mid-afternoon, and the café – serving ice cream, sorbets, tea – was full of women in black chadors, family women. (At this time, in the amusement park, there would be the young girls in black, and the Guards in green watching them and walking among them.) About the café and the women there was a latent elegance. It was as though the yearning in women for beauty and style couldn't now, at this level, be suppressed in Iran; it was like a kind of disobedience.

We sat in a window alcove, and it was part of the civility of the place that though we sat there a long time, and though after a while I began to make notes, no one looked at us or made us feel uncomfortable.

Arash's family had been in Tehran for only two generations. They had been a farming family, and there was still a distant branch of the family on the land, which was to the west of Tehran. They kept cattle and sheep and had two *ghanat* wells, without which there could be no farming in the desert. These wells follow old underground water-courses running down from the mountains; Arash said the water-courses had to be repaired and cleaned four times a year.

Arash's father's father, when he came to Tehran, became a military man in the service of Reza Shah, the father of the last Shah. This was in 1931. Afterwards, when his military service was done, he ran a housing or real estate agency in Tehran.

Mehrdad broke into his own translation to say, 'They were *exactly* middle-class people.'

When Arash volunteered to fight in 1984 he became what was known as a Basiji. Basijis were known by the headbands they wore. These headbands could be red, or green, or white, or black; though what was usually shown on television in Iran and abroad was the red headband. Red was the symbol of blood and sacrifice and the faith.

Arash took part in eleven advances as a Basiji. For seven of these he was at the front. At the start of his time, in 1984, at the mid-point of the war, there was still the custom for religious chanters to come to the front before every advance and whip the men up. The chanters would chant, and the men would beat their chests rhythmically with one hand or – if the war situation was serious – with two hands together. Sometimes the chanters could be very famous, known all over Iran. A very famous chanter came to Arash's section before Arash's fourth or fifth attack.

Even if no professional chanter came before an attack, there would always be someone among the men who could do the chanting and lead the others in the ceremony. The chanting was done in as melancholy a voice as possible. What was being chanted was not the Koran, but devotional songs, and often devotional songs made famous by famous singers.

Mehrdad said, 'If you go to a school there is always somebody who knows these rhythms, these sad songs. And he can lead others in chanting.' (Later that evening, in the hotel room, when I was checking my notes with Mehrdad, he gave me a demonstration of the kind of chest-beating Arash was talking about. In less than half a minute, and even as he was talking to me, explaining what he was doing, he made the room seem small with his hypnotic drumming.)

The chanting ceremony usually lasted two hours. When the very famous chanter came to Arash's section the chanting went on for six hours, because this famous man had the voice and lungs and stamina.

The chanting filled the men with thoughts of death and martyrdom and going to paradise and having freedom. After this the men were quiet for half an hour or longer, but never for more than ninety minutes. And then the attack began, usually at 2.30 in the morning. In the quiet period between the end of the chanting and the start of the attack the men wrote letters and wills, and fixed their shoes and made sure their underpants were clean.

Mehrdad said, 'Many people had religious ablutions before an attack, because they thought that an attack was a holy action, and that one should be nice and clean for it. And since it could end in martyrdom, they would see their God in a clean body and clean clothes.'

There were officers among the Basiji, but they had no badge or epaulettes or distinguishing mark; though of course the bushiness of the beard – the Prophet was said to have spoken against taking a razor to the skin – told who the higher men were. The Basiji, Arash said, were always informed about their situation; their questions were always fairly answered.

After two years of voluntary service as a Basiji, Arash went home, and then almost immediately it was time for his regular military service. After two months of training he went to the front again.

I asked Arash, 'You were going to do your military service anyway. Why did you volunteer as a Basiji?'

'It was what my friends did. Twenty-five per cent of them. They put it in our heads.'

'They?'

'The television and radio, and the speakers outside mosques. Magazines, newspapers, everything.'

They made him feel he was fighting for Islam, first of all. And then nation and family, both together.

Mehrdad said, 'The word he is using is a very strong word. It is *namoos*. It suggests a protective feeling for the women of one's family. It is a word that might be used for one's feeling about one's country – or one's gun. There is a funny story. It comes from the time of the Shah's father, Reza Shah. He was inspecting some soldiers. He asked one of them, lifting up the man's gun, "What is this in your hand?" – "This is a gun." Reza Shah became angry and said, "Akbar, this isn't a gun. It is your *namoos*. It is your mother, your wife, your daughter. You must keep it and protect it." He goes further down the line and reaches Ahmed. Ahmed is a Turk from the north, or something like that. Iranians make jokes about the Turks. Reza Shah lifts Ahmed's gun and says, "What is this?" Ahmed says, "This is Akbar's *namoos*. This is Akbar's mother, wife, daughter."'

When he left the Basiji and joined the army for his military service, Arash was selected, after his two months' training, for a special commando regiment. He went to the supporting line about twenty kilometres from the front. He slept that first night or day until noon. He was on a hill. He woke up and began to go up the hill to the 'assembling place'. (Mehrdad had trouble with the last word: his first rendering was 'yard'.) A rocket hit about six metres down the hill from him, and he was blown eleven metres away. He was unconscious for about a day. When he came to, there were drips stuck into his arm, and he felt a numbness down his side.

He said, in the window alcove in the café, with the traffic outside, and the middle-class ladies in black chadors having ice cream and tea at the other tables, 'And I still feel something.' And – nine and a half years after his wound – he passed a searching, caressing hand down his left thigh.

He was in the field hospital for seventeen days. They didn't let him go back to Tehran. He said to them that the Basiji could go back to their home cities when they wanted. They didn't listen. They sent him back to the assembling place. The very first day he got there he thought there was 'the smell of an attack being prepared'. He decided to escape.

He knew the area from the previous year. He knew that the mountains were in the north, and he knew there was a village or small town behind the mountains. He thought it was thirty kilometres away. In the afternoon he took his money and his things and began to walk to that village. He walked until nightfall. He came to a shepherd's tent. The shepherd was driving sheep to pasture. In the winter the sheep were driven down the mountains; in the summer they were driven up. They were driving the sheep up now.

In the tent there were an old man, a baby, a woman, and six young girls. They gave him hot milk and some traditional animal-fat ointment for his aches. He told them that he had got separated from his regiment and become lost in the mountains, and was now walking to the town or village on the other side of the mountains. They said to him, 'It's a long walk. There are a lot of wolves about. And you're walking in the wrong direction.' They made him sleep that night there, in the tent, with everybody else.

At six in the morning he left them. He walked until two in the afternoon. He came to the village. He stopped a van and offered to pay for a ride. He had money on him, because – before the rocket fell and damaged him – he had just come back from two weeks' leave. He reached a big city. He took a bus there and came to Tehran. His father was shocked by his condition and didn't want him to go back to the front.

It was fourteen days before Nowroz, the Persian new year, an ancient, pre-Islamic festival, and he stayed with his family until the end of the holiday.

Mehrdad said to me, 'One reason he probably decided to escape was that he didn't want to be engaged in an attack with Nowroz coming. Everybody here wants to celebrate Nowroz with his family, in his own way. I say this, because he is now saying that immediately after the holiday he went back to the front.'

And there Arash found that there had been no attack after all. But there was going to be one now. It was a very big one, and it started four days after he got back.

Altogether Arash walked away from the war on three occasions, and there seemed to have been no trouble for him when he went back.

A special memory he had was of the time when for some days they were directly facing the Iraqi positions. He saw a glint from the Iraqi side: the sun catching a wristwatch, he thought. He saw the glint again, and decided it wasn't an accident. He flashed back with his own watch; and there was an answering flash. They played that game for a while. On later days they used binoculars to flash at one another.

It was like the stories from the First World War of the passing fraternisation between men fighting one another on the western front. Arash wouldn't have known about that. His story spoke of the great weariness on both sides towards the end. But he didn't make the point; he made no point at all. He told the story simply as an oddity of the war.

When his obligatory military service was over he stayed on in the army voluntarily for four more months. He had made friends there, and he left with one of his friends. They went together to Shiraz. They slept in a park. In the morning they heard that the Imam Khomeini had died. That was the saddest moment of the war for Arash, and for other people as well.

Arash said, 'I remember my friend being rebuked by his mother for eating an apple. Just as though Khomeini's death had created something like Ramadan.' Ramadan, the fasting month.

And Tehran now, at the end of the war, was a great let-down, just as it had always been during the war. 'In Tehran it was wedding parties. Two of my friends had been martyred. And there, in the same alley, with that funeral, there was a wedding party. At the front it was Islam and war. Here in Tehran people were talking about fashions and music. On the Voice of America we could hear Iranian people asking for new records to be played. In Tehran nobody cared about the war. Everybody was looking for money.'

Worst of all, he found that in Tehran the Basijis had a bad reputation. They hounded people for violating Islamic rules and they extorted money from them.

Mehrdad said, 'They are people who think they have lost something.

They think the rich people have stolen it from them. So they can be aggressive.'

Arash had spoken with great openness. But something was missing. The war he had told us about was a war without death, and with very little blood. He had spoken of his own wound from the rocket; he had spoken of sheep being driven across minefields to detonate the mines. But that was all. Even when we asked him about the martyrs' battalions he said only that during the attacks the martyrs' battalions went first, then the regular battalions, and behind them the supporting battalions. He wanted to talk about the war, but he didn't want to talk about death.

Later, when we had left the café and were in the car, and daylight had gone, I asked him directly, 'Did you see many people killed?'

He really didn't want to answer. But he said after a while, 'A regiment of fourteen hundred men went on an attack. And only four hundred came back.'

'What do you think of that now?'

'I am indifferent.'

It was like what Mehrdad had said to me; and, as with Mehrdad, Arash was really saying that he couldn't express his pain.

'I feel you are a lonely man.'

'I prefer to be alone.' A little later he said, 'Everyone was looking for Ali's justice. But after a while they saw it wasn't getting done.' Ali, the son-in-law of the Prophet, the fourth caliph of Islam, known for the wisdom of his judgements, murdered on his way to the mosque in AD 661, and ever since the focus of Shia reverence and grief.

I said, 'Do you think you can get such a thing as Ali's justice in the world again?'

'Never. Even in those days he had many difficulties. He was a great man, and in a short period of time he had many enemies, and he couldn't do it. It is always like that.'

He had reached that conclusion when he was twenty. Mr Jaffrey, the Indian Shia, had had intimations of the same thing at the end of his active life; and his sweet dream had, indirectly, caused untold misery to the co-religionists he had left behind.

Mehrdad said later, when we were talking of Arash, 'Don't you think he was a simple man?'

I hadn't thought of Arash in that way at all, simple or not simple; but

I didn't have Mehrdad's Iranian eye. I had liked Arash's openness, and had seen him as a stoical man, perhaps even a good man, whose goodness could have been used in other ways.

He was altogether different from the other fellow we tried to talk to about his war experiences. This man was sent to us by a publisher who was bringing out books about the war. The veteran, if indeed he was that, was a small, neat man with a neat black beard and bright, unreliable eyes. He thought he had been sent to us to lie, and he lied and lied about everything. He was an architect, he was a doctor; he had held dying martyrs in his arms. There was no concrete detail in anything he said, and I doubted whether he had even been at the front.

He began after a while to make religious signals to us. He made us see that his sleeves were buttoned at the wrist; that was a sign of piety. Before he sipped his tea he bent low over the table, shifty eyes swivelling away, and very clearly spoke the word of grace, *Bismillah*. I asked him about the devotional songs that had been chanted at the front. He said Iranians were a poetic people; poetry came easily to them. He himself, when he was at the front, had written his will in verse. A soldier at the front, if he was by himself, could chant religious songs all day.

He broke off then and, in the same tone of voice, asked Mehrdad, 'He is asking about brainwashing?'

We decided he was a trouble-maker, and got rid of him.

Afterwards Mehrdad and I flagged down a route-taxi. It had one passenger, a plump and very clean-looking young man, well dressed and with a full beard. He was in the back seat. Without saying anything he got out and sat next to the driver, so that Mehrdad and I could sit together – it was taxi etiquette in Tehran.

I wanted to talk about the man who had written his will in verse. Mehrdad brought his brows together and nodded towards the back of the bearded young man. Soon afterwards the young man got out; and it was Mehrdad who pointed out to me that as soon as the young man had gone the driver had turned on the car speakers: jumpy music, either on a cassette or on the radio, from the Voice of America or from Israel. Music was un-Islamic and illegal now, and men with beards were on the side of the law.

One morning my breakfast was brought up by the chambermaid. She was fat and brassy, with a shiny, unwashed face, and a definite smell from wearing so many clothes, some of them perhaps of synthetic material. The Persian cheese (from Denmark) came with a slice of toast, a thick piece of purple-tinted, lacklustre onion, cut some time before, and a leaf of lettuce, curiously supine, which might also have been laid out some time before. Onion and lettuce leaf (typhoid was about) immediately suppressed appetite; and the Nescafé sachet was good only for one lukewarm cup. Hip-swinging and aggressive in her monk-like garb, the maid came in again after a little while to take away the tray; and when, not long after, she came for the third time, to ask whether I wanted the bed made up, she was chewing toast – everything in her mouth showing, though she was over-covered everywhere else – and I believed the toast was from my breakfast tray.

Early that afternoon – I was working in my room – the laundry came back, the shirts laundered and nice in plastic bags. The other clothes came in a fancy cardboard box printed with the name of the hotel. The box was new to me. I thought it out of character with the austere style of the hotel and the Foundation for the Oppressed; and when I opened it I found my clothes unlaundered, absolutely as I had sent them in the morning. I telephoned the concierge. He sent the laundry manager up. The laundry manager was embarrassed. He took away the clothes and, in absurdly quick time, brought them back again, ironed and warm (even if not washed) and in new plastic bags.

When at last I went down to the lobby I found that the DOWN WITH USA sign was no longer above the Omega clocks. After fifteen years the awkward, angular characters had been unscrewed, leaving spectral impressions along the screw-marks. The moment seemed to me historic; perhaps it meant that things were going to change in some way. But the next day a much longer, flowing, copper-coloured line of Persian went up above the clocks, and it apparently said the same thing with more style.

Variable sun and moving clouds modelled and re-modelled the mountains to the north, lighting up this section, then that, showing up spaces between ranges, revealing an unsuspected ridge here, a valley there, revealing range behind range, and the textures of rock abraded by winter snow. Sometimes a rain cloud, shredding on a high range and filling the indentations and striations of rock, looked like snow.

4

Salt Land

ALI, A MAN of about sixty, had made his fortune as a developer in the Shah's time. At some time in the early 1970s, before the great oil boom, he had had the luck – and wisdom, and money – to buy a big tract of salt land in Kerman. He bought at one *touman* a square metre, ten rials, about fifteen US cents; three or four years later, when the boom had come, and cities all over Iran were growing fast, he sold some of his salt land as building land for four hundred *toumans* a square metre. So – just to play with extraordinary figures – an investment of no more than ten thousand dollars, say, had turned after three or four years into a little fortune of four million dollars.

Such a fortune would have been enough to keep most people calm. But Ali moved the other way. He became a supporter of the revolution. He said, 'Now that we had the money, the financial security, we wanted liberty. It was the one thing we didn't have.' As a student in the United States, in the 1960s, he had become passionate about politics, even local American politics; and he had grown to feel ashamed that he came from a country that wasn't free. He had never lost that feeling. So when the revolution appeared to be coming in Iran Ali supported it morally and financially. He did this through an ayatollah who had become his friend.

Ali's ideas of revolution came from his reading, especially of history. But there was also – though he didn't say it – a supporting or congruent touch of religion. He said, 'We expected a revolution based on heavenly laws and laws of nature.' Heavenly laws: it was like his own

version of Mr Jaffrey's *jamé towhidi*, and Arash's search for the justice of
Ali – Ali the fourth caliph, the Shia hero-saint.

Many different ideas and impulses had appeared to run together in
the making of the revolution. So when the revolution came there was –
just below the apparent unanimity, the general feeling of release – any
number of conflicting interests. And Ali, as a rich man, had suffered;
the revolution had treated him roughly for three years. He had been
kidnapped more than once; arrested and imprisoned many times; even
tried. He had been bled of tens of millions of dollars.

After three years he had learned how to live with the revolution, just
as, in the time of the Shah, he had learned how to live with that
régime. The business of survival, the dealing with the various strands
and levels of authority, now took up a fair amount of his time. He knew
his way now; in almost any situation he knew how to move.

He was slender, of middle height, his Persian features quite regular.
Physically he was not remarkable; it might have been part of his camouflage. His quality as a man was something that grew on you. His
slenderness, for instance, might have seemed natural to him; in fact, it
was the result of regular exercise. His work, his business, his almost
angry wish to survive, had kept him healthy and alert. The strains of
survival showed more on his wife, compelled now to live an unnatural,
imprisoned life. She had lost much of her hair; she still had a graciousness, but it lay over a deep, wounded melancholy.

His ideas of revolution, in the time of the Shah, had been touched with
religion: a dream of heavenly laws and natural laws. And he came from
a religious background. His father and his father's father were mullahs;
and there were mullahs in his father's mother's family as well. His
mother's family were what Ali called 'city people'.

His father was born in 1895 (though Ali wasn't sure of the Christian
year). When he was sixteen he went to the theological school in
Mashhad. In those days (and for a long time afterwards) many boys from
the villages went to schools like those at Mashhad and Qum, because
they were given a small room of their own, food, and sometimes even
a little stipend by the ayatollahs whose students they became. The ayatollahs got no money from the schools; such money as they had, or gave
to their students, came from their followers. So there was a fairness
about the system: the people gave, and the people got something back.

In 1911, when Ali's father went to Mashhad, the theological schools were, besides, the only places in Iran offering higher education. There were no universities or higher schools; Iran under the Qajar kings had fallen very far behind, had almost dropped off the map.

After four years at Mashhad Ali's father became a mullah and went to the town of Kerman. He became a teacher there, and that was how he might have ended, like his father before him. But the Qajars were overthrown; the Shah's father, Reza Shah, came to power (with British help); and in the mid-1920s the legal system in Iran was changed by Reza Shah. A ministry of justice was set up, and the French code was incorporated, without much trouble, into the traditional Islamic system. The new system was more formal. It required courthouses, judges, lawyers.

It was easy enough for Ali's father, with his training in Islamic jurisprudence, to fit into the new system. He became a judge first of all – he was not yet thirty – and then a lawyer. He prospered. He began to speculate in land in various parts of the country. Because he knew the old law and the new law very well, and because many of the land titles were complicated, he was often asked to establish a title; and his fee would sometimes be a parcel of the land in question.

So, in an unlikely turn of events, during the dictatorship of Reza Shah, the world opened up for Ali's father in a way the mullahs of his family of earlier generations couldn't have imagined. And, ironically, when Ali's father seemed to have made himself quite secure, the world grew dark for Reza Shah. In 1941 – the outside world breaking in, in every way – the Allied powers occupied Iran to keep it from falling under German influence. Reza Shah, thought to be too friendly to the Germans, was deposed, and taken by the British to South Africa, where he was soon to die: a strange prefiguring of his son's own tragedy thirty-five years later.

The occupation didn't affect the rise of Ali's father, and it wasn't bad for the country. In the eleven years between the deposing of Reza Shah and the restoration of his son the country knew a semi-democracy, Ali said, and a semi-chaos as well, because the central government couldn't impose its will everywhere. But Iran was free in a way it had never been before. So Ali, who was five or six when Reza Shah was deposed, grew up knowing nothing but freedom. And – the generations marching on – Ali, as the son of a rich and famous and admired father, was far more privileged than his father had been as a boy. But his father was strict; and Ali, with a remnant of old manners, accepted this strictness.

When Ali was eighteen his father said to him, 'I have been paying your expenses up to now. But now I want you to look after yourself. I am going to give you a sum of money. You can use it either to go into business or to go to a university.'

Ali used the money to go to the United States. He did various technical courses; then, when the money ran out, he did a course in the humanities with the help of a scholarship from a university. Altogether he spent eight years in the United States.

He was nearly thirty when he went back to Iran; and he had known nothing but freedom. It was a shock to go back to Iran, to the Shah's autocratic rule, and to Savak, the Shah's secret police.

Ali said, 'In this kind of régime you have to know how to manage. If you come new or raw to the situation, you make all kinds of errors and you can suffer.'

I asked him, 'What kind of errors did you make?'

'One day I was trying to catch a taxi. A taxi stopped. There were two men in the back, one man in front. I was sitting also in the back. I got involved in heavy politics, criticising Shah. Later on I found out it was a set-up. They wanted to check me. They had started the political discussion deliberately. I was very naive and expressed my ideas right away. I was glad the car stopped when it did. Otherwise I might have gone to a café with them and been made to say many things, and they would have got me into trouble. When things like this happened you realised this is not America; you can't tell your mind right away. We learn we have to live a double life. So when the revolution happened here we already had the experience of living a double life.'

What Ali learned especially, and very fast, was that the Shah was sacrosanct. Other very high people could be criticised; but not the Shah. 'There was a saying: "If you leave out the Shah, you can do anything in this country."'

Ali's job in Iran, when he got back, was with the government. He was in the planning department. His first duty was to make a report about a government cement plant that was losing three million dollars a year. He did some simple research and discovered that a successful private cement plant had been set up for three million dollars. He recommended that the government plant should be closed down; he said that the three million dollars the government spent every year on its own plant should be given to private people to start new plants. This made economic sense; but in every other way, as he discovered, his advice was wrong. He was treading on too many toes. He should have thought about the managers of the plant, their families, their connections; he should have thought about the workers. These were considerations he had been expected to take into account.

Soon he saw that the planning ministry was a sham; that, whatever its stated aims, it was required to do nothing or very little; and that, as an adviser, he was expected to abide by the old unspoken rules, the old ways of patronage and friendship and family. He saw, too, that one of the chief aims of the ministry was to keep its highly paid staff out of the mischief they might get up to elsewhere.

He resigned, and became a translator. It wasn't a step down. Because of the oil economy and the import-export boom there was a lot of translating to do. Ali did his translating mainly for Iranian exporters. He dealt with the consulates and high officials of many countries. He got to know the ropes as well as anyone, and it occurred to him that it was wrong for him to continue being a translator when with his accumulated knowledge he could do more. He set himself up as a kind of middle man. For 15 per cent he offered to place the goods of an exporter with a foreign buyer. This suited everyone. At very little extra cost it simplified matters for the exporter; and it enabled Ali, who had no capital of his own, to go into business. He did so well that soon he was able to start a company of his own and secure warehouses at the southern ports. This enabled him to buy outright from exporters and to increase his margins.

Then he had bigger luck. He bought the big tract of land in Kerman State. It was poor land, salty. But – he was a country boy – he knew its potential. He became a farmer. He took advice from the agricultural institute set up by the Shah. He began to 'wash' the land of salt; it was a process that would take seven years. He did the washing in this way. He dug a trench a metre or two deep around a field; the winter rains washed the salt from the earth into the trench; and that trench led to another, which led to a salt river. While the land was being washed he could grow certain crops on it. The first year, for instance, he grew a sweet melon that did well on salt soil. (Some of that melon variety was on the table at the end of our dinner that day: white, firm, succulent, sweet, with a feeling of earth and summer.) He sold the crops he grew while they were in the ground; he sold wholesale and the price included delivery to the buyer; so he sold a lot. Later he grew alfalfa grass and became a cattleman.

Then there was the oil boom of 1973. The income of the government, which had been three hundred million dollars in 1961, rose to twenty-two billion in 1976. The cities expanded. Land prices jumped, and Ali was able to sell portions of his salt land for four hundred times what he had paid for it. He also became a developer in his own right. As an amenity in one development he thought he should have a mosque – Ali's religious background came out in many ways. He didn't know how mosques had to be built, and he took advice from an ayatollah, a very educated man. The ayatollah introduced Ali to an engineer who specialised in building mosques. The mosque was built, and a friendship developed between Ali and the ayatollah. A year or two before the revolution the ayatollah, who was working against the government, got into trouble with the secret police and was imprisoned. The ayatollah's followers brought the news to Ali, and Ali with his connections and money was able to do various things and to get the ayatollah released some months later. The friendship of this ayatollah became very important for Ali when the revolution came; without this friendship things would have been very hard for him indeed.

Some people Ali knew, supporters of the revolution, turned against it after the first month. Ali thought he should give it a little more time. But then, about two months after the revolution, when the executions began, he had serious doubts. People who had done nothing were arrested and taken to jail. Many of them disappeared. 'Then they started charging into people's houses, confiscating their properties. We had no security for our property or our children or our wife.' I felt that the word in Ali's mind was the word Mehrdad had introduced me to: *namoos*.

A Revolutionary Court, the Court of Islamic Justice, had been set up about a month after the revolution. One of Ali's best friends was second-in-command in that court, and Ali used to go every day to see what he could do to save people he knew.

'That court was going almost twenty-four hours a day. Khalkhalli was the master of that court.' Ayatollah Khalkhalli, Khomeini's famous hanging judge. 'He used this court as the instrument of his executions. It was in Shariati Street. Before the revolution it was a military court.

The Shah had set up this court to try his opponents. Almost the same people who had set up this court were now tried in it, in the same building. My friends were in the court for about two years.'

But long before that time Ali had given up on the revolution, and he was deep in his own torments.

'We expected something heavenly to happen, something emotional. When we were kids of twelve and thirteen we used to read accounts of the French Revolution, the American Revolution, the Glorious Revolution in England. And the Russian Revolution. But we were always fascinated with the French Revolution. It was something done by *God*, you know. In the last generation most of the Iranians who had studied abroad had French culture. We were hypnotised by their stories of the French Revolution. We all thought revolution was something beautiful, done by God, something like music, like a concert. It was as though we were in a theatre, watching a concert, and we were happy that we were part of the theatre. We were the actors now. For years we had been reading about Danton and Robespierre. But now we were the actors. We never thought that those killings would start afterwards.'

It took a year for the communists and the Islamics to move away from one another. But the Tudeh, the Communist Party, had infiltrated every branch of the new government. They even went to the Friday prayers in the mosques. They showed themselves as people of God. The Communist Party in those early days put itself entirely at the service of Khomeini. They said, according to Ali, that they didn't want executive power; they were content to be counsellors. And they were behind the nationalisation of banks, insurance companies, factories. They gave the Soviet-style aspect to government and official demeanour which the visitor could still notice.

After six months of the revolution Ali was insecure and bitter. Life wasn't easy. It was impossible to work. The new officials were hostile; they looked upon Ali as part of the old régime. Some people in Ali's company began to agitate against him. Two or three of them would come to Ali's office to 'question' him. He had to buy them off. And at the end of the first year he was kidnapped.

'This was in Kerman. I was on my land. We were building houses. They came in a car, three or four of them. They asked me to help them in a building project they had. I got in the car, and they drove me away. They kept me fifteen kilometres away in a desert area and questioned me as in a court. It was in a little shanty house, a shepherd's shelter.

They were young boys. They had seen a lot of cinema. Now they had guns in their hands and they felt really big.'

The guns were from the armouries of the Shah's army. When the army collapsed, and it collapsed suddenly, many people ran to the armouries to get guns. For four months after the revolution the guns were piled up in the university and were being given away to anyone who asked for it and could show an ID card. Many people offered Ali guns, but he soon realised that guns were no use to him, because he couldn't kill anyone, even to protect himself. And perhaps if he had had a gun and had tried to use it at the time of his kidnapping, he might have been harmed by his boy kidnappers.

He thought now to move carefully with these boys, in order to find out just how many more were behind them. Perhaps there was no one else. Perhaps there were four thousand, and they were planning to hold him for a ransom. They talked for ten hours in the shepherd's hut in the desert. At last they said they were going to release him, but he had to pay them. He didn't want to pay them too much; he didn't want to encourage others. He promised very small sums. The boys were enraged. They threatened to kill him. They threatened to destroy his building company. But he didn't promise more.

He said, 'I was very strict.'

And in the end he was released. But this kidnapping added to his insecurity. There were four million people in Tehran; and it seemed that any four of the four million could come with guns to demand money. And all the time now there was trouble with local officials. They began to occupy his land and housing developments. They said they were government property and had to be given to the people.

'The local government man actually confiscated many properties in Kerman, mine and other people's.'

'What was he like? Did you get to know him?'

'He was connected to the Mujahidin group. Very leftist, 100 per cent against capitalists.'

'What was he like physically?'

'He was about thirty-four, short, fat. Full of resentment. An educated man, an engineer. I am sure he was beaten by Savak. And he was full of resentment. He caused me a lot of damage. Millions. Many millions. I met him a few years ago. He came to my office. He was poor. He had been kicked out of office. The government had put him in prison. He came to me and asked for a job. He came and kissed me and asked for pardon. He was then about forty-five. He had an old jacket. I told him that every kid had toys, but there is one toy that is the special toy. "I too have toys. I have been used to living well, to enjoy myself, and every night, all through my life, I have had lavish food. I am still doing that. And that is my favourite toy. If because of what you have done I didn't have my lavish living for one night, I would never forgive you. I would never pardon you. But what you did was like a little fly walking on my skin. It couldn't hurt me." '

A lawyer friend of Ali's had come into the room where we were and was sitting with us – it was a Friday morning, the Muslim sabbath – and I felt that the presence of this third person was encouraging Ali's unusual passion.

I asked, 'Did you give the man the job?'

'I didn't give him the job. Because people of this kind can never be straightened. If they had the chance again, they would hurt me again. So they should be kept away.'

And now, a year into the revolution, Ali was being pushed from every side, by government people, by communists within the government, and by simple agitators. He was kidnapped three or four more times.

'I wasn't much afraid to go with them, because I knew that my reasoning was stronger than theirs. The first time you think it's a wild animal, it's going to tear you apart. But once you tame this animal, you can order them around.'

There was now, too, a constant harassment from the Revolutionary Guards, jumping into the garden and looking through the windows to see whether anyone was looking at television or videos, or breaking into the house to search for alcohol or ham or women's dresses or men's neckties, all now forbidden things.

'And if you were cleanly dressed, they didn't like it. They would attack you. It was like Pol Pot, but not so extreme. Ten per cent. It was a full revolution.'

'A full revolution?'

'The reins of government went altogether out of the hands of government, out of control. It was anarchy and terror. The reason was Khomeini himself. About three months after the revolution I was taken by my ayatollah friend to meet Mr Khomeini. The ayatollah friend had explained to Khomeini that I was a developer and a technical man and could help with housing problems. I and the ayatollah friend and

Khomeini were sitting together on the ground in Khomeini's house. The door opened. Some mullahs came in. Khomeini started talking with them. Later some more mullahs came in. And it went on and on until the room was full of mullahs, two hundred of them. And they all wanted money to take to their students and religious organisations in their own towns. Khomeini said he didn't have money to give to all of them. Then he said, "Go to your own towns. Find the first man who is rich or the first man who has a factory or a huge farm. And force him to pay you."'

This language from the head of the government shocked Ali. And this was when he realised that Khomeini was leading his people to chaos.

The lawyer sitting with us said, 'His mental discipline was different from other people's. He was a man of the people. He understood the majority of the people. The majority were not educated. They wanted to get money and things. They didn't want revolution. They wanted money, and Khomeini knew that.'

Ali said, 'The majority wanted to loot.'

The lawyer said, 'So he made disorder in the country and let them loot. He did what they wanted.'

Ali said, 'When he said, "Follow the law," it wasn't the law of the country. It was his law, the law in his own mind. Before the revolution he said it was un-Islamic to pay taxes to the government. After, he said it was Islamic to pay taxes to the government. He wanted complete chaos. That day in his house I realised this man is not a man of government. He was still a revolutionary. He couldn't control himself. Until the very last day he was making disorder.'

I wondered whether this disorder, this constant 'revolution' (a word with misleading associations), wasn't an aspect of Shia protest. But when I made the point neither Ali nor the lawyer took it up. They were disillusioned men; they spoke out of a great torment; but they were so deep in Shiism; it was so much part of their emotional life; that they couldn't take this step back, as it were, and consider it from the outside.

They began to talk instead of the Islamic law of necessity, in whose name Khomeini, always acting religiously, had said and unsaid things.

Ali said, of this law of necessity, 'To protect yourself, you can sometimes do something wrong. The aytollahs can mediate between the first level of laws, which come from Allah, and the second level. When the need arises, the ayatollahs can for a short time issue secondary orders.' The example he gave was close to him. 'In Islam the protection of people's property belongs to the first level of laws. But during Khomeini's régime, while he was alive, there was a shortage of land for housing. So Khomeini said, "Using my privilege of ordering the second order of laws, I am going to grab plots of land that belong to anybody in the town, without paying any compensation, and I am going to subdivide it and give it to the people who need it. Because there is necessity."'

And now, to prove that this action of Khomeini's was excessive, the lawyer began, as I felt, to take me down the lanes and ancient alley-ways and tunnels of Islamic jurisprudence such as was taught in the theological schools of Mashhad and Qum.

The lawyer – delicately eating small green figs whole, and, in between, peeling and eating other fruit – said, 'About a hundred years after the birth of Islam one of the caliphs in Mecca wanted to take land around the holy place. People were living in houses around this holy place, the Qaaba. But the law didn't allow the taking of the land. Protecting people's property was a duty of the caliph. So the caliph invited the big muftis to his house, to find some way. The best opinion was that of a direct descendant of Prophet Mohammed, the fifth Shia Imam, Bagher. He said, "You can take those houses around the Qaaba because the Qaaba came first. Value the houses, and pay the owners, and send them away."'

Ali said, 'Khomeini has set a bad example. Every ayatollah now can claim necessity, as Khomeini often did, and break the law.' And Iran was still living with his Islamic constitution, which gave him supreme power, and established the principle of leadership and obedience. The constitution provided for an elected assembly, but there was also a council, which could override the assembly.

Ali said, 'He had an instinctive brain. He was instinctively intelligent. An instinctive, animal intelligence. Because of this he could command the people. He did not have an educated intelligence. He didn't become emotional. He was very cool.'

At our next meeting Ali had a memory to add to his story of being in Khomeini's house, three months after the revolution. The two hundred mullahs were in the room, asking Khomeini for money, and he had told them to go back to their districts and take it from the first rich man they met. That had appeared to satisfy most of the mullahs. But – as in an Arabian Nights tale – one of the mullahs had said, 'My town is very poor. In my town there is no rich man.' Khomeini, in a kind of reflex, had touched Ali's sleeve, and for a terrible moment – long enough for Ali to remember it sixteen years later – Ali had thought he was about to be sacrificially offered to that very poor mullah.

And, in fact, something like that happened fifteen months later. Ali was arrested by the revolutionary court in Kerman. A number of charges were made against him: strengthening the royal régime, grabbing millions of square metres of people's land, exporting billions of US dollars, directing a failed *coup d'état* against the government, directing an anti-revolutionary organisation. The accusations were not specific; they were formal, standard accusations, and they were made against many people.

Ali said, 'In the Kerman area, if you are a little active everybody knows you. I was very active before the revolution. I was known. I was a little Shah, the symbol of power there. When they set up a branch of the Revolutionary Court in that city they came after people like me. The Guards were all from rural backgrounds. They have their own special accent. They were very young, and happy with their trigger. Many of them later died in the war. I would say that there was a mixture of 40 per cent Mujahidin, and 60 per cent Muslim groups. The Mujahidin, Marxists, had infiltrated the Revolutionary Courts from the very beginning. They didn't identify themselves; they pretended to be Muslim.'

Ali could identify the Mujahidin and the Muslims, because he, too, was pretending: he was pretending to be a Muslim revolutionary. 'My life was in danger, and I had to make friendship with them regardless.' Very soon Ali discovered a third group who had infiltrated both the Mujahidin and the Muslims. 'They were people who simply wanted to grab some money for themselves. But they acted Islamic.' And they in their turn soon understood that Ali was also acting, and he was not a Muslim revolutionary. 'These people became friends of mine because they knew I had money, and they told me gradually what is going on in the court, and who is who.'

Ali was arrested many times and held for four or five days. Once he was held for six months. The revolutionary prison was an old factory shed that had been divided up. There were a few cells for people being kept in solitary confinement; two big compounds for social prisoners, people like opium smugglers and thieves; and a big cell for political prisoners. Ali was put at first in a solitary cell, one metre wide by two and half metres long, with only half an hour a day outside to go to the toilet and wash. The first day he read a sentence on the wall written by somebody before him: *The prisoner will eventually be released, but the prison-keeper will be forever in the prison.*

'And that was an encouraging sentence because it told me that the man before me had been released. Even now, after fifteen years, though I have been released for so many years, and have been so free to go on so many journeys anywhere in the world, and I have gone and enjoyed myself, even now, when I have certain things to do, and I go to the prison in that area, although the place has changed, and the prison is not the factory shed, I still see some of the prison-keepers there. So they are the prisoners. Not us. They were the prisoners.'

Some of the Revolutionary Guards in the factory-shed prison introduced themselves to Ali. He found out that they were the sons of labourers who had worked for him in his building projects.

They said to him, 'In the past you wouldn't look at us. You were so proud. Now you are behind bars here and we have to feed you. *Allah ho akbar!* God is so great!'

They went and told their fathers about Ali, and to their surprise their fathers said that they should do everything in their power to help Ali, because in the past Ali had helped them by giving them jobs.

'And those boys helped me a lot. They didn't have a lot of power, but they could tell me things. They could post letters and bring letters from my wife. They would give me the best quarters in the prison and give me the best food.'

It was because of these new friends that Ali was taken from the solitary cell and put in the political section. All the anti-government people in the jail were there, forty-five or fifty of them. They talked about politics all the time because they had nothing else to talk about, and Ali found that people had political views according to their background. There were some people from the Tudeh Communist Party, although their leaders were cooperating with the government. There were Mujahidin groups, although the Mujahidin had not yet started their war against the government. There were extreme Maoists. The government, in fact, was quietly beginning to destroy the left. There were also, in the political section, some generals and colonels of the Shah's army;

certain big landowners who had links with the Shah; and, curiously, two sexually corrupt mullahs who had flourished in the Shah's time. One of these mullahs said he had a talisman for women who couldn't bear children; he used to take the women to his house and have sex with them. The other was a fortune-teller.

'Both were actually executed. We used to see the executions from very far. When they had the executions somehow we would find out the night before. We would turn off the lights very early in the evening and pretend we were asleep. Then about twelve at night the lights would go on in the garden in the courtyard, and we could see the executions from far without the guards knowing about it. There was a local mullah who had those high powers in the Revolutionary Court – confiscation, imprisonment, or death.'

'What effect did the executions have on the prisoners?'

'No one liked it, whatever his group. They didn't feel it was justice that was being done.'

From time to time the revolutionary inspectors would come to the jail and some of the political prisoners were taken away with them to be 'investigated' (Ali used no stronger word). These investigations would last from two to five hours, and then the prisoners would go back to the jail. The investigations were polite.

Some of the prisoners became jealous of the privileges Ali appeared to be enjoying because of his new friends among the Guards. In fact, these friends were bringing Ali so much fruit and candy that he used to share it out with the cell.

The day came when some of the communist boys could stand it no longer. They said to Ali, 'This is a wedding party for you. But wait. Wait until we take power. We don't bring your kind of people to the court and to prison. We will take the court and the executioner to your street and to your house, and we will try you in front of your house and execute you right there.'

Ali said to them, 'Thanks be to Allah that you are in prison, and you will stay in prison and cannot do anything to me.'

After some time Ali's trial was announced. People were invited to make whatever charges they wanted to against him and submit whatever incriminating documents they had. There were seven sessions in the mullah's court, and the case against Ali was dismissed.

The mullah-judge said, 'I am not a man of Islamic revolution. But I have made this revolution to bring Islam. There is a distinction between the two. I want to make a house in heaven. I don't want to make a house in hell. A rich man is not necessarily guilty, unless I find some guilt in him. You may not be a good Muslim, but I find you not guilty.'

Things became quieter for Ali after the trial. There were still problems, many problems. Life was never easy now, and perhaps he would never feel secure. But the kind of revolutionary who had prejudged him as a rich man and tormented him during the first three years of the revolution was not so dominant now in the courts and government departments. The government had got rid of many of the wilder people, and those who had remained in office had become less hard with the years. Power had corrupted many of them. Some of them had made a lot of money and gone into business for themselves. People in power could still be obstructive; but they were easier to read now, and there were ways of dealing with them.

And after all of this there was melancholy in Ali's house. It showed in his wife's face, which spoke of an unassuageable grief for what had really been a lost life.

On the mountains to the north morning light cast shadows in the dips and hollows. Every irregularity, of abraded rock, or rockfall down a slope, was picked out. Morning light also showed the extent to which the lower mountains were built up; and, at various places, the cutting of new terraces – cement-coloured below the beige – for further building. In the evening small broken lines of lights could be seen on what should have been bare mountainside. In the morning those lights disappeared, and there seemed to be nothing. Lower down, poplars looked fresh against the darker green.

5

The Jail

PAYDAR, GROWING up in poverty in the poor north-west, was possessed by the idea of revolution from an early age. He was tormented by what he saw every day and every night of the suffering of his widowed mother. She stitched clothes and made socks and stockings for a living, and often sat at her machine until two in the morning.

In time Paydar joined the Tudeh Communist Party. The Tudeh hoped to ride to power on the back of the religious movement, and in the early days of the revolution it was the policy of the party to adopt an Islamic camouflage. That was easy enough: the themes of justice and punishment and the wickedness of rulers were common to both ideologies. But the Tudeh party destroyed itself. It gave a Soviet-style apparatus to the Islamic revolution, and then it was destroyed by that apparatus.

Ali, in his provincial factory-shed jail in 1980 and 1981, had seen the beginning of the round-up of the left. Though the enraged communists in the political section of Ali's jail were still threatening to hang Ali outside his house when they came to power, their day in Iran was really over. Two years later, in 1983, the Tudeh party was formally outlawed by the government. And two years after that, Paydar, who was in hiding, like the surviving members of the party, was hunted down and taken away to a jail outside Tehran.

Paydar didn't know then in what part of the country the jail was; he didn't know now. For two months, as he calculated, he was kept in something like a hole, without a window, 'without a speck of light', and questioned. And it was in that darkness and intense solitude, that disconnectedness from things – at first in the hole, and then in a cell with fourteen others, where he spent a further year – that he began to think dispassionately about the idea of revolution that had driven him for so much of his adult life. And he arrived at an understanding – especially painful in the circumstances – of why he had been wrong, and 'why revolutions are doomed to fail'.

'I thought that people are much too complicated in their nature to be led in a simple fashion, with a few slogans. Inside ourselves we are full of greed, love, fear, hatred. We all carry our own history and past. So when we come to make a revolution we bring with ourselves all these factors in different proportions. Revolutions have always disregarded all these individual differences.'

So, in the jail, he had rejected the idea of revolution. It had been his great support, the equivalent of religion; and no other idea quite so vital had come to him afterwards. He was like a man in whom something had been extinguished. He was a big man from the north-west. It was possible to imagine him full of fire. Now he was strangely pacific; his suffering, old and new, was always there to make him watch his moods, consider his words, and make him take the edge off passion or complaint. He was trying now – exposed as he was, and liable to be picked up again at any time – to make a cause out of his privacy, his family life; though day-to-day life was hard, and in the economic mess of revolutionary Iran, and with the decline of the currency, the value of his earnings as a teacher went down and down.

He said, 'I was attracted to revolutionary thinking when I was eighteen.' This would have been seven or eight years before the revolution. 'There was a man in our town who had just come out of prison, and we loved to go and talk to him. But he didn't want to talk to us because of security problems. Finally he must have had a good impression of me, because he chose me to talk to. He was thirty-eight, and a close friend of a famous writer who was drowned in our river. He trusted me and started to talk to me.'

I asked Paydar, 'Where did he live? What sort of house?'

'A very small and ordinary house, such as you get in the north-west, with a little yard and two bedrooms. He lived with his mother and his two sisters. He told me lots of things about injustice and how he would eliminate it.'

'Were you working at the time?'

'I had just left school and was working in the bazaar market. At the same time I was writing little stories for the magazines. I wrote about thirty, and most of them were published.'

'What did you write about?'

'About poverty, about people suffering. My father had died when I was twelve, and I experienced poverty afterwards. My mother worked sixteen hours a day to keep us. There's a gloomy picture I have of her: waking up at two and seeing her dozing at the machine.'

Paydar's new friend, the former political prisoner, gave Paydar books by Russian writers. Paydar was especially moved by Maxim Gorky; he was fascinated by the novel called *The Mother*. The friend also introduced Paydar to revolutionary Iranian writers, some of whom had been in prison. The friend didn't want to talk about his own time in jail. He had done three years, and Paydar would have liked to hear about it. But the friend preferred to talk about his political ideas.

He said they were Marxist ideas. Paydar understood later that they were Marxist ideas of a very crude sort; but at the time he was excited, and those crude ideas became his. Still later it became clear to Paydar that those were the only political ideas the friend had; the friend had not tried to find out more.

I said to Paydar, 'And yet he had a saintliness in your eyes?'

'Yes. What I felt was pure emotion. I felt, yes, that what the man was saying about revolution could be done, but it required sacrifice. So I started to prepare myself for revolution. I started even to think that I might lose my life.'

'How long did it take you to get to that stage?'

'All this took just a year.'

'And your mother?'

'She knew. She knew he was teaching me his way, and she didn't say anything. She was the type of mother we do have here. They believe in their sons and believe in what they are doing. This usually happens in those families where the father has died and the son has replaced the father. The mother – not strictly obeys – yields to her son.'

'You talked of revolution and sacrifice almost in a religious way.'

'I am not sure about my religious feeling. My father was atheist. My father was not a religious man. Nor was my mother. It couldn't be typical Iranian. My mother did believe in God, but she believed more in humans. I remember something very nice from her. "If you ask a little child not to do a bad thing, and reward him if he doesn't do that, it is okay, because he's a child. But if he grows up and understands himself, and you still reward him for the good things he has done, you are insulting him." '

In the late 1970s Paydar went to England to do a higher degree at a provincial college. He went with his wife and their two children, and he might have done so on a scholarship, though he also had his savings. In England they lived in rented rooms. And – though he didn't see it then, and didn't say it now – this course of study in England was a tribute to the Shah's Iran. It spoke of the mobility that had come to people like Paydar, born in poor and backward areas; it spoke of the economy that had kept him in work, and given him savings; and it spoke of the strength and purchasing power of the currency.

I wanted to know what was the first unusual thing about England that Paydar noticed.

'In England I looked at things with a sort of prejudgement. I thought they were capitalists. I was very cynical. I thought they were responsible for our miseries in history. Which of course to some extent they were.'

'Did you notice the buildings? Did you like any of them?'

'I closed my eyes to lots of things. Those revolutionaries who thought like me did the same thing.'

And soon enough the revolution came.

'It was 1978. People were on the streets and I had to take sides. As someone who had always wished to be with people in the streets for freedom and equality my side was chosen. I took part in demonstrations in England. I handed out leaflets to people passing. At that time Khomeini was getting popular with the revolution.'

I said, 'We heard about him quite late in England. I felt the religious people were keeping him secret.'

'He wasn't there at first, in the revolution. It was only in 1978 that people started to hear about him.'

'They had kept him secret even from you?'

'Even from us, who were struggling. And at this time I had to make a difficult decision. I was not a religious person. I was a Marxist. But Khomeini was a religious man who was heading the revolution. The only party which would side with Khomeini at that time was the Tudeh party. And automatically I was attracted to that party. Which of course – apart from taking sides with Khomeini – had lots of popular intellectuals in its leadership. Some of them we *loved*, for their intellectual work, before we knew what they were politically. I was stuck in a conflict at

that time. I decided in the end to be with Khomeini. But I had a lot of
misgivings. I would tell friends, "We may win the revolution, but culturally we will go back a thousand years."'

'What did your mother say?'

'She was *very* pessimistic. She said, "You will never gain anything following these religious people. We have known them. We have seen
them. These are the people who didn't let me learn reading and writing." She was right, because a clergyman went to my grandfather's
house and said, "You should never send your daughter to one of these
schools. These schools are satanic centres for women." This would
have been in 1925, when my mother was seven years old. And my
mother never forgave them because my mother loved knowledge and
books.'

But Paydar managed to convince her. He was her son, and she loved
him. And then he gave up his studies – he thought it was a waste of
time studying while the revolution was going on – and went back to
Iran. He wanted to be in the arena, with the people.

The revolution was over when he got back. The Shah was in exile,
and Khomeini was in power. Paydar found a job as a teacher. He had
had his doubt about the drift of the revolution, and soon things began
to be bad. There were religious regulations. Women had to wear the
chador and the full headdress; music and cultural events were banned.
There were restrictions on the press. In August 1979 *Ayandegan*, a non-
religious, liberal opposition newspaper was closed down. And after
two years Paydar's teaching job came to an end. There was a 'cultural
revolution', as it was called; all the universities were closed.

He took a series of temporary jobs in different parts of the country.
It was the start of a wandering life for him and his wife and their two
children. He worked mainly as a translator for private import–export
companies.

Paydar said, 'The tragic point here is that I came to a conflict with
the Tudeh party as well.'

'What about the man who had first talked to you about revolution?
When you were eighteen. The man who gave you the Gorky
books.'

'He was not active after the revolution. And that was very strange –
if I had paid attention. He got a teaching job. Still he is a teacher. And
now I know that he was very wise.'

'But he didn't advise you?'

'He didn't do that. Maybe he thought I was too young. Maybe he had his own doubts. Maybe he was ashamed he himself wasn't taking part. Actually I went to him long afterwards and said, "You were very wise. Why didn't you advise me?" He said, "I myself was not so sure about what I was doing. After the Shah's régime this was a new régime, and I had no ideas about it, no certainty about it. I was just living through it."'

'What do you think of that now?'

'It was a fair answer.'

'Your mother?'

'She surrendered to what I thought. She accepted what I said.'

The conflict he had with the Tudeh party was about their unquestioning support of the Khomeini government. When he objected they said that Khomeini was heading a popular movement; since the party believed in the people, they couldn't be far from the people. So the party had to be with Khomeini; internationally that had always been their strategy. This was in 1983, the very year when the Tudeh party was outlawed, and people from the party began to be arrested.

'I was in great turmoil. I was in danger. They started to search my lodgings. At the university I had made some statement. I had said I was with the Tudeh party. They searched for me in the town where I was and I just managed to escape. Just by accident. Someone had been arrested there, and he had later told his family that the Guards were talking about me. That family came to me to let me know, and I escaped with my family. Those days! Yes! From that time on I was living in hiding. I used to come and see my family once a month and bring money. I took different jobs. I disguised myself. I took jobs in restaurants. Manual jobs, simple jobs. Always in a far place. My relations and friends helped me. My mother was the centre of information.'

After two years of this life he thought that things had settled down, and that he could come out of hiding. No one appeared to be following him. The newspapers reported fewer arrests. So he began to live with his family again and took teaching jobs. He lived like this for a year. One night there was a telephone call. It was from the Revolutionary Guards. They said they wanted him to come to their headquarters for a few minutes to answer a few questions. Later he discovered that they had been going through his records and had found out where he was living.

He asked the man on the telephone, 'Will it be really a few minutes?'

The Guard said, 'Oh, yes. Surely you won't be here for more than an hour.'

Paydar kissed his wife and children. He told them he was saying goodbye for a long time. His wife told him he was wrong. But he was right: he didn't come back for a year.

He went to the Guards' headquarters, and introduced himself. He was sent to a room. The Guard there was expecting Paydar. He gave Paydar a questionnaire and asked him to fill it in. One of the questions was: *Have you engaged in any political activities in the past?*

I asked Paydar, 'What was the Guard like?'

'A strongly built, bearded, tall man with a cruel face. He had big hands with very thick fingers. They were the first thing I noticed, the thick fingers. Maybe I was thinking of his beating me.'

'How old would you say? And in uniform?'

'About thirty. In uniform. Khaki.'

'Educated?'

'Not educated. Not at all. This was quite obvious from the way he spoke.'

'And the office?'

'One of those ordinary *komitehs*. It's what we call them. I said to that question about political activities: "No." He said, "Are you sure you didn't have another kind of belief?" And then I told him fully about the way I thought. No other information. And he grinned. He said, "We knew that." He blindfolded me and put me in a small room. It was nine in the morning.' (In Paydar's narrative time had jumped: the whole night seemed to have been taken up with this interrogation. But I didn't notice this jump until much later.) 'And it was spring. April or May. From there the next day I was sent to prison. First to Evin.' The great prison of Tehran. 'After a week I was sent to another place. Where it is I still haven't discovered. And there I was questioned for two months, and I was sentenced to a year. In Evin it was tolerable. It was a modern place. The other place was terrible. It was very old. Just like a hole. Then the prison was all right for the rest of the year. It was a commune of fifteen people in the room. That year it was better because they didn't have so many prisoners. It used to be very bad. And the situation outside had cooled down.'

That was when Paydar began to think, in solitude, and from a distance, about revolution. He considered it was the most important year in his whole life.

'Your mother?'

'She had died two years before that. Fortunately quite quickly. I started to think about the revolutionary stuff and all my beliefs. Now it was the time to think for myself, and to think of subjects that to some extent were forbidden to me.'

'You had forbidden them to yourself.'

'I had forbidden myself. For instance, for me Arthur Koestler was a reactionary. So I didn't read anything by him. That's it. It was as simple as that. And George Orwell was a reactionary. I had people in two groups only. Revolutionary people, and reactionary people. Now I thought especially of my mother and what she had done without being aware of these ideologies. For me she was the symbol of the real human being. She was loved by everyone. Anyone who knew her loved her. It was something very strange. When she died in the hospital all the nurses and the doctor himself cried. The reason was, she cared about everyone there. She would say, "Nurse, what happened to your gentleman caller? Did he come?" And she would ask another nurse, "How's your mother? Is she getting better?" All the time she was busy with them, helping them, although she was ill.

'I thought that ideologies are only a small part of our intellect which can help us in life. The main source lies in our cultural way of thinking. And natural behaviour of people like my mother. The revolution I worked for didn't understand me as an intellectual or my mother as a person.'

There was no systematic physical maltreatment in the jail. Paydar was handled badly only twice. The first time was when Khomeini had died, and there was a nervousness in the Guards about a possible attempt to free the prisoners. They blindfolded all fifteen and led them out to a minibus and ordered them to bend down and keep quiet. The man next to Paydar asked in a whisper, 'Where are they taking us?' Paydar put his finger to his lips and said, 'I don't know.' But the Guard heard. He came and hit Paydar with his gun on the back of the neck; and he began to beat Paydar with such frenzy that Paydar thought he would die. He was ill for a week afterwards. He lay in the cell without attention. They just brought his food. Somehow he lived through it.

On another occasion he was slapped. He had said something about the Mujahidin, the left-wing religious people who had once been with the Guards (and were among Ali's tormentors in the early days). A Guard slapped Paydar and said he was never to use that word *Mujahidin* again. He was to say *Monafegheen*, which was a bad word and meant 'hypocrites'.

Paydar said, 'I devote myself to my teaching work and am more useful to my people in this way, just trying to educate them. I wish I had thought that right at the beginning. But we were in the middle of things, with the dust above us. And the earlier régime is responsible for what has happened now. They deprived us of freedom and good education, and enabled these others to come up.'

On the low hills to the north, tawny in certain kinds of light, and with a soft texture, there were terracings, sometimes with little green dots of recent tree-planting, and with retaining walls, marking the site of future development, as I had thought. And then I learned one day, walking in the area, that one of the low tawny hills, to the left of my hotel window, was Evin prison, the scene of many executions. The address of the Azadi Hyatt was Evin Crossroads.

I had noticed the beginnings of terraces in one place, had seen a path winding up in another; a kind of stepped great wall going up and disappearing around one side of the hill; and reappearing far away on the other side. I had felt that the stepped walls on both sides were linked, but I didn't know what I had been looking at. This was partly because of the play of light on the mountains that had so enchanted me.

It was only in the morning (when the eastern sun filled the valleys and dips with shadow) that the stepped wall to the right – its height now revealed – cast a broad diagonal of shadow tapering up to the top and there disappearing. At other times, when no shadow was to be seen from where I looked, the high stepped wall was like the colour of the hill, showing at the top only as the merest serration, which was what had made me think that it was a retaining wall, to prevent landslips and movements of earth.

If the stepped wall to the right showed up plainly only in early morning shadow, it was just past the middle of the day when the wall to the left became in its turn a wall of shadow, and showed in a great toothed curve where before I had seen no wall.

And now that I had seen, I always saw; and the serrations of the wall to the right and left, and the half-hidden tips of serration in places in the middle, were to me like the iron teeth of a giant old man-trap.

Now that I knew it was a prison, I was amazed that though I had looked at it for many days, I had seen it merely as part of the view and hadn't wondered about it: a monstrous concrete hangar of a building, sand-coloured, rising above the green of poplars and *chenars*. Over the next two or three days the plan of the prison and the prison grounds became clearer, detail by detail. The asphalt road winding up through the deceptive green to the guard-house at the entrance; the long low buildings like railway sheds – perhaps workshops – at the foot of the hangar; and, a little lower, concrete apartment blocks, staff quarters no doubt, not quite as residential as they had seemed to me. I had thought of those blocks as developers' clutter on a beautiful hillside; they – or the idea I had had about them – had helped to camouflage the prison.

At night there were further clarifications of the mountain view, and they seemed more sinister, if only because sinister things happened in prisons at night: the big zigzag of blue road-lamps marking the climb of the asphalt road to the prison; the high, big, very white prison lights above the hangar-like building; and, everywhere else, lights.

The prison was so extensive, such a large part of north Tehran, that it took a long time to read.

One afternoon, allowing my eye to follow the shadowed wall down the hill to the left, I saw that it led to another, between trees, and this wall led down to a wall running transversely from left to right at the foot of the hill. This wall at the foot of the hill was very high; and in it were high, blue gates, through which no doubt, after the revolution, the trucks came out at night with the bodies of the executed. Against the green and the brick and the concrete the blue of the gates was noticeable; it made you wonder about the choice of the colour.

Below the beautiful, many-charactered mountains, this presence: the great prison of Tehran, more awful and frightening than the castle of Prague. What came to me when I found out was like what had come to me in the British embassy in Dakar in West Africa, when I found out that the wall of the embassy tennis-court was the wall of the morgue next door, which explained the daily crowd of grieving Africans in Muslim caps and gowns.

Ayatollah Khalkhalli, Khomeini's hanging judge, used to sit in judgement in the Revolutionary Court, the Shah's old military court, in Shariati Street, Ali had said. In the early days after the revolution that court used to be sitting almost round the clock, and Ali used to go every day to try to save people he knew. The prisoners would probably have been taken to Shariati Street from Evin.

In August 1979, when I first went to Tehran, the court was still in full flow. Khalkhalli, in an interview with the *Tehran Times* – Mr Parvez still the owner and editor, and Mr Jaffrey sitting at his high standard typewriter and rapping out peppery calls for the ayatollahs to get back to Qum – Khalkhalli, in that interview in August 1979, said that he had 'probably' sentenced three or four hundred people to death. On some nights, he said, the trucks had taken thirty or forty bodies out of the prison.

They would have left through the blue gates.

6

The Martyr

MEHRDAD AND I met Abbas in the office of a book publisher. Abbas was twenty-seven, and a war veteran. He had volunteered – giving up school to do so – when he was fourteen, in the second year of the war; and he had served right through. He didn't seem now to have a settled vocation. After the war, driven by spiritual need, he had done theological studies at Qum for three years; but then he had felt let down by Qum. Later, to please his girlfriend's family, he had done his high-school diploma and gone to the university. Now he was learning about films; he was making very short, poetic, *haiku*-like films, lasting no more than a minute. He was also travelling about the country, gathering interviews from war veterans like himself, for the publisher in whose office we were meeting. The publisher seemed to have a line in books about the war.

There were any number of veterans, and Abbas, with his military training, had worked out his own procedures for getting many interviews at the same time. When he got to a new place he would call veterans to something like a public meeting, hand out printed questionnaires, and tell war stories of his own, deliberately simple stories, about simple things, to encourage the veterans to lose their shyness or self-doubt and write down their own memories.

He told us now one of the stories he told the veterans. Mehrdad, still close to his military experience, was so fascinated he didn't translate the story for me. Mehrdad's eyes shone; he never took them off Abbas.

Abbas was an arresting man, small, fine-limbed, classically handsome, with a neat trimmed beard and a full, barbered head of neck-length hair. He had dressed with care for this meeting with us in the publisher's office. He was wearing a green shirt with broad, shiny vertical stripes over a patterned light-and-dark ground. His spectacle-case, clipped to his waist, was part of his style. The style was affecting, because the man had been damaged in the head, and had clearly overcome a great deal to be still so much himself. His eyes were bloodshot, unemotional, strangely staring; he moved his head slowly; he said his legs still hurt.

And yet, after an hour of eating fruit and drinking tea and talking, I had got nothing new from Abbas, had not been able to get beyond his gaze and what seemed to be his formality and pride; had not been moved to make a note or even to take my notebook out from the breast-pocket of my jacket. And when the electricity failed in the neighbourhood, and everything was suddenly dark all around, it seemed time to leave.

We stood up to say goodbye. It occurred to me, in the darkness, to ask whether in the course of his interviews he had met anyone from a martyrs' battalion who had survived. He said a few had survived. When we asked whether we could meet one of them, he didn't say anything. And then – it might have been the effect of the darkness, seeming to muffle life in the neighbourhood, making us speak softly, with the voices of children still playing in the street below suddenly very clear against the roar of the boulevards not very far away – it might have been the drama of the power cut that made Abbas say, hesitantly, 'I shouldn't say this, but I was one.'

And then we stayed and stayed. Abbas talked at first in the darkness, and then by candlelight. The publishing house had a stock of candles, for these power cuts.

I made no notes. Later that evening in the hotel Mehrdad and I reconstructed what we had heard. I made my notes then.

When Abbas said that he had been in one of the martyrs' battalions, much of what he had been saying earlier fell into place. He had volunteered at the age of fourteen. He had been taken close to the war, and then, on his own initiative, he had picked his way to the murderous Dezful front – the frontier town of Dezful had been utterly destroyed by the fighting. What had made him volunteer? He said that a government organisation for development had sent speakers to his school (and Mehrdad told me later, in the hotel, that this school was one of the very best in Tehran). The speakers said they wanted to take boys to the front to show them the war, and they asked for volunteers. So Abbas volunteered.

He had no business, even as a Basiji, to be on his own in Dezful. The soldiers wanted to send him away, but he begged them, did things for them, and they allowed him to stay.

He was at Dezful at the time of a big Iranian attack. For twenty-two days there was the sound of artillery and planes. And this was the time when Abbas had his first sight of death or martyrdom on the battlefield.

An ambulance came back from the front – a glimpse there of Iranian organisation – and people ran to it. Abbas ran with them. At first he thought the people in the ambulance were only wounded. When they were placed on the ground he saw they were dead. Two of the dead men he had seen alive only two hours before. And he thought, 'I was looking for my friends. But these are not my friends. My friends are somewhere else.' He felt then that death was an exalting and wonderful thing, and he knew that one day he would have to have the same experience and go where his friends were.

It was an intense spiritual moment, and it was heightened when he was washing the cartridge belts and harness straps of the dead men. That was one of the things he used to do at the front. Every day he used to go to the morgue – officially called *Meradj*, the place of ascension – and collect the equipment from about forty dead men. He would clean the equipment in the evening. There was a shortage of equipment at this time because so many men were involved in this big attack. There was also a shortage of shoes. Another thing he did during the day was to help unload the supply trucks when they came up to the front. He did that unloading with a lot of zeal; it was one reason why the soldiers didn't send him back.

The cleaning of the equipment of the dead men was a spiritual exercise for him because he would think that the pieces he was cleaning belonged to men who had gone to a place which they didn't quite know. And it was possible – Abbas's words were ambiguous here – that he also meant that though the men didn't know where they were going, they had gone there straight and with determination.

A year later Abbas joined the army properly, and he was a member of one of the martyrs' battalions. People who volunteered as martyrs proclaimed themselves ready for any job. They wore no special clothes when they were in ordinary battalions; they made themselves known to the officers by their extraordinary zeal. One martyrs' battalion literally fought to the death; no one survived.

Before an attack there was 'a goodbye ceremony'. Someone might sing; someone respected in the battalion, like a clergyman, a commander, an old man, or a popular man, might address the men. This person would stand on a podium or a chair and say, 'Tomorrow we have an attack.' That was how the goodbye ceremony began. Some people would burst into tears right then; others would cry later. Generally there was a lot of weeping and wailing. The speaker would say, 'Some of you might not come back tomorrow. We might not see each other again. Some people would see God tomorrow.'

Then there would be music and chanting. Abbas heard this as something in the background. Nobody could focus on it. Everybody was emptying himself of all feeling, pouring feeling into a common pool. In that pool there was a collection of miseries and worldly difficulties and family problems, a pregnant wife perhaps, a sick baby, financial problems, quarrels with parents. Everything went into that common pool and was disappearing. Joining this ceremony was like joining a ship. Whether you liked it or not you had to go with it.

Abbas was wounded twice. Though it would be truer to say that he talked of the two occasions when he was wounded. The first time was during an Iraqi counter-attack at noon (the Iranians had attacked early in the morning). The people who were caught up in that counter-attack were the injured, the martyrs, and a few other fighters who wanted to delay the enemy advance. A rocket exploded near Abbas. He was hit in both legs and fell unconscious. It was night when he awakened. He heard Arabic voices and saw Iraqi soldiers apparently standing on guard at twenty-metre intervals. They were a picket line at the head of the Iraqi advance. Abbas found a hand grenade and a machine gun. He threw the grenade at the Iraqis and killed four of the men, and then he ran the fifty metres to the Iranian side. He was fired at but he zigzagged and wasn't hit.

The second wound was more serious. It occurred a year later, at night, during one of the biggest Iranian attacks: attack after attack for more than a month. Again there was a rocket burst near him. A bit of shrapnel struck him on the back of the head, and he was thrown on the ground. He fell on his head and was hurt badly. He passed in and out of consciousness many times. Finally he was taken by plane to the big military hospital in Shiraz.

There they inserted a bit of artificial bone in his head. After a while he lost his sense of balance; then he couldn't see. He had a clot on his retina, and there was a danger that he might lose his sight altogether. A day came when the authorities wanted to take some of the patients to the shrine of Shah Cheragh, one of the famous shrines of Iran. Abbas wanted to go. He was in a wheelchair now. The doctor said Abbas wasn't well enough to go, and Abbas shouted and began to quarrel with the doctor. The doctor relented, and Abbas was wheeled to the shrine at eight in the morning.

There was singing and chanting as on the battlefield, and Abbas made a vow: 'Allah, I accept whatever you wish, and I like whatever you like. But I cannot tell a lie to you. I need my eyes. If you give me back my eyes, I will use them to go back to the front.'

At twelve Abbas left the shrine with the rest of the patients and went back to the hospital. At two the nurse came to his room; he was taking about twelve pills every six hours. As the nurse opened the door Abbas saw the light and shouted. Doctors and nurses ran up. They saw that the clot on the retina had gone, and they didn't let him sleep. They called other doctors to look. None of them believed that that kind of religious miracle could happen. Word got around. Something got into the papers. But Abbas was nervous of letting too much be known.

The publisher's assistant, constantly serving us tea, said, 'And a good thing, too. If people had got to know about his cure at the shrine they would have rushed to him and torn bits of his clothes for keepsakes and magical purposes.'

I had heard something like that in 1979 about people who had been shot by the Shah's police during the demonstrations before the revolution. Even a slight wound could be fatal, because when a man fell his fellow demonstrators ran to him to force their hands in the wound in order to stain them with the warm blood of a martyr.

Some time after that evening in the publisher's office I was in Shiraz. I went to the shrine of Shah Cheragh at dusk. It was like a fairground in the streets outside, with the lights and the stalls and the strolling crowd, and there was something of that atmosphere inside as well, with people walking about in the diffused light and soft shadows of the courtyard, while in the mosque proper, in the brighter light around the railed grave of the saint, other people were praying and asking for boons.

To see what Abbas had seen, to enter the common pool of feeling here, you had to bring some feeling of your own. You had to bring the faith, the theology, the passion and need.

A tall Indian on the road outside was asking for alms in his own way. He had spotted me when I was on the way in; and he had dropped everybody else and concentrated on me. '*Bhaiya, bhaiya*, brother, brother,' he had said, bunching up his soft lips and screwing up his small eyes like a film actor working at grief.

He was young and fat, in white shoes that were quite startling in the dusk, and in loose cream-coloured clothes that caught him on the protruding lower belly. He was dandling a screaming baby and appeared to be with a woman with many attendant children. He said he was from Dubai. He had come to Shiraz to pay his respects to the saint, but bad people had stolen all his money, many lakhs, and all his papers. As he spoke he dandled the baby against his cream-coloured clothes and with every shake and dandle of his lower belly he twisted his thumb and finger against the poor baby's bottom and the baby screamed.

After I had walked about the shrine courtyard I went looking for him to find out how he had fared that evening. But he and his baby had vanished, and the woman with him and the children with her.

In the publisher's office, by candlelight now, Abbas spoke of the effect of his experience on his faith. I had asked him.

He said, 'It made me go deep in myself. I have some findings for the spiritual part that I think nobody has.' This was Mehrdad's translation of a difficult idea, later in the hotel, and at the end of a long day: let it stand as it was spoken. 'On the battlefield we could see a lot of things that cannot be described in a materialist way. When I saw people running with an arm blown away it was unbelievable. There are lots of people here on the street who have a little injury on their arms, and they lie down in the street. But over there, the enemy was coming, and this boy was running from the enemy with one arm blown off. It showed me what's possible. And at the moment I don't care about my aches at all. I pay no attention to it.'

He wanted after the war to stay close to the spirituality he had discovered in himself. To him this spirituality was like a treasure. Not many people on the street possessed such a treasure. 'People on the street', *mardom to khiyabom*: it was the second time, speaking of his spirituality, he had used the words; as though spirituality was the true divider and differentiator of men. Of course those people on the street were not less than he was, but they cared about things he didn't care for. Their idea of religion was not letting women be without the veil or the *hijab* headdress; which was something he didn't mind about.

'The Koran says that we do things according to our capacity. So I would do whatever I can, and they would do whatever they can.'

He felt he should improve his spiritual feelings, and he thought he could do this with study and scholarship. Since childhood he had liked to study. So he went to the holy city of Qum, and enrolled in a five-year course. He completed it in three years. And by then he had had enough of study. He didn't feel he had got in Qum what – perhaps innocently – he had been hoping for. Study was study; the spirituality he was concerned with was more personal; it didn't come through study. There were many examples of people with much religious learning but without spirituality.

In the outside world there was, a year or two later, another test for him. He fell in love with a girl and wanted to marry her. He went to her family and asked for her hand. They told him that he had to go to the university first; their daughter was a university student. This was a hard thing to ask of Abbas, Mehrdad said; because in Iran you couldn't be considered for a university place if you didn't have a high-school diploma; and Abbas had left his very good Tehran school at the age of fourteen to go to the war.

But Abbas, always now with his spiritual idea of what men could do, always now with that picture of the half-dead boy with his arm blown off running away from the enemy, Abbas set to work. This was two years ago, and Abbas had already got his diploma and his university place; and his family and the girl's family were getting ready for the wedding.

It was only now that it occurred to me to ask about his family: Abbas had always seemed so absolutely himself, so secure, so handsome and fine.

'My father worked for the bus company here in Tehran.'

'What did he do?'

'He was a simple worker.'

Mehrdad, with his feeling for the social grades of Iran, said, 'A mechanic?'

And Mehrdad was right. He said later that the bus company for which Abbas's father had worked was a poor company, a very poor company; and to be a mechanic there was to have a poor kind of job. But the mechanic had educated all his children. One now ran a factory; another was a professor at the university; the youngest was an engineer. So Abbas's family was one of the success stories of the revolution.

I wanted to know how he had discovered the spirituality in himself.

He said it began with his name. His name had always been precious to him. The first Abbas in Islamic history was the cousin and principal commander of Imam Hussain, the son of the great Ali; and this Abbas was one of the seventy-two who had stayed and died with Imam Hussain at the battle of Kerbala. This Abbas had been, literally, the standard-bearer of Imam Hussain.

So at the Mohurram celebrations when he was a child – Mohurram the blood month, the Shia mourning month for the martyrdoms at Kerbala – the young Abbas, even when he was six, had wanted to live up to his name. He wanted to carry the flag or standard at the Mohurram procession. He never wanted to put it down on the ground; to him that was a kind of sacrilege.

Was that all? Hadn't he been told something by his father or someone else? Were there books he had read?

He said he couldn't explain any more. His family was religious only in an ordinary way. There were books in the house, but they didn't belong to his father.

I asked, 'If there had been no war, what do you think would have happened to you?'

The publisher's assistant said, 'That's the question we all ask. Without the war we might have gone to Allah in a roundabout or much longer way. Some of us mightn't even have reached Allah in the end.'

Abbas said, 'I would have continued my studies. I loved *pure* physics. It is related to philosophy. The study of matter.'

And this was interesting to me because it showed how, even within the rigidities of a revealed faith, a feeling for the spiritual might prompt wonder; and science and the search for knowledge would have begun. It was like the understanding that had come to me some years before, in India, in the south of the country, of the ways in which certain brahmin families, priestly proponents of antique ritual and taboos, had in two generations in the twentieth century arrived at high science, made ready for that intellectual journey by the very complications and demands of their theology, and its curious, shut-away purity.

I told Abbas something of this.

He might not have followed. But he said (still with that battlefield picture of the boy with the blown-away arm), 'I wanted to see how things were made. And what they are made of. I wanted to know about the essence of things.'

The lights had come on again in the office and the streets. It was past eight, and we had been in the publisher's office since 4.30. The publisher's assistant wanted to clear away the fruit plates and close the office. The children had long ago stopped playing in the streets; through the window, while the daylight lasted, I had seen them beating up and stripping a *chenar* sapling, climbing up the slender trunk and pulling down the branches.

Abbas's bloodshot eyes were almost friendly now. He said, 'I have said more than I should. I have talked like a drunk man.' (That was Mehrdad's first translation when we were in the hotel. But then right away he said, 'No, that's too strong. It wouldn't be good for Abbas.' He thought and said, '"A drunken man doesn't know what he says, and I feel I have been like that." That would be better.' I didn't see the difference, but Mehrdad said, 'The second one is softer.')

The publisher's assistant was switching off the lights, using this new darkness to push us outside. Abbas talked of the two one-minute films he had made. Each film had three sequences. The first began with a man making footsteps in the snow; another man walks in his footsteps; a third man begins to do so, but then hesitates, and finally turns off in another direction, leaving his own footsteps in the snow. In the second film a man is being married; then a farmer is tilling the land; and finally there is a field of waving wheat.

Mehrdad said, 'In Iran wheat is the symbol of generation.'

The films were transparent in a way that Abbas might not have known. His own idea of himself showed through: he was the man who had struck out on his own, and he was the man to whom life had come again.

In the taxi Mehrdad said, 'You noticed? He didn't mention Khomeini once.'

I said, ' When he was talking about Qum he said there were many examples of religious learning not going with spirituality. I would like to ask him a little more about that.'

But Mehrdad didn't think that was a good idea – he meant it was an idea with some danger – and I didn't say any more about it.

Mehrdad said a while later, 'He is to me a real hero, Abbas. In the war and in civilian life. The way he does things.'

Mehrdad was thinking especially of Abbas going back to school in his mid-twenties, to get his diploma, in order to go to the university, in order to marry his girl.

On a wall in a side street we saw in very big letters the English words FAITH NO MORE. Mehrdad said it was an album of American 'heavy-metal' songs. But the letterer knew English well, and his English or Roman letters were done in a way that no one knowing only the Persian script could manage. (Even Mehrdad wrote the English script awkwardly.) In spite of what Mehrdad said, I thought the words were a kind of protest, like the playing of the popular music of the Shah's time, which you often heard coming out of flats and taxis.

Then, on a pier of a road bridge there was a big daubed sign in Persian in red and green: MARTYRS SAY (in red): (in green) WHAT HAVE YOU DONE SINCE WE WENT AWAY? That was critical, Mehrdad said. But Basijis had that privilege. They could daub what they wanted on the streets; no one stopped them.

In the hotel room – with the big window giving a clear view of the spread of lights, blue and brilliant white and orange, of Evin prison – we reconstructed the evening. I asked Mehrdad, when we came to that stage of Abbas's story, whether Abbas and his brothers, the mechanic's sons, wouldn't have moved forward anyway, even if the revolution hadn't come; and whether the revolution hadn't really been wasteful of talent.

Mehrdad said, 'People are like ships.' (Abbas had used the ship metaphor, too, but in a different way, when he was talking about the goodbye ceremony on the battlefield.) 'When the first ship goes in one direction, the others just follow. It's like the firing squad, when they have to shoot a thief.' (Memories there of Mehrdad's recent military service.) 'The first shot is the important one. The others just follow. They hear the sound and they all pull the trigger. I have seen it many times.

For example, in the swimming pool. In the military service I was a life-guard at a swimming pool. The little boys who came were all nervous, but the minute the first boy jumped in, all the rest jumped in, not caring how deep the water was or whether they knew how to swim. And at the university. A professor is teaching badly, is known to be a poor professor. Nobody does anything. But one day some student gets up and objects to something, and then there is chaos. Everybody starts objecting to the teacher.

'That is my feeling about the revolution. My parents attended four or five demonstrations. But they didn't know why. They didn't know what they were doing. My father is not brave. He is not brave at all. Now when you ask him he says that he didn't go to the demonstrations. But I remember it. We had a lot of books in our house. There was a pictorial one, full of colours. It was published by the Shah. It was about the royal family. It was a prize to my sister from her school. My father – I said he was not a brave man – he tore it up and put it in the dustbin. He said, "Maybe when the revolution comes they don't want to see such things in my house." I said, "Nobody cares about your house." He was just doing what everybody else did. He was innocent – and fright-ened. Others had a lot of sin, but he was innocent.' Mehrdad thought of himself as iconoclastic, but his language could still be religious.

I said, 'There was something you didn't translate. The story Abbas told the veterans when he handed out the questionnaires about their war experiences.'

'There were two friends at the front. One of them was always talk-ing about sport and the jobs he had done in the city. He didn't feel he was at the front. The other man was a spiritual person. He didn't want his friend to lose touch with the spiritual side. He thought a lot about how to turn the friend from town talk to spiritual concentration. At last he got a notebook from one of the PBXs at the front. For ten days he wrote down whatever his friend said. At the end of the tenth day the sixty pages of the notebook were filled. He took the notebook to the friend and said, "Here you are. Here is your talk for ten days. I have written down everything. Read it and see whether you have been doing a good thing, a bad thing, or an indifferent thing." Two days later the friends met. The sportsman took the spiritual man to a silent and hidden place, brought out a plastic bag which was filled with burnt paper, and said, "This is my past. I understood what you wanted to say, and I won't repeat the same mistake again." After a time, whenever he began to tell one of his old stories, he stopped himself and said, "Oh, forget it." And he was famous as "Mr Oh, forget it." '

I said, 'The story fascinated you.'

'Abbas said that whenever he told this story to the veterans they began to laugh, but this laughter turned to weeping as they remembered the war and their own friendships. This story, Abbas said, was just to show the veterans that a simple story could be effective when they were filling in their questionnaires about their war experiences.'

I said, 'What do you think of the story now?'

'I have no feeling at the moment.'

A little later he said, 'It's an Iranian story, because of the affection between the two soldiers. It is hard to tell a friend about his failings. The story was about a friend who found a good way of doing that.'

7

Qum: The Punisher

WHEN I went to Tehran in August 1979, Ayatollah Khalkhalli, the hanging judge of the revolution, was a star. The Islamic Revolutionary Court in Shariati Street was sitting almost round the clock, as Ali had said. People were being killed all the time in Evin prison and trucks were taking away the bodies through the blue gates at night.

There was nothing secretive or abashed about this killing. Some revolutionary official was keeping count, and regularly in the *Tehran Times* there was an update. In the beginning the counting was to show how clement the revolution was; later, when the killing became too much, the counting stopped. In those early days official photographs were taken of people before they were killed and after they were killed – killed and, as it were, filed away, naked on the sliding mortuary slab, in the giant filing cabinet of the morgue. These pictures were on sale in the streets.

Ayatollah Khalkhalli, the ruler of the Islamic Revolutionary Court, was open to the press. He was giving many boastful interviews. I went with an interpreter to see him in Qum. It was Ramadan, the fasting month; and Qum was where the ayatollah had temporarily retired to fast and pray. It was August and very hot in the desert. When we got to Qum we had to wait for more than five hours until the ayatollah had finished his prayers and broken his fast. This was at nine in the evening. We found him then sitting on the floor of the verandah of his modest house, at the centre of a little court also sitting on the floor: his guards, some Iranian admirers, and a respectful, formally dressed African couple (the man in a light-grey suit, the woman in a chiffon-like, sari-like garment) who were visiting.

The ayatollah was white and bald and very short, a clerical gnome, messily attired. He liked, perhaps because of his small size, to clown. His jokes were about executions, and then his court threw themselves about with laughter. He also liked – and this mannerism might have come with his hanging duties – abruptly to stop clowning and for no reason to frown and grow severe.

He was from Azerbaijan in the north-west. He said he was the son of a farmer and as a boy he had been a shepherd. So, going by what Ali had said, Khalkhalli would have been just the kind of village boy for whom, fifty years or so before, the theological schools had offered the only way out: a room, food, and a little money. But Khalkhalli had almost nothing to say about his early life. All he said, with a choking, wide-throated laugh, was that he knew how to cut off a sheep's head; and this was like another joke about executions, something for his little court. Perhaps, because he had never learned how to process or meditate on his experience, never having read widely enough or thought hard enough, his experience had simply gone by, and much of it had even been lost to him. Perhaps the thirty-five years (as he said) of theological studies in Qum had rotted his mind, pushed reality far away, given him only rules, and now with the revolution sunk him in righteousness and vanity. He was interested only in the present, his authority and reputation, and in his executioner's work.

He said, 'The mullahs are going to rule now. We are going to have ten thousand years of the Islamic Republic. The Marxists are going to go on with their Lenin. We are going to go on in the way of Khomeini.'

Revolution as blood and punishment, religion as blood and punishment: in Khalkhalli's mind the two ideas seemed to have become one.

And, in fact, that double idea, of blood, fitted revolutionary Iran. Behzad, my interpreter, was a communist, and the son of a communist father. Behzad was twenty-four; with all his Iranian graces, his scientific education, and his social ambitions, he had his own dream of blood. His hero was Stalin. Behzad said, 'What he did in Russia we have to do in Iran. We too have to do a lot of killing. A lot.'

On the way back through the desert to Tehran, in moonlight, we turned on the car radio. The news was about the closing down by the government of the liberal or non-religious paper, *Ayandegan*. The news caused Behzad's mood to grow dark. Whatever was said by the communists at the top, however much for the next year or so they continued to claim the religious revolution as their own, Behzad knew that evening that the game was up.

I thought now, sixteen years later, that I should go to Qum again, to look for Khalkhalli, and, if it were possible, to get from him some new angle on old times. It also occurred to me, after what I had heard from Abbas and Ali, that when I was in Qum I should try to talk to a student, a *talebeh*, to understand the kind of person who nowadays, after the revolution, was going to the theological schools.

Mehrdad didn't think I should go to see Khalkhalli. I had so far kept my nose clean; going to see Khalkhalli, or trying to see him, would be too political a thing to do, too intrusive, and there might be trouble. And, indeed, when I asked around I was told that for various reasons Khalkhalli mightn't want to be disturbed. He had been cast aside by the revolution long ago as one of the old brigade, and was living in retirement; he had also recently had some sort of heart trouble.

In spite of Mehrdad, I put out feelers. And the news that came back was good. There might have been official discouragement, but Khalkhalli had been reached. He was ready to see me in his house at eleven o'clock on a certain day. His house was in a little lane in Qum, the Kucheh Abshar; and the person who would take me there would be a *talebeh*. The *talebeh* had been a student in Qum for many years and would, besides, be willing to talk to me on his own. I was to meet the *talebeh* at the Marashi Library in Qum; it wasn't far from where Khalkhalli lived. I would have no trouble finding the Marashi Library. It was very famous and everybody in Qum would know where it was.

It was too complicated an arrangement; too many pieces had to fall into place. As a traveller I knew that much simpler arrangements, in simpler places, could unravel. So I went to Qum with a kind of half-faith.

There was a new road to Qum. It went past the Khomeini shrine: the copper-coloured dome, the decorated minarets. Kamran, the driver, who had earlier taken Mehrdad and me to the shrine and the Martyrs' Cemetery, asked ironically, 'You want to go again?'

We were in desert, but where there was irrigation there were green fields. The land was flat. Then we came to true desert, and the land, red-brown and bare, was more broken: now a series of cracked mud knolls, now a line of low cliffs worn down in certain places to rock, the rock showing in twisted, cracked layers. It was wonderful, from the car. But Mehrdad said, 'We think it is very bad land. It is salt land.'

To the left, far away, was the great salt lake. In 1979 Behzad, my guide and interpreter, had told me that Savak used to dump people in the lake from helicopters. I heard now from Mehrdad that the lake was so salt nothing sank in it. Mehrdad talked more about the oil that was said to be below the land. Officially, Mehrdad said, it was given out that the oil in this salt land was of poor quality; but the story among Iranians was that there was a lot of oil there, and it was to be kept in reserve. So, though the land was salt and bare, it was fabulous, as Qum itself was fabulous, on a site no doubt ancient, since all sacred sites go back and back, to earlier religions.

Sometimes now to the left we could see the old, slow, winding road to Qum. The hard land softened, opened out into a plain; scattered tussocks appeared. In the distance a jagged mountain range was amethyst-brown in the glare. Two or three times in the wilderness there were garage stops: black smears in the desert: the black of tyres stacked one upon the other, the black of oil on the bare ground.

Sheds like factory sheds along a local road some way to the right announced the nearness of Qum; and soon the dome and minarets of the famous shrine of Qum began to show above the nondescript spread of dust-coloured brick houses. In 1979 Qum was a small town; now, after the revolution, it was three times the size and had a population of a million and a half.

We came to a roundabout, well watered, green. It was the end of the desert and the beginning of the town.

Kamran said in his ironical way, 'We are entering the Vatican.'

At the side of the road there was a big board that looked like a municipal welcome board. But it offered no welcome. What it stated had caused much distress, Mehrdad said. He gave this translation of what was written in the bold, flowing Persian script: 'The whole practical philosophy of the law is governing.' The word used for 'the law' was *fiqha*; it meant 'jurisprudence' in a very wide way, and was one of the principal subjects studied in Qum. As with so many things in Persian, Mehrdad said, the statement on the board was ambiguous.

The politer meaning was: 'Our rule is based on study and religion.' The real meaning was more brutal: 'We at Qum are here to rule you.'

Not long after the revolution the people of Iran had voted in a referendum for an Islamic Republic. This was in 1979. The principles of the Islamic Republic hadn't yet been worked out, and most people thought that they were simply voting for freedom and justice. The principles of the Islamic Republic had been worked out now by the scholars, and this rule by Qum was one of the principles. It was an aspect of the fundamental idea of the Islamic state, the idea of the Leader and obedience to the Leader, which was now never to be questioned, even indirectly.

A later board, in three languages, was softer. It was about the shrine of the much-loved woman saint, Masumeh, 'the innocent', the sister of the eighth Imam.

And now, after the desert, and in the holy city, the women in black chadors in the streets made an extra impression. They were brisk, solitary-seeming, noticeably small. Some of them held the chador over their face with their hands or bit an end of it between their teeth; they looked like people who were muzzling themselves. You didn't think of the woman saint of Qum; you thought of the principle of obedience.

Without the dull gold of the dome of the shrine the town would have been quite ordinary; but always there was the dome. And now, further into the town, we began seeing the students with their turbans and variously coloured tunics and their black robes. We saw more and more of them, and Qum became more than a town in the desert, more than a place with costumes.

It was as though we had switched centuries. As though, by some cinematic or computer device, we had been taken deep into a play by Marlowe (say), had begun to walk old streets, live with old assumptions, and had gone back to an old idea of learning, with all its superseded emblems of colour and dress.

(Superseded, but oddly familiar: fragments of that academic idea, originally imported from the Islamic world, had survived in the Oxford I had entered, just like that, one afternoon in 1950, and was soon taking for granted: the long black gowns of lecturers and scholar-students, the shorter gowns of commoners, ordinary students.)

The Marashi Library was not as well known to ordinary people as we had been told. Different people had different pieces of information. We began, almost, to be led on corner by corner. We had sped through the desert on the new road; we were losing time now; we were going to be late for Khalkhalli.

At last we came to the library. And I could see why we had had such trouble getting to it. We had been asking about it as though it was a landmark. It wasn't. It was a new building in brown brick, a little too Islamic in its arches and windows and decoration; and it wasn't all that big or noticeable. Its upper façade had a Qum camouflage of strings of coloured bulbs, and new posters and the remains of old ones were on its lower stone walls. The big board that stuck far out over the busy street was like the board of a commercial enterprise.

We left Kamran in the car and went to look for the man who was going to take us to Khalkhalli. It was now past eleven, and eleven was the time Khalkhalli had given.

As soon as we went through the arched entrance to the library, I knew we were in trouble.

The tomb of the Ayatollah Marashi, the founder of the library, was just to the left after the entrance. It was in a curious kind of aluminium cage with a green cover, like a big parrot cage. (And the aluminium was for the modernity, Mehrdad said later; silver would have been more usual.) Even as we hurried in from the busy, bright street, some devout people in great need, and some very ill people, were leaning quietly against the cage. Next to this, and raised a little above the marble floor, was an open carpeted area, and more people were sitting or praying there, below a big colour photograph of the Ayatollah Marashi in extreme old age.

The Marashi Library, here, seemed to be also the Marashi shrine, with its own devotees and concerns. And it didn't surprise me that in the little office at the end of the hall they knew nothing about us and our meeting with Ayatollah Khalkhalli.

We were shown to another office, and there they didn't know anything about us either. From there we were taken to the office of the son of the great Ayatollah Marashi.

He – the director of his father's library, and the guardian of his father's busy shrine as well – was a big, dramatic man with a fine big black beard with two grey streaks. He had a black turban and a tunic and a robe, and his office was imposing, full of books and files and paper. He said he didn't know who we were or why we had come. He

knew nothing about *talebehs* or Ayatollah Khalkhalli. I said I had
Khalkhalli's address: it was the Kucheh Abshar. I showed it to him in
my notebook, in case I had got the pronunciation wrong. He said it
wasn't an address; there was no number. I said the lane might be a short
one and people there would almost certainly know where Khalkhalli
lived.

He was having none of that. He began to fire off questions. 'What is
your name? Where do you live? How many books have you written?
What kind of books? What agency are you connected with? Are you
from SOAS?' I didn't know what SOAS was. He didn't like that; he
didn't like anything I had said. He said I was to write down my name
and address. Oddly civil after that, he made me sit down, while
Mehrdad went out to telephone people in Tehran and to telephone
Emami, the *talebeh* who should have been waiting for us at the library.

Mehrdad wasn't long. When he returned he said that Emami was
going to telephone back. I thought that was bad news. But Mehrdad –
anxious now to console me – said that while we waited for Emami we
could go and have a look at the manuscripts in the library. We were
going to be very late for Khalkhalli, but Mehrdad didn't seem to mind.

As we were going up the steps to the manuscript room Mehrdad said
that the director of the library had stood up when we entered his
office. This was a gesture of respect in Iran; the director wouldn't have
done that if he hadn't known about us.

And then, beyond an iron-barred door, we were in the quiet of the
manuscript room, and among old things of great beauty. So that,
abruptly, after the disorder of the streets, and my nerves, and the
obstructiveness downstairs, we were again in another world.

It was already 11.30. Even if Emami came now we would be an hour
late for Khalkhalli. I began mentally to write that meeting off, and
thought that, rather like the people downstairs leaning against the aluminium cage to get the healing emanations of the dead holy man, it
might be good for me, after all, to linger here for half an hour or so, in
the calmer emanations of an older world. I thought of the library of the
University of Salamanca in Spain, another collection of idle learning, or
its mirror image, almost from the same period. But without warning
the English-speaking guide who had been deputed to show us round
was taken away, and there came a young cleric in a tunic and gown
who, small and frowning, saying nothing, marched us from case to
case, the skirt of his robe swinging above his small, light-coloured

slippers, and finally marched us out of the manuscript room, closing the iron-barred door with a bang behind us.

He led us then without speech or friendliness to other sections of the library: printed books, conservation, fumigation, copying. And then to rooms with more and more printed books: the unending stream of Islamic theology, elaborated without haste in places like Qum, and put out in 'sets' of many volumes, uniformly and garishly bound: so many sets they made you wonder how far they had been checked and proofed, whether they were intended to find readers, or whether they were issued as sacred objects, the emanations of a revered ayatollah, their publication or manufacture being somebody's act of piety or charity.

So many sets to see, now, in the company of our surly attendant, that at last I said no and stopped. I felt that we should be content with the adventure we had had, should go and look at the shrine of Hazrat Masumeh, eat lunch or something, and drive back to Tehran. Mehrdad agreed. He thought we had drawn too much attention to ourselves. It worried him that I had written down my name and address; and he didn't think that we should hang around.

We broke off from our attendant, walked down two floors to where the library proper began. And found Emami, the *talebeh*.

He was relaxed and easy, a tall and slender man of about thirty, and he didn't seem to know that he had kept us waiting an hour. He wasn't in tunic and robe and turban, but in trousers and a silky or shiny white shirt with a textured pattern. No word from him – or Mehrdad transmitted none – about how he happened to be where he was, or why he hadn't telephoned, or even why he hadn't been there an hour earlier. All that came from him, in his calm, soft way, was yes, he knew where Khalkhalli lived, and would take us there.

I asked about his clothes. He said he was entitled to wear the tunic and the robe and the turban of the *talebeh*, but he didn't like wearing them. He presented this – or so it came out in Mehrdad's translation – as an aspect of his modernity; he saw himself as a modern man.

We went to the director's office to say goodbye. The big man in the black turban was civil but distant; his business with us was over. The white office pad with my name and address was still where I had left it on his desk, on a pile of papers and old books. It looked glaring and noticeable; I could understand Mehrdad's worry.

Downstairs, we passed the visitors to the shrine sitting or praying on the carpet below the photograph of Ayatollah Marashi or pressing their faces against the aluminium cage of his grave. Outside, on the busy sunlit street, we passed an open-fronted bookstall or shop: Persian books in a glass case, two very young students in turbans and tunics and gowns excitedly buying what appeared to be a concise textbook from the stall-keeper, and looking like people who had found treasure. Perhaps the little book was a simple question-and-answer book. The scene was like a stage set, with props – new books of antique learning, a shop of such books – that had ceased to be props, and with costumed actors – bookseller, students – who had become their roles. It would have been nice to stop and look, and to play with some of the fantasies the scene suggested. But we were already an hour late for Khalkhalli.

We found Kamran and the car some distance away, on the sunny side of the street. When we were all inside, the car wouldn't start.

We all pushed, even Emami in his shiny white shirt, Kamran demonstrating even at this speed his capacity for handling his car recklessly, now steering out without warning into the traffic, now pushing directly against the traffic. He had Iranian luck; no one hit us. After about a hundred or a hundred and fifty metres the car bucked and started. And then Kamran and Mehrdad and Emami – in spite of what he had said, he didn't absolutely know where Khalkhalli lived – asked and asked the way, doing what we should have done on our own earlier in the morning. Everyone knew the ayatollah's house, and said it was very near. But it took some finding.

At last we came to a short residential street: white houses, newish, the houses with high fences or walls in the Iranian way. Emami pressed the bell of one house. Nothing happened. Emami pressed the bell of a second house and talked for a little into the intercom. The gate of the first house opened, and a very old woman, not in the black chador of Qum, but with a light patterned scarf (which she was tying around her head), came out to the pavement and pointed to a third house.

Emami pressed the bell there. Mehrdad also pressed, and after a while a man opened. He was not in uniform; but Mehrdad observed – and told me later – that the man had a gun at his waist, below his shirt. He said he didn't know anything about a meeting, but he would go in and ask the ayatollah. The ayatollah was reading. He came out again after a while and said, 'The ayatollah was expecting you. He was expecting you at eleven.' (But Mehrdad didn't tell me that until the end of the day.)

We went through the tall gate and found another guard. He was in dark-green trousers and shirt, the old-style uniform of the Revolutionary Guard *komiteh*.

A small front courtyard, a short flight of steps, a verandah: I remembered something like that from 1979, but I couldn't be sure that it was the same house, because the surroundings seemed to have changed so much. In 1979 Khalkhalli's house was at the edge of the town, in a new street with young trees; the desert felt close. This lane looked established and was deep within the town.

We took off our shoes and went into the reception area. To the right was a library or study with bookshelves packed with books in sets. To the left was the sitting room, a formal, almost empty area spread with carpets. The walls were a pale grey-green. Green-striped oblong cushions were propped against the inset radiators in one wall. A thin palliasse on the carpet, oddly intimate, showed where at one stage the ayatollah might have been resting (or waiting for us). On the other side of the room were four or five dark armchairs. On the lace doily on the side table next to one of the chairs were three or four toothpicks or toothsticks: the master of the house, no doubt. That must have been where he was, reading, when we pressed the buzzer on his gate.

Hanging on the wall with the radiators was a ready-wrapped black turban, looking somewhat thin and squashed and pathetic; and, above that, were photographs of the ayatollah with Khomeini. The photographs were high up on the wall – perhaps to prevent them from being pilfered – and it wasn't easy to see the details. One photograph was a candid-camera, black-and-white shot of Khalkhalli and Khomeini, both in turban and robe, both frowning, walking purposefully in snow at the back of a car: a street scene, no doubt. Khalkhalli's robe came down almost to his ankles, outlined his belly, and didn't stress his shortness; in fact, striding beside Khomeini, he didn't look much shorter. A formal group portrait to the left of that was of Khomeini, his son, and Khalkhalli; Khalkhalli had been the teacher of Khomeini's son and was proud of the distinction. Next to that was a colour photograph of Khomeini and Khalkhalli, both men laughing this time: Khomeini on the right reclining on what looked like a *chaise longue*, Khalkhalli leaning conspiratorially over him from the left, Khalkhalli turbanned and black-gowned and with his thick-lensed, black-rimmed glasses. Khalkhalli's black gown – like a protective wing over Khomeini – occupied much of the left side of the photograph. The photograph was not properly focused or had been badly enlarged: there was a kind of blue-white halo around Khomeini's chair. It was a disturbing photograph: Khalkhalli the jester making his master laugh. It was the only photograph I had seen in which Khomeini was laughing, and the laugh altered the face, stressed the sensuality.

Khalkhalli was now out of everything, people said; he had been pushed aside. The photographs on the wall were like proof of his power in the old days, his closeness to the Imam, the leader of the revolution. But in a time to come the photographs on the wall might say something else: the busy men of the revolution frowning in the street, laughing in private.

He came in now. And it was an entrance. He was barefooted, in simple white, like a penitent, and he moved very slowly. A short-sleeved white tunic, wet with perspiration down the middle of his chest, hung over a loose white lower garment. Step by dragging step he came in, very small, completely bald, baby-faced without his turban, head held down against his chest, looking up from below his forehead, eyes without mischief now and seemingly close to tears, as though he wished to dramatise his situation and needed pity.

He invited me to sit in a chair. He sat next to me. We were separated by the little side table with the lace doily and the tooth-sticks.

I didn't know how to start. I really wanted to hear about his work as a judge, and to hear what he had to say now about the revolution. But I didn't know how to get to that. I thought an indirect approach, with questions about his childhood or his early days, would begin to take us there. But, as in 1979, he didn't want to talk about his life.

If we were to go back so far, he said, it would tire him. He had had a heart operation, a triple bypass. And, either because it was hard for him to sit on the chair, or because he wished to show he didn't like my questions, he got up from the chair next to mine and moved to the palliasse on the carpet.

I asked when he had become a revolutionary. He said he had always been a revolutionary, ever since he knew himself; he had always hated kings.

The guards brought in tea in little glasses. They sat and listened to our talk. I felt they liked the break in their routine.

And social graces came to Khalkhalli. He said he had learned a lot from Nehru. This was meant as a courtesy to me: he saw me as some-one from India. He had especially liked Nehru's book, *Glimpses of World History*; in the Persian translation it was in three volumes. I reminded him of his interest in the Polisario movement in 1979, and asked what he thought would be the future of societies that were rev-olutionary today. He said, in Mehrdad's translation, 'Reality will always prevail.'

Reality: for him it meant truth. It was to be set against false systems, false gods, fraudulence. It was hard, though, to get him to talk con-cretely; he turned everything to abstraction. As an ayatollah that was his talent. It pleased him to be baffling my purpose; and as he talked in his ayatollah's way about reality and fraudulence his eyes – seemingly so close to tears when he entered – brightened, began to twinkle: a glimpse there of old mischievousness, with something of the man of 1979 showing through.

He said to me, 'Are you going to see Ayatollah Montazeri?'

I said, 'I don't think so.'

When Mehrdad had translated this, Khalkhalli looked at him and said, 'He should see Montazeri.'

Mehrdad set his face and did the translation. And it was only later, putting together various things I heard, that I understood that this question about Ayatollah Montazeri was a political question, and pos-sibly even an attempt by Khalkhalli to involve me in his cause. Khalkhalli and Montazeri had both been important in the early days of the revolution (Montazeri at one time had even been Khomeini's second-in-command); and both men had made themselves known for their virulence. If Khalkhalli was the hanging judge, Montazeri, as Khomeini's second-in-command, had sometimes been even more zeal-ous than his master. When Khomeini had said that the revolution should concentrate on the young, that people over forty were useless, Montazeri had gone one stage further. Pensions were useless, he had said; dead trees should be cut down. People still remembered that. Both those men, Khalkhalli and Montazeri, had been cast aside by a later generation of people in power; both were now kept quiet and harmless.

But nearly all of this I got to know later. So when Khalkhalli asked whether I was going to see Montazeri I missed the point of what he was saying, and I couldn't take it up. Instead – and it would have been disappointing to him – I asked what he had been reading when we came: I said that the guard who had come out to us had said that he was reading. Was it a religious work?

It was only the paper. He said, in his lecturer's way, 'The world doesn't stand still. There are always new things. That is why I read the papers.'

The words he was using were not meaning much. They didn't tax him and they were enabling him to assess me. Sitting on the palliasse on the carpet, he had been looking up at me from below his forehead, and I became aware now of his counter-probing, between his rambling, abstract talk. How old was I? Did I have children? I said no. He asked why. I said if I had had children it would have been hard for me to do my work. He said many Persian writers had had a hundred children and written a hundred books. How many books had I written? Did I make a living? It was hard for a writer in Persian to make a living. Was I connected with some agency? What was my religion? He asked about India and Kashmir, and paid no attention to what I said.

He had become unhappy about me. He had been used to another kind of interview, something more political and immediate (and perhaps something offering more immediate publicity). He didn't know what I was after. And perhaps I had lost my way. Perhaps the misadventure at the Marashi Library had made me too cautious.

It might have been better if I had asked him directly about his reputation as the hanging judge of the revolution. But I didn't want to do that; I thought that a question like that would have made him close up or give a set answer or grow hostile, and would have achieved only the obvious. I could have asked him about the photographs on the wall. The photographs interested me, and they were important to him; he might have wanted to talk about them, and that might have led to other things. But that idea, about the photographs, came to me only many weeks later, when I was considering my notes.

I went on in my groping way. I asked how he assessed the revolution now. He talked for some time, clearly using a lot of meaningless words, and Mehrdad's short translation of what he said was that a beginning had been made. How much of a beginning? Thirty per cent. I saw an opening; and he must have seen what was going to come. Because, before I could ask about the 70 per cent that still had to be done, he said he was tired. The eyes that twinkled while he talked or lectured became dead, the expression melancholy, empty. He dropped his head, pressed his chin against his chest, stood up slowly, the sweat showing on the front and back of his short-sleeved white tunic. Step by step he moved to a side room.

The interview was over. And now we had a problem. We had no car. Kamran had gone off to find a garage to mend his ignition. He had said he would be back in half an hour, but that wasn't meant literally. We could only wait for him. It was the middle of the day and it was too hot to wait in the lane outside. So, waiting for Kamran, Emami, Mehrdad and I continued to sit in Khalkhalli's reception room with his guards, and we talked.

To talk to Emami had been part of my purpose in coming to Qum, to find out about the *talebeh* or students who were coming nowadays to Qum. Emami had already spent fourteen years as a student. He had started at a Tehran theological school when he was sixteen, and he had moved to Qum after being accepted by an ayatollah. He was married now, with a two-year-old child. His grant from his ayatollah was two thousand *toumans* a month, about fifty dollars. He earned a little extra doing a little teaching himself, and doing translations from Arabic. It wasn't an easy life. Qum was dusty and hot. He endured it because from an early age he had wanted to be a propagator of the faith. He wasn't the classical *talebeh*, he said, the son of the poor family looking in Qum for free food and lodging. His father was a businessman; they were middle-class people.

But when was all this studying going to end? When was he going to go out into the world? It wasn't like that, he said. Some people could remain students for fifty years. Khomeini used to say that he was learning every day. But that didn't explain how movement might come to a cleric's life. How did people begin to stand out? He said people stood out because of their learning and personality. There was no end to learning. And with all the commentaries, and the commentaries on the commentaries, on theology and philosophy and jurisprudence, all those book-sets in the Marashi Library, it was possible to see what Emami meant. People could also stand out because of their ability, in this thicket of scholarship, to make fresh or interesting judgements. Khomeini, for example, did that with his statement that the game of chess was not against the law, provided there was no betting on the outcome. That was a judgement that people in Qum still talked about.

He himself wasn't famous, Emami said. He was content to be what he was, one of the foot soldiers, as it were, of the faith, one of the propagators. That was his vocation. He wasn't rich, but he didn't mind. He didn't care too much about eating. I said I thought he was putting it too strongly. I didn't think he was too deprived. He had a fine physique; I was sure he played some sport. He smiled; he said he exercised every morning.

There was little more to be got out of Emami. He had this idea of the vocation; it was sufficient explanation of his fourteen years of study; he couldn't step outside himself to consider his life and motives. His world had rigid limits. What passed with him for learning was really only a way of learning the rules. To know the rules was to simplify life, and Emami was a profoundly obedient man. It was what was required by the faith and the revolution; every day in the newspapers there was a message like that.

We had been talking for about half an hour or forty-five minutes in the ayatollah's reception room, below the ayatollah's turban and photographs, waiting for Kamran, listening for the sound of a stopping car, and going out from to time to time to the verandah to check. And then Khalkhalli came in again, slow, sad, his loose top tunic wet down the middle. Mehrdad explained about the driver and the car. Khalkhalli asked whether we wanted some bread and cheese, Persian bread, Persian cheese.

This seemed to me a good idea; it might give me a chance to talk in another way to the ayatollah. But Mehrdad said with some firmness that the offer of bread and cheese was just a form of words, a courtesy, that the ayatollah was asking us to leave.

We stood up to say goodbye. If we wanted to see him again, Khalkhalli said, we would have to make an appointment. It would have to be next week, on Thursday; that was the day he wasn't teaching. And this time we were to keep to the hour. His melancholy face began to alter with irritation. And we were to make notes. Nobody could remember everything. Talk without notes was a waste of time. We had been playing with him. I said that I made notes, but not right away; I hadn't felt that our earlier conversation had got to the note-taking stage. Next week, he said, his irritation beginning to melt; and we were to telephone beforehand. He gave the number and pointed to one of the guards: he would answer the telephone.

I began to feel that if we hadn't been so delayed, and if things had gone better, he really wouldn't have minded talking. But the moment had passed. We went out to the verandah, put on our shoes, and went out of the gate in the high wall. We crossed the street to the little strip of shade near the corner, and we stood there, waiting for Kamran.

Mehrdad said, 'Did you see the gun?'

Emami said, 'He has many enemies now.'

Mehrdad said, 'They are like enemies to each other. The old timers and the new people.' Then Mehrdad said to me, 'He asked you about Montazeri. I hope you are not going to try to see him. That is the way of death.'

He spoke with genuine dread. I did what I could to calm him down.

I said, 'But these men are back numbers. They are very old, and they can't be dangerous to anybody now.'

He said, 'In this situation even the dead are dangerous.'

And standing there, opposite Khalkhalli's house, I thought that even if I did come next Thursday – and if everybody remembered, and there was a meeting – there would perhaps be little to add to what I had seen that early afternoon: the justicer of the revolution, old and ill and anxious, subjected himself now to various controls, sitting below his photographs, which were more sinister and condemning than he knew, and with guards with guns, one of the guards wearing the old dark-green uniform of the early *komiteh* and making it look like old clothes.

There had been guards in 1979. I could still remember – the desert sunset all around us at the end of the long August day – the heavily built man with a gun at the low front gate of the exposed house in the half-made lane; and the heavy frisking hands of that man; and his closed, foolish, exalted face. The revolution still belonged to the country as a whole, and all that business of guards and searching had been principally for the drama: the pretend idea of the revolution in danger, part of the excitement and celebration of the early days of the revolution. Now – though it was part of his restraint – he needed the high wall and the man with the gun.

Mehrdad said, unexpectedly, 'It was very nice of him to say that he was tired. Iranians don't do that. They don't say things so openly. He is very old. But very clever.'

★

We waited in the shade at the corner. Mehrdad thought we should walk to where we could get a taxi, do what we had to do with Emami, and arrange to meet Kamran at 4.30 on one of the well-known bridges of Qum. We could leave a message with Khalkhalli's guards. We pressed Khalkhalli's buzzer again, and the guard who came out, the bigger man with the moustache, didn't mind at all being disturbed again.

We began to walk in the glaring white streets, Emami guiding us and talking at the same time about what was wrong with the philosophy course at Qum: too much old philosophy, not enough about contemporary matters, too much about Farrabi and Avicenna – an enchanted name to me: strange to hear it spoken so casually – who had taken their ideas, many of them wrong ideas, from ancient thinkers like Ptolemy and Aristotle. This criticism of Qum was approved thinking; Emami, though he saw himself as a modern man, ready to dress in a modern way, was not a rebel.

Surreally, as in a dream, after some minutes of walking, we saw Kamran's car coming down the empty white street towards us. He had had his troubles with that ignition; he had gone from garage to garage, and then from car shop to car shop, looking for a replacement.

Now that we didn't have to walk, Emami wanted us all to have lunch with him at his flat. He insisted. Mehrdad agreed, and we stopped at two or three shops in dusty streets to buy fruit and other things for the lunch. It was hot and still. There were twenty-five thousand students in Qum, Emami said. He showed us the big hostel for foreign students; they were mainly Indian, Pakistani, and African; there were few Europeans. There were also a fair number of Arabs. A little later, as if apologising for the dustiness of the town, he said the Arabs made the place dirty. He spoke conversationally, without malice, like a man saying something that everyone would accept: always with Iranians, and in unexpected ways, this uneasiness about Arabs, who had been both their conquerors and the givers of their religion.

We passed Khomeini's house, the house where he had lived when he was a teacher in Qum. It was at a bend in a busy street. A policeman was watching the traffic; the street might have been less busy when Khomeini lived in it. The house was low, unassuming, the colour of dust, partly hidden by its street wall. But, as so often in Iranian houses, that blank, almost unnoticeable wall would have concealed a courtyard, with a pleasant play of sunlight and shade, removed from the racket and glare of the street.

Emami lived at the very edge of the expanding town, in a new development that seemed to have been set down just like that in desert and dust. The streets were not yet made. For some time we bumped over rubble and brickbats, and I began to worry about Kamran's car, which had just been mended. At last we stopped. A scrap or two of plastic on the street, an empty packet caught in broken brick and stone: the effect was, already, one of civic neglect. But behind the blank door of Emami's house there was, even here, a little courtyard: shade, order after the unmade streets, and steps from the courtyard to the two rooms Emami rented: his home for the last four years.

The concrete front room was bare, apart from the shelves of books on one wall. Emami went and borrowed a chair from a neighbour for me. The bareness of the room – speaking not so much of poverty as of the simplicity of the theological student, concerned only to propagate the faith – so staggered Mehrdad that he made a note of it in his notebook. On the shelves were various sets of books on theology, philosophy, and jurisprudence, among them the five volumes (in cream-and-green binding) of Khomeini's great work of jurisprudence on all aspects of buying and selling (not known to me until that moment). The philosophy books included a Persian translation of Bertrand Russell's *Problems of Philosophy*. (No royalties for the Russell estate, though: Iran didn't belong to the international copyright convention.) Emami said, when I asked, that the books students like himself used were published by various foundations, and the prices were reasonable. But his library would still have taken up a fair portion of the stipend he had got from his ayatollah.

Emami, now our host, and in his own dwelling, grew in graciousness and courtesy. The two-year-old son we had heard about was sleeping; otherwise, Emami said, the boy would have already been with us. He was busy but discreet in his attentions to Mehrdad and Kamran and me, and in his instructions to his wife, unseen, somewhere in the background, preparing the fried eggs and tomato that had been decided on by him and Mehrdad as the general dish, with Persian bread and white cheese (imported from Denmark, but halal) for me.

He brought in and spread an oilcloth on the floor. This oilcloth was a sacred thing, Mehrdad said, because bread was wrapped in it. It had to be clean and it had to be kept in a high place. Emami then began to bring in plates and other things. From time to time he stopped and talked with us, squatting on his knees and heels, his trousers tight over his muscular thighs, the silvery shirt showing his exercised shoulders and his flat stomach. He was content, he said again, when we began to eat. He was doing the work, the propagating of the faith, that he wanted to do.

I asked whether he knew about the loss of faith in some of the young, as was reported. He said it was no secret. 'Our enemies know our weakness.'

A gentle knock on the door, as from someone who didn't want to create too much of a disturbance. This time it wasn't food that was being sent in by Emami's unseen wife, but her son, rested and at peace but a little shaky after his deep sleep, which still showed in his face.

Watermelon followed the egg and tomato. I asked Emami who were the enemies he had mentioned earlier. He said the countries of the West; they wanted to wipe out Islam. He said this with the same gentleness he had said everything else.

Our lunch was over. The dishes were cleared away, and Emami folded the oilcloth with deliberation, bringing the four corners together, twice over, before taking it outside. Then he passed his son back to his wife. After that – all distractions now out of the way – he and Kamran began to talk. They talked about the war. Emami said that in the last year of the war he went to do Islamic propaganda at the front. How often? He said he went on four occasions; altogether he was at the front for about two or three months. He gave some lectures. Kamran asked whether this was all that the clerics did, give lectures. Emami said no, he knew some clerics who fought. But he himself hadn't fought. For him the war was a spiritual experience.

He was content, but he knew he hadn't done enough. His house was far away from the teaching schools, and travel and household jobs took up much of his time. But recently he had got a bicycle; that was a great help.

Emami wanted to take us after lunch to one of the theological schools. We had no one to say goodbye to – his wife had remained unseen, and the boy had been taken away – and we stepped down without ceremony into the little courtyard, and then almost at once we were in the bright rubbled street in the desert. We drove back towards the centre of the town, to the school Emami had in mind. The principal wasn't there, and the guard couldn't give permission for us to look around.

Emami directed Kamran to another school. It was a modern building in yellow brick in a wide street lined on both sides with trees and a water channel. Some students – a flurry of gowns, tunics, and turbans in the yard beyond the water channel – had arrived for a class; some more were riding up on motor-scooters. They looked clean and healthy and – there was no other word – prosperous. Emami came back. He had seen the principal: we could look around.

We took off our shoes in the entrance hall, put them in big pigeon-holes for shoes, and walked up on fitted carpet to the floor above. All the time students came in. Some of them had a drink at the water cooler before they took off their shoes. They were soon quite a crowd. They didn't talk; some of them looked anxious. The sound that came from them as they went up the wide carpeted steps in their socks was the sound of their clothes. In the carpeted open area at the top of the steps students who had failed in a certain subject were sitting on the floor and writing their examination again. There was an element of punishment and public shame in this public rewriting of an examination. The students had no desk or writing boards, and some of them were in extraordinary writing postures: sitting on crossed legs and leaning so far forward to write on the floor that all the upper body seemed stretched out.

The principal was an old and kindly man, impressive with his turban and dyed beard, a figure of antique wisdom. He introduced us in his small office to three of his lecturers, sitting formally side by side. One lecturer did Christianity (and spoke English), another did Islamic Sects, and the third did Islamic Theology. Mehrdad said that 'theology' was not a correct rendering of the Arabic word, and there was a little amiable dispute about this between Mehrdad and the three lecturers, the principal looking benignly on. What that subject was, rather, Mehrdad said, was an analysis of the traditions connected with the Prophet: old learning, hardening century by century, and commentary by commentary, into what might or might not be considered true traditions, important because they could be used to establish or challenge laws.

The principal then took us on a tour of his new college building. It was rich and splendid. In the lecture rooms the chairs and desks were new and solid. In the library there were sets and sets and rows and rows of new books, with here and there a student sitting on the floor beside the bookshelves.

The lower floor was for what the principal called special projects. One scholar and one special project to a room. After having gone through the lecture rooms one by one, I didn't feel I could do the special-project rooms. I said so, but Mehrdad might have softened what I said, because the principal seemed to pay no attention.

He pushed open a door, the first in the corridor. We surprised the scholar resting or napping on the floor, with a blanket and a pillow. There were books and slips of paper everywhere, on the floor, on the table, on the shelves. The principal said the scholar in this room was an historian of repute (and someone I later talked to in Tehran said that this was so). The historian, horribly surprised, reached out for his white skullcap and pressed it on his head. He was middle-aged, even elderly. He scrambled up as best he could, gathered his brown blanket around him, and, slightly bowed, came to the door. He had a fine old face; his skin was light-brown and smooth. He held the brown blanket around his middle the way the women in the streets held their black chadors below their chin.

The principal said that the historian was writing a book called *The Political History of the World*.

The historian, recovering fast from his surprise, said to me, 'Do you know a book about Gandhi and the Muslims?'

I didn't know of any. But, to encourage the historian, I said, 'It's an interesting subject. The man who first called Gandhi out to South Africa in the 1890s was an Indian Muslim merchant. So you might say he started Gandhi on his political life.'

The historian paid no attention. He said, 'Send me the book.' He went back a couple of steps and took a piece of paper from the top of a pile of books. 'Here. Take my name and address. Send me the book.'

I said he might get the Indian embassy in Tehran to advise him.

He appeared not to hear. Coming close up to the door again, he said, 'Take it as a memory. Take it as a gift. You know, I have been doing a certain amount of work on Zionism for my history of the world. I have begun to feel that while the Zionists made the United States their first idol or false god, they are turning India into their second idol. I don't know whether you know that the crown of India was handed to the British by a Jew, Disraeli. The fact isn't as widely known as it should be. The British sword was sharpened in India by Jews. I very much fear that the Zionists are going to wound India again. They will kill Gandhi again and exile his thought again.'

Mehrdad, translating, broke off to ask me, 'Was Gandhi exiled?'

I said, 'Perhaps he's speaking symbolically.'

The historian, plucking at his blanket and cap, and politely stepping back during this exchange between Mehrdad and me, came forward again at the end of it and looked ready to go on. But we decided – to the principal's clear, if well-mannered, relief – to get away and leave the historian to his rest.

We went to the shrine of Hazrat Masumeh. Kamran, in spite of his cynicism about things generally, had begun to grumble that in the morning, at the start of the journey, he hadn't put anything in an alms box, hadn't made that offering, as he should have done. That was why he had had the trouble with the ignition and had to do all that running about from garage to garage. Now, making it as much of a performance as he could, he stuffed a folded old banknote through the slot of one of the alms boxes in the street outside the shrine. And, as though that wasn't enough, when we were in the shrine courtyard he left us and went to the tomb, to say a prayer for a safe run back.

While Kamran was doing that, a man took Mehrdad to one side and asked about me. 'Is he a Muslim?' (It might have been my dark glasses and Banana Republic felt hat.) Mehrdad said yes, to save trouble; and the man was satisfied. But there could have been trouble. Technically the shrine was a mosque, and non-Muslims shouldn't have been there, not even in the courtyard. There had been no question like that from anyone in 1979; Behzad, my guide and interpreter, had taken me everywhere. I became unhappy in the courtyard after this. Revolutionary Guards were about, and I didn't want to be stopped.

We didn't stay long. Kamran came out from the illuminated tomb, his prayers said, his expression tight and chastened. We started for Tehran. The sun went down round and red behind the salt cliffs. When we were closer to Tehran than to Qum, Kamran began to talk about Emami and his trips to the front. He said, 'They' – the clerics – 'didn't get the real meaning of the war. Let's even say Emami went six times to the front. Two days going, two days coming back. So he would have spent twenty-four days travelling. The rest of the time he would have been preparing people to fight. He would have been talking. He would have simply doing his job.' When we got nearer Tehran Kamran became more irreverent about Emami. He said, 'Emami is doing quite well, in that little flat, whatever he says. He is living there on his own. I am still living with my parents.'

A little later, the lights of Khomeini's shrine now beginning to be seen, he raised the matter of his payment for the long day. I thought Mehrdad had settled that beforehand, but Mehrdad now said he hadn't. He said in English, 'It is better to do these things in a friendly way.'

Mehrdad said something in Persian to Kamran. Kamran didn't reply. Instead, he put on the car's roof light, pulled back his left sleeve, and raised his forearm to show a long, jagged shrapnel wound.

Mehrdad said to me in English, 'We must do this in a friendly way.'

We made certain calculations, pricing kilometres and then hours, adding the two figures up, and knocking a little off the rather large sum that resulted. For a while – Khomeini's shrine now behind us – Mehrdad kept this figure secret, kept Kamran dangling. When the lights of Tehran began to show he put the figure to Kamran. It was immediately accepted. I counted the notes out and put them in an envelope. Mehrdad gave Kamran the envelope. Kamran put the envelope on the dashboard and talked no more about money.

8

Cancer

MEHRDAD HAD a friend called Feyredoun. Feyredoun, who was in his early twenties, like Mehrdad, was doing his military service in the air force. He came home to Tehran at weekends. He was tall and slender and sharp-faced. His English (like Mehrdad's, all acquired in Iran) was fluent, once he got going, and capable of great complexity. Feyredoun, having grown up in the isolation of revolutionary Iran, was hungry for books, ideas, philosophical discussion.

After one such discussion I said to Mehrdad, casually, when we were talking of something else, that his friend Feyredoun was a religious man. I meant only that he was a man of faith; but the word 'religious' rankled with Mehrdad. He raised the matter some days later when we were driving about Tehran; and it was one of the things I thought we should talk about more fully when I went to his house.

We went there late one afternoon. We surprised his mother. From the reception room, as we entered, we could see straight through an open door to a side room where she was lying on a bed. She knew we were coming, but she must have misjudged the time. She half stood up, half rolled off the bed. Her head was bare, and she bit at the lower end of her chiffon-like headcover. She was short and plump and matronly, though she might have been only in her forties; she radiated kindliness. She came from the north-west and was light-eyed.

Mehrdad's father was there, too, just for a little, to be introduced to his son's guest. He was tall, darker than his wife, as handsome as his son, but a little more frail, even willowy. I might have thought him a man of low energy, perhaps with a medical condition. But his son had said, twice, that his father was not a brave man, was a man who always looked for safety and ran with the crowd (now displaying pictures of the Shah, now destroying a book of his daughter's, a school prize, which had pictures of the royal family). And this was the man I saw, the man who was not brave; though, really, he had shown himself a man of resource after the revolution had done away with his safe banking job. He had picked himself up and gone into business in a small way, buying and selling, and had done well enough to give his family this middle-class house in an outer district of Tehran. But the difficult everyday things that people do can sometimes be taken for granted by their children.

The reception room was big, with carpets spread side by side – a confusion of pattern and colour, as in some Persian painting – to cover all the floor. The dining table, with flowers and fruit, was in a corner, and it was there, until dinner time, that Mehrdad and I sat and talked.

Mehrdad said, 'What do you mean by a religious person? I have a problem with the word you use. You called Feyredoun religious, and he himself thinks he is a pagan.'

I asked, 'What does he mean by pagan?'

'A pagan is someone outside the public religions. Here we have ways of judging whether a person is religious. The first way is their appearance. Beards. It has been recommended in Islam that men must have beards. There are special rules about shaving the beard and cutting the moustache. You can cut the beard with scissors, but not razor blades.'

'It's in the Koran?'

'No. *Hadith*, the traditions connected with the Prophet.'

'Did you hear about it when you were growing up?'

'Yes. But the recommendation became more known after the revolution. I have known people who, when they have to send in photographs for job applications, especially grow their beard. There are other rules. If they are growing a moustache it mustn't be so long that it gets wet when they drink water. This is also a *hadith*. All these things are written in *Bahar-al-Anvar* and other *hadith* books. In the old days religious people had long hair. But now they don't.'

'Why?'

'Nobody knows. There is something else. It isn't general. If you bow down to pray you rest your forehead on a cake or tablet of earth from one of the holy sites of the faith. Even in Qum they make a lot of these cakes of earth. After a time your skin darkens or alters colour where it rests or falls on these earth-cakes. They say their prayers five times a day, and sometimes there are special night prayers. These special night prayers involve a lot of bowing and rubbing of the forehead against the earth.'

It was something he had pointed out to me in Qum about Emami, the darker central part of his forehead, another aspect of Emami's piety as a *talebeh*, like the bare concrete front room of his apartment. But you had to know about the practice before you could look for signs of it. Once you knew, it was easy to spot. Some very pious people had something like a scorch mark on their forehead; this was because they heated the cakes of earth for their prayers.

Mehrdad said, 'There is something else. Religious people use rose-water on their body. They smell of it, during Mohurram especially.' Mohurram, the Shia mourning month. 'And they are shy people – for the sake of appearances. When they are talking to a woman they put their head down. Of course, looking at a woman has special rules. Let me see how many rules there are about it in Khomeini's book.'

He went and brought back a big paperback: yet another book of rules by Khomeini, in addition to the five volumes I had seen in Emami's library about buying and selling.

Mehrdad said, 'This one is called *Resaleh* or *Tozih-al Masa-el. Rescript* or *Explanation of Problems*. There are ten basic rules about looking at women in this book of Khomeini's. The book itself deals with three thousand problems.'

'Are people looking up things all the time? Do those rules really help people?'

'To me the rules about beards have no logic. They don't say why. They just say, "Do it." And I cannot be a religious person because I listen to most kinds of prohibited music. We have asked them a lot about it. They say that music is prohibited if it changes your mood or feelings. That's nonsense. Because you cannot listen to music of any sort and keep your mood.'

'What kind of music is prohibited?'

'Music for dancing. The music of love songs. Western music is prohibited, apart from the classics. Indian popular music is also prohibited.

There was a time when buying musical instruments was prohibited. Let me look it up. Here. It is Khomeini's problem number 2067. And I don't say prayers. So I'm not a religious person. I never fast. I never go to a mosque. And I don't obey any of the rules, though I know most of them. I have studied law and know most of them. Some of the rules I make fun of. For example, there is the rule about blood money. This is: if you kill somebody you pay blood money to his family. The rule now is that a woman is worth half as much as a man. If you kill a man you pay the full price. At the moment the full price is two million *toumans*, twenty million rials. About five thousand dollars. You pay half of that if you kill a woman.'

'You think people need these rules?'

'I'm coming to that. After we see the problems of life we begin to think. We try to stand on our own feet and try to get to some kind of resolution. Religious people don't like it. Because it means we are putting the whole system away. We believe in God most of us, but we think like Voltaire.'

That was what I had meant when I had said that Feyredoun was a religious man. But in Iran, as I now saw, words like 'religious' and 'pagan' had Iranian meanings.

Mehrdad said, 'God is needed for life. But not those meaningless rules. People don't worry about it. We have rules about young people being together. It is illegal, but people do it. I have a friend. She is having troubles with her boyfriend. She is not a virgin. By this same fellow. He is now going away; he is going to leave her. And she is praying regularly. When the pressure is on, people turn to religion. We need God. In a poor country with a lot of problems we need someone at the top.'

'Why do you think the religious people place such stress on rules?'

'They are the rule-makers. If you deny the rules you are denying the rule-maker. If you put the rule-maker away you are against the Leader. If you oppose the Leader you are against the Holy Prophet. If you are against the Holy Prophet you are against the Holy Book, and the Holy Book comes from God. Someone against God must be killed. But who does the killing? Only the rule-maker. Not God.'

There were rules; everything was controlled. It wasn't only the chador and headdress for women; or boys and girls not walking together; or women not singing on the radio and television; or certain kinds of music not being played. There was a complete censorship, of magazines, newspapers, books, television. And helicopters flew over North Tehran looking for satellite dishes; just as the Guards walked in the park to watch the boys and girls; or entered houses to look for alcohol and opium; or, as I was to see in far-off Shiraz, the local morals police did the rounds even of the tourist hotels to make their presence felt.

In 1979 and 1980 the missionaries of the Islamic revival, echoing one another, as though their copy had been provided by a central source, had endlessly said that Islam was a complete way of life; and in Iran now it was possible to see political Islam as a complete form of control. Mr Parvez, the founder-editor of the *Tehran Times*, had said to me not long after I had arrived, 'They want to control, your way of sitting here, and your way of talking.' I don't think I had understood what he was saying. It took time to understand how far the restrictions reached, though it was easy enough to state what they were; and it took time to understand how they were deforming people's lives.

Mehrdad's sister was unmarried, and had little chance of getting married, since too many men of suitable age had been killed in the eight-year war. She simply stayed at home when she came home from work: silent, full of inward rage, her unhappiness a shadow over the house and a source of worry for her parents, who couldn't work out a future for her. It was too difficult for her to go out; and now she had lost the will. In this she was like the fifteen-year-old daughter of a teacher I had got to know. This girl had already learned that she could be stopped by the Guards and questioned if she was alone on the street. She hated the humiliation, and now she didn't like to go out. The world had narrowed for her just when it should have opened out.

In February 1980 I had seen young women in guerrilla garb among the students camped outside the seized US embassy: Che Guevara gear, the theatre of revolution. I remembered one plump young woman, in her khakis, coming out of a low tent on this freezing afternoon with a mug of steaming tea for one of the men: her face bright with the idea of serving the revolution and the warriors of the revolution. Most of those young people, 'Muslim Students Following the Line of Ayatollah Khomeini', would now have been dead or neutered, like all the other communist or left-wing groups. I don't think that young woman with the mug could have dreamed that the revolution to which she was contributing – posters on the embassy wall and on trees were comparing the Iranian revolution with the Nicaraguan, making both appear part of a universal movement forward – would have ended in this way, with an old-fashioned tormenting of women, and with the helicopters in the sky looking for satellite dishes.

The very gear and style of revolution now had another meaning. The beards were not Che Guevara beards, but good Islamic beards, not cut by razors; and the green guerrilla outfits were now the uniform of the enforcers of the religious law.

No one I met spoke of any kind of revolution as a possibility. That idea, so loved by Iranians of an earlier generation, had been spoilt now, as in the old USSR; 'revolution' was a word that had been taken over by the religious state. No one ever spoke of the possibility of political action. There were no means, and no leaders in sight. No new ideas could be floated. The apparatus of control was complete. The actual rulers, though their photographs appeared everywhere, were far away; government here, as someone said, was 'occult'. And still, in the general inanition, there was a feeling that something was about to happen. It made people nervous.

One afternoon, as we were driving up into the mountains above Tehran, Mehrdad, after seeming to say that people had learned how to live with the restrictions, abruptly said the opposite. He said, 'Everybody is frightened. I am frightened. My father and mother are frightened.' (Poor father, again.) 'They are not sure what the future will bring for them or for us, their children. They are not so worried for me. I am an adult now and can look after myself. But my brother is very young. The eight years or so he has to live before he becomes an adult are going to be very dangerous years.'

With this insecurity, certain fantasies had taken hold. The most extraordinary was that Khomeini had been a British or European agent. I had heard it first from Mr Parvez, and had thought it part of his paranoia. But then I had heard it from many other people. There had been a meeting in the French West Indian island of Guadeloupe, according to this story, and the Powers had decided to foist Khomeini on the Iranian people. The Iranians were simple people; they could be persuaded by skilled propaganda to demonstrate for anything; people had joined the demonstrations against the Shah not out of conviction, but simply to do what everybody else was doing. The establishing of an Islamic state in Iran was an anti-Islamic plot by the Powers, to teach Muslims a lesson, and especially to punish the people of Iran. And, as if answering those fantasies, there were even signs of the faith being questioned in certain aspects.

Mr Parvez had said, 'The war [against Iraq] was fought in the name of Islam. It was a blessing in disguise. Without the war people wouldn't have got so fed up with Islam.' That had seemed extreme. But then I had detected wisps and shadows of religious uncertainty in some people's conversation. Just as – in these fantasies issuing out of a people stretched to the limit by revolution, war, financial stringency, and the religious state – it was said that Iranians were not really responsible for the Iranian revolution, so I heard that Iranians were not really responsible for the more dramatic aspects of the Shia faith. The bloody scourgings of Mohurram, the mourning month: the idea was really imported from Europe, from the Catholics; it had nothing to do with the original faith.

I talked about this to Mehrdad. He said, 'It's something habitual. Our enemies are always responsible. Blaming others, not ourselves.'

I had been given the name of Mrs Seghir. She lived abroad now, part of the Iranian dispersion. She had returned to see her elderly parents, and had been in Tehran for some time. When I telephoned she invited me to lunch; and she and a woman friend came to the hotel to take me to the apartment. This was to conform to the rules: it wouldn't have done for Mrs Seghir or the friend to come alone to meet an unknown man.

The apartment was in an American-style block where things had decayed. The lift opened into a narrow little lobby that served two apartments. The lobby was more than shabby; it was dirty, with a nasty scrap of carpet. The gloom continued inside. In the sitting area of the open-plan room old Louis XVI reproduction chairs and a settee were like things not sat on. A wall, ridged with old lines of electric cord, was hung with a set of European miniatures of no value, flowerpieces or landscapes, one to a frame, in two unsteady, widely spaced rows. A long dining table was at the other end of the room, next to the kitchen. The kitchen looked very much used.

In a small room beside the kitchen a man was sitting at a table just inside the open door. He was very old – but very old – with the pigment gone in irregular patches from his face. He sat at an angle to the table, with his back half to the door, and with the side of his face showing. This was Mrs Seghir's father; he was ninety-one. Mrs Seghir's mother, in the sitting area of the room, told me that; she herself was eighty.

Mrs Seghir's friend, who had come with her to the hotel, was now busy in the kitchen with Mrs Seghir. The friend was divorced. She was friendly and fat, bursting out of her long skirt, and she had fat, greedy lips, made for food alone. She was delighted to help in the kitchen, and was fast on her high heels.

There was a French window from the sitting area to a balcony. It was half open, and the traffic noise was very loud. I looked out. One side of the balcony was a jumble of old cardboard and brooms and cleaning material, and on the other side there was a covered easel or chest, or so it appeared. This was the satellite dish. Mrs Seghir needed it for the news; she would be quite lost in Iran without the world news. The camouflage was to protect the dish from the helicopters; they were searching even now.

The food was laid out, in a smell of warm oil: *coo-coo*, which was a kind of Iranian quiche, rice, mashed aubergine. The old man – his face dreadfully damaged by age, his eyes very dark and shadowed below the pigment-less forehead and beside the blotched cheeks – came to the table, a belt around the trousers, some inches below the waistband and the belt-loops. He was helped by his wife, Mrs Seghir's mother. She, very small and thin, her eyes weak behind her glasses, was still wifely and solicitous: such emotions go on to the end: it was affecting.

The fat lady talked about the north of England. A relation of hers lived there, a professional woman married to a professional man from Bangladesh. She had gone to visit the couple and had been taken with the good manners of the English. She spoke as though she really knew; yet I felt that what she was saying about England hadn't come so much from her own experience as from the television she might have watched when she was over there.

The *coo-coo* was cut up for the old man by his wife. He helped himself to other things; but at the very end he lost control and, holding his head low over his plate, appeared to have an accident, to be a little sick. He got up after that – he had never spoken – and made his way back to his room. Carefully, he eased himself down into his chair, sitting again at an angle to the table, with his back to the open door. He had become very slow; the accident had wearied him; and now with painful deliberation – his world reduced to the performing of these small acts – he took out a pen, took up a folded newspaper, undid one fold, was content with that, held the paper down, and seemed ready to go on with the crossword puzzle.

I now noticed a Qum silk carpet on the floor, and a purple velvet cover on the coffee table with heavy, old embroidery, three lines of roses and vines done in silver thread mixed with gold: something done a long time ago for the extravagance, the luxury, the expense. Mrs Seghir said that the embroidered velvet cover had been a gift to her from her mother. There were cut glass dishes on the cover with sugared jelly-balls and a saffron-coloured candy made in Qum.

Later, when Mrs Seghir was in the kitchen again, helping the fat lady with the dessert, the mother pointed to the chandelier and said 'Qajar arms'. I had seen the chandelier and, as it were, not seen it, finding it too oppressive. Mrs Seghir's mother said again, 'Qajar arms'. The Qajars, the dynasty overthrown in the 1920s by the father of the late Shah. I got up and looked at the engraving of the Qajar arms, quite hard to see, on the many glass chimneys of the chandelier. There was a circle of those chimneys, and they were like the chimneys of old-fashioned oil lamps; and within and below that circle were tinkling cut-glass pendants of varying size, intricately worked. Mrs Seghir's mother said, 'Baccarat'. I saw for the first time that – in this small low room that needed paint and less clutter on the balcony and less noise from the traffic – there were two of these chandeliers. They filled the upper space. To be aware of the two was to feel choked.

Mrs Seghir, her smock dancing over her chunky hips and her black hose, finished her kitchen work at last and came and sat with me. I asked about her husband. He had died from cancer, she said. I had touched a grief that was still raw. He had become frightened after the revolution, she said. He was an engineer, highly trained, with an important job with the government. He hadn't lost his job, but the stress had destroyed him. Five years or so after the revolution he had complained one day of not feeling well, and they had gone to the doctor, as they would have done for some minor complaint. Cancer was diagnosed in the colon. It called for immediate surgery. The operation was done within days, and was successful. But then a later X-ray showed that there was cancer in the lung as well.

On a little oval table, a reproduction piece, set not far from the half-open French window, were photographs of the family: Mrs Seghir herself at different ages, her daughters, and, in a large frame, a photo-graph of her husband taken some time before his illness (he hadn't wanted his children to see him when he became very ill). The photo-graph was of a handsome, good-natured man, immediately attractive and fine. The photographs, in varying frames, were close together on the little oval table, like the picture-holders among the elms and pines and oleanders and the fading flags in the Martyrs' Cemetery. And they too, in a way, were martyrs of the revolution.

Feyredoun was going to be home on leave that afternoon, and Mehrdad and I went to his family flat. The flat, in a city street, was much smaller than Mrs Seghir's. It was darker, much less opulent in intention, and now clearly with little money; but it had something of the same atmosphere. It had too much furniture, the remains of old family style. The flat was on the first floor, and it was full of traffic noise, not the roar that came to the top of Mrs Seghir's block and through her half-open French window, but a more immediate and more jagged noise that came in all the time through the open metal windows. There were two dining tables in the small sitting room. The longer one, which was at right angles to the other, was prepared for us. It had chocolates in a glass dish, fruit in a larger dish, and tea in small, gilt-decorated glasses with handles.

Feyredoun's mother was in the kitchen. She called Mehrdad. He went to her, and they talked for a while. When Mehrdad came back to the sitting room he was distressed.

He said, 'I've been hearing miseries. Sometimes I think I can't bear any more.'

Feyredoun's mother worked as a pharmacist in a hospital. There was a gardener there whose son had gone to the war. The boy hadn't returned, but the gardener never believed that his son was dead. He always said that his son was going to come home again. The gardener was a devout, bearded man, so bearded and devout that people at the hospital thought he might be an ideological spy, keeping an eye on the staff. The war at last ended. Prisoners began to return. Lists of return-ing prisoners were printed, and the gardener always came to ask Feyredoun's mother whether his son's name was among them. The name never was.

About three months before, there had been a mass funeral for three thousand unknown martyrs whose remains had been recovered from old battlefields. The air force had flown the boxes to the Martyrs' Cemetery. Each box was covered with the Iranian flag (green, white and red with the emblem of Allah in the middle). The boxes were stacked up in pyramids. Mehrdad had seen the ceremony on television and had been overwhelmed. The men whose remains were being buried had died in army uniform; Mehrdad, doing his military service, had worn that uniform; he had felt linked to the dead men. Telling the story in the sitting room, he plucked at his shirt, to indicate how much the uniform had meant to him.

One of the boxes contained the remains – 'two bones', as Mehrdad said – of the gardener's son. Up to that moment the gardener had been fortified by his faith. Now he began to grieve. Just a week or two ago the gardener had died. There had been an autopsy at the hospital a few days before; it showed that the gardener's stomach had been eaten up with cancer. That was what Feyredoun's mother had wanted to talk to Mehrdad about. That was what had sent Mehrdad out to me saying, 'I've been hearing miseries.'

When, many days before (which now seemed to me like many weeks before), I had asked Mehrdad what he felt about the war, he had said, 'I feel nothing about it.' He hadn't meant that. What he had meant was what he had just said: 'Sometimes I think I can't bear any more.'

There were rules and more rules. But young people, those who had known nothing but the religious state, were learning their own ways of disobedience. They had their bodies; their bodies were their own. There were stories of a sexual revolution among the young; and there were other forms of disobedience.

Feyredoun's brother was nineteen. He was just five or six years younger than Feyredoun, but he belonged to a different generation. Feyredoun was a philosopher, a doubter, intellectually curious. Only a wall, he said, separated him from his brother. But while there were serious books on Feyredoun's side of the wall, on his brother's side there were photographs of football teams and a 'heavy-metal' pop group, and a swastika. Feyredoun's brother was a Nazi. He said that as an Iranian he was Aryan; therefore he was a Nazi. And he took being a Nazi seriously.

Sitting at the big table in the main room of the flat, Feyredoun told me that his brother and his friends had driven out the Jewish family who used to live next door. They had slashed the tyres of the family's car and broken their windows. The family had not only left Tehran; they had left the country.

Iran was not Europe or the United States. Iran had its own stresses, and the story Feyredoun was telling, with his own strange innocence, wasn't just about young Iranian Nazis. His story was more about the difference now between the generations, the difference that five or six years had made. There was another aspect of this difference: Feyredoun's Nazi brother and his friends were not frightened. Their principal sport now was to go out taunting the Guards, challenging them to arrest them. There were consequences: Feyredoun's brother had often spent a day or so in jail.

The brother had been in the sitting room when Mehrdad and I arrived. He was sallow and very thin. I didn't know anything about him then, and hadn't thought about his black clothes. He had been polite but withdrawn, and I had seen him as someone else deprived and poor and lost, without an idea of a future, and more desperate than his brother or Mehrdad. Now that I had heard about him I wanted to talk more to him. But – and this, as Feyredoun said, was another sign of cultural change, a break with the past – the boy had gone out of the flat without telling anyone.

The revolution had bred strange children.

Feyredoun and Mehrdad took me to a new part of Tehran that was booming. It was like another city. It served the new rich, the people who had done well out of the revolution. It was in the north-east of Tehran, and was about ten years old. There was a new commercial centre with expensive shops that served the new condominiums going up on one side. The people who lived there were traders and people who were cutting deals, Mehrdad said; not productive people. But in the commercial centre their daughters moved with an ease and an allure that were immediately noticeable: high-heels, slender legs in stone-washed jeans, stylish short chadors.

'And the skin,' Mehrdad said, with his own sensitivity to the beauty of young girls. The good skin that came with good air and good food and an idea of the future: the skin his own sister didn't have.

Another kind of person, another kind of disobedience. In the high, well-lighted watch-post at the entrance to the commercial centre, a young girl stood blank and unabashed before the Guard. 'He's got her,' Feyredoun said. Some un-Islamic behaviour; something against the rules, something perhaps about showing too much of her hair. Mehrdad said, 'He'll talk to her and let her go.'

When we were in the coffee shop Mehrdad showed a girl in the reflection in the glass. He said, 'She's drugged.' The girl's eyes were blurred, unfocused; her scarf had fallen very low at the back of her head. In the corner a khaki-clad Guard was talking to the proprietor. It was the big, yellow-jacketed waiter who came to the girl and told her to watch her chador. She merely touched the top of her head; and after a while the Guard, perhaps not wishing to make a scene, or to appear to have been challenged, went away. A little later, when the girl staggered out, I saw that her long chestnut hair was hanging out of her scarf at the back. It was a fashion, Mehrdad had told me some days before, and also a display of disobedience.

Later, on the road outside the commercial centre, we saw a group of young people who had just been searched by the motor-cycle Guards – for videos, compact discs, drugs, or other forbidden things.

9

The Two Tribes

ISFAHAN AND Shiraz, famous cities with romantic names, were receiving foreign tourists once again. I went to Isfahan first. I had no idea what to expect. No special tourist or cultural motif attached to the name. Java, much further off, had the mystical Buddhist pyramid of Borobudur and the Hindu towers of Prambanam; India had the Taj Mahal and the sculptured temple towers of the South. But Isfahan, like Samarkand, was its romantic name alone. Such ideas as I had of its glory had come indirectly, through Indian painting. From certain over-wrought imperial Mogul pictures I knew that for the emperor Jehangir (who ruled from 1605 to 1627) the India of his empire and the Persia of Shah Abbas (who ruled from 1587 to 1629) were the central powers of the globe; no other country really mattered. Britain (even after Queen Elizabeth, and the defeat of the Spanish Armada, and Shakespeare) was far away, on the margin; the ambassador sent by King James in 1618 had a hard time getting attention from Jehangir.

A Hindu artist of Jehangir's court spent six years with a Mogul embassy in Isfahan doing portraits of Shah Abbas, to enable Jehangir to understand, and at the same time to be at ease with, his great rival. It was those – sometimes deliberately shrunken – portraits of a short-legged Shah Abbas (with a curved sword almost too big for him), rather than any concrete idea of his great city, that I carried in my head. So – such is the power of caricature – I was not ready for the splendour and extent and cosmopolitanism of Isfahan, its breathtaking confidence and inventiveness and, always, the rightness of its proportions: the immense main square (bigger than St Mark's in Venice), the bridges, the domes of both mosques and of churches, the delicately-coloured tiles in whose colour and pattern and effects large and small one could lose oneself, the mighty halls of audience. It was possible to understand Jehangir's uneasiness: so much of Indian Mogul architecture was already here, in Shah Abbas's Isfahan, in addition to so much else.

Such glory here; a kindred glory in India. Yet in less than a hundred years after Jehangir the Mogul glory was over in India; and a hundred years after that India was a British colony. Iran never formally became a colony. Its fate was in some ways worse. When Europe, once so far away, made its presence felt, Iran dropped off the map. Its great monuments fell into decay (and never became as well known as the Indian monuments). And by the end of the nineteenth century its rulers were ready to hand over the country, and its people, to foreign concessionaires.

India, almost as soon as it became a British colony, began to be regenerated, began to receive the New Learning of Europe, to get the institutions that went with that learning. The first great Indian reformer, Raja Rammohun Roy, was born in 1772, before the French Revolution; Gandhi was born in 1869. Iran was to enter the twentieth century only with an idea of eastern kingship and the antiquated theological learning of places like Qum. Iran was to enter the twentieth century only with a capacity for pain and nihilism.

There was glory in Shah Abbas's Persia, but the glory was flawed. This, though, was not an idea I could put to my host and guide in Isfahan. He was a retired diplomat; he was full of his country's pain. His life hung between two poles. In the 1960s his father had wished to turn him into someone of English education. In the 1980s, after the revolution, and after he had retired from the foreign service, he had rejected the idea of travel abroad: in the wider world the humiliations of having an Iranian passport were too great. He lived on the remnant of a private income; and he also did a little teaching. Revolution and war had damaged him and exhausted his country; the old diplomat knew that. But he was a divided man still; he saw both the revolution and the war as necessary, and his stories of pain were ambiguous.

He had a friend, a teacher. The teacher was a Europeanised middle-class Iranian of the Shah's time. When the revolution came the teacher was in his late thirties; and the teacher's son was eleven. The boy's name was Farhad; it was the kind of old Iranian name – rather than an Arab or Islamic one – that middle-class people had been giving their children since the time of the reforms of the Shah's father.

After the revolution the teacher began to feel that his son was drifting away from him. In the second year of the war, when he was fourteen, the boy finally rejected his family and their ways. He discarded the name of Farhad and gave himself the Arab name of Maissam. Maissam was one of the early followers of the Prophet; he died a martyr. That was the road the teacher's son wished to travel.

Khomeini had said that the revolution had to concentrate on children and the younger generation. People over forty (like the teacher) were useless. (And Ayatollah Montazeri, the second-in-command, had gone further and said in poetic metaphor that dry trees should be cut down.) The words were not idle. Much energy had gone into indoctrinating the young; with the war, the needs of the revolution were great.

The old diplomat said, 'Young boys like to play with guns. So they would take them to the mosques and they used to show them the Israeli Uzi sub-machine-gun and other guns. These boys were fascinated, and at the same time they chanted slogans and prayers while someone related the story of the martyrs of Kerbala.' The unequal battle of Kerbala, the Shia tragedy and passion, unendingly rehearsed. "The victory of blood over the sword. Because the martyr wins eventually. And some of those young people used to inform on those of their friends who were Mujahid or belonged to the communist groups. They would ask them to bring news from their house and the houses of their friends, as a sort of revolutionary act.'

And then one day, without telling his parents anything, the teacher's son went to the mosque and volunteered, and was sent to the front.

'From what I heard later he became the commander of a small group defusing the land mines. He was a Basiji. In the beginning they didn't know how to defuse the land mines and they would send hundreds of the Basiji to defuse the mines. They had special shows for them before they joined. They would make up a man with some phosphorescent material, to suggest that the Imam Mehdi had been seen at the front on a white horse galloping in the distance.' Imam Mehdi: the Twelfth Imam of the Shias, for some centuries in hiding somewhere, waiting to return to the faithful. 'And they would give the Basiji a key round their

necks, which was a key to paradise. In those days there were jokes about
the keys to paradise being made in Japan, mass produced and imported.
But I should tell you that those boys *wanted* to go. I had some students
who volunteered. I remember the day the bus took them away. The bus
was waiting and one boy was trembling in my arms. I told him, "If you
are not sure you don't have to go." He said, "I have to go, but I'm
scared." They would put them in the buses and drive them around the
city, and they were heroes, going to fight Satan and open the way to
Kerbala.' Kerbala, giving its name to the ancient sacrificial Shia battle,
but still the name of a real place in Iraq.

'It's the custom in Iran when somebody goes on a journey that he
should pass under the Koran two or three times. The Koran is kissed by
the head of the family and held over the head of the person going away.
But for those Basiji, when they were sending them to the front, a
mullah would do that, kissing the Koran and holding it above the head.
And then they would give them the headbands, red or green. Of course
it's a nice ceremony of farewell. When I was young and had to go away
my mother would do that ceremony over me with the Koran. When I
got into the car she would pour a vessel of water behind me on the
ground. Prayers would be said over the water before it was poured, and
they would blow over it. Water is a sacred element in Iran, and the ceremony is almost certainly pre-Islamic.'

After some time the teacher heard that his son had been wounded
and was in hospital in Tabriz. He went there and brought him home
and nursed him. When the boy was well enough again he went back to
the front. This happened many times.

'After six years he finally returned home. The war was over. He was
quite depressed. His parents didn't know what to do with him. He
spent most of the time in his room. He didn't want to see other people.
At last one day the teacher went into the room. He saw the boy sitting
cross-legged in the centre of the room, and the carpet was spread with
photographs, group "All these people are dead." They were his friends
at the front.'

The war was receding; things were cooling down; there was less of
the old frenzy or zeal. Slowly, yielding to his parents' love, the boy
recovered. He changed his haircut; he began to wear European or
international clothes again. He joined a university. The Basiji were
privileged; they could get into universities even if they didn't pass the
entrance examination. Piece by piece, then, the personality which he

had discarded six or seven years before as a boy was restored to him as a young man. He went back to listening to pop music. He dropped the Arab name he had given himself and became Farhad once more.

The diplomat said, 'He thinks now he'll be a doctor. It's all been a dream. He doesn't talk about the war. I know that many of them – boys like him – were disappointed. But as there were special privileges for them as Basiji they now have a split personality.'

A split personality for Maissam-Farhad; and a split personality for the old diplomat as well, because to be Iranian was to have a special faith, a special version of the Arab faith; and the old diplomat knew in his bones – and it was part of his pain – that, draining and inconclusive and terrible as the war had been, it had to be fought.

He said, 'If those boys hadn't done those sacrifices Saddam and the Iraqis would have eaten up a quarter of Iran. In a way Khomeini can be regarded as one of the makers of Iranian nationalism. He revived the old Arab-Iranian confrontation after so many years. One of the names Saddam had given himself was "Victor of Ghadessiah". That was the big Iranian defeat at the hands of Arabs in the very early days of the Muslim invasion. In the time of the caliph Omar, ten years after Mohammed. And Saddam called Iranians "Magis", Zoroastrians.' Worshippers at the fire-temple, adherents of the principal pre-Islamic religion of Iran.

The old diplomat was a wise and cultivated man; yet the Iraqi taunts – which were like taunts in a schoolyard – still had the power to wound him: the taunt about the Iranian pagan past, the past of fire-worship and unbelief, the past before Islam, and the other taunt, about the way Islam had come to Iran, with conquest by the Arabs, energetically propagating their new faith. The battle of Ghadessiah had taken place in AD 637, but it was as fresh as the defeat at Kerbala. Persia had a long history; for close on a thousand years before Ghadessiah it had been a power; it had challenged Greece and wounded Rome. But that past was dead; it might have belonged to another people; it didn't make up for the defeat at Ghadessiah. The Iran in people's consciousness began with the coming of Islam, began with that defeat. It gave a special edge to the faith in Iran, and a special passion to the people.

The teacher's son had lived out the contradictions of that passion. Rejecting his family's Shah-inspired Europeanised ways, embracing the faith, he had given himself the name of a very early Arab martyr. That had led to the Basiji headband, the key to paradise around his neck, and the war against the Arab who called himself the victor of Ghadessiah.

Children, too, had a split personality, the diplomat said. It was how they resisted whatever was too crushing and preserved some part of themselves.

He told a story of a couple he knew, people like himself, suffering, disaffected, but still nationalist. They had a nine-year-old daughter in a local Hizbullah school. One day they received a summons from the school principal. When they went to the school they found that their daughter had become the best reciter of the Koran at school. She was so good the school had decided to give her a prize in the presence of her parents. The parents knew nothing of this talent of their daughter's. In fact, when they had received the summons they had been frightened. They had no idea what their daughter might have been saying about them.

The diplomat said, 'It's a strange way to live now.'

These were the stories I heard while I walked and drove about Isfahan, while I considered domes and tiles, arches and vaulting, and, at night, the lights of the arcaded bridges on the river. Much had been restored; but much seemed perishable. Brick was perishable; and in some dirt alleys the bare brick back of fine buildings seemed about to return to clay. In some such unsettling way a great pain, physical and mental, lay below the civility of the old diplomat. Pain was really the subject of his stories; and sometimes a story, though presented as the experience of someone he knew, had a quality of folk myth, something fabricated out of the general need, just as, at certain times in communities, jokes appear and make the rounds, made up by no one but contributed to by everyone. Such a story was the story about the 'piece of meat'.

An eye specialist was asked by a middle-aged lady in a chador to examine the eyesight of a patient, a young man, who was in the local hospital. When the specialist was taken to the patient he saw that the boy was just 'a piece of meat', mutilated beyond rehabilitation, without hands, without feet. Every day the lady in the chador came to the eye specialist and took him to see this patient. The specialist wondered whether there was any point in restoring the sight of a person who would never get well again or return to any sort of life. But he didn't want to wound the lady in the chador. She was always in the hospital ward. There were two or three like her, not more.

The specialist made inquiries. He found out that the woman in the chador was not the boy's mother; she was only a neighbour. The boy's mother came to the hospital every day, but she didn't stay long. After some time the specialist won the confidence of the lady in the chador, and one day he asked why she wanted the mutilated boy, who was not her son, to see again.

The lady in the chador said, 'My own boy, my own son, was executed because he belonged to an anti-revolutionary group. The person who reported him was this boy here, this neighbour's son. I am happy that my own son is dead. He was executed, and that was all. I want to keep this piece of meat alive to take revenge. I want his mother to grieve for him every day.'

The Shah had proclaimed the pre-Islamic past, in order partly to link himself to the great rulers of that past. Like Alexander two thousand years before, he had made a ceremonial pilgrimage to the tomb of Cyrus at Pasargadae. After the revolution gangs of revolutionaries had gone to the tomb and the palaces (and fire-temple) nearby; but they had done little damage. It was also said (with what truth I don't know) that Ayatollah Khalkhalli, Khomeini's hanging judge, had been appointed to a committee to work out the best means of destroying (or simply defacing) the ruins of Persepolis. But then there had been the war, the long Sacred Defence. And now tourists came again to Shiraz and took a car to Persepolis and a few got as far as Pasargadae.

The nihilistic revolutionary moment had passed. The revolution had taken hold; there were no more enemies; the world had been remade (though Ayatollah Khalkhalli thought that only 30 per cent of what had to be done had been done).

There was an Islamic entrance examination for the universities. Mehrdad said it was getting harder. Five years ago students didn't have to memorise parts of the Koran; now they had to. In all government offices there was now an Islamic organisation; and all candidates for jobs had to be interviewed by that organisation. They asked political questions, but they were also interested in how well people knew the Islamic rules.

Mehrdad said, 'Not the ordinary rules, but very detailed ones. They say that all Muslims must know these rules. They ask you about the prayers. We have five ordinary prayers a day. But you also have another kind of prayer – the frightened prayer, to be said in an emergency. Or the Friday prayers. Or the prayer for the dead. All of them have rules. And a man like me, who doesn't say his ordinary prayers, he cannot know the extraordinary prayers.'

At the universities a special subject was Khomeini's Will. It was worth a credit and it was obligatory even for non-Muslims; it had to be done regardless of what subject was being offered.

Mehrdad said, 'The subject is called *The Imam's Will.* I got twenty out of twenty. Our professor came to us with a summary in ten hand-written pages. Khomeini's way of speaking is complicated. Even a simple sentence has a complicated grammar. A ten-year-old boy can see a sentence painted on a wall and know it's from Imam Khomeini. On the whole it's nice, but to read forty pages would have been tough. The professor's summary made it easy. It is all about keeping the revolution alive. It cautions against America and imperialism, and it tells how to keep the mosque and Islam safe.'

The world had been remade. Where once Mehrdad's father had photographs of the royal family on his wall he now had a silhouette of Khomeini (done by Mehrdad: he liked using his hands). The country had been turned inside out, eviscerated, by war and revolution. Some people had come up; very many more had been destroyed; and no one could say for sure that a larger cause had been served. All that could be said was that the country had been given an almost universal knowledge of pain. There was no general will to action now; with the exhaustion that had come with their pain people were only waiting for something to happen. People like Mehrdad and his family were living on their nerves. It might have been like this in the time of the Shah. So that perhaps history here was curiously circular. Every great action – the war, the revolution – had to be. And every great action led back in a chain to itself.

On my last day in Tehran I talked to Ali about the revolution against the Shah. Could something else have happened?

People like him needed liberty, Ali said. They were well off under the Shah, but they had to live like mice. When they compared themselves with their counterparts in other countries they felt humiliated.

No man could be at ease with that kind of humiliation. It was people like him, not the poor, who made the revolution. And there was the cultural side, the Islamic side.

Ali said, 'I have to go back. In the 1940s, when Iran was occupied by the Allies, a lot of people started migrating from the villages to the little towns. And a lot of little businessmen in little towns moved to the bigger cities.'

In the towns the migrants outnumbered the older population. This older city population was secular. The migrants had deep-set Islamic ways. They didn't like what they saw in the cities: drinking shops, cabarets, women in short skirts, cinemas showing blue films, half-dressed women singing and dancing on television. Right through the 1940s and 1950s there was this movement from the villages to the cities.

In the 1960s the Shah started his land reform. 'The rich land was left in the hands of the old landowners. The infertile or semi-fertile land was divided among the farmers, the people who had always worked the land. Traditionally the farmers had a landowner they looked to. He sucked their blood, but he was their patron. He would lend them money, give them seed, and he would help when there was a disaster. When the land distribution happened the farmers lost their patron, and the government didn't attempt to replace the patron by a banking system. The farmers couldn't make ends meet. They left their farms and moved to the cities.'

These people were also conservative and religious. Their sons grew up in the cities and became educated. They went to universities; they took advantage of scholarships given by the Shah's government. But this second generation was still under the Islamic influence of its fathers. Ali thought it took two to three generations to change a village way of thinking. Iran didn't have the time for that. Things were moving too fast. This second generation had no earlier generation to compete with and as a group became powerful. They got jobs in the government; they became teachers. Many of them went to the bazaar and became businessmen.

'Mentally they were Muslims. And since they were from poor families they had the mentality of leftist socialism. That is why the Mujahidin had a good appeal: Marxism and Islam was their ideology. An irony: materialism and Allah. These people, first and second generations of people who had migrated to the cities, had links with their farmer families who were left in the farms and little towns and villages. These people were the leaders of the new movement. I knew so many of them in Kerman. So when the revolution started the leaders were already in the cities, and the masses they needed for revolt and demonstrations were in the villages and little towns.'

Away from this, and as if in another world, were the Shah's people. They were the sons and daughters of the older city population. Many of them were wealthy and had been educated in European or American schools. They spoke many languages; they could talk about Western philosophy and European politics. They knew the history of France and Spain and Germany better than they knew the history of Iran.

'They were about 5 per cent of the population. Maximum. The others, below, were the 95 per cent, reading Koran, Arabic – the real people, the masses. They had no communication with the 5 per cent. They were two tribes living in one country. Shah was surrounded by this 5 per cent. Especially later, when he married his last queen, educated in France, with complete French culture. They resented the Islamic tradition exactly as the other group resented the Western tradition that was forced on them.'

In the 1970s there was the oil boom. Iran's income became fifty times what it had been. This was wealth beyond imagining, and it made matters worse.

'This new wealth came to the cities, and the majority of the people lived in the rural areas. The younger generation of the farmers who had migrated to the cities realised that they were being cheated. More and more, from 1970 on, Islamic organisations started mushrooming in universities and in every city. And especially in the bazaar. The Islamic organisations were acting as a replacement for political parties. The Shah didn't allow political parties to take root. And these Islamic groups also expressed people's ideas about the Shah and his group, that they were not Islamic. The Shah and the Queen and her group started having artistic festivals. They invited musicians, poets, dancers, and all kinds of artists from abroad. There was one group that was completely nude, and they danced. There were many of those occasions. It was like putting gas on fire.'

Now, almost two decades later, the Shah and his group had disappeared. The colour photographs of the religious leaders were everywhere. They, too, required absolute obedience. The country was full of Islamic rules, and the Guards and Basiji were there to enforce them, in the afternoons in the park, at night on the highways. Young people like Feyredoun's brother had known nothing but religious rule. He had become a Nazi, in his innocent, dangerous way; he and his friends went out on some nights to mock the Guards. There was a sexual revolution among the young, and a falling away from the too-strict, too-pervasive faith. Of that falling away Emami, the *talebeh*, had said in Qum, 'Our enemies know our weakness.' After all the pain, a new nihilism seemed to be preparing.

Ali said, 'The two tribes of Iran still exist. If there is no marriage between them, I don't know where they are going.'

III

PAKISTAN
Dropping off the Map

1

A Criminal Enterprise

THERE WAS much to see in Persepolis, more than could be considered in a day. And not many visitors were ready after that to do the extra forty kilometres or so to Pasargadae, where there was comparatively little, and what there was was bare and scattered and picked clean: the sunken tower of a fire-temple, the palace of Cyrus, and the tomb of Cyrus. Mehrdad and I had the place to ourselves. The sunburnt old guide at the site entrance (perhaps also one of the watchmen), small and lean and unshaven, dressed in an old jacket and pullover for wind and dust, got on his motor-scooter and, wordlessly, began to act as our outrider in the desolation, stuttering on just a few yards before us, kicking up dust and blue smoke, and – like a beguiler in a modern version of some old myth – smiling and beckoning whenever our driver hesitated.

So we came to the remnants of Cyrus's palace. Large sections of the white floor, made up of big, irregular, interlocking marble blocks, had remained as level and close-jointed as they had been when set 2500 years ago. At one time the palace had been quarried for its stone. Some of this – used in a mosque in another place – had been recovered in the Shah's time and brought back to the site. These blocks, carved with Arabic letters, served no purpose now; they were just there as sacred relics, in what had been a seat of world power in the century before Herodotus, more than a thousand years before Islam. The flat land all around was full of wild grasses and flowers, dry and crisp after the summer, and alive with the song of unseen birds.

A short time before, the guide said, about thirty or forty people from India had come here in a bus. They had stood before a pillar with a cuneiform inscription high up – *I am Cyrus, son of Cambyses, and this is my palace* – and they had said prayers of some kind. Then, for about twenty minutes, they had wailed. When that was done they had got back into their bus and gone away.

The guide didn't know who the people in the bus were. But it was an easy guess that they were Parsees, Zoroastrians, followers of the pre-Islamic religion of Persia, and descendants of the people who had left Persia after the Arab conquest and the coming of Islam. They had found refuge in Gujarat in India; Gujarati had become their language. They were a small community and had remained more or less intact until this century. Now, with the intermarriage that had come with the general opening up of the world, they were melting away. This remembering by some of them of old glory, this ritual grief in the ruined palace of Cyrus, was like a miracle; though the ancient prayers might have been ill-remembered, and the ritual made up.

Not many days later I went to Pakistan, to Lahore. I put up at the Avari Hotel. The Avaris were Parsees, part of the dispersion; the partition of the Indian subcontinent in 1947 had left some Parsees in India, some in Pakistan. In the lobby of the hotel were large colour photographs of Mr and Mrs Avari, the founders. At the entrance a plaque honoured Mrs Avari. It told of her life and work. It ended like this: *She died on 25th November 1977 at Boston (USA). May the Almighty Ahura Mazda Grant her Soul eternal peace in heaven.*

This made Zoroastrianism like a version of Christianity or Islam. Had the old Iranian religion been like that? Perhaps it didn't matter. What mattered was what remained in the hearts of the people who had put up the plaque. The classical world had been overthrown and remade by Christianity and Islam. These were universal and not local religions; their religious and social ideas touched everyone and could seem familiar even to outsiders.

In Iran the pre-Islamic past was irrecoverable. It wasn't like that in Pakistan. Vital fragments of the past lived on in dress, customs, ceremonies, festivals and, importantly, ideas of caste. Islam reached Iran just after the Prophet's time. It was nearly four hundred years later that north-west India began to be penetrated (the conquest of Sindh in the south-west is something apart). By AD 1200 (giving very rough dates) the Muslims were a power in the north of the subcontinent; in 1600 this power was at its peak; by 1700, with the decline of the Mogul empire, Muslim power in India was more or less broken.

There had never been anything like an overall or settled conquest, as in Iran. In fact, the extraordinary peoples who came up after the Mogul decline – the Mahrattas, the Sikhs – were in part championing their own faith against the Muslims. It was the British, religious outsiders, who subdued both those peoples, and became, by a mixture of direct and indirect rule, the paramount power in the subcontinent.

The British period – two hundred years in some places, less than a hundred in others – was a time of Hindu regeneration. The Hindus, especially in Bengal, welcomed the New Learning of Europe and the institutions the British brought. The Muslims, wounded by their loss of power, and out of old religious scruples, stood aside. It was the beginning of the intellectual distance between the two communities. This distance has grown with independence; and it is this – more even than religion now – that at the end of the twentieth century has made India and Pakistan quite distinct countries. India, with an intelligentsia that grows by leaps and bounds, expands in all directions. Pakistan, proclaiming only the faith and then proclaiming the faith again, ever shrinks.

It was Muslim insecurity that led to the call for the creation of Pakistan. It went at the same time with an idea of old glory, of the invaders sweeping down from the north-west and looting the temples of Hindustan and imposing the faith on the infidel. The fantasy still lives; and for the Muslim converts of the subcontinent it is the start of their neurosis, because in this fantasy the convert forgets who or what he is and becomes the violator. It is as though – switching continents – the indigenous people of Mexico and Peru were to side with Cortés and Pizarro and the Spaniards as the bringers of the true faith.

A lawyer told me of the Muslim slogans he heard as a child of three, in a small town in the Punjab, at the time of the agitation for Pakistan. They had moved him as a child; they moved him still. The lawyer (whose father had been a famous liberal in pre-partition days) was presenting himself to me as someone just as liberal as his father. If people out there, the lawyer said, lifting his chin (a little hesitantly) towards the street, knew how liberal he was, he would be 'strung up in half an hour'.

But he was an old fanatic, really. He wasn't content to possess his faith; he wanted it to triumph in an old-fashioned way. I could tell that as soon as he began to recite the slogans of 1947. His voice trembled, his eye gleamed: he was a child of three again in Lyallpur, playing with visions of sending the infidel to kingdom come.

> *Darté naheen dunya mayu Musalman kissee sé –*
> *Ja poochh Ali-sé.*
> No fear in the world the Musalman knows – go and ask Ali.

The translation – liquid Urdu turning, word by word, to English stone – cooled him down. He said in half-apology, reverting to his lawyer's manner, 'As poetry not very good, perhaps. But clutching at my heart.'

We were sitting in the lawyer's dining room. It was much used and strangely dark, as though it had sunk a little too much below the level of the land outside. There was a bad smell from the street ditch: perhaps something wrong with a sewer pipe. The lawyer apologised for it; it seemed, though, to be something he had got used to. The refrigerator was in a corner of the room, perhaps as a check on the servants. The tall and sullen Pathan servant, in the very dirty clothes that servants in Pakistan are required to wear, came in every two minutes to get something from the refrigerator or to put something back. This was distracting to me, but not to the lawyer. His eyes were bright, far away. The Pakistan slogans of 1947 had given him a lift; I felt they were still singing in his head.

At last we began to sip the bad coffee the dirty servant presented, and – as in so many of the houses I had been to – we contemplated the ruin of the state.

The new state had been hurriedly created and had no true programme. It couldn't be a homeland for all the Muslims of the subcontinent; that was impossible. In fact, more Muslims were to be left behind in India than were to be in the new Muslim state. It seemed rather that, over and above any political aim, the new state was intended to be a triumph of the faith, a stake in the heart of old Hindustan. Someone (not the lawyer) remembered this taunting slogan of 1947:

> *But kay rahé ga Hindustan,*
> *Bun kay rahé ga Pakistan.*
> As surely as Hindustan will be divided,
> Pakistan will be founded.

In Lahore in 1979 I met a man who tried to tell me what the creation of Pakistan had meant to him as a child over the border in India. He had to feel for the words. At last he said, 'To me it was like God.' To many, or most, of the Muslims of the subcontinent the state that had been won out of India came as a kind of religious ecstasy, something beyond reason, beyond quibbles about borders and constitutions and economic plans.

And then, almost at the moment of partition, some people saw that there was a certain amount of money to be made out of the new state as well. All the land in the west – ancient and not-so-ancient seats of Hinduism and Buddhism and Sikhism – was finally going to lose, or be cleansed of, its Hindu and Sikh populations. They would leave and go to India. As communities, the Hindus and Sikhs were rich; it was said that they owned 40 per cent of the wealth of the region. When they left, many debts were wiped out; and all over Pakistan, in villages and towns large and small, an enormous amount of property needed new owners. Fortunes were made or added to overnight. So at the very beginning the new religious state was touched by the old idea of plunder. The idea of the state as God was modified.

It didn't have to pay its way. It became a satellite of the United States; its various régimes were shored up right through the Cold War. It didn't develop a modern economy; it didn't feel the need. Instead, it began to export its people; it became in part a remittance economy.

Thirty-two years after partition there came the war in Afghanistan against the Russian occupation. This could be entered into as a kind of religious war; and, again, the loot was prodigious. American arms and Afghan drugs followed the same route for eight years; hundreds of millions of dollars stuck to the hands of the faithful all along the way. The corruption was too gross; the state was finally undermined. Public faith and private plunder made a circle. There was no point now at which that circle could be broken into, and a fresh start made. After the cynicism and intellectual idleness of four decades, the state, which at the beginning had been to some like God, had become a criminal enterprise.

★

No real thought had ever been taken for the running of the new country. Everything was expected to flow from the triumph of the faith. But Islamic identity, though powerful as a cause of pre-partition protest ('a very powerful evocative factor', as the lawyer said), couldn't by itself hold the unwieldy, two-winged state together. Bangladesh, with its own language and culture, soon fell away; and even then everyone looking for political power in what remained of Pakistan promised to be more Islamic than his rival.

The procedural laws inherited from the British, master law-makers of the subcontinent, were interfered with in a half-hearted and impractical way. Certain Islamic appendages were tacked on. The lawyers couldn't always make them work; and the legal system, already damaged by political manipulation, became a little more ramshackle. Women's rights ceased to be secure. Adultery became an offence; this meant that a man who wanted to get rid of his wife could accuse her of adultery and have her imprisoned. In 1979 provision was made for Koranic punishments; and though there had never been any amputations (the doctors said no), people had loved the public floggings and run to see them.

The Islam defined by these laws was restrictive and severe and simple. The laws might not always be implemented. Like the public floggings in 1986, they might be suspended (in spite of the public demand); or, like the laws about drinking and gambling, they might be bypassed. But the laws all remained on the books; and they changed the nature of the state. They gave encouragement to the backward-looking. They made for uncertainty. They outlined the kind of tyranny that, in a crisis, people might talk themselves into.

It was an accident that, with the breaking away of Bangladesh, the part of the subcontinent that was now Pakistan was the least educated part. It had fallen late to the British, and had had less than a century of British rule, from the mid or late 1840s to 1947, with the disturbance of the Indian Mutiny (1857–60) near the beginning of the period and the independence movement at the end. (The British Raj here, by another accident, coincided more or less with the life of its most famous chronicler, Rudyard Kipling, who was born in 1865 and died in 1936.)

British institutions sat lightly on older local systems, the tribal systems in the north-west, the feudal chieftaincies in the half-slave south. After less than fifty years of Pakistan those older informal systems were beginning to show through again. The inherited modern state could be felt as a recent and needless burden.

Always in the background now were the fundamentalists who – fed by the ecstasy of the creation of Pakistan, and further fed by the partial Islamisation of the laws – wanted to take the country back and back, to the seventh century, to the time of the Prophet. There was as hazy a programme for that as there had been for Pakistan itself: only some idea of regular prayers, of Koranic punishments, the cutting off of hands and feet, the veiling and effective imprisoning of women, and giving men tomcatting rights over four women at a time, to use and discard at will. And somehow, it was thought, out of that, out of an enclosed devout society with uneducated men religiously tomcatting away, the state would right itself, and power would come, as it had come to Islam at the very beginning.

The case for Pakistan was made seriously for the first time in 1930 by a poet, Mohammed Iqbal, in a speech to the conference of the pre-partition Muslim League. The tone of the speech is more civil and seemingly reasoned than the 1947 street slogans; but the impulses are the same. Iqbal came from a recently converted Hindu family; and perhaps only someone who felt himself a new convert could have spoken as he did.

Islam is not like Christianity, Iqbal says. It is not a religion of private conscience and private practice. Islam comes with certain 'legal concepts'. These concepts have 'civic significance' and create a certain kind of social order. The 'religious ideal' cannot be separated from the social order. 'Therefore, the construction of a polity on national lines, if it means a displacement of the Islamic principle of solidarity, is simply unthinkable to a Muslim.' In 1930 a national polity meant an all-Indian one.

It is an extraordinary speech for a thinking man to have made in the twentieth century. What Iqbal is saying in an involved way is that Muslims can live only with other Muslims. If this was meant seriously, it would have implied that the good world, the one to be striven after, was a purely tribal world, neatly parcelled out, every tribe in his corner. This would have been seen to be fanciful.

What is really in the background of this demand for Pakistan and a Muslim polity, what isn't mentioned, is Iqbal's rejection of Hindu India.

His hearers would have understood that; and both they and he would have had a concrete idea of what was being rejected. It lay all around them; they only had to look; it was an aspect of the real world. What didn't exist, and what Iqbal's proposal didn't even attempt to define, was the new Muslim polity that was to come with the new state. In Iqbal's speech – which was momentous – this polity is an abstraction; it is poetic. It has to be taken on trust. The Prophet's name is even used indirectly to recommend it.

The speech is full of ironies today. Pakistan, when it came, disenfranchised the Muslims who stayed behind in India. Bangladesh is on its own. In Pakistan itself the talk is of dissolution. The new Muslim polity there has turned out to be like the old, the one Iqbal knew: you don't have to go down far before you find people who are as voiceless and without representation as when Iqbal made his speech in 1930.

2

The Polity

ONE DAY six months before, this woman's husband and his nephew, both labourers, had got hold of her and 'butchered her nose'. The husband had then fettered her. Somehow she had freed herself, and then she had run away. She went to the big city of Karachi. She had a friend there. The friend got in touch with a human rights group in Lahore that ran – with foreign subsidy – a shelter for battered women.

It was in the office of that group, in the waiting room, that I saw her. Among the very quiet women there – the passive, half-dead faces of women taken by suffering beyond shame and perhaps even feeling – she was noticeable. A veil of gauze-like material was pulled tight over her lower face, to hide the wound. Above the veil only her eyes and eyebrows showed. I thought they looked like the eyes of a child; this made the thought of her disfigurement more painful.

But she wasn't a child. She was thirty-five. I found that out when I came back to the office some days later to see her. Her face was uncovered this time. The tip of her nose hadn't been cut off, as I had feared; it was more as though it had been pinched with a pair of hot tongs. On either nostril there was a wound, raw pink edged with dark-red; but she was now used to it and didn't try to hide it.

She was small and thin and dark. She had got married when she was nineteen. Her father was ill at the time, and her mother thought she should get married. It was against Islam for a girl not to be married. She had got married without a dowry, 'only for God'; this meant that the only dowry she could take to her husband was the protection of God.

She had got married to a man who was an occasional labourer. She didn't know the man and she didn't know why her parents had chosen him. She had just done what she had been told; she was helpless.

Farzana, the human-rights lawyer who was translating, said, 'She is a victim of feudal society.'

The woman herself couldn't see it so clearly. She only knew that the husband who had been found for her worked for the landlord that her father worked for. Her husband worked as a cook. He got three hundred or four hundred rupees a month, ten or twelve pounds. He also got food from the landlord. The landlord had a lot of land. She had got to know the landlord, had got to know who he was, because both her mother and her father worked for him. He was a respectful man, and very nice.

There was a school in the village, a primary school, but she didn't go. Her parents didn't allow it. They were both illiterate. Her father had left no money when he died. He died penniless. He was a servant of the landlord, that is, he served the landlord when he was required to serve him. When the landlord went hunting he used her father. He would kill birds for the landlord and take care of the dogs. He lived in a mud hut in the landlord's yard. She didn't really know how many people lived there. There might have been twenty-five families, but she didn't know. All of them were servants of the landlord. There was a mosque in the village and they all went there often.

Talking about the mosque, the woman smiled. She had thought the question about it was a trap question, and she was glad to have seen through it. She felt, too, it was the only good thing she had said about herself.

There was no furniture in her parents' hut. There was a box; there were a few utensils; there was an electric fan. So there was electricity in the hut; and the fan, extravagant though it appeared, proved how bad the summers were. There was nothing else that she remembered.

Her marriage had gone well for a while. She had three children, two boys and a girl. She used to work as a servant in people's houses. But then two years ago her husband had become a heroin addict. He wanted her to bring home more money. There was trouble when she couldn't. One day there was a quarrel between her children and her husband's nephew's children. Her husband's nephew was a labourer also, but on another estate. She beat all the children. The husband's nephew's children complained, and when her husband came back he beat her very badly. She went with one child to her in-laws' house. Her husband followed her. She wanted to go to the police, but one of her husband's relations told her not to. He made her go back to her husband. That was her mistake. The quarrel about the children was only a pretext. Her husband was angry about the nephew, and then the two men got together and butchered her nose.

She smiled when she said she knew the landlord's family. That was clearly, in her own judgement, the second good thing she had said.

Her own children, the two boys and the girl, used to go to the school. But then they left and they forgot how to read and write. They forgot 'each and every thing'. But they went every day to the mosque; she made them do that. She thought now that her children were being treated very harshly. Her husband's father and mother didn't like the children.

The landlord didn't help her in her trouble. She didn't ask him. She didn't think of asking him. Her landlord didn't know of her trouble. There was no one to tell him. She had no family in that village any more. Her brothers and sisters were not interested in her any more.

She was living in the shelter of the human rights group. They had found a job for her, working two days a week in a bandage-making factory.

She wore plastic shoes; her feet were restless in them. She constantly adjusted her pink skirt which had a flowered pattern. A block-printed headdress was the only touch of style.

She said that nothing gave her pleasure now. All she wanted was to get her children back. But something had happened since she ran away from her husband: she was not frightened now.

Farzana said, 'She is callous.'

Strange word. Perhaps Farzana meant 'calloused'.

But 'callous' might also have been right, because when Farzana asked again, the woman said, 'I am not supposed to feel pleasure or happiness.'

And suddenly she began to laugh. She was laughing at me, my strange questions, my clothes, the fact that I needed an interpreter to talk to her. The laughter had been building up inside her, and when it came she couldn't control it, remembering only, for manners' sake, to turn aside and cover her mouth and butchered nose with her palm.

The Moguls had built forts, palaces, mosques and tombs. The British in the second half of the nineteenth century had put up buildings to house institutions. Lahore was rich in the monuments of both periods. Ironically, for a country that talked so much about Islamic identity, and even claimed to be a successor to Mogul power, it was the Mogul monuments that were in decay: the fort, Shah Jehan's mosque, the Shalimar Gardens, the tombs of both the emperor Jehangir and his great consort Noor-Jehan. It was as though two Versailles, at the very least, were being allowed to rot away. This was due in part to a general lack of education, the idea of earlier centuries that what no longer had a purpose no longer required attention. But there was also the Muslim convert's attitude to the land where he lives. To the convert his land is of no religious or historical importance; its relics are of no account; only the sands of Arabia are sacred.

The British administrative buildings live on. The institutions they were meant to house are still more or less the institutions the country depends on. On the Mall, the central thoroughfare of Lahore, these big buildings stand, a little artificially, one after the other, each in its splendid grounds, as though the British here, out of their experience elsewhere on the subcontinent, knew from the beginning what they had to set down in central Lahore: the civil service academy, the state guest house, the college for the sons of local chieftains, the governor's house, the British club, the public gardens, the courts, the post office, the museum.

The courts were always busy. But, with all their apparatus, they didn't deliver, the lawyers said. There was too much political interference, too much litigation; there were too many false witnesses; the judges were overworked. But there was no earlier local system that could be restored. There was a peasant story of justice under the Mogul emperors. Night and day, in this story, a rope hung outside the palace wall. The poor man who wanted justice only had to run to this rope and (if there wasn't too much of a crush, of if he wasn't stopped or cut down) pull on it. The rope rang a bell; the emperor appeared at his window, and gave the peasant justice. This story – really a serf fantasy about the mercy of the master – had got into Pakistani schoolbooks as a fact, and was used to make a point about the grandeur of the old Muslim rulers. But according to Waleed Iqbal, a lecturer in law (and a grandson of the poet who proposed the idea of Pakistan), the law here before the British, in the days of the Sikhs, was 'vague'; and going back further, to the times of the Mogul (the times of the rope and the bell), the law was simply dictatorial. The British-given courts, and the British procedural laws of 1898 and 1908, were still all that the country had. They met a need; that was why they had lasted.

I went to see the courts with Rana, a junior lawyer in an important practice. Rana was twenty-nine, and from the Punjab. He was the son of a small landowner who had sold his land, lost the money, and lost his status. Rana had decided quite late to become a lawyer. He wanted power; he wanted to protect himself. At the same time – and this was his unwitting tribute to the institution – he thought that in the law, and in the practice of the law, he was going to find something like purity, something separate from the disorder and unfairness of the country, something in which a man was judged as a man.

The law had been a double disappointment to him. The disappointment showed in his manner; he was a brooder. He was handsome and slender; he had many friends among the young lawyers. They were pleased to see him in the yard and Victorian Gothic corridors of the courts, and the lawyers' tea room (like a railway station buffet). He was more buttoned up than his friends. I don't think he liked wearing the black suit of his profession; I think that, as a junior, he had grown to think of it as a livery of servitude.

In the half-broken street at the back of the courts there was a forest of lawyers' boards or tins, in the swaggering Urdu script, black on white, or red on white, and hanging like shop signs on the rails and on the concrete and metal electricity poles. The crowd in the yard of the lower courts was in constant movement, like a school yard at recess; part of the swirl, and barely noticed, was a prisoner being led on a chain by a policeman. In the arches of the verandahs of the main building, on the lower floor and the upper, people stood at rest, draped in loose Punjabi costume.

Small, beaten-up rooms: small courts perhaps, some with a few people, some with hardly any. I wasn't sure what I was seeing; Rana didn't talk a great deal. But then we came to the main hall, and Rana became respectful. He found a chair for me and made me sit on it; he stood behind me, near the door. The ceiling was high, with hammer beams; the floor was of marble. Books were in trays or baskets on the floor, and paper slips were in the books. Lawyers in black jackets stood at lecterns before the bar, and attendants all the time brought in trays and files. Two judges sat below a fringed brown-cloth canopy; it was like an emblem of majesty. 'What is the number of the ordinance?' one of them said, turning the pages of a big book. At the back of the judges and their canopy were curtained Gothic windows; above the doorways were Gothic arches. And once again, considering the careful Victorian Gothic decoration of the hall, the Mogul motifs of the side doors, the scales of justice above the fireplace (now with electric or gas heaters), it came to me, as it had come elsewhere in the subcontinent, that the architects of the Raj had always been on their best behaviour in these public buildings, taking pains with details which might not be noticed individually but which added to the overall effect. The big-bladed fans did not hang from the ceiling; they were fixed vertically to the walls; in this autumnal season they were still.

The judge began to read his judgement. It was in English, and in a mumble that I found hard to pick up. He repeated certain words as he read. He was finding against a district commissioner who had ordered the silencing of the loudspeakers on a mosque. '. . . It cannot be countenanced. It is not in his power . . .'

It was possible to see – in this fine hall, with the judges below a canopy, and the lawyers in black at their lecterns, with the formality of debate and judgement, and the laws all printed in big books – it was possible to see how, even with things going wrong in the country, Rana could have this idea (as I read it, from his conversation) of the purity of the law.

He had for some years wanted to be a policeman. That was for the sake of security, to protect himself in the Punjab, where the police had such power over simple people. He was ten or eleven when he had found out about this power of the police. He had been cycling in a careless way on the public road and had caused an accident between a rickshaw and a car. The police had come for him at home and taken him to the police station. This was in the small town where Rana's family had lived before they moved to Lahore. His father and mother were not at home; they had gone to Rana's father's village; some relation was very ill or had died. So Rana had to get in touch with an uncle. The uncle said he was coming over right away. Rana told the sergeant, and the sergeant said to him very roughly, 'Go and sit there.' A little later, still waiting for the uncle to come, the sergeant said to Rana, 'Go and wash my plates and spoon.' Rana, without thinking about the consequences, said, 'No. I am a Rajput.'

It was the pride of his family and clan that they were Rajputs, ancestrally of the Hindu warrior caste. The ancestry was in his name, Rana; the actual pride had come to him in his father's village. He often went there with his father. His father at that time still had his land, and everywhere Rana and his father went people treated them with regard. They would say to Rana's father, 'Rana Sahib, how good of you to pay a visit to us here.' The people who said that were peasants who worked on Rana's father's land. Rana was stirred by their respect; he grew to enjoy it; in this way he had got to know what being a Rajput meant.

That was why when the sergeant in the police station in the town asked Rana to wash his plates and spoon, he was able to face the sergeant squarely and say, 'I don't like the job. I don't want to do it.'

The sergeant didn't do anything to him. He could have; he could have been brutal. It might have been Rana's manner, or the fact that Rana's uncle was coming. The uncle had to pay up when he came: five hundred rupees to the sergeant to hush up the matter, and a further five hundred for the rickshaw owner.

When they were leaving the station the sergeant said to Rana's uncle, 'Wait a minute.' He told the story about the plates and the spoon and said, 'This boy is only ten, but he is already a goonda.' A thug. The uncle, though he approved of Rana's behaviour, said to Rana, when they were outside, 'This is how the police will behave. In future you should be careful.'

That was the incident that made Rana want to be a policeman. A little while afterwards some policemen raided the house of a neighbour. This made Rana want to be a policeman even more. As a policeman he would be protected, his family would be protected; and, of course, it was a government job. A government job made a man secure. When he was thirteen or fourteen he began to think of himself quite seriously as a future police officer. He felt the instinct to power in himself. Then one day this changed.

He had a cousin who was a policeman, an ASI, an assistant sub-inspector, in a small village about forty miles outside Lahore. An ASI was a low rank, but Rana had always been proud of this cousin, had seen him as a successful man. Just as, in his father's village, he had grown to feel pride as a Rajput and a landowner's son, so the possession of an ASI cousin, when he began to understand about these things, made him feel 'superior'. He was about sixteen or seventeen when he thought one day that he would go and visit this cousin. There was no reason; he just wanted to say hello to this successful man, to be in his presence. In his cousin's police station he saw men in handcuffs, men in chains. He saw that the police had been trained to treat ordinary people like criminals. He remembered that, though his cousin was very nice with his friends, he was very rough with his family. Rana didn't like what he saw; he decided he didn't want this kind of power. He gave up the dream of being a policeman. It had been with him for a very long time; he had nothing to put in its place.

It was not long after this that Rana's father sold his land in the village in order to go into business. The business failed almost immediately; everything was lost. And Rana discovered then that the respect he had grown to enjoy in the village as his father's son was no longer there; even close family became distant. He wanted not to see people. He felt that his dream of power over people was wrong.

His father pulled him out of this gloom. He insisted that Rana should do some higher training. Rana's father had always believed in education for its own sake. He used to tell Rana when Rana was a child, 'I will kill you or throw you out of the house if you don't go to school.' Another thing he used to say was, 'Illiteracy is death. Literacy is life.'

He suggested now that Rana should go to a law school. Out of the ruin of his fortune he found five hundred rupees a month for the school fees. Gradually, in the study of law, Rana found a kind of philosophical solace. It introduced him to another idea of power.

He spoke of this when he came with a friend to see me, some days after our visit to the courts. He said, 'The more I learned about the law the more I felt that all power doesn't lie with the policeman. Anybody who is a man of means, and well educated, and with an awareness of his rights, can be a stable man, a man who can face any kind of consequences.'

His law studies lasted three years. Near the end of that time he became involved with a girl, and after the law examinations he thought he should spend a little time away from his family. He went to Islamabad and the mountain places, Murree, Kagan, Naran. The girl didn't marry him. She married someone with money. He didn't hold it against her; it still made him proud that she had liked him. And again it was his father who came and pulled him out of his melancholy. He found Rana in one of the mountain places and said, 'Enough is enough. Come back and file your papers for an advocate's licence.'

And now Rana, who had learned about the law, began to learn about the legal life. In his eyes he had made himself an educated, sensitive person; he expected people to respect him for that, to respect his sensibilities. He found, when he began to do his six-month probation, that there was no respect at all for him. His seniors treated him like a clerk or office messenger, a peon. He changed his firm. The senior in the new firm said, 'I will pay you fifteen hundred rupees in the beginning. After fifteen days I will pay you two thousand. And after four or six months money will become immaterial.' Rana didn't even get the fifteen hundred starting pay. It wasn't that the senior didn't like Rana; he liked Rana very much; he just didn't think he should pay him.

Rana said, 'Money became immaterial in the other way.'

Sohail, the friend who had come with Rana, said, 'The problem with Rana is that he's not a yes man.'

Rana said, 'Now I am living like a yes man. Eighty per cent I am a yes man now.' But he smiled. He was out of office hours, and not in his lawyer's black suit; he was more at ease. He could make little jokes.

Seniors were one thing. There were also the clerks to whom you had to give little tips before they did what, according to the law, they had to do. Rana's senior said, 'This is part of the job'; but Rana didn't agree. Then there were clients. They wanted lawyers with experience or a reputation. The better clients wanted lawyers who could speak better English than Rana could; in Pakistan everything to do with the law was in English. And after all of this there were the judges. Rana didn't think they cared as they should about words and the meaning of words; they cared about personalities.

The first time Rana appeared in court on his own was over a petition for bail. The law, Rana thought, was that when injuries were not on the vital parts, and not grievous, bail should be granted. He stated his case. The judge said, 'Young man, have you finished?' Rana said, 'Yes, sir.' The judge said, 'I will give a decision after a few minutes.' Rana turned and made to step down from the dais. The judge said sharply, 'Listen to me.' Rana turned and looked at the judge. The judge said, 'I have dismissed your petition.'

Rana went back in a gloom to his office. He talked with friends about giving up this branch of the profession. It didn't make him feel any better when the next day a senior from the firm went before the same judge and the petition for bail was granted.

When as a boy he had thought of power he had thought of exercising it. Now he saw power from the other side, from below. One day he was in the district courts. Two young boys, ten and twelve, and their mother were charged with drug trafficking. The mother was crying. Rana went and talked to her. She told him that the policeman who had brought the charge against her and her sons had been pestering her to sleep with him. Rana believed her.

Sohail said, 'There are two kinds of people who are living well in Pakistan. People with names, and people with money. Everybody else are like insects, worms. They have no power. No approach. Powers are in limited hands, and money is also in limited hands.'

The day came when Rana thought he could take no more. He wanted to leave Pakistan, get away. He thought – with a curious wilful ignoring of immigration laws – that he would go to England, do a job there, improve his English, learn more about the law. When he went to the British consulate to get a visa the man at the counter didn't let him finish his story. He threw Rana's passport back at him. Rana remembered the insult; telling the story, he acted out the official's throwing gesture. But he could do nothing about it. He had to stay where he was, and stick it out in the law.

Sometimes now he told his father that he was going to give the law just one more year. Then his father would say, 'You have spent a lot of time on the law. You better stay in, because at least you are earning something.'

He was living now on his nerves. There were all the strains of the profession and then there were the difficulties of daily life.

Once there was a lot of transport in Lahore, Sohail said. There were nice Volvo buses. Then they – the unknown 'they', who were responsible for so much – stole the air-conditioning systems and the carpets and the cushions. Then they began stealing parts of the engines. Now the depot was full of useless buses. And there were only minibuses on the roads. These buses had only fifteen seats, and there would be twenty or thirty people at the bus stop.

Rana said, 'Sometimes I wait for an hour. How can you blame people if they want to take the law in their own hands? If they want to take the Kalashnikov. There are some basic requirements for life – you give people a chance to have their edibles, to travel in an easy way, to have other opportunities.'

Sohail said, 'The people don't know about their rights.'

Rana closed his eyes and nodded. There were ten in his family. He was the eldest son. Once, for the sake of his own security and the security of his family, he had dreamed of power over people. Now he talked of their rights.

I asked about his mother.

'She is a simple woman. From the village.' It had been an arranged marriage, a Rajput caste affair. 'She just tells me to wait. And wait.'

It was one of the grand lawyers of Lahore who suggested that I should go to the Hira Mandi, the Diamond Market, the area of the singing and dancing girls, the prostitutes' area. The lawyer's office had something of the formality of the higher courts. Whenever the lawyer entered the outer office all the clerks and assistants stood up and fixed their eyes on him. This regard for rank and personality in the law was what Rana hadn't expected, and suffered from; but it worked the other way with me. I knew at once from everything that surrounded this lawyer, and from what I saw in people's eyes, that the lawyer was a man of weight. The lawyer had a very good guide to the Diamond Market for me. One of his clients, he said, knew the area well. And the client was there, in the inner office: a big man in a loose peach-coloured long-tailed shirt.

The dancing and singing began late. My guide was to come to the hotel at eleven that evening. He came fifteen minutes after that. He was fatter than he appeared seated in the lawyer's office. He had a muscular man with him, and when we got to the van in the hotel drive there were two other men inside it, a dark pock-marked man with a baseball cap and another muscular man, with designer stubble, in a red and blue striped jersey.

The Diamond Market was in the old walled city, some way beyond the end of the Mall, and at the back of the Shah Jehan mosque. It was strange – just at the end of a short van ride – to see the girls in the lighted rooms, with the men passing in the dark streets all the time, with rubble and dust all around, and food shops and sweetshops.

My guide in the long-tailed shirt walked with authority. People knew him. It was his area; the lawyer was right. The man in the red and blue jersey said, 'He is terrorist of this area.' When my guide, in the peach-coloured long shirt, greeted someone, the man in the jersey said of the man greeted, 'He is small terrorist.'

So it went on, past the lighted rooms, with the musicians seated on the floor, the girls in groups or singly, with careful, worrying, blank expressions. Always above the lighted rooms were balconies, sometimes with girls, sometimes with young men. The guide said, 'Their agents.' He offered everything that was going: sweets, food, the girls themselves. Always, with this, glimpses of derelict people, lepers, men withered away to almost nothing.

They wanted me to try a milk sweet. They took the thing they had in mind from a display in front of a shop; there was no objection, only compliance and a smile. I tried it with them, nervously. And then there was a meal in a famous restaurant or eating house. It was quite a big place. Chicken and goat simmered in pots outside. A table and chairs were wiped down for us in an inner room. As in ancient Rome – where a famous floor mosaic was of food scraps thrown down – they threw bones on the floor when they had finished chewing them. The big man in the long shirt used bits of naan bread to scoop up the liquid from the chicken and goat stew. He went then, as though demonstrating his power, to get some more from the pots outside.

When he came back I asked, 'How many terrorists in this area?' His friend, in the striped jersey, winked at me and said, 'Only one.' The big man talked of his time in London, in Whitechapel. He had got to know two African or black terrorists there, he said.

At the end they washed their hands at a tap over a sink and wiped their fingers dry on a towel. The big man pointed to the photograph of the girl on the calendar next to the sink. 'You like her? You want to f— her?' Food had made him expansive. 'On me. You f—. I have the money.' He slapped his side.

We walked again, past the hypnotic lighted rooms. It was hard not to be worried or frightened, with all the stories of the kidnapping and torture of women and girls.

For the first time that evening there was a police jeep, moving cautiously in the narrow lane.

The big man said, 'The police are rubbish.'

They all agreed.

The big man said, 'They come at 12.30, when everything closes down.'

He was in trouble with the police. He was on a murder charge and had spent a year in jail before being released on bail. That was why that morning he had been in the lawyer's office.

He said, 'Justice is rubbish. Law is rubbish. Law is only for the poor, not for the rich.'

We went up the steps to the lobby of a movie house. The lobby was empty; the cinema looked closed. The big man showed the still photographs on the display boards, and his friend in the jersey said, 'All these girls are pros.' Again as though they were being offered to me. I said I was embarrassed. The friend – a sudden, unexpected fellow feeling arising between us – said, 'I know very well what you mean.'

We went back to the van. An absolute derelict had been watching it. He came out of the darkness and, shrivelled, skin and bone, hardly a man, asked for money, which, wordlessly, but without disregard, the men gave.

The big man said, 'Last round.'

We drove slowly down and up and down the narrow lanes again. Rich men came and took away the girls, they said. Right at the end of our last round, pointing to a dark thin man in a dark *shalwar-kameez*, drugged-looking, pulling at a cigarette, the big man said, 'A broker. Those three.' He meant the girls in the lighted room. The dark man was standing in the dark street just in front of the room.

The big man said, 'Now where do you want to go?' I said, 'Back to the hotel.' They were all disappointed.

In the old days I would have grown dizzy with excitement here. Up to my mid-thirties I had been attracted to prostitutes and sought them out. My memories of those times were not really of pleasure, however; they were more of the enervation that came after the dizziness. The men in the van might have thought that I was pretending – prostitutes in Pakistan had a recognised place in lower-middle-class and upper-class life: there would have been no dishonour for me – but I now had no brothel urge. My ideas of sexual satisfaction had changed.

The big man picked up a bottle-shaped cut-out that was standing against the windscreen. It was of Nawaz Sharif, the opposition leader, broad-waisted in long shirt and unbuttoned waistcoat. The big man said, 'He is my leader.' The cut-out figure was the leader, in fact, of all the men in the van. I was, to my surprise, among politicians of a sort.

Politics and sexual repression and cruelty and captive women and music and grime and lepers wasting away and exposed food: many ideas and sensations were in conflict in this pleasure area. Everything was to be distrusted; everything cancelled out.

The big man wasn't lying, I learned later. He was as important as he said he was. He had done the things that important men in this kind of area did, and some people wanted to get him. We might easily have been fired on that evening, from one of those dark upper windows.

3

Rana in his Village

ON FRIDAY, the sabbath – it had been declared the sabbath only in 1977, as part of a political auction in Islamic pledges between a prime minister and his challengers, in which it could be said the prime minister had both lost and won: he had been deposed soon afterwards and tried and hanged, but the Friday sabbath had stayed – on Friday, when Rana didn't have to put on his lawyer's black suit and black tie, he took me to his father's ancestral village.

His father had no land there now. But the village was full of relations, and Rana had arranged for an uncle to receive us. Five uncles of Rana still owned all the land. They had the same grandfather; they were brothers or cousins. There were four or five hundred houses in the village, Rana said. Each house had from eight to ten people, and at one time most of those people would have worked the land for the landowners. Now a few had gone abroad, to Saudi Arabia, Kuwait, and other places; and a few had started businesses of their own, small poultry farms, little shops, an ice factory. Life there still followed the old pattern. Everybody got up before sunrise, whatever the season and the weather. They worked until noon. The field workers took their food in the fields; they didn't return home until the end of the working day.

It was this old and beautiful way that Rana wanted me to see. He made his own arrangements for the car. It was a friend's car, and the friend was the driver. The friend was shorter and stouter than Rana. He was as young as Rana, but things were already moving for him. He had his own business in a small town. He made and exported garments, still in a small way, but he had dreams. They made him talkative, until we hit the bad roads and the drive became a trial.

The way out led for some time past a tree-lined canal, and then we were on the very flat plain of the Punjab. It was the area of Raiwind, Rana said; every summer religious scholars met here. They were more than scholars; they were missionaries. I remembered the gathering in 1979: like an immense fairground in the flat land: the roads and glinting cars seen from far and diminishing in the distance; the hummocked spread of tents; the waterlogged ground as springy as a mattress, breaking at every footfall into minute cracks that sealed up again as soon as the foot was lifted; and then, in the enclosed space of the tents, the accentuated perspective view of tent-poles leaning this way and that and going back and back, smaller and smaller; a great restless seated crowd in the aqueous covered light; with shifting and very white gashes above, where the tent-covers didn't absolutely meet, and the sky showed.

The Raiwind gathering that year had come at a time when the country was having its first taste of religious terror, under General Zia. He had hanged Mr Bhutto, the Friday sabbath man; he had gone then to Mecca to do the little pilgrimage, not the full one, but he had still come back with a hundred million dollars of Saudi money. Government offices in Pakistan were required to stop for all the pre-scribed prayers; Islamic whipping vans were being sent out to deal with the wicked. People were cowed. Some of them felt they couldn't be good enough; they felt they had to do more and more; and all around Raiwind, even after the ecstasies of the missionary tents, people could be seen on the roadside saying more prayers.

The land – on this Friday morning, when we were driving to Rana's village – was so flat and the air so clear that people could be seen from very far away, two or three villages at once: very small figures, some playing cricket on this holiday morning, some running or walking: the sharpness of the detail, and the small size of the figures, giving the eye a kind of pleasure. The houses were of clay brick and were the colour of the earth. From time to time there were the fat, tapering chimneys of brick kilns, with disordered or broken-into brick-piles around them.

There was a short cut, Rana said. If we could find out where it was we would get to the village in an hour. He couldn't remember where the short cut was, and he didn't know what condition it would be in after the floods. We began to ask. Rana was right. There was a short cut, and two or three people told us that the floods hadn't done it too much harm. But the short cut, when we came to it, was nothing like a real road. It was full of ruts and wide puddles, and at every village there was a jam. The shops at these village intersections were set far back on their plots; on the trampled, muddy space in front of the shops goods were displayed. This illusion of extra space encouraged people to make wide manoeuvres and added to the confusion. Once for about ten minutes we couldn't move at all, because there was such a tangle of horse-drawn tongas, carts, cars, bicycles, buses.

Many of the carts were driven by very young boys, sitting on the very edge of their carts and smoking like men, allowing themselves to be bounced up and down a little more than was necessary, and handling the reins with something like dash: the labour still new and exciting, a proof of manhood. On a dreadful stretch of stony, half-made road we saw a narrow-backed boy of about ten pushing hard at a little handcart behind the horse cart of his father. The boy was having trouble. He leaned to one side of the cart and then to the other, making the hand-cart tack from side to side on the stony road.

I asked Rana, 'What will happen to that boy?'

Rana said, 'His future is lost.'

After two hours of the short cut – always villages, always jams – Rana said we would come back by the other road.

At last we came to the little town that served the village. And then a while later to the village itself. Brick-walled plots; gutters on either side of the road; many pools for waste. Rana showed a building which he said was the girls' school, but we didn't stop. We drove on to the uncle's house.

He was waiting for us, and when we entered the outer courtyard where he received people we saw him. He was a fine-faced, slender man all in white except for the black shoes – white turban, white dhoti and *koortah*: country clothes – and with a well-trimmed white beard.

The small house was at the end of the courtyard: a dirt-floored verandah with brick columns supporting the roof, and a wide dirt-floored room with concrete walls and wooden doors. There was a reed mat on the dust of the dirt floor in the verandah, and a string bed in the inner room. A ceiling fan hung from the timber ceiling; the cross-beams on which the ceiling rested looked like iron rails. A new bed frame, as yet unstrung, stood on its end against one wall. Big nails on a wall for clothes; two wall niches, one above the other.

Two extra string beds were brought in for us by men who suddenly appeared. A string chair was brought in for Rana. A cousin in a dhoti and singlet, and with a towel over his bare shoulder, came in then and offered salted *lassi*, buttermilk. This serving cousin was much smaller than Rana or the uncle in white.

A young boy, carefully dressed in a khaki-coloured *shalwar-kameez* and black sandals, switched on the fan. It was too cool for the fan. We turned it off. The boy who had turned the fan on was another cousin. He was mentally defective. Rana told the story. When the boy was about a month old another cousin had accidentally dropped a block of ice on him; the boy had been like that ever since. And perhaps the ice had come from that ice factory Rana had mentioned.

The boy had a booming voice he couldn't control. He was full of attention for the visitors, and when he attempted to talk in his booming voice he became the centre of attention, with Rana looking tenderly at him, and the uncle looking at him.

Other people began to come, to pay their respects to Rana. The *patwari*, the man who kept the village land records, came on his motorbike. He was dressed formally, in an olive-grey *shalwar-kameez* suit. He was in his own way an important official; his position and duties had been defined in Mogul times. The taxes a landowner paid depended on the *patwari*'s records. But he wasn't properly introduced, and he said nothing at all; he just stayed in the room.

A high brick wall divided the outer courtyard, where visitors could be received, from the inner courtyard of the family house, where they couldn't go. A little girl in a flowered green long dress peeped round the wall, as if to find out whether visitors had really come, as she might have been told. When she saw us she pulled back as if frightened. A neem tree grew on the other side of that wall, and smoke rose from a fire of some sort in the inner courtyard.

A loudspeaker voice came nearer and nearer down the main village road. The loudspeaker was on a van selling blankets for winter.

Our driver, the garment-maker, was stretched out on one of the string beds, absolutely at ease now after the hard drive. It was as though he knew the village, knew Rana's uncle, the house, the bed itself. He talked to Rana about his garment business and his dream of exporting. Then, through Rana, he talked to me: he thought I could help, spread the word about him. His Urdu was spattered with unexpected English words: 'designs', 'latest designs', 'fashion design', 'total design', 'models'.

The loudspeaker could be heard returning. No words now, only film music.

A hookah was brought in. The worked brass bowl, sharply flattened out at the bottom, rested on small legs.

Among all these cousins anxious to attend and serve, Rana was indeed like a prince. He did not let his relations down. His manners were perfect. He was a stage or two higher than they were, or perhaps four or five stages higher.

A cousin brought a gun and cartridges, and offered shooting. Rana explained what the cousin had in mind. There was 'jungle' nearby, 'jungle' here, as elsewhere in the subcontinent, meaning not thick tropical forest, but a simpler kind of wilderness. The gun and the cartridges were like fine artefacts in the bare, dirt-floored room, a touch of luxury, like the hookah, something for the visitors. But they were also a tribute to Rana's uncle. He farmed two hundred acres, all in sugar cane, and four hundred people worked for him. He meant by that, Rana said, that those people were available for him; he could use them as he needed them.

Cocks began to crow outside, though it was past midday, and there was the chatter of children. A little boy in a black suit, already dusty, came and stood in the doorway.

Our lunch was now ready. The middle string bed was manhandled and placed end up against the wall. From the house in the inner courtyard brightly coloured cushions and two proper chairs were brought out, and a low table with a patterned Formica top. When the man or boy lifted the table into the room, the simple wooden frame of the table showed below the pretty Formica top, and some of the big new nails that had been driven clean through both the Formica top and the wooden frame. And suddenly there were lots of extra hands, lots of people doing things. A tablecloth or spread – a yellow floral spray on a dark-red ground – was set on the Formica table; they tried to flatten it out, but the ridges and dips of the folds remained. Rana said, 'Hand-stitched'. And when the china and tray were brought out, more and more hands appearing as they were needed, Rana said, 'These things are being brought out for us.' As though he didn't want the courtesy of his family to be unnoticed or to be taken for granted.

Whole fried eggs, each in a china saucer; a plate of mango pickle; a basket of wholewheat parathas wrapped in cloth to keep them warm; milky tea, already sugared, in a china pot. The parathas were done in village-made ghee or clarified butter; the wheat, though ground in a mill somewhere else, was from the fields around us.

Rana said, 'You might want to wash your hands.'

We did that outside, standing near the brick wall. One cousin poured water from a jug for us. Only the visitors ate. The others sat or attended on us. The more important among our hosts sat. One man simply stood holding the water jug.

The food was as good as it looked. We washed our hands again. And then it was time to go to the fields, to do the shooting that had been promised us. Another gun had appeared, as well cared for as the first.

The brick house next door, blank-walled, with a door from the lane, was the house of a relation of Rana's. Opposite was the smaller mud house of labourers. It was more open, and two or three people were lying on string beds in the shade. Once these people would have been the landlords' workers; now they were self-employed.

In the lane the dust was thick. The gutters, on both sides, were green with the flow from buffalo or cow pens. In one yard a woman was cleaning a drain with her hands; the muck lay thick and green on her hands up to the wrist.

The fields began just outside the village. From time to time we saw, from far away, small groups of women, three or four in a group, coming from the fields towards the village. They looked festive in the distance, like part of a wedding procession. Their clothes were red and yellow, and the baskets on their heads were covered with bright red cloths: they might have been baskets of flowers or ceremonial offerings. Near to, the women were small, thin, sunburnt: no connection, it seemed, between them and the colours they wore. Sometimes they hid the lower part of their face with their headcover. Not part of a wedding procession; they were only labourers coming back from the fields. Bright colours were worn by unmarried women, Rana said; married women wore duller colours.

We saw a new brick house a little way ahead, in the middle of fields. This was a school. One of Rana's uncles had given the land. But there was no teacher for this school or for the other three schools in the village, including the school for girls that Rana had pointed out when we had arrived. No male teacher wanted to come to the village, Rana said, because of the 'environment'. Village life had pleasures only for people who belonged there; it held nothing for outsiders. And women didn't want to come and teach in the village because they were frightened of being kidnapped by the big landlords; though, as I had seen, Rana said, the landlords of this village, who were his relations, were good and kind. And the school building, when we came closer to it, turned out to be less than a shell. It had no roof and no walls at the back.

We walked on the bunds or low walls between the sunken fields. Occasionally we jumped across little ditches. It was early November, cool, with a slight breeze. The fields were varied: nearly ripe sugar cane, tall but not yet ready for cutting; fields of young maize. Wheat fields had been harvested. Cotton fields from a distance looked like fields of white and pink roses, with the pink of the cotton flowers and the white of the cotton. Some fields still had their stubble; others had been ploughed and flooded. How long would they stay flooded? Rana asked someone of the party, and the answer was that the field would be flooded for three or four days, and then the water from the irrigation channel would be turned off. Rana asked, 'How is the irrigation done in England?' And if this flat part of the Punjab was all that you knew it would have been hard to imagine a country where agriculture depended only on rain.

We were now far from the village. Yet the fields were never absolutely empty. There were labourers going home. Tiny donkeys, half hidden by their great wide loads of grass, were sure-footed on the trampled-and-dried bunds. Sometimes mongrel dogs stood a field or two away and watched us. They were not at ease, and the whistles of our party made them nervous. They feared the cruelties associated with those whistles; they kept their distance.

Once we passed what looked like a small village: a cluster of mud or brick dwellings with dung-cakes on the walls. It wasn't a village, Rana said. It was the house and outbuildings and pens of one branch of the family. They had quarrelled with the main branch of the family; they preferred now not to 'talk', and they lived here by themselves. A two-stroke engine chattered away in the verandah: a machine chopping up grass for the animals. Rana said, 'The modern world.' And, in spite of the family quarrel, he waved at the man and boy looking after the chopping machine.

I had thought we were walking to the 'jungle' for the shooting. But at a certain stage Rana sent two of our party to a sugar-cane field, and they began to cut canes. We left them doing that, and we walked on. Rana pointed to a house below trees some distance away and said we were going there. There was a grinding mill there. We would grind the canes and have fresh cane juice.

We walked on and on, always seeing people. Once we saw a whole family, five or six people, squatting in a field and cutting tall grass. A small bare-backed boy was among the grass-cutters; he was about five, and, childlike, he stood up in the tall grass to see us. The rest of the family kept their heads down, cutting.

I said to Rana, 'Do they really need the labour of the little boy?'

Rana said, 'It is hard to cut grass.'

We were now near the house and the trees Rana had pointed to. We left the bund and struck across a bare field, wet in the depressions, but elsewhere caking and cracked. The dogs of the house began to bark. But they didn't show themselves, and it was some time before I saw them among the buffaloes.

The cane-grinding machine was on a slight rise and near a shade tree. A small pile of bleached, sun-dried cane husk showed that some-one else had been there perhaps a week or so before. Irrigation water made a pond and separated us from the house with the buffaloes and the dogs and the shade trees; dung-cakes were drying on the top of the outer mud wall.

The two cane-cutters came up, the master cutter holding the knife, the assistant carrying the long cut canes on his shoulder. A string bed was brought over from the house. We, the visitors, were to made to sit on it in the thin, scattered shade of the tree and watch the others get the grinding machine ready. One of the men with the guns spotted a grey, yellow-tinted bird on a tree about forty or fifty feet away. The bird was on the very end of a branch, as though it wanted to look at us and what we were doing. The man took aim; a dreadful bang; but the bird flew away unharmed; and no further shot was fired. The guns were forgotten. All energy went now into preparing the cane juice.

The grinding machine was cleaned with water from the pond. The long peeled bough that was to push the grinder was found; one end was fitted into the slot for it. This bough could also have rested as a yoke on the necks of two bullocks, and the bullocks would then have moved in a small circle and turned the grinder. But now some of the men of our party were to do the pushing; while two others were to sit at the grinder and feed in the cut canes. Someone from the house came to help, and the grinding began. It was a joke for the party: three men pushing the yoke as though they were bullocks, with the two men feeding in the canes ducking low, even while they squatted, every time the yoke made a circle.

At last a whole jugful of the juice was ready. It was grey, warm, with no pronounced flavour; possibly a deeper flavour would come after a while. Rana drank a tumblerful, a cousin standing with the cane-juice jug as he had stood with the same jug, when it held water, while we were having lunch. The garment-maker drank. Then the others drank.

Our entertainment was over. There was no shooting. We began to make our way back. In the cities of the subcontinent cane juice could be had from stalls with simple hand-turned grinders. For a version of that everyday pleasure, for the sake of drinking fresh cane juice in the fields, a whole train of people had put themselves at Rana's service; and perhaps some part of the pleasure lay in the ceremony, the crowd, the memory of old times. I asked Rana whether he had gone shooting with his father when they came to the village when he was a child. He said no; he had been too young. His pleasures in the village had been the pleasures of looking. He would go into the fields on his own and look.

He was in white *jama* or loose trousers and brown-gold long coat. The style was princely. It appeared more so in the fields. In my own eyes he had been growing in elegance and graciousness. He had no land now, but the people served him willingly still. It was service like that over many years that had given him the idea and pride that he was a Rajput.

It was possible to understand what he had said about the twin personalities he had in the city. The Lahore lawyer in the black suit and black tie felt the law as a daily humiliation; he had expected, in his grand profession, a higher form of the courtesies of his village. The man who was divided in this way was impatient at everything that didn't work in his country. He always said 'in my country'; he never said 'in Pakistan'. In his moodiness he had become part of a great underground rage that few of the politicians yet understood.

From far away we could hear the loudspeakers in the village. They were not selling blankets now. They were the loudspeakers of the mosque, and the preacher was speaking, Rana said, of the virtues that could come to people living simple lives, such as the people of the village; though for the children of the village, as Rana might have said, the future was something already lost.

As we entered the village a boy in ochre-coloured clothes was throwing earth at a tethered donkey, and the tormented animal was kicking back.

Rana went to the inner courtyard of his uncle's house to say goodbye to the women of his uncle's family. We had seen nothing of them, apart from the girl in the green dress right at the beginning, who had peeped from a safe oblique distance at the strangers, and had scooted.

Towards Lahore and the two sides of his personality we then went. We went by the other road, not the short cut. There were as many villages on this road as on the short cut. But there was an asphalted strip. It was wide enough for only one vehicle, and that made for delays. But it was the easier way. Rana had said it would take an hour and a half. It took two.

4

Guerrilla

IN 1945, at the end of the war, when Shahbaz's father was demobbed from the British Indian army, he thought he would settle in England. This was the kind of thing that some Indian princes did before the war; their money and their titles gave them a kind of exotic dignity, even if India was a colony. It was perhaps in Shahbaz's father's mind that the coming independence of India and Pakistan would give an equivalent dignity to a Muslim settler in England. Other Muslims from the sub-continent thought so, too; they distrusted independence for various reasons, and saw residence in England, a land of law, as a way out.

So, though Shahbaz was born in the year after independence, he hadn't grown up without colonial and racial stress. He had gone to both primary school and public school in England, and he had suffered especially at the public school. He was the only Asian, the only Muslim, the only one who didn't eat pork and go to the chapel. It didn't help when his father became insolvent. For three terms Shahbaz's fees couldn't be paid, and it seemed at one time that he would be asked to leave. That didn't happen, but it made Shahbaz feel separated from his friends.

Shahbaz's father gave up the idea of settling in England. He began to prepare for a return to Pakistan. He started a business in the interior of the Punjab. When he was twelve or thirteen Shahbaz went in the school holidays to see this business of his father's. They visited certain feudal families in the area. These 'feudals' were great landlords who owned whole villages. The sons of some of those families had been students in England, and Shahbaz's parents had looked after them. Shahbaz now saw that on their home ground the sons of these feudals didn't act like Oxford or Cambridge graduates. They treated their workers and peasants like serfs. The peasants would touch the feet of their landlord in submission and greeting; it was more submission than greeting; and the landlord would not ask the peasant to rise. Shahbaz, fresh from England, wanted to weep.

His last three years at the public school in England were very happy. He was on his own. At half-term and in the holidays he stayed with friends or in paid accommodation. Once he stayed with a rector in Oxfordshire and he had a platonic romance with the rector's daughter. Life was good for him; and though he was now more English than Pakistani or Muslim, though he hardly knew Pakistan, the poetry he began to write was all about poverty and beggars and cripples and people in the streets.

When he finished the public school he went back to Pakistan, to Lahore, to do a degree. He took an interest in local politics; he was against the rule of the generals; he was a man of the left. But his true political life began when he went back to England. He went to a well-known provincial university to a do a degree in English literature. The place was hot with politics. It was 1968; it was the time of the Vietnam movement; and, as he remembered twenty-seven years later, 'very emotional'. Everybody was saying that the 'system' was rotten and had to be changed. He said it; sexy Latin American girls said it. There was 'a lot of smooching around'. University life was 'a kind of carnival'.

There were close Pakistani friends at the university. Many of them were doing English literature, like Shahbaz; it was one of the lighter courses, possibly the lightest, and at this time it was very political and restricted. It was encouraging Marxism and revolution rather than wide reading. So Shahbaz and his Pakistani friends in their Marxist study group read the standard (and short) revolutionary texts, Frantz Fanon, Che Guevara. And while they read certain approved Russian writers, they didn't read or get to know about the Turgenev novels, *Fathers and Sons* (1862) and *Virgin Soil* (1877), which dealt with conditions not unlike those in feudal Pakistan, but questioned the simplicities of revolution.

Shahbaz said, when I asked about Turgenev, 'The fiction I was not relating to my political development.' As though his ideas about Marxism and revolution, however formulaic, were personal to him, part of his development.

There were similar Pakistani study groups at other universities in England. They came together and began to have meetings every two weeks in Cambridge or London. In London they linked up with Indian leftist groups. Earl's Court in London was the leftist area, with bars and restaurants with a leftist tone. Leftists from all over the world met there, and in this international atmosphere there were discussions and all-night parties. It was 'exhilarating'.

A cousin of Shahbaz's was part of the larger London study group. She had been to Cuba and had cut cane there for six weeks and had met 'Fidel'. Shahbaz was half in love with this cousin. She was a good-looking girl, and her stories of the equality in Cuba and the medical services made him love the idea of the collective even more. He became impatient for the revolution. But then, after the university, the beautiful cousin began to regress. She went back not only to having peasants cut her canes in the Punjab; she went back at the same time to a mullah-like passion for Islam. Shahbaz said, as though he was speaking of a medical condition, 'She went through a complete regression.' To round off this regression, she even married a 'creep'. Now in Lahore, on those social occasions when they were in the same room or place, she didn't recognise Shahbaz.

But there was someone else for Shahbaz, another Pakistani girl from his own university. With this girl he fell fully in love, and she was apparently in love with him. Shahbaz said, as though he was talking of making love or baking a cake, 'We wanted to go back and make revolution together. It was marvellous.' This idea of the future supported Shahbaz right through his time at the university. But then, at the end, when it came to packing up and leaving home and going off to the guerrilla wars, the girl found she couldn't follow Shahbaz.

Shahbaz said, 'She couldn't make the political break with her family.'

The thought of their love kept Shahbaz warm through the ten long guerrilla years, in the deserts and mountains of Baluchistan and Afghanistan, to which, somewhat to his surprise, he found he had committed himself, in those exhilarating all-night discussions and parties in Earl's Court and Cambridge and his own university. Ten long celibate years, because although a man might be in Baluchistan fighting for the Baluchis, he had to stay away from the women. Adultery among the nomads was a murderous business. A man thinking of adultery had to go to a woman's tent, awaken her without awakening her husband, lead her out past relations and past the family flocks, make love to her, and then take her back, all without being discovered. This kind of adultery was like a guerrilla war within the guerrilla war, Shahbaz said; and, though the most successful adulterers made the best fighters, Shahbaz was content to observe it from a distance. All of this, though, and his own long celibacy, lay in the future.

One of the things his Marxist student group used to discuss was the 'nationality question' in Pakistan. Punjab was the dominant province; people in other provinces felt left out. Iqbal, the poet who had proposed the idea of Pakistan, had thought, with his convert's zeal, that Islam would be identity enough and cause enough for people in the new state; and that historical ideas of clan and caste (like Rana's Rajput pride) would disappear. Iqbal was wrong. Regional feeling was bubbling up, especially in the east; Bangladesh would soon secede.

It was the idea now of Shahbaz's Marxist group that Marxism and revolution would do what Islam had failed to do. Shahbaz explained the idea in this way: 'You needed a revolution from below. From within all the nationalities. And the process of revolution would cement the nationalities.'

Shahbaz didn't think the idea was too abstract; it was taken from Marxist literature, and the group had spent a year and a half working it out. And they knew, too, where the revolution should start. It should be in Baluchistan, a big, near-empty desert province to the west. The population was small and backward, many of the people nomadic. There had been three uprisings since independence, and the people were still disaffected. It was a difficult area to police. It was, all in all, the place where, in the more abstract and scientific-sounding language of revolution, 'the contradiction between the state and people was very clear.'

The group was now dominated by a South African Indian. His family had moved to Karachi and had a shop there. He met the group when he came to London on a visit. He was very young, nineteen or twenty, but he said he had been a Marxist all his life, and he was full of revolutionary and guerrilla stories. He said that he and all his family belonged to the African National Congress; he himself had been underground in South Africa. He had done more, young as he was: he had been underground in Pakistan itself, in Baluchistan. That shut the Pakistani Marxists up completely. The South African had no formal education, and they liked it when he abused them for their privileged backgrounds.

Shahbaz thought him inspiring and 'charismatic' (that was one of Shahbaz's words). He was a good-looking man, short and very stocky, with piercing eyes. He had no time for people's personal problems. To him the cause was all. This was another relationship that was to end badly for Shahbaz. The South African was to try to kill Shahbaz. The piercing eyes that attracted Shahbaz turned out to be the eyes of a paranoiac. Twenty-five years later, when all guerrilla wars were over for him, and he was back in Africa, in Zimbabwe, he committed suicide after trying to kill his son. This was something else that was in the future.

One day in London in 1969 the South African was especially abusive of Shahbaz's university Marxists. That was his way of bringing them to order. Then he said, 'You guys should stop talking and start acting. If you are serious you should give up everything and make Baluchistan the focus of a revolution in Pakistan.'

This was like the revolution from within the nationalities that the group had discussed. The primary aim of that had been the cementing of the nationalities. The South African was far more ambitious. He was aiming at total revolution, and he said he was following the precept of Lin-Piao, Mao's second-in-command during the cultural revolution. The countryside, Lin-Piao had said, could be used to swamp the cities; the countryside was where you could start guerrilla war against the cities, which was where the state was.

They were all awed by the South African's vision. Che Guevara of Argentina, Cuba and Bolivia, Frantz Fanon of the French West Indies, the African National Congress, and now Lin-Piao: it seemed to Shahbaz's study group that, late though they had come to revolution, all the great and tried forces of revolution had begun to run unconquerably together for them and in them. They all began to dream of Baluchistan and guerrilla war.

The next year Shahbaz graduated. He told his parents then that he was going to a film school in Yugoslavia. He came secretly back to Karachi, spent a night there, and went by train and bus to a small town in Baluchistan. They were met by a Baluchi tribesman. He took them to a training camp in the mountains. The South African was there, and someone from the London group.

Baluchistan here was like Iran, desert plateau and bare mountain,

with very little water, very little vegetation, and extremes of temperature. This was where Shahbaz was to spend ten years. For the first
three years he and the others were learning the language and trying to
start social services for the Baluchis.

But I felt that the narrative had become too fast here. I felt when I considered my notes that certain things had been elided. I telephoned
Shahbaz; he didn't make difficulties. I went to see him again. I wanted
to hear more about those very early days in Baluchistan. I wanted to
hear more about the first day.

Shahbaz said, 'I took the train from Karachi. I was met at the other
end by two tribesmen on the platform. They were more urbane than
the tribesmen I was to meet later. We took a bus for ten miles. We got
off the bus and walked for two days. It was my first walk through
mountains. Very rough terrain. I was dressed in *shalwar-kameez* and
shoes, and a turban I was not used to. I was carrying a rucksack I was
not used to carrying. On the way we made bread, and ate dry bread,
and I spent my first night out in the open. It was summer. We just lay
on the bare earth. It was exhausting. I got blisters. I was in pain. My
whole body ached. When I arrived at the camp I was exhausted.

'Five days before, I was at university in England. Now I was suddenly
thrust into a camp of thirty to forty tribesmen, fully armed, speaking a
language I didn't know. It was like sitting in the movies. It was like
meeting Martians. I had not mentally prepared myself for the shock of
this meeting. That first night I was given a gun and put on sentry duty.
Five days before, I was at university in England. They killed a goat to
celebrate my arrival. We had meat that night with a lot of fat, very rich
meat. It made my stomach run. And going to the toilet in the bush, as
it were, was also initially difficult.'

A reading of Turgenev would not have prepared him for Baluchistan,
but it might have prepared him imaginatively, as a revolutionary, for this
meeting with Martians.

What Shahbaz had got to was a training camp. There was as yet no war;
that was to come three years later, after the training. The Baluchi leader
in the region, Shahbaz's field commander, was a clan chief. There were
tribes among the Baluchis, and clans within the tribes; rivalries between

clans and tribes made it hard for Shahbaz and the other outsiders to have an overall picture of what was going on. There were five outsiders in the training camps. A few others were in the cities, to see to supplies and money matters.

For the first three years Shahbaz and the others were 'integrating'. (There appeared to be a technical term for everything a guerrilla did. This would have been reassuring for some beginners, who, now that they were in the field, in the vastness of Baluchistan, might have begun to feel small, and perhaps even idle.) So they integrated for three years. They learned the language and set up social services for the tribesmen. The tribesmen were nomadic. Life was not easy for Shahbaz when they were on the move. He lived on dry bread and slept on the ground, on a shawl spread over grass. In the summer they built shelters and slept in the open. In the winter they lived in caves with an overhang of rock. In the winter the outsiders slept in sleeping bags. Shahbaz also had a radio and a typewriter and books. He and the others had stored a lot of books in caves, but when the camp was moving about he could carry only two.

Life was hard, but Shahbaz and his friends felt 'incredibly creative'. They were among nomads. In England when they were talking about revolution they had talked about workers and peasants. These Baluchis were certainly not workers, and they weren't at all like Punjabi peasants, who were the peasants Shahbaz knew. These nomads were people whom the modern world had never touched. That was why they had seemed to him like Martians at the beginning. He knew it was not the way a revolutionary should feel. But in this period of integration he had thought of what Mao had said: that the peasants were a blank page, and that whatever you wrote on that page the peasant became. That was how he had grown to think of his nomads; though, as an intelligent and fair-minded man, he worried that as a revolutionary he was being vain and perhaps even cruel, thinking that he could bring up these people any way he chose.

Twenty years later he excused himself. He said, 'You really felt you were on the cusp of change in the life of a nation.'

Shahbaz was a man of generous spirit. It was said in Pakistan that Pakistanis, because of their uncertainty in the wider world, always tried to bring their fellows down. Shahbaz wasn't like that; he readily offered admiration to Pakistanis as well as to other people. Perhaps his isolation in England and his time in the English public school had given him both a need for other people's approval and a capacity for hero-worship. Just as he had surrendered to the South African in London, so now in Baluchistan he surrendered to the clan chief who was his immediate commander.

The clan chief was illiterate, a shepherd from a family of nomads. He had fought in the 1963 Baluchi uprising against the Pakistan military government. Shahbaz was enchanted by his humility, his moderation, his calm, his gift of language. The clan leader had the illiterate's unclouded instinct for the character and mood of people, and he knew in every situation how people needed to be talked to. He was a natural leader, and Shahbaz and the others had hopes that he would be the Mao or Ho Chi Minh of the Baluchi, and perhaps also Pakistani, revolution.

So they began, as they thought, to educate him politically, to educate him, as Shahbaz was to say twenty-five years later, in the ways of the world and the politics of revolution. His response was all they could have wished. It was a proof – this time in far-off Baluchistan – of the rightness and universality of Marxist revolution. It washed away any doubt they might have about their mission. Shahbaz thought the Baluchi clan leader took to his education 'like a duck to water'; though Shahbaz, if he hadn't been so anxious for an admired man to respond well, to pass this critical test, might have paid a little more attention to the illiterate man's sense of what was required of him.

Shahbaz said, 'We didn't see ourselves as leaders. We saw ourselves as creating leaders for the people.'

Shahbaz's Marxism and longing for revolution was 'emotional'. The South African was different. He wanted power, Shahbaz thought. Perhaps he wanted (this was my idea rather than Shahbaz's) to be in Baluchistan what, as an Indian, he couldn't be in South Africa, in or out of the African National Congress. And Shahbaz appeared, in his generous way, to think that the South African's wish for power was all right, because he was 'leadership material'. Power, in this argument, was something the world owed the South African.

There was another outsider whom Shahbaz admired and felt especially close to. This was a Christian boy from Karachi, the son of a senior air force officer. He had been part of the London group; and he had given up his accountancy studies to join the revolutionaries. He was emotional like Shahbaz; he was intelligent, and well read; he cried easily, like Shahbaz. He cried for the poverty and injustice he saw. This boy, as a Christian in Pakistan, had spent much of his life as an outsider; he might have been (though Shahbaz didn't make the comparison) as much an outsider as Shahbaz had been for many years in England. This boy had a great sense of humour, and Shahbaz remembered his 'fantastically loud laugh'. Shahbaz remembered him as very thin, very dark, very Bengali-looking.

Shahbaz, when he spoke of this boy, became filled with the mood of elegy. This boy was killed six years after he had got to Baluchistan, in the third year of the insurgency. He had gone to a small town to meet someone he trusted, and was betrayed by this person to the army. He was captured with his deputy, a tribesman. The army said nothing at all about his capture; so the insurgents never got to know. They learned later that he was interrogated and tortured for many weeks and then thrown out of a helicopter. It tormented them that they didn't know when he had been killed. Shahbaz, though he spoke of this boy in elegy, never thought to look for his family afterwards.

The revolution began, after three years of preparation, with dozens of uprisings all over the wastes of Baluchistan. And, quite miraculously (for someone so emotionally attached to the idea of revolution), the area in which Shahbaz had been moving around (and having a hard time) became, in technical guerrilla language, a liberated area. The leaders of the revolution were clan chiefs, like the one Shahbaz admired, who had become guerrilla commanders. The war was scattered, reflecting the divisions of tribe and clan. There were five or six separate fighting groups in the tribe to which Shahbaz was attached. He was running a camp for one of those groups. His camp had from fifty to two hundred fighters. His business was not fighting. It was to educate the people in his area, to train them in medical skills, to adjudicate in disputes, and (curiously, for a public school man) to deal with matters concerning farming and the flocks.

But there were two sides to the war. It soon became clear that, after the secession of Bangladesh, the government of Pakistan, under Mr Bhutto, was going to deal with the Baluchis and their tribal chiefs with extreme severity. Shahbaz thought that at one time one hundred thousand troops were in Baluchistan. In London the South African had dazzled them with the name of Lin-Piao and with his theory, from the Chinese cultural revolution, that guerrilla war in the countryside would swamp the cities. What they hadn't expected, what no Marxist primer or revolutionary handbook had prepared them for, was this: a well-trained professional army moving with overwhelming strength to flatten the frail social structures of a nomadic people.

Shahbaz's misgiving or bewilderment on the very first day, at his sight of the 'Martians' of Baluchistan, had something in it after all, however much, with the help of the thoughts of Mao, he had rationalised it away later. The nomads were not the workers or peasants of Marxist literature, rooted people. The nomads were wanderers; they travelled light; they could be brushed away.

Shahbaz, telling the story, didn't say a great deal about this. I felt there was more to say about the brushing away of the nomads, and when I went to see him some days later I asked him.

He said, 'People were dying all around you. People had lost their livelihoods and their families. The economy of a nomadic family is so fragile. It depends on flocks. All you have to do is to destroy the animals. Which they did. They shot them, rounded them up in big sweeps, thousands and thousands of sheep and goats and so on. And once you do that, people have nothing to live on.'

The army didn't move in the summer; the heat was too great. The army moved in winter, and at the end of the second winter the revolution in Baluchistan was more or less over. All the partying and lovemaking in London, all the discussion of sacred revolutionary texts with sexy Latin American girls, all the preparation and education in Baluchistan, had come very quickly to nothing.

Shahbaz was for some time in one of the few liberated areas holding out. Soon as an administrator he was on his own. The South African had left not long after the actual fighting had begun. This hadn't worried Shahbaz. He still had faith in the South African, and he knew that the South African was going to Europe to do important work: to raise funds (from Russia, Germany, and India, though Shahbaz didn't say this), and to plant stories about Baluchistan in the left-wing press. The South African kept in touch, but he never came back.

Such publicity as Baluchistan got abroad was because of the South African, but it was very little. Baluchistan never became one of the big international left-wing causes. One reason might have been the quick collapse of the revolution; another reason would have been the silence in Pakistan about the uprising and the army operations. The government said nothing; no Pakistan newspaper printed anything; and

journalists who wrote about Baluchistan were jailed. The revolutionaries in the cities did put out a little clandestine bulletin, stylishly called
Jabal (a Baluchi word meaning 'mountain'), but it was rough and
cyclostyled and it came out once a month. It would have looked a little
too much like what it was, a voice in the wilderness, and its message
didn't carry.

At the end of the second winter of the army's operations the Baluchi
clan chief – in whom Shahbaz and the others had seen a possible Ho
Chi Minh or Mao of the Baluchi revolution – decided to leave
Baluchistan, and to take some of his abandoned and derelict nomads on
an unusually long walk across the border to Afghanistan. There were at
one time about twenty-five thousand of these refugee nomads, Shahbaz
said; many of them were women and children who no longer had men
to support them.

The winter after that, the Christian boy from Karachi, who had the
'huge smile and huge laugh', and wept for the poor, and had been
studying in London to be a chartered accountant, was captured and tortured and dropped from a helicopter.

The army was now pressing very hard. Shahbaz said, 'Terrible.
Massacres. Starvation. Bombing. Seeing many of the people you had
raised up and trained die in front of you.' But he never doubted the
cause. 'No. The disasters made me wiser.'

He had constantly to decide what to do with various groups of
non-combatants, whether to send them north to Afghanistan or east to
Sindh, or to keep them where they were. It was important not to send
everybody away, because a depopulated area ceased perhaps to be a liberated area.

The army watched all the routes. Shahbaz was closely blockaded in
his liberated area. Extraordinarily – after all the planning for a guerrilla
war in the countryside – food had to be smuggled in from the cities.

Shahbaz was still game, still excited, in spite of the failure and tragedy
all around him, still seeing the revolution as part of his personal development. He said, 'It was an intensely creative time.'

Wheat was what they most needed. Shopkeeping in Baluchistan had
been something the Hindus did once upon a time, but after partition
they had been run out of all the towns. Tribals had taken over, and
they were relatives or distant relatives of the insurgents. They organised
camel trains. These camel trains, sometimes with guerrilla escorts,
had to pass through various army checkpoints. There were disasters,

especially in winter, the time of the army offensives. Guerrillas would be taken in by the army; shopkeepers would be taken in; precious food would be lost. There were times when Shahbaz and his people were eating one meal every two days. They travelled with bits of bread in their pockets; that kept them going.

The army moved up one winter to the mountains where Shahbaz and his group were. They had to get out fast. They moved at night, to avoid being spotted by the army helicopters. They were moving with a lot of food, reserve stocks. They couldn't lose that. For a whole day Shahbaz and his group hid in a nomadic settlement. They were fed and looked after, and in the night they moved out. The army at this stage wasn't using helicopters alone; it was also using trackers, army scouts and local Baluchi trackers. These trackers led the soldiers to the nomadic settlement. They asked questions. 'Who was here last night? Who made all those tracks outside, coming up to your houses?' Everybody in the settlement was killed, sixteen people.

Shahbaz was disturbed for weeks after he heard. The Baluchis with him were more stoical; they comforted him.

Shahbaz said, 'Because nomadic life is hard, they have a great capacity for absorbing calamities. I learned that stoicism and patience from them.'

Three years later – the interlocking wheels of all the various Greek tragedies and revenge tragedies of Pakistan grinding away – Mr Bhutto, who had unleashed the army against the Baluchis, was deposed by a general and tried and hanged. This general declared an amnesty, and the war in Baluchistan was over.

Shahbaz was now in Afghanistan with the other refugees. He had walked there over the mountains from Baluchistan. There were two camps for the refugees in the south of Afghanistan. The clan chief who had led the refugees to Afghanistan was still there, still a man of influence. The revolutionary movement also had various flats in Kabul. For the many weeks that Shahbaz was in Afghanistan he moved between the refugee camps and the flats in Kabul.

It was in Kabul that Shahbaz met the South African again, after six years. The revolutionaries, those who had survived or were still interested, were meeting in Kabul (especially safe for them, with the Russian occupation) to talk about the future of the movement. Shahbaz and some of the others also wanted to talk to the South African about what he had been doing in Europe for six years, and about the money he had raised.

There were tremendous arguments, 'huge fights'. At the end Shahbaz and the South African were not talking to one another. The South African began to say that Shahbaz and the others were traitors; they had betrayed the revolution and should be killed. Shahbaz was shocked. He was even more shocked when the clan chief – in whom they had once seen a future Mao or Ho Chi Minh – called him and said he could no longer guarantee Shahbaz's safety: the South African would now be trying to poison Shahbaz. Shahbaz thought it better to leave the Baluchi to deal with the South African. He went back to the mountains. This was how Shahbaz said goodbye to the two men he had most admired.

The movement had now broken up. The Baluchis didn't want to have anything more to do with outsiders. They were not interested in revolution now; they had become separatists. The South African finally went back to London. That was where after a while Shahbaz went, too, returning to Kabul from the mountains to take a plane. From London he got in touch with his parents, who had felt betrayed by him, and made it up with them.

He was deaf in one ear because of the war. He had lost all his teeth. He had had hepatitis, and couldn't drink alcohol now. He had annual bouts of malaria.

He said, 'I have no regrets. That was and always will be the most creative, stimulating part of my life. Where I was most energised, and where I learned so much. I was disappointed by the end result, but that doesn't make me bitter.'

The angle was unexpected. Didn't he feel now – time having passed, and leaving aside his parents and the Baluchis – that he had misused his privilege and betrayed himself intellectually?

'No. I came to maturity when all this was going on.'

'All this?'

'Guerrilla wars all over the third world.'

It was his idea of education. It was the strangely colonial idea of his generation in Pakistan, born though they were after independence. Education wasn't something you developed in yourself, to meet your own needs. It was something you travelled to, without fear of prejudice now, and when you got to where you were going you simply surrendered to the flow.

As a Marxist he thought he had been unconventional. He hadn't wished to impose the standard Marxist kit on the Baluchis. He thought that there was much about the tribal culture that was good and positive and should be preserved, like the legal system, and the common ownership of pasture land. Now the whole tribal structure had been destroyed. There was no longer traditional law; there was no access to the courts; and there were now two to three hundred blood feuds among the leading families. So things in Baluchistan were now much worse than they were in 1970, when he had gone there from Karachi, by train and bus and on foot, carrying revolution.

This was the story Shahbaz told over many hours. Stories told in this way can have elisions and jumps, but as I read my notes over the next day or two I felt that certain things were missing. There was no sense of the passing of time, though Shahbaz had spent ten years in Baluchistan and Afghanistan. There was no reference to water, no true sense of a landscape. And the tribesmen were not there. They were the people to whom Marxism was being taken; they were the people who were being ravaged; but they were not there, not even as costume figures. Only the Baluchi clan chief and the South African and the Christian boy with the big laugh were there.

Shahbaz was surprised by what I had said about the tribesmen. It hadn't occurred to him, and he had no explanation. The tribesmen had been present to him while he spoke. 'I see them – the tribesmen – all the time. But my description may have been one-sided.'

About the passing of time he said, 'It was ten years. Hard to encapsulate. People here find it difficult to relate to the passing of time. Time passes slowly for many people and they find it difficult to pinpoint. People are not used to rapid changes and that affects their attitude to time. Lives have changed – dramatically – but it has been a very slow, cumbersome process. I don't think it's Islam. People don't have the mechanism to remember when the dish reached their village or when they saw their first naked girl on MTV.'

What he said about water was puzzling, considering his silence about it: 'Everything was dominated by water. The search for water was the most important thing in the world. The tribesmen knew where the water was, but not in what quantity, or how clear it was, and whether it could support a hundred men and the animals with them. Or whether there would be springs or rivers or pools. So we sent scouts ahead to find out. And sometimes at five the scouts would come back and say the water wasn't good enough or wasn't enough, and so we had to walk on into the night. It was also like this for the military. The extremes of temperature were enormous.'

The experiences and the emotions were there, but they had not come out in the earlier account. It was as though, in this story of revolution, he had wished to strip people down to their Marxist essentials. (In some such way the Islamic zealot wanted converted people to be the faith alone, without distorting history and traditions.) He had seen the tribesmen not as men but as tribesmen, units, and the clan chief as a leader rather than as a man with affections and human attributes.

He had been just as hard on himself; he had left out much of his physical suffering, which had been very great. His eardrum had been punctured by an explosion at the very beginning; and his ears had bled for many months. He had been tormented by hepatitis; every bout lasted two months, and it made the long marches 'killing'. Hepatitis came from the bad water; the tribesmen were less susceptible than he was. (This was probably why he had never talked about water the first time.) There were no fruit juices to help with the hepatitis; the food was mainly bread and meat, sometimes lentils, and sometimes damaging things like milk and clarified butter.

All of this he had left out as inessential, with the faces and costumes of the tribespeople, and the tents, and the camels, and the baggage, and the landscape.

He said, 'It was a very personal account. I very rarely speak about these experiences.' Later he said, 'I didn't talk about my own suffering because the people I was with were suffering more.'

That vision of suffering, though repressed, was there. It came out now, when he talked of what had happened afterwards.

The clan leader he had admired had quarrelled with the *sardar* or chief of the tribe. The *sardar* had not wanted to 'take the movement forward', and the tribe was now badly divided. The clan leader had gone back to his own area, and he was hard up. His people were hard up.

Shahbaz said, 'You should remember that the people have remained totally impoverished because of the loss of their flocks. Thousands of them have come down to Sindh and Punjab to look for work for daily wages. So the economic life of the tribe, and other tribes as well, has been destroyed.' The *sardars* blocked development. 'They are greedy. They want commissions. The *sardars'* own economic life has been destroyed. No flocks of his own, no gifts of sheep from his followers. So the *sardar* depends now on government handouts.'

Afghanistan, with the Russian occupation, had been a safe place for Baluchi refugees during the insurgency. But that war in Afghanistan had turned out to be calamitous for the Baluchi people. A million Afghan refugees had been settled in Baluchistan, and they had been like locusts. They had come with their own very big flocks, and they appeared to repeople the land. They cut down the trees and their flocks grazed on the best pasture. The Baluchis could do nothing. They had become a minority in their own territory.

'Those refugees were Pathans. So the Pathans today are in a much stronger position than the Baluch in Baluchistan. The Pathans brought with them their fundamentalist trend. *Madrassas* [Koranic schools] and so on – totally alien to the Baluch culture. This happened after the war. Friends still keep coming here and talking about how bad it's become.'

And still he didn't feel responsible. Still he thought of himself as a carrier of the truth.

'The ideology was supplied by the 1968 movement. But the urge was a local urge, to do something for my country, especially after the loss of Bangladesh. Today the people who think they have the answer are the fundamentalists.'

5

Penitent

THE FUNDAMENTALISTS were known to English-speaking people in Pakistan as the 'fundos'. They were to that extent a presence now. They were still in the background, but they pushed and pushed, and always wanted more.

The Indian subcontinent had been bloodily partitioned to create the state of Pakistan. Millions had died, and many more had been uprooted, on both sides of the new frontiers. More than a hundred million Muslims had been abandoned on the Indian side, but virtually all the Hindus and Sikhs had been chased away from Pakistan, to create the all-Muslim polity of Iqbal's casual poetic dream.

That should have been enough. But the fundamentalists wanted more. It wasn't enough that this large portion of the ancient land had ceased, after the millennia, to be India; and – like Iran, like the Arab countries – had been finally cleansed of the older faiths. The people themselves now had to be cleansed of the past, of everything in dress or manners or general culture that might link them to their ancestral land. The fundamentalists wanted people to be transparent, pure, to be empty vessels for the faith. It was an impossibility: human beings could never be blanks in that way. But the various fundamentalist groups offered themselves as the pattern of goodness and purity. They offered themselves as true believers. They said they followed the ancient rules (especially the rules about women); all they asked of people was to be like them and, since there was no absolute agreement about the rules, to follow the rules they followed.

The most important of the fundamentalist groups was the Jamaat–i–Islami, the Assembly of Islam. It had been founded by a religious teacher and zealot, Maulana Maudoodi. Before partition he had objected to the idea of Pakistan, for strange reasons. The poet Iqbal, presenting the case for a separate Indian Muslim state in 1930, had said that such a state would rid Indian Islam of the 'stamp which Arab imperialism was forced to give it'. Maudoodi's ambitions were just the opposite. He thought that an Indian Muslim state would be too limiting, would suggest that Islam had done its work in India. Maudoodi wanted Islam to convert and cover all India, and to cover the world. Iqbal had said that an important reason for the creation of Pakistan was that Islam had worked better in India than in other places as 'a people-building force'. Maudoodi didn't think so. He didn't think the Muslims of the subcontinent and their political leaders were good enough, as Muslims, for something as precious as an all–Muslim state. They were not pure enough in their belief; they were too tainted by the Indian past.

Maudoodi had died in 1979. But the attitude of the Jamaat was still that the people of Pakistan and their rulers were not good enough. If Iqbal's Muslim state had had its calamities, it wasn't the fault of Islam; it was only the fault of the people who called themselves Muslim. In the fundamentalist way of thinking this kind of failure automatically condemned itself as the failure of a false or half-hearted Islam. And the Jamaat could always say – its cause ever fresh – that Islam had never really been tried since the early days, and that it was time to try it now. The Jamaat would show the way.

The Jamaat headquarters and commune was in a twenty-eight-acre site at Mansoura, on the edge of Lahore, on the Multan road. Among the people in the commune were some penitents, expiating sins of varying magnitude.

One of the penitents was Muhamad Akram Ranjha. He was fifty-eight. Penitent though he was, and devout, he was not a solitary. He was living at Mansoura in a rented house with his rather large family. He was a man of rough feudal background. His father was a rich man, with five hundred acres, and with some political influence even in the British time. But Muhamad Akram had received no formal education as a child. There was a reason. He had had typhoid when he was very young, and his father had vowed that, if his son recovered, he would never be sent to a secular school, but would be educated in the Koran. The boy recovered; but the father forgot one half of the vow, and the boy (though receiving simple religious instruction from a mullah) grew up like someone of an uneducated feudal family, spending his time on horses and tent-pegging and polo, and gambling and hawking, and going to local festivals.

When he was twenty-three Muhamad Akram became involved in a serious family quarrel. The quarrel was about a woman and land. The woman was a cousin of Muhamad Akram's. She was an educated woman, the first in the family to get a degree. When her father died she inherited six hundred acres. She was twenty-three. Her uncle, her father's brother, an old-fashioned man, wanted her to stay in purdah; he also wanted to marry her off to his eight-year-old son. She wanted none of that. She had studied in Lahore at Queen Mary College, a famous coeducational school run by Christians; and she was used to freedom. She was also in love with Muhamad Akram's brother, her cousin. He was twenty-six and unusually handsome and spoke well. He was already married, with two sons. But she ran away with him and became his second wife.

The uncle (with the eight-year-old son) was enraged. He threatened to wipe out Muhamad Akram's branch of the family. This was very much the local feudal way, and the uncle was a man of local power. Muhamad Akram went to the uncle and asked for pardon. 'Please don't kill us. I promise that we will find out where my brother and the girl are, and we will bring the girl back to you.'

Muhamad Akram found the runaway couple in Karachi. He asked them to return to Lahore. When they were there he and three or four other male members of the family kidnapped the woman at gunpoint. The woman's husband, Muhamad Akram's brother, was not cowed. He went to the police station and filed a charge against the kidnappers. This show of spirit in the husband, this bringing in of the law into a rough feudal dispute about land and honour, must have been unexpected. And it was at this stage – perhaps to resolve the overlapping issues of land and honour, before the police did what they had to do – that the kidnapped woman was shot dead. It was never established who actually did the killing.

All the kidnappers were arrested and tried. The law moved fast – this was in 1960, during the rule of General Ayub – and less than two months after the killing all five kidnappers were jailed. Muhamad Akram was sentenced to fourteen years, a life term.

He was sent to the jail in the city of Multan. He was offered a choice of cell-mates. He could share with a well-known Lahore thug of the Gujjar tribe (and, though this wasn't said, risk being sexually assaulted); or he could be with the secretary-general of the Jamaat-i-Islami, who was doing time as a political prisoner. Muhamad Akram chose the man from the Jamaat.

The two men talked. In a matter of months Muhamad Akram underwent a change of heart. He began to read the writings of Maulana Maudoodi. He saw the error and emptiness of his feudal ways. His jail-house conversion to the cause of the Jamaat became famous. Soon he began to study. Matriculation, bachelor of arts – the young feudal didn't want to stop. He became legendary as a reformed prisoner. His sentence was cut from fourteen years to six, and on the very day of his release his master's diploma in Urdu literature arrived in the post.

Muhamad Akram's son, telling this story of his father's conversion (larger in this account than the dead girl's own tragedy), said, 'He went to jail as a feudal, and came back as a Muslim revolutionary.'

It was twelve years, though, before Muhamad Akram made the move to the Jamaat commune at Mansoura. First he enrolled in a law college, with the help of the distinguished lawyer who had defended him at his trial in 1960.

(I met this lawyer in Karachi in 1979. He was by then very rich, quite crazed with religion, vain, and hoping for political power. It was a very religious time – Mr Bhutto had been deposed and hanged, the Islamic whipping vans were being sent out to punish the wicked (and everybody was running to see), and everything stopped for prayers – and the lawyer thought that it was important for him to make a show of his piety. He muttered his prayers all the time I was with him and clacked his prayer-beads. I didn't respond. He said, 'I suppose you're thinking that I should be in a monastery.' I had no intention of encouraging him. I said, 'I am not thinking that.' He clacked his beads and muttered and clacked his beads again and then, ratcheting his piety up a notch or two, said, 'I'm God-intoxicated.')

This man not only helped Muhamad Akram get into the law college; he also became his unofficial spiritual adviser. And so it happened that when Muhamad Akram started his law practice in his home area of Sargodha he also became politically active on behalf of the Jamaat. This was a break with the past; the feudals here had always been·supporters of the people in power.

But the past was not buried. Blood feuds here never absolutely died. In 1975 scores were settled with Muhamad Akram's brother, who fifteen years before had filed a case against the kidnappers of his wife and had caused them all to go to jail. This brother, now only forty-one years old, was killed by persons unknown. Four years later Muhamad Akram moved to the Jamaat commune at Mansoura; two years after that he got his son to move there; and the year after that, 1982, he moved the rest of the family. In that year the son of Muhamad Akram's murdered brother killed someone on the other side; and Muhamad Akram for an unstated reason gave up politics.

Security and piety and penitence and the cause of the Jamaat now ran together for them all at Mansoura. It had become their world.

The killing was never discussed in Muhamad Akram's family. Saleem, the only son, conceived in the year of the killing, and born in the first year of his father's imprisonment in Multan jail, said, 'We don't have courage to talk about it to my father.'

Saleem was now thirty-four, and important in his own right as a senior customs officer. For him the drama – his father's conversion and repentance, the studying in the jail – marked the beginning of the family's intellectual rise. He came one Saturday after work (Friday now the sabbath – the hanged Mr Bhutto's weekly memorial – and Saturday the first working day of the week) to take me to Mansoura. He was a tall man wearing a tie and a light tweed jacket (for the Lahore winter) and from certain things he said I felt he was expecting me to be surprised that a man living in Mansoura should be wearing such 'modern' clothes. He came in his office car, with a driver, and on the back seat were *The Economist* and other serious magazines.

The mistake was not to accept his offer of air-conditioning. It was early evening, and I feared a chill. But it was also the rush hour. By the time we got to Mansoura, stopping and starting at traffic lights all the way, the main road misty all the way with dust and brown fumes, I was quite choked.

I had heard much about Mansoura and its fortress-like atmosphere, and I had expected something more hidden away. But it was just there, beside the main road, in the heat and fumes and dust, and with fluorescent strips; and just at the entrance, on the left, as if in immediate demonstration of who they were, the faithful were at their evening prayers in the Jamaat's mosque, below a kind of netting or open frame which might have been used for a cover when it was too sunny or when it was raining.

Saleem, in sudden haste, took off his tie and threw his jacket on the car seat and went to join the prayers, first telling the driver to take the car back a little so that I could have a better look. One little boy in miniature *shalwar-kameez* was extremely energetic with the prayers, bouncing up and down on flexible joints.

It was quite dark when the prayers were over. Saleem then took me on a tour. There was a board with a map of the settlement. Each of the houses on the map had a number and a list on the right gave the names of the occupants. This kind of order was unusual in Pakistan, Saleem said; I felt it was another aspect of the modernity of the Jamaat about which people talked with foreboding.

Away from the lights of the mosque, we walked on broken paths. We came to the famous hospital. It was built at the time of the Afghanistan war. People spoke of it with awe, but the waiting room or casualty room or emergency room that Saleem showed me, opening a flimsy door from a dark lane, was dimly lit and empty. It looked roughly finished and seemed already to have fallen into something like Pakistani informality. The library and research unit, with all its modern computer facilities, was closed until the morning. But the cassette shop was open. It sold sets of Maulana Maudoodi's speeches, and a number of cassettes about Kashmir, including one in English called *Crush India*. Saleem, like a man in a toyshop, began to buy, possibly for friends, pointing to this cassette and then that one, and at the end the man in the shop put the ones Saleem had bought in a small, white, modern, plastic bag.

We came to the family house. It belonged to someone from the Jamaat; Muhamad Akram was renting it. It was a narrow house on two floors, and Saleem said there were two places where we could talk: the dining room or his study. His study, on the upper floor, had no furniture, only carpets and cushions.

I needed a table at which to sit and write, and I thought we should look at the dining room. It was on the other side of an open lobby or staircase area, which was very narrow and squashed. There were sacks of paddy in this area; one of the sacks had burst or had been opened and some of the golden-coloured grain was on the concrete floor. The paddy came from 'the farm', Saleem said; so the family still worked land at Sargodha. The dining room was narrow and not deep. The furniture in it left no open space, and the fluorescent light seemed to press on my forehead, just above my eyes. There were altogether twenty big, carved armchairs, a matching set, very much in the rustic feudal style (and also the Indonesian bourgeois style). All these chairs had their backs against the wall. Twelve were in the reception area proper, six facing six across low wide tables, with the other eight tight and almost touching around the dining table.

Saleem said, going perhaps by the way the chairs were arranged, that visitors were expected. And so - past the sacks of rice, and with a glimpse now of the servants at the back, the thin and dingy shadow people of every Pakistani household, even here at the Jamaat – we went up the steep and narrow concrete steps to Saleem's study and library.

It was a very small room about twelve feet square and about eight or nine feet high, or so it felt. The air was hot and dusty; the room was entirely sealed. It was carpeted and with bolsters, as Saleem had said; and there were bookshelves on the walls. Half the wall facing the door carried those Islamic sets in decorated binding which I had got to recognise at Qum. Other shelves were more informal. But I soon stopped looking at the books. I began to choke in the stale, enclosed air. I felt I was becoming ill. On the floor what looked like a pouffe or a stool was an air-cleaner; it was turned on, but it would be some time before it made an impression on the room.

I asked for a window to be opened. Saleem called down to the servant, who was bringing one of the big dining-room chairs for me, and feeling his way up the narrow, steep steps behind his awkward load. The servant, coming into the room and putting the chair down, pushed at the window. It was a sliding metal-framed window, and it appeared to be stuck. Saleem lent a hand, or perhaps a finger, with the catch. The servant kept on pushing, and at last the window opened. There was a screen behind it; there was no view. The traffic roared from the Multan road. The air outside was gritty and almost as hot as the air in the room. The servant dragged the chair next to the open window, and there for a while I sat, breathing in, rather like the pious sitting beside the rails of the tomb of a saint, to take good from the emanations. The window looked over part of the flat roof above the lower floor; this explained the great heat inside and out.

Saleem said he was a cricket freak. He knew the names of minor, forgotten Indian spin bowlers from Trinidad: S. M. Ali, Inshan Ali, Imtiaz Ali, Rafiq Jumadeen. This was an offering to me, I knew; but cricket wasn't the only thing on his mind. All the bowlers he mentioned were Muslim, and he knew more about them than I did.

The servant came up the steep steps again, this time with tea and pakoras, hot fried savouries, and a milk-and-almond sweet, condensed and solidified, perfectly delicious and quite unexpected, as though somehow in the cramped pieties of this Jamaat house an artist had broken free in the kitchen.

Then the father came up, the penitent. He was in a pale-brown *shalwar-kameez*, and I saw in it the colour of penitence. He was shorter than his son, and heavy, and the steps had strained him. He was only fifty-eight, but in his family – Saleem was immediately deferential – he was the old man; and he filled that role.

He sat on the carpet, very close to my chair, almost touching it, and looked up at me, with extraordinary trustingness. His brown skin was clear and smooth; his forehead, unmarked, appeared to shine, as if from years of oiling. One light-coloured eye was bad; a cataract had been removed the year before. Even with that, his expression was benign. Something was wrong with his hearing. He leaned forward when I spoke, and, with his lips slightly parted over small, sound-looking teeth, he appeared to smile.

Saleem explained who I was and what I had come to do in Mansoura.

And in no time they were launched, father and son, speaking of their Mansoura faith. They wanted an Islamic state. Pakistan wasn't an Islamic state. It wasn't enough that a state for Muslims had been created in the subcontinent. An Islamic state was one in which the most righteous man ruled and, as in the earliest days of Islam, led the people in prayer.

This was like what I had heard in 1979, at the time of General Zia, who had tried to Islamise; but, like others before him, hadn't known how to convert a personal faith into the apparatus of a state; and had in the end settled for a personal tyranny. He was now dismissed as a hypocrite. But, after all that had happened, the dream was still here at Mansoura, the dream of restoring the golden age at the very beginning of Islam, when the manageable, pure congregation was at one with itself and the ruler.

And now father and son spoke together in a kind of duet, exchanging ideas about that golden Islamic age. After the talk in the car about the modernity of the Jamaat in matters of dress and organisation, after the tweed jacket and the tie and *The Economist* and the talk of cricket, it was strange to see Saleem, the customs officer, matching his feudal father phrase for phrase.

Did I know, Saleem's father asked, about the time one of the early caliphs was rebuked for wearing an extravagant cloak? And he, the father, asking the question, looked up at me and brought his face very close. Saleem, more casual, sipping tea, picking at a pakora, and half lying on the carpet, propped on a cushion, took the story about the caliph forward. The caliph told his questioner that a relation had given his ration of cloth to make that cloak. Imagine that, Saleem said. And imagine that, his father said after him. Imagine the ruler of an empire stretching all over the world; and yet, Saleem said, completing the thought, a member of the assembly could ask him that question. (So, in this vision of the golden age, the cards could be shuffled, and the simplicity of the single, manageable Islamic congregation could be set beside its reward: a world empire.)

No, no, Saleem said, a Muslim state wasn't an Islamic state; many people made that error. No, no —

He was interrupted by the servant, one of the Pakistani shadow men, bringing up fresh pakora, this time pieces of fresh cabbage fried in chick-pea batter, hot and crisp and then soft and delicious. Behind the servant was Saleem's young son, Muhamad, thin, used to attention, forward and then shy and clinging, with big dark eyes and the Mansoura pallor. His father fondled him; his grandfather fondled him; he was offered pakora. But he didn't want to stay, and he went down again with the servant.

I asked them about General Zia, the Islamic terror of 1979. Hadn't he done enough? What remained to be done?

There was a great deal, Saleem said. There was still Hindu influence to be got rid of, and (this was perhaps Saleem's *Economist* reading) remnants of British colonialism. And there was the question of marriage, the father said. The Koran said a man could be married four times; now there were these women's groups trying to tamper with the Muslim family law. He spoke like a man aggrieved, denied his due; he looked up at me with his sweet expression and complained as though he knew I would want to help him. And there was the question of usury; something had to be done about that.

Still, the father said, Pakistan and Iran, as countries, were closest to the Islamic ideal; that had to be given them. Saleem agreed about Iran, saying that the only thing wrong about Iran was its quarrels with its neighbours. There was Sudan, too; that had to be considered as a country working towards Islam; but Saleem wasn't sure about Sudan.

I asked whether he wanted something like the Iranian Revolutionary Guards in Pakistan. Lying against the cushions, Saleem said with some severity that a religious state had to encourage the good and deter the bad. All countries had police forces to do that. I said that this would be interfering with people's liberty. Saleem said that there was no free will in Islam. And his father, smooth-skinned and benign, said that the very word 'Islam' meant obedience, submission.

I asked how the state would define what was Islamic. That had given General Zia a lot of trouble, in spite of his Islamic Ideology Council. There would be debate, Saleem said. He added, surprisingly, that everybody didn't have to agree. He, for example, didn't always agree with his father. His father, again surprisingly, said, 'There is freedom in Islam.' What they wanted, the father said, was a state where everyone accepted Islam voluntarily, with all his heart. And I began to understand how freedom and submission could run together.

Saleem said, 'Islam hasn't been tried.'

I was half expecting to hear this. I said, 'Is vanity or pride wrong in Islam?'

Saleem said, 'Yes.' His eyes became uncertain, as liquid and melting as his son's.

'How can you cast this slur on all the millions who have gone before you? How can you say they have not been good? How can you make this claim for yourself?'

I had touched something.

His father said, 'We can only be as good as we can be.'

The boy Muhamad, Saleem's son, came in again. Saleem said the boy had begun to go to school.

Saleem's father said, 'He is learning the Koran already.'

They asked him to recite the opening suras. He was pleased to be asked, but he clung and pressed to his grandfather and had to be coaxed a little more before he began to speak the words in his child's voice.

Saleem's face was full of pride; and there was pride, too, in the old man's good eye.

Saleem said, 'He is going to learn the whole Koran by heart.'

'The whole Koran,' the old man said, picking up the duet with his son.

I asked, 'How long will that take?'

Saleem said, 'Five or six years.'

I couldn't stay. My breathing had become very bad. Downstairs, the servants, thin and dark and dingy, behind the sacks with the spilt golden paddy. Outside, the fumes and grit of the Multan road. Saleem's driver drove me back to the hotel. Saleem didn't come with me.

On Friday, poor Mr Bhutto's sabbath, I went to Mansoura again. I went this time in daylight and saw that the compound, which had a kind of parking-lot barrier at the entrance, and was full of idle bearded men in Friday clothes, was bigger than I had thought, a little campus. The place was also much dustier. The main road outside was absolutely broken, unpaved, and a cloud of dust and brown motor smoke hung over it.

Saleem's family house looked more informal in daylight, a rough village building, with a shed or garage to one side, and other little added-on areas. Many servants, thin and poor and on call, quite separate from the bearded exhibitionists at the entrance in proper Friday clothes, were standing about outside and inside; it was hard to imagine where they all slept.

A handsome man with well-groomed wavy hair was so friendly and open that I thought he might be a relation of Saleem's. He was one of the house servants, and he was friendly because he had seen me six days before. He told me that Saleem and his wife were still at the prayers, and he led me – the sacks of paddy from the 'farm' still in the lobby, one sack torn – up the narrow concrete steps to the study.

For some reason a sheet or cloth was hung over the window, and the air-cleaner was working away. I asked the friendly servant to put on the air-conditioner, and he did so.

Saleem, when he came, was in white *koortah-shalwar*, a loose cotton outfit, a man at rest. We went over the details of his father's kidnapping case. The case obsessed Saleem; it had marked his life. As a child, for his first six years, he had gone once or twice a year to Multan jail to see his father. Then, when his father had come out, the whole family had lived together in Sargodha for twelve years, before the father had moved to Mansoura. Saleem was twenty-two when he had joined the commune. For three years as an adult, no more, he had been on his own.

He said his religious feelings had developed outside the commune. He said of the commune, 'They don't push you. We have a dish.' A satellite dish, which the Jamaat didn't like. 'Sometimes our ladies "meet".' He meant they met strangers; this was something strict Islam forbad.

His wife, Tahira, came. In the hotel the day before, when she had come to see me with Saleem, she had looked bright. Now there was something extinguished about her expression. It might have been the absence of make-up; the Jamaat didn't like make-up. She was handsome without it; and she had the heaviness of the lower body that came to women of her class after they became mothers, from the many days of lying-in after each birth, and the extra-rich foods they ate.

She said she was troubled when she first came here. She would have liked a better house. For the first three or four years she had been a little upset, not at all satisfied. But now it was all perfectly all right, though she would have liked a separate room for the children. She would have liked a house like the house at Sargodha, with a proper drawing room, a proper dining room, and a proper guest room.

She said, 'Here we have a lot of servants. Fourteen or fifteen. A lot of guests. Very upsetting.'

Saleem said, 'What she really wanted was a nuclear house.'

She said, 'Now it's all right. I am used to it. I don't wish any more.'

The air-conditioner gave a *whoomph* and a whine, and died. A power cut: and there was something like a silence all over Mansoura, like the silence in a mountain valley just after a snowfall. An unsuspected door was pushed open to the left of the sheeted window, and we could see that the door opened on to the flat roof. It would have been very hot, perhaps unbearable, up here in the summer.

Saleem's sister came in. And it was an entrance. She was a big woman in a khaki-gold *shalwar*, and all her head and face was covered with a loosely wrapped, light-coloured, lightweight cotton cloth, which had a small, scattered decorative motif; so that she called to mind the bandaged Claude Rains in the lovely old film of *The Invisible Man*, and perhaps, like Claude Rains, she too had wrapped herself up to conceal a vacancy.

She had gone into purdah, Saleem said. (But this was not proper purdah. Proper purdah would have kept her away from Saleem's study.) I could ask her anything I wanted about Mansoura and religion, Saleem said; it was their way. He himself had spent the first five years here without saying the prayers. He said them now, but there had been no compulsion.

The sister was twenty-seven; so she would have been born the year after her father had come out of jail. She couldn't absolutely say why she had gone into purdah. She had just felt one day she should go into purdah. And she was much calmer now. She didn't say much more; and perhaps there was nothing more to say.

Perhaps there was no mystery, nothing to be elucidated; perhaps places like Mansoura, by the prayers and outward forms of piety, and the repetition of forms, and the self-awareness that came to people through simply being here (Mansoura was like Oxford in this respect: it was an endless topic of conversation to people there), perhaps places like Mansoura, which could dull someone like Tahira, Saleem's wife, could at the same time give quite simple people this possibility of constant personal theatre. It was possible to imagine the drama of this sister of Saleem's going into purdah. 'Have you heard? Saleem's sister is thinking of going into purdah.' – 'She is going into purdah.' – 'She's gone into purdah.' – 'It's a question everybody asks me. I just thought one day I should go into purdah. I feel much calmer now.'

Muhamad, Saleem's elder son, who was going to learn the whole Koran by heart, came in; with Ahmed, the younger son.

There were visitors. They were a young couple. The woman was very handsome; the man was big and strong and, young though he was, looked like a man of authority. The young woman said she came from a political family. I knew the family name, from the newspapers; Saleem was of a feudal background, and well connected.

The woman said she hadn't been to Mansoura before. She hadn't wanted to, because she didn't think she would like it. She couldn't like something that took away her freedom. And yet, though she came from a family with a name, she had given up her studies when she got married.

Her husband, the strong man, said, 'It was against the custom of the society.' And since that sounded harsh, even to him, he said, 'In another society it would have been different.' As though it was all only a matter of his wife's luck.

We talked – the eternal subject – about Pakistan.

The woman's husband said in his blunt way that the modern state was giving way to 'separate fiefdoms', as in the past. And in his blunt way he said that it would be good for business. He spoke with no regret for the passing of the state. And I could see how for him, with his tribal background, the modern state had simply been a burden without reward, a consumer of energy, a series of snares.

All the ideas – of freedom and the loss of freedom, religion and the state – were linked. It was where Iqbal's convert's dream of the pure Muslim polity had led, back and back to the death of the state in the region where the man had come from, and to Mansoura here.

After some delay the tea was brought up the difficult steps by the servants. The power came on. And soon there was nothing more to say. We had exhausted Mansoura as a subject. Saleem's sister, in her own style of purdah, had gone down unnoticed.

6

Loss

FOR MOST of the Muslims of the subcontinent the partition of 1947
had been like a great victory, 'like God', as a man had said to me in
Lahore in 1979. Now every day in the newspapers there were stories of
the killings in the great port city of Karachi. That was where many of
the Muslim migrants from India, townspeople, middle class or lower
middle class, had gone after partition. Nearly half a century later the
descendants of these people, feeling themselves strangers still, unrepre-
sented, cheated, without power, had taken up arms against the state, in
a merciless guerrilla war.

In Iqbal's convert's scheme Islam should have been identity enough
for everybody. But the people of Sindh (the province where Karachi
was) didn't like seeing their land, half empty and half desert though it
was, overrun by better-educated and more ambitious strangers. The
land of Sindh was ancient, and always slightly apart. The people had
their own history and language and feudal reverences. They had set up
political barriers, some overt, some hidden, against the strangers from
India, the *mohajirs*. And in Pakistan the *mohajirs* had nowhere else to go.

Partition, once a cause for joy, had become like a wound for some of
these *mohajirs*. For some the memories of those days still lived.

Salman, a journalist, was born in 1952. He was tormented by, and
endlessly sought to reconstruct, the events of four days in 1947 in the
town of Jalandhar, now in Indian Punjab. At some point in those four

days, between 14 and 18 of August 1947, the absolute beginning of independence for both India and Pakistan, his grandmother was murdered in her house in Jalandhar, with others of the family. On the fourteenth she was alive, protected by Hindu neighbours. On the eighteenth Salman's mother's father, who had been hiding somewhere else, went to the house, a middle-class Indian courtyard house, and found it empty, with blood spattered on the walls but with no corpses.

Salman's grandfather ran away. He must have been about fifty at that time. He managed to get on a train going to what had become Pakistan – just a short run away, along lines that until four days before had been open and busy. The train was attacked on the way. He arrived in Lahore buried under dead bodies. He was one of the few survivors.

Salman got to know the story when he was fifteen. Until that time he had lived with the idea of the Hindu and the Sikh as the ultimate evil. But when he heard this story he felt no anger. The story was too terrible for anger. It didn't matter then who had done the killing.

The blood on the walls of a house he didn't know (Salman had not been to Jalandhar or India) and could only imagine, the absence of bodies: the details, or the blankness of detail, from a time before he was born, worked on Salman, became the background to his life in Pakistan. He could spend minutes wondering, when the story came back to him, how the people in the house had actually met death. Had they been cut to pieces? Had they – dreadful thought – been abused?

There were other stories of that time which he got from an uncle: of the uncle (and no doubt others) hiding behind oil drums and taunting the Hindu and Sikh rioters, who didn't want India to be broken up.

> *But kay rahé ga Hindustan!*
> *Bun kay rahé ga Pakistan!*
> Divided Hindustan will be!
> Pakistan will be founded!

In the 1960s these stories, of death and riot, began to rankle with Salman. 'I would think we had lost so much for this country, and this is what we are doing to it now.'

But there had been a long serene period in the new country. The family had lost everything in Jalandhar, but Salman's father, a civil engineer, was working for the government – he was in Baluchistan at the time of the riots in Jalandhar – and so there was money every month. In 1952, the year of Salman's birth, his father left the government to set up on his own. For ten years and more his practice flourished. He brought up his family in a religious way. All the rituals were honoured, and there were Koranic recitations. Salman as a child knew many prayers by heart. Religion was part of the serenity of his childhood.

In 1965, when he was thirteen, Salman became aware of another kind of Islam. This was at the time of the short, inconclusive war with India. 'There were songs exhorting *Mujahids* to go to war and promising them paradise, heaven. Mobs of people from the city of Lahore, armed only with clubs, set out to fight the holy war against the infidel Hindu. They had to be turned back. They had been charged up by the mullah. The interesting thing was that the mullah was not leading those people. He was sitting safe in his mosque.'

In this way Salman was introduced to the idea of *jihad*, holy war. It was a special Muslim idea. He explained it like this: 'In Christianity Christ died for all Christians. He can ensure heaven for them. In Islam Mohammed can only make a submission in your favour for being a follower of his. It is only Allah who makes the final decision on the merit won by good deeds. Nothing is greater, so far as goodness goes, than *jihad* in the name of Allah.' *Jihad* was not meant metaphorically. 'The word of the Koran is taken very literally. It is blasphemous even to think of it as an allegory. The Koran lays great store by *jihad*. It is one of the sayings of Mohammed – not in the Koran, it's one of the traditions – "If you see an un-Islamic practice you stop it by force. If you not possess the power to stop it, you condemn it verbally. If not that also, then you condemn it in your heart." As far back as I remember I have known this. I think this tradition gives the Muslim licence to act violently.'

In 1965 he saw for the first time the idea given a public, mob expression. And though he saw people then doing 'silly things', he understood both their need to win merit as followers of Mohammed, and also their fear of hell.

'Endless whipping with fiery flames, and fire beyond imagination. Having to drink pus. It's very graphic in the traditions. In the Koran there's just mention of the fires and the endlessness of punishment.'

In 1968, when he was sixteen, and in his first year at Government Science College, Lahore, Salman found himself part of just such a mob. There was a review in *Time* or *Newsweek* of a book called *The Warrior*

Prophet. Two or three copies of the magazine with the review had somehow got to the college and were passed around. No one had seen the book, but the boys decided to take out a procession to protest about it. It was during a break; the boys were sitting outside. There was no particular leader. The boys were all as religiously well trained as Salman. The idea of the public protest simply came to them, and they became a mob. Salman went along with them, though he remembered very clearly, all the way through, that he hadn't found anything obnoxious about Islam or the Prophet in the review. The weather was good. It was winter, the best season in Lahore, and they shouted slogans against the United States and broke up a couple of minibuses.

The mullah who in 1965 had charged up his congregation, and sent them off to the front to fight with sticks, had stayed behind quite safe in his mosque. It wasn't his business to fight. His business was to charge people up, to remind them as graphically and passionately as he could of the rewards of *jihad* and the horrors of hell.

He was like the mullah I heard about (from someone else) who had been drafted in, with other mullahs, to campaign against Mr Bhutto in 1977. This mullah was short and fat, in no way personable, and known to be unreliable. But that didn't matter; he was a wonderful preacher, with a powerful voice. There was a curfew at the time, but it was relaxed (as it had to be) for the Friday prayers. The people who went to the mullah's mosque found themselves listening to more than prayers. They heard stories, from Islamic history, of heroism and martyrdom, in the mullah's famous voice and wonderful declamatory style. He asked them to be worthy of the past, to take up *jihad*, and not to ignore the forces of evil around them. 'Say to the enemy, "You test your arrows on us, and we shall test our breast against your arrows."' It sounded like poetry, and authoritative for that reason, though no one could place it. The actual words didn't mean anything, but they drove people wild; and at the end of those Friday prayers poor Mr Bhutto's curfew had been rendered harmless. The congregation went away full of religious hate, determined to earn a little more merit in heaven by sending Mr Bhutto to hell.

That the mullah was unreliable, and not a moral man in any recognisable way, was not important. He was not offering himself as a guide. It was his business as a mullah to keep the converted people on their toes, and when there was need to charge them up, to fix their minds on hell and heaven, and to tell them that when the time came only Allah would be their judge. This was an aspect of the religious state – the state created for converts alone, where religion was not a matter of private conscience – that the poet Iqbal had never considered: that such a state could always be manipulated, easy to undermine, full of simple roguery.

There was something else that Iqbal had never considered: that in the new state the nature of history would alter, and with that altering of the historical sense, the intellectual life of the country would inevitably be diminished. The mullahs would always hold the ring, would limit inquiry. All the history of the ancient land would cease to matter. In the school history books, or the school 'civics' books, the history of Pakistan would become only an aspect of the history of Islam. The Muslim invaders, and especially the Arabs, would become the heroes of the Pakistan story. The local people would be hardly there, in their own land, or would be there only as ciphers swept aside by the agents of the faith.

It is a dreadful mangling of history. It is a convert's view; that is all that can be said for it. History has become a kind of neurosis. Too much has to be ignored or angled; there is too much fantasy. This fantasy isn't in the books alone; it affects people's lives.

Salman, talking of this neurosis, said, 'Islam doesn't show on my face. We have nearly all, subcontinental Muslims, invented Arab ancestors for ourselves. Most of us are *Sayeds*, descendants of Mohammed through his daughter Fatima and cousin and son-in-law Ali. There are others – like my family – who have invented a man called Salim Al-Rai. And yet others who have invented a man called Qutub Shah. Everybody has got an ancestor who came from Arabia or Central Asia. I am convinced my ancestors would have been medium- to low-caste Hindus, and despite their conversion they would not have been in the mainstream of Muslims. If you read Ibn Battuta and earlier travellers you can sense the condescending attitude of the Arab travellers to the converts. They would give the Arab name of someone, and then say, "But he's an Indian."

'This invention of Arab ancestry soon became complete. It had been adopted by all families. If you hear people talking you would believe that this great and wonderful land was nothing but wild jungle, that no human beings lived here. All of this was magnified at the time of partition, this sense of not belonging to the land, but belonging to the religion. Only one people in Pakistan have reverence for their land, and that's the Sindhis.'

This was what lay all around Salman's serene childhood. These fantasies and illusions, which to some extent were also his when he was a child, were to become his subject when he became a writer. They took time to discover; they needed the adult eye; they required him to stand a little outside himself.

But even while he was still an adolescent Salman began to have intimations of being somewhat apart. Just a few months after he had gone along with that schoolboy demonstration about *The Warrior Prophet* (feeling all the time that it was unjustified), and in that little afternoon *jihad* had helped to break up a couple of minibuses, something happened that unsettled him.

It was Ramadan, the fasting month. He had been told, and he believed, that if he stayed up praying on one particular night during the last ten days of Ramadan, he would be cleansed of all his sins; he would become a new man. They told him he would feel lighter; that was impressed on him. That year the big night was the night of the twenty-seventh. He and his brother and his sister and the rest of the family stayed up praying. In the morning he didn't feel any different. He had been looking forward to a great feeling of lightness. He was disappointed. But he didn't have the courage to tell anyone in the family.

His disappointment, and the worry about it, might have been greater at this particular time because, after a decade and a half of success, his father's civil engineering business had begun to fail. The actual work was holding up, but Salman's father had begun to make a series of misjudgements about people. Salman was still at school; his father's business troubles would have worried him.

Two or three years later — Salman's father's business going down all the time — there was another incident, this time at the end of Ramadan. Eid is the great festival at the end of Ramadan, and the Eid prayers are always in a congregation. Salman's father had taken the car to go to the mosque he always went to, and Salman and his brother were going on foot to look for a mosque in the neighbourhood. Salman said to his brother, 'What a waste of time.'

The brother said, 'Especially when you don't even believe in it.'
Salman said, 'What? You too?'

The brother said, 'Our elder sister doesn't believe either. Don't you know?'

Salman had a high regard for his brother's intellect. The worry he had felt about losing his faith dropped away. He didn't feel he was letting down the people who had died in the riots in Jalandhar in 1947.

All three children of the family had lost religion. But, as his business had gone down, Salman's father had grown more devout and more intolerant. One of the festivals the family had celebrated when Salman was a child was the Basant or Spring festival. Now Salman's father banned it as un-Islamic, something from the Hindu and pagan past. There were great quarrels with his daughter when she came from Karachi, where she lived. She was not as quiet as Salman and his brother. She spoke her mind, and the arguments could become quite heated. One day, when Salman's father's brother was also present, Salman's father said, 'Let her be. She's an apostate. Don't get into these arguments with her.' And he walked away in anger.

The house would have been full of strains.

Salman's father wanted Salman to be an engineer. But Salman's mathematics were bad, and just before his twentieth birthday he joined the army. He had developed an interest in guns. He had no religious faith now, but he was the complete Pakistani soldier. He was passionate about going to war with India, though there had been the Bangladesh defeat just the year before.

'It was in my mind that we – or I, personally – had to get even for the murder of my grandparents and my two aunts. It must have been with me always, but this was a very cold feeling. Like a seasoned murderer going in for his hundredth kill. I wasn't excited or emotional about it. It was just something I had to do. I didn't talk about my grandparents, but I was very vocal about going back to war with India. This was with my army companions. Not at home.'

After two or three years this feeling left him. He also fell out of love with the army. He couldn't find people to talk to, and he was rebuked for talking about books and trying to impress. Three years later he was able to leave the army. He joined a multinational company in Karachi. The job came through an army friend whose uncle was the number two in the company.

So Salman went to Karachi, the *mohajir* city. Life was not easy. He lived in the beginning as a paying guest in a family; after that there was a shabby little rented room with a kitchen. He moved up the ladder slowly. He had a friend in the company. One day when they were talking Salman mentioned the *Reader's Digest*. The friend laughed. Salman said he wanted to learn. The friend was pleased; he began to guide Salman, and Salman looked back on this as the start of his education.

After five years he married, and then, like his father, he gave up the security of his job and became self-employed. He did so at a bad time. Karachi had grown and grown since independence; it had received immigrants from India and from all parts of Pakistan; and now the Sindhi-Punjabi-*mohajir* tensions were about to turn nasty.

In January 1987, less than four years after he had married, Salman and his wife lost all their money. A friend had told them that at their stage in life they should be thinking of the future and making some investments. They had put their money in different investment companies; they had been careful, as they thought, to spread the risks; but one day all the companies just vanished. The friend had persuaded them to invest in a company run by missionary mullahs. These mullahs were not militant; they wanted only to make Muslims good, to bring strayers back into the fold, and to win fresh converts. The friend said to Salman and his wife, 'You may not have faith, but this is the only company that's truly reliable.' That was where most of Salman's money and his wife's money went.

This tragedy was matched by the tragedy of the streets. 'Things were getting bad in Karachi and Sindh during this time. Between 1987 and 1989 this terrible thing began to happen in Karachi. A solitary pedestrian at night would be approached from behind by a motorcyclist and stabbed in the back. There must have been fifty or a hundred-odd cases. They would happen once every week or so. Just an isolated incident somewhere. I do not recall reading anywhere that any one stabber had been apprehended. I was getting more and more upset about it.

'In July 1987 this incident happened. I had to drive my wife to the airport at two in the morning. On the way back I ran out of petrol. I knew there wasn't enough when I started, but I thought I would buy at one of the many points. This was a city that never really slept. But every single petrol station was closed for fear of armed robberies. I took my wife to the airport. My petrol was now very low. On the way back, about two kilometres from home, the car stopped. It would have been just after two in the morning. So I parked the car and started walking.

'I have never felt such a raging fear – it was surging inside me. I still very distinctly remember looking at the walls at the side of the road to see which one was easier to jump over, and escape, in case I was attacked. And then I heard this motorcyclist coming up from far behind. *Put-put-put.* I was utterly and completely terrified. And in this scramble of thoughts the only thing I remember was this desire to escape, to go over a wall. I don't know what kept me there. And the *put-put-put* came nearer. I looked back. He was a lone rider. The attackers were always two. So I knew he wasn't one. But still the fear was real. I stopped walking. And he came *put-put-put.* He said, "What are you doing on the street at this time? Don't you know it's dangerous?" I told him. He asked where I was going. When I told him he said, "Get on, I will drive you home." He was an Urdu-speaking man. I laughed and asked him, "You said it's dangerous. What are you doing on the street?" He said, "I'm on the way to the Indian consulate, to be first in line for the visa." Just after two in the morning. That is what people had to do. He must have had relations in India. He was going visiting. He wasn't getting away from the danger.'

Salman and his wife had been playing with the idea of leaving Karachi and going back to Lahore. This experience decided him. Later that morning he telephoned his wife and said, 'We really have to get away.'

'It wasn't really fear. Fear for my own life. It was the sorrow of living in an unjust, cruel society. Everything was collapsing. It's as though those poor people who died in Jalandhar died in vain. Why should my aunts and grandparents have to pay with their lives – for nothing? There was no bitterness. Just a sense of the unfairness in it all.'

About six months after the motorcycle incident, people who were suffering in Karachi, like Salman, organised a peace rally. There were about five hundred at the rally. They were people who had lost hope. It was winter time, very lovely and pleasant in Karachi. The people in the rally smiled and nodded at one another. Many had tears in their eyes.

'There was an immense feeling of brotherhood, of belonging. No slogans. It was just a walk for peace in Karachi. And all along I had this lump in my throat and I thought I would break out crying. Everybody knew that we were all partners in this grief, for whatever was happening to that city. Everybody used to have this feeling for that city. It never went to sleep. And people used to say – the Punjabis and the Pathans – that it was a kind-hearted city, especially good to its poorer inhabitants.'

That year, in the first week of September, there was a massacre of some three hundred people in the city of Hyderabad, the second city of Sindh. Unidentified gunmen opened up, and in ten or fifteen minutes killed those three hundred. It was part of the *mohajir* war. Sometimes the *mohajirs* did the killing, sometimes the army.

Salman met some friends that day. They said to him, 'You look sick. Has someone died?' He said, 'No, no. No one's died.'

On that day Salman and his wife decided to leave Karachi. It took them three months to wind up their affairs.

It wasn't easy for Salman to make a living. The restricted intellectual needs of the country offered him few openings as a writer, didn't encourage him to grow. He was poorly rewarded for what he did.

He had become a kind of wanderer. He found solace now in wilderness. The country at least offered him that; there were great tracts of desert and mountain where a man might feel no one had been before.

He carried the old torment with him: the first four days of independence in 1947, from 14 to 18 August, and the empty courtyard house in Jalandhar with blood on the walls.

He had not been to India, and he was beginning to think he should go there. There was a journey he wished to make. He wanted the journey to start on 11 August, and he wanted it to start in the Himalayan hill station of Solan. From Solan on 11 August 1947, his aunt (who was to be murdered within a week) had written to her husband that it was getting very dangerous in Solan; he was to come at once and take her back to Jalandhar. He went and brought her down in the train. He said later (he was one of the survivors) that the hatred and tension in the railway coach was something they could feel. But they got without trouble to the house in Jalandhar on 14 August.

That was the journey Salman wanted to do again one year, within those dates, if he could get an Indian visa. 'To mark the beginning of this thing.'

7

From the North

RAHIMULLAH WAS a Pathan of the Yusufzai clan, and he carried the clan name as his surname. A Pathan clan was descended from a remote ancestor; the Yusufzai, as the name suggests, were the sons of Yusuf. Some Yusufzai families had full family trees, but Rahimullah could trace his family back only three generations. His grandfather, he said, would know more.

The past went back only as far as people's memories; people didn't have the means of assessing or fixing the past before family memory. Time here was like a river; it was hard to mark any precise point in the flow. People didn't always know how old they were. Rahimullah gave 1953 as the year of his birth; but on his birth certificate the year was 1954. As for Rahimullah's young servant, small and dark and smiling, with nice strong teeth and a very full head of wavy black hair, he could be eighteen or nineteen or twenty; no one could now tell.

Rahimullah's father was born in 1918 (as his son said) to a poor farming family. Shortly after he was born both his father and his mother died (possibly in an epidemic, though Rahimullah didn't say); so the boy was literally an orphan. He made a living as a shepherd, looking after other people's cattle. At the same time, up to the age of thirteen or fourteen, he got some schooling; he got as far as the eighth class. When he was of age he joined the British Indian army as a sepoy. He was tall, over six feet, and fair, with blue eyes. In the second world war he saw service in Egypt and Libya. In 1953 he was in the Pakistani army contingent that took part in Queen Elizabeth's coronation. He retired from the Pakistan army as a *subedar*, a junior commissioned officer, in the military transport section.

It had been a long and good career. But then, unexpectedly, it went wrong. He was not long back in his village when he was recalled because of the Bangladesh situation. He was sent to the port of Chittagong in Bangladesh as part of the reserve. The war was lost; Bangladesh seceded; the Pakistan army in Bangladesh laid down its arms. So, at the very end of his army career, in his retirement, Rahimullah's father became a prisoner of war. For a long time his family didn't know whether he was alive or dead. At last one day there was a letter from him from the prisoner of war camp in Rampur in India.

When, two years or so later, he came back to his village, Rahimullah's father took up social work. He got people to start a bus service; he campaigned for electricity to be brought to the village; he set up the first flour mill; he got people to build their own approach roads; and he had the village well cleaned. At the Friday prayers in the mosque he took his chador round to collect money for various causes. Some members of his family objected. They said, 'You are asking for alms. This is below your status.' He said, 'No, no. I am doing God's work.' But it must have been held against him, because when the time came and he stood for the local elections, he lost; another member of the family won.

Rahimullah's father would have liked his son to be an officer in the army, and he did all that he could, with his limited means, to educate him in proper schools: up to the sixth class in the English-medium cantonment school in Peshawar, then for two years in a Catholic convent school in Jhelum, then for three years in a British-built military boarding college. But at the end, big man though he had become, and a basketball player, Rahimullah didn't pass the medical test: his eyesight wasn't good enough.

Father and son were both very disappointed. The father said, 'You can't help it. It's God-given.' He thought then that Rahimullah should become a doctor. And for two years and more Rahimullah studied science, at first locally, and then at a Parsee-founded science college in Karachi. In the examinations Rahimullah missed the first division by a mark or two. This meant that he couldn't get admitted to a medical college.

It was at this time that Rahimullah's father became a prisoner of war.

Only part of his salary was paid to the family (the rest was kept back for him). Rahimullah had to give up thoughts of his own career and go back to the village to look after the family. It would have been a dark moment for him; it would have seemed that the world had altogether closed up. But then, when his father came back, the world slowly opened up again, and in a way that no one could have foreseen.

When he was a student in Karachi – and living with an older cousin – Rahimullah, to pay his way, had worked from six in the evening to two in the morning as a proof-reader for a newspaper. This had earned him 180 rupees a month, six pounds, and had left him free to go to classes during the day. He had got in this time to like the idea of newspapers. And now, out in the world at last, and with the established professions closed to him, he looked for jobs on newspapers. He became a sub-editor; he did reporting. He moved between Lahore and Karachi; he changed newspapers; he worked his way up slowly.

The Afghanistan war, and the long factional fight afterwards, was his great opportunity. As a Pathan and a man of the frontier, he knew the issues and the personalities. He was in demand; he did much work for foreign organisations. He thought he had become one of the best-paid journalists in Pakistan.

Though there was nothing in Rahimullah's eyes to match the glory of the army officer, he could feel that he had redeemed himself. Now, on land near his ancestral village – the village that twenty years or so before had rejected his father at the local elections – Rahimullah and his younger brother had built a big and stylish house for their big joint family. The house had been built away from the village because the village was overcrowded. It had been built twelve years before, when Rahimullah was only thirty; so, in spite of checks, he had moved fast.

The wall was of unrendered concrete, and decorative: a series of upright oval cartouches with raised edges that made a scalloped pattern top and bottom. The main gate was tall and imposing. It was painted green and yellow, and there was a spiked railing at the top. The pillars were faced with marble. Below the spiked railing *Shelter* was carved in Pashto, the Pathan language; and the names of Rahimullah and his brother were carved in Urdu on the pillars.

A second metal gate protected the inner family courtyard with its big two-storey brick house and water-tower. The outer courtyard was the general reception area. There every Friday village people who had

needs or wanted certain things done came to see Rahimullah.
Rahimullah was now based in Peshawar, a couple of hours away by car;
he made a point of being in his house every Friday for these meetings.
In this social-political work Rahimullah was consciously following his
father and honouring his memory.

The family had made an immense journey during the century; and
the family houses here were almost like stations in that journey. The
ancestral village was only three kilometres away, in the mountains. In
that village, and high up (and without water), was the small and poor
house where Rahimullah's father had been born. Much lower down,
next to the mosque, was the more spacious house Rahimullah's father
had moved to after he had retired from the army. Still lower down was
the courtyard house – once a Hindu shop-and-house: always in these
villages these reminders of the cleansing of 1947 – where Rahimullah's
father had had his cow-pen and storerooms; later they had built six
shops there and rented them out.

Rahimullah's father had been to Libya, Egypt, London, Bangladesh;
Rahimullah had moved between his village and Peshawar and Lahore
and Karachi; Rahimullah's younger brother had done well in the
United Arab Emirates. They had needed the world outside; they had
fed on it; without it they would have rotted here. But it was to this
sacred, choked place – where fields and distances were small, and where
both Rahimullah and his father had been forced to change their house
because of the overcrowding – that they wished to return, to shake off
the world, as it were, and to be truly themselves; and to be buried.

There were burial societies among Pathans in the big cities and
even in the foreign countries where they had migrated. The graves
here were decorated, and not as plain as Islam said they should be; and
women, yielding to old tribal feeling, broke the strict purdah of the
Pathans to go to the cemetery to recite verses from the Koran and to
leave money for the poor to pick up later, and sometimes also to leave
coloured flags and pictures and salt on the graves of people they
especially honoured.

They – Rahimullah and his brother – had built this big new house
about two years after their father had died. So, though Rahimullah
didn't say, the father had died with the knowledge that his eldest son
had, after all, done well. The house was on the edge of a five-acre plot,

and they had bought the plot because it was near the main road and the irrigation canal. In all they owned about twenty-five acres. Not all of it was irrigated; much was *barani* land, rain-fed land, which gave only one crop a year.

The courtyard for strangers was to the left of the main gate. The guest house was set at the end of the big dirt yard. The verandah or loggia had brick pillars and brick arches and a patterned marble floor. It was like a much richer version of Rana's uncle's guest courtyard – Rana the young country-born lawyer – in the village near Lahore; as often in the subcontinent, it was possible to see in a small area the living peasant origins of more princely building ideas. Where in the poorer place the floor of the principal room, beyond the verandah, was of dirt, here it was terrazzo; where in the poorer place there were big nails on the wall and niches, here there were high wall cupboards with glass doors. Where two or three string beds were the only furniture, here there were two proper wooden beds with decorated headboards, and, in addition, a big dining table with a set of ten chairs, and side tables with a set of six armchairs.

Rana's uncle felt far away, in style and confidence. And yet Rana's uncle had land, was a man of influence in his own way, with people in the village who depended on him. So it was possible in Rahimullah's male guest house to get some small idea of the layers of reverence in the country, and to understand the great distance he and his father had travelled. It explained the quiet coming and going in the courtyard that Friday morning. Some people stood outside in the early-winter sun; some stood in the verandah; some sat easily in the armchairs in the inner room. It was as if there were accepted levels of familiarity. The visitors didn't talk directly to Rahimullah for very long, and most of them didn't really need to; Rahimullah would have known what most of them wanted. What these Friday-morning visitors were offering was their presence.

Rahimullah talked of crops and the weather. The monsoon had brought good rains, but now people with *barani* land were waiting for rain, so that they could start sowing wheat. When things became bad people went barefooted to the fields and prayed for rain. There were special prayers that were said in fields, mainly to bring rain, but sometimes also to keep off disease. There were other, older rituals.

'If you blacken someone's face and take him round to the houses, and collect alms and cook some food and give it to the poor, it may bring rain. It may be done very soon. There are very superstitious people here.'

Rahimullah's younger brother, and Rahimullah's eldest son, brought in tea and biscuits and a sweet cream-of-wheat dish. The brother was pink-faced, big and broad-shouldered. He said, 'Are you happy?' It was his greeting, part of his courtesy. He said no more, stood about civilly for a while, then withdrew.

A small, dark, moustached man came in and, without saying anything, sat down in one of the armchairs. He was wearing the flat, pie-shaped, felt cap of the frontier and the mountains. He was the *nai*, the barber, Rahimullah said, and he had come to find out whether anyone in the house wanted a trim or a shave. His name was Qaim Khan. He came every Friday, and sometimes on other days as well; there were certain households that he served. This explained the ease with which he had come in and sat down, while others appeared to wait. He was in a pale-blue *shalwar-kameez* with a raw-cotton gilet. Rahimullah and his brother and his son were in pale peach; the colour spoke of cleanliness and sabbath rest. For the barber, though, the sabbath was a busy working day, and the blue he wore could more easily disguise dirt and wear.

And, indeed, as Rahimullah began to tell me, the barber didn't only cut hair. He had other duties, and he was available all the time. He could act as a cook when there was a wedding or a death; he would bring his big pots and tubs and cooking implements to the house, create a cooking place in the yard, and cook rice and other simple things in quantity. He was also a messenger; he took round wedding invitations; he broke the news of deaths. He could do circumcisions. Qaim Khan had an extra, inherited skill. He could sing and play on the flute, and people sometimes asked him to perform. His wife also sang. She and Qaim Khan's mother and sister were also always on call, to serve the women of the households in certain ways, taking messages for them, or accompanying them when they went out.

In the transplanted Indian community in Trinidad, on the other side of the world, the village barber (where Indian villages existed) had ritual duties like this (though not all of them). This went on up to fifty years ago, when I was growing up. So what Rahimullah was saying was half familiar to me; and I thought it remarkable that in a shaken-up and much-fractured colonial community this ancient kind of messenger and go-between and matchmaker should have reappeared; and that in that other world people of this caste calling, not a high one, should have declared themselves.

The *nai* Rahimullah was describing was also, I thought, in some ways like the village *koum* of converted Java: the handler of dead bodies, and also the cook, a man of low Hindu caste absorbed into Islam. Though the *koum* had been given the dignity of leading the Muslim congregation in prayer — as if in this new incarnation he destroyed older caste ideas — his other functions were still, after five hundred years, recognisably part of the old Hindu order.

In some such way, here in the frontier, the *nai*, as Rahimullah was describing him, seemed to be part of the Hindu past, a thousand years after conversion. (Though here, too, there were fantasies and a general neurosis about racial origins and the history.) Sitting in Rahimullah's guest house, considering Rahimullah and the blue-suited *nai*, the one man big and scholarly-looking and gracious, the other small and dark and with respectful eyes, I felt I could see how, when the older religion lost its footing, the antique social order had been lifted with small adjustments into the new religion. It was as though in the subcontinent the idea of caste was ineradicable.

Qaim Khan had no land and no house. Many *nais* had become well off now, but few of them had their own house. Qaim Khan would have loved to buy some land and build a house, but he had no money. To earn money he would have to go away. He wouldn't mind going to local towns like Mardan and Peshawar. But — he was speaking through Rahimullah — he didn't want to go too far. What he really wanted was to live and work here in the village.

When I asked — Rahimullah translating for me — whether he wouldn't like to go outside the village and open his own barbershop, he fixed Rahimullah with his eyes, familiar yet respectful, as though the question was Rahimullah's own, and he began to look very small. He said that if he went to Peshawar or Karachi and found a job in a shop he would make thirty-five rupees a day at the most, less than a pound. With that kind of wage he wouldn't be able to save. A number of his friends and relations had gone to Karachi. He himself had once gone to Karachi. He worked for somebody who had a barbershop, a richer relation from the village. He was the servant of this family, and he got twelve hundred rupees a month, forty pounds. It wasn't enough for him, so he came back.

He had gone to school until he was eight or nine. He had reached the third class. He had had one daughter, and she had died. That was his story. He had nothing else to say, and he was content after that to sit in the armchair and say and do nothing.

Rahimullah took me to see his family courtyard. It was a great courtesy; purdah was strict here. But two masons were at work on the family house, and proper purdah arrangements would already have been made. The house, for fifteen people altogether, was of brick and on two floors. On the lower floor – I was considering it from a distance – there were four rooms at the back of a big verandah with a marble floor and brick arches. The water tower (with the television aerial) and the upper floor were reached by open concrete steps on the left. The women's quarters were on the upper floor, and the verandah there was screened by pierced and patterned concrete blocks.

The yard was unpaved and dusty. It was full of fruit trees, planted apparently at random and not creating the effect of an orchard. Between the trees were a number of beds and tables and drums and baskets and junked pieces of furniture. A miniature hut was where the chickens roosted. There was a well in one corner of the yard; it had a concrete cover and an electric motor. The kitchen was in another corner, with chopped wood on the flat roof.

Separate from this, and in its own little cleared area, was a traditional clay-walled cooking place of northern India, the *chulha*: something again which the Indian immigrants of a hundred years before had taken to Trinidad and which I had known as a child. So for me in Rahimullah's family courtyard, though the *chulha* here had another name, it was a little bit like finding pieces of my past. Even the disorder – the bed, the drum, the basket – was like the disorder I had known in my grandmother's houses.

I asked Rahimullah whether the masons who were at work on the house were also going to pave the yard. I asked that because of the apparent disorder; it seemed temporary; it seemed that soon everything in the yard was going to be put away again. But Rahimullah said no; what was there was good enough. And though it seemed strange then, a little later I understood: the people in the house would know where to find everything.

Rahimullah's younger son came out of the house and ran up to me, firing an imaginary pistol. He said in English, 'You! You! You are a

British policeman!' It might have been the effect of television, or my jacket; or his father might have told him about their guest.

The animal pens were at the back of the main house. Just outside the walls were the dung heaps and the fields. The family's five acres here, irrigated land, were sharecropped. Sugar cane, corn, fodder, vegetables: half of everything was for the family.

We – Rahimullah and I and the little party who had attached themselves to us – began to walk towards the main canal. We walked on the new concrete walls of the feeder canal or drain, between sugar-cane fields; sugar cane here was the most profitable crop. We saw, some fields away, the sugar-cane patch of another family and their low mud-and-brick house. That was a barber's house, they told me. Not Qaim Khan; another barber.

I said, 'Rich family?'

No, no, they all said in a kind of chorus, as though the poverty of that family with the mud-and-brick house was very well known.

The main canal was smaller than I expected. But it looked clean and controlled, a sudden touch of order, and the flowing water was refreshing to see. It was lined with young trees. The government looked after the canal; the government even looked after the trees. Water and trees in the foreground and the well-kept, variegated fields stretching away in sunlight made for deep, romantic views. The openness and distance was a surprise after the crowded sabbath roads and the cluttered shops and the bicycles and the people walking to market. And yet that sense of crowd remained, in the aspect of the precious irrigated land, parcelled out in small pieces.

I asked whether the barber, Qaim Khan, was of the Yusufzai clan. Rahimullah said no; Qaim Khan had no land, and land mattered. Only the blue-blooded Pathans were landowners, and they preferred to buy land here, high as the price was, rather than buy a house in a town like Peshawar, though the house in Peshawar was the better investment. Until quite recently barbers and other artisans, carpenters, blacksmiths, goldsmiths, washermen, weavers, were not allowed to buy land. They were able now to buy land for houses, but it was rare for them to own agricultural land. They were not considered part of what Rahimullah called the mainstream; the mullahs were above them; and the blue-blooded Pathans were at the top. Rahimullah didn't make much of it; but it was interesting in this account to find the mullah slightly downgraded.

Rahimullah said, 'Since the *nai* is living among the Pathans, and has to survive in this male-dominated and very tough society, he actually has come to regard himself as part of it, and he strives to live by the same standards and principles. An artisan might say, "We are Pathans." And they might be accepted as such outside the province, but the blue-blooded Pathans will not accept them as such. They will not let their daughters marry them.'

So we talked, as our party picked its way along the concrete walls of the smaller canal back to Rahimullah's house, and the outer courtyard. When we were in the guest house again, among the beds and the armchairs, he talked of the Pathan idea of honour. He was proud of this idea. When we had first met, in the hotel in Peshawar, it was what he had talked about. He had told a story about a Pathan girl who had run away with a male servant of the family. The couple had been hunted down – no place in the frontier for them to hide – and tied to a tree and shot; the police had stood by and done nothing.

Rahimullah sought now to codify the Pathan idea of honour. Language, home territory, hospitality, sanctuary, revenge: honour extended to all of these things. Though in some of its details the code here would have been purely of the region, there was a general, related idea of honour in the subcontinent. It was something I had always understood, growing up in the Trinidad Indian community. It was one of the things that had given that community a reputation for murder in the 1930s. I knew, though, that murder wasn't always simple murder. When men know in their bones that governments are malign, and that there are no laws or institutions they can trust, the idea of honour becomes vital. Without that idea men who have no voice or representation in the world can become nothing. The poor, especially, need the idea.

Rahimullah said, 'It's only yesterday that somebody was killed. Four years ago a local poet was killed, and yesterday revenge was taken. His son had hired assassins to kill the murderer, and they have done it now. They waited four years. They can wait for twenty years.'

A wrinkled old man, thin and dark and white-capped, was sitting in one of the armchairs. He appeared to be listening, but I don't know how much he understood. Rahimullah said he was a cousin; that might have been only a courtesy. The old man had a son in Dubai; the son wanted to come back to the village. The old man thought Rahimullah could help; that was why he was there.

A small, dark young man with wavy hair, and in a grey *shalwar-kameez*, came in.

Rahimullah said to me, 'Do you know this guy?'

The young man shook my hand. His hand was wet and cold. His name was Kimat Gul. He was Rahimullah's servant, the only one. He looked after the cattle. He hadn't gone on the walk to the canal with us because he had gone to the sugar-cane field to get fodder for the buffaloes and cows. The guest house was where he lived. He slept here and he watched television here. The television set was on the big dining table; Rahimullah had bought it for him in Peshawar.

Kimat Gul was an orphan and no one knew when he was born; he could be eighteen or nineteen or twenty. His father had remarried, so Kimat Gul was absolutely on his own. He had stayed with relations before coming to Rahimullah; then he had left Rahimullah to go to Karachi. Everybody here went to Karachi. They loved the land and the village, but the land couldn't support them. Kimat Gul didn't stay long in Karachi; he had come back to Rahimullah.

Someone in the guest house said in English, 'He is a barber.' Another *nai*, then. And, in fact, he was the brother of Qaim Khan, the earlier young man in blue.

Rahimullah said, 'He wants to become a driver. He says, "I will drive your car." But right now I have another driver. Kimat Gul is getting six hundred rupees plus food and room and clothes and TV. He has been with us since he was very small. If he stays with us we will arrange for his marriage and provide him with a house. We have three houses, two houses here and one in the village. For the marriage he will be able to get a girl from his relations. He has to keep to his relations. He can marry, but he will have to pay for that. Clothes and household goods.'

In Karachi Kimat Gul had worked in a barbershop. It wasn't a good job. And there was the trouble in Karachi. It was dangerous moving about to look for another job. He moved from a locality called Landhi to another called Sher Shah: Karachi for him was these names, and the memory of danger. Even going to work was risky. People were killed. A policeman he knew was killed; the policeman's name was Ayub.

Qaim Khan, Rahimullah's sabbath barber, the man in blue, came back from whatever he had been doing and sat down open-mouthed in an armchair. Perhaps he wasn't even listening. He would have known the story very well.

There used to be strikes, Kimat Gul said, still talking about Karachi.

Nobody came to the barbershop. There was no work. So he came back here.

He was barefooted. His wavy hair, hanging down his neck, was black and thick and shiny. He had a deep, almost booming, voice. He had a ring on the fourth finger of his left hand. If you wore a ring, the fingers didn't get diseased. It was a silver ring and it stood out against his very dark hand. The dark white-capped man, with the son in Dubai, was also wearing a ring like that to keep his fingers healthy.

Rahimullah said, 'I am the only one not wearing a ring.'

I asked Kimat Gul, 'Are you happy here?'

He said in his extraordinary voice (and Rahimullah translated), 'I'm happy. But where else can I go?'

There were laughs all round, and Kimat Gul laughed too, showing his big teeth. He didn't like barbering, he said, though he knew how to do it. He preferred feeding the cattle.

It was time for the midday prayers. Rahimullah got up and, wrapping his big sand-coloured chador or shawl about him, went out into the sunlight of the guest courtyard, and at the far end turned behind the small bougainvillaea bushes and small trees – one day perhaps a proper hedge and screen – into the family courtyard.

Later the two men who had been working on the house, the mason and the son of the shop assistant, came and sat on a string bed in the arcaded verandah and shared food with Kimat Gul, the herdsman and servant who lived there and watched television.

After lunch – thick wholewheat *roti*, vegetables, chicken, mutton pilau, apples and grapes – we went the short distance to Rahimullah's ancestral village of Shamozai. Just outside Rahimullah's gate a young girl was playing in the dust: the first girl, the first female, I had seen since I had arrived. Purdah was soon going to fall on her; the rest of her life was going to be spent in that void where time was without meaning.

In a half-open hut not far away some men were making coarse brown sugar, and we stopped to watch. The cane was crushed in a simple steel grinder worked by bullocks. The cane juice simmered in a big, shallow, saucer-shaped iron pot; the fire below, in a kind of tunnel, was fed by trash and wood and dried cane-husk. The sun was bright outside, and the heat here was great. A man used a long-handled ladle to skim off the cream-coloured scum and to lift this waste into wicker baskets; from time to time he used a rake to scrape the upper wall of the black pot. It took about two and a half hours to make the sugar, crumbly and aromatic, delicious on its own when fresh, and quite unlike the refined product.

It was left to Rahimullah to tell me that though the area was poor, the men making the sugar came from outside. Local people, with their own idea of what was fitting, wouldn't want to do that hard and very hot job.

Shamozai was spectacular. It was surrounded on three sides by rocky, abrupt, sharp-edged mountains which were part of a mountain range. In the foothills of this range the settlement lay: from a distance, flat-roofed, flat-walled, a pattern of rock and wall and sun and shadow, cubist in appearance. The house where Rahimullah's father had been born in 1918 was high up. A narrow lane wound down the steep hill; near the bottom, next to the mosque, was the house Rahimullah's father had established as his own. Not far away was the circular stone-stepped pool or tank fed by the spring that ran down the mountain.

The site, with the mountains and the spring and the pool, was clearly special. It felt even sacred, like the hot springs of Pariyangan in Sumatra, where the Minangkabau people were said to have come out of the earth; like the volcanic ground at the foot of Mount Merapi in Java which the poet Linus felt to be sacred, suffused with the emanations of the Hindu and Buddhist monuments a few feet below the surface. There would always have been a settlement at Shamozai; below the surface here, too, would be ruins that would take the human story back and back.

The main lane was crowded. There were children and more children everywhere, lank hair and smudged faces and dusty little limbs, as though the village houses could no longer hold them in. It gave a touch of fantasy, almost, to the shut-away setting, considering how desolate the abrupt mountains looked from not very far away. A *nai*, in his mid-forties, already had ten children; a farmer had eight. All the families who could afford it had moved out of the village. But the village was still full of Rahimullah's relations. He shook hands all the time; the narrow lane (with its twelve or thirteen shops, small and dark and low, some of them dirt-floored) was like one extended family hall.

On the way back we passed Rahimullah's wife's family house: a tube-well at the end of the lane, a blank brick wall before that, with a half-open gate revealing the cow-pens at the back of the living quarters.

The family were originally better off than Rahimullah's, with more land (and they too had moved out of the old village); but they were not as well educated, and Rahimullah and his brother were able to buy some land off them.

Rahimullah's father had arranged the marriage, though Rahimullah chose his bride. She was a distant relative and used to come to the house, and he used to go to her family house, the blank-walled one we were looking at now. She was in purdah, but since the families were on visiting terms they could see each other; though they didn't actually meet and talk. The most he said to her, when she came to his house, was 'Welcome'. They met properly only on the third night of their wedding. They were both very shy. He didn't know what to say. He could only say, 'How are you? Are you happy? How do you feel in your new house.' She didn't reply. Now she lived just a short distance away in the new house Rahimullah and his brother had built, her life completely defined.

A splendid white-capped figure was waiting for us in the guest house. This was Mutabar Khan, another cousin of Rahimullah's. He had spent all his working life outside the frontier, and now he had come back for good, to the twenty acres that his family had, in different pieces. He was born in Shamozai in 1930 and he had left the village and gone to Karachi when he was sixteen. Now, a little like an actor who had made up for the last act, he had a great parted yellow-black-grey beard. When he spoke of his life outside, he compressed it; it was as if it had occurred in a kind of parenthesis.

That life, as he told it, was reduced to the names of places, Karachi and Dubai; to two employers, a Hindu grain merchant in Karachi, and an Arab in Dubai who owned an orchard; and the money they paid. There were no details, no pictures, no suggestion of the passing of time, the passing of life. But time here was an unconsidered flow; and to his fellows Mutabar Khan was a man who had seen the whole thing through and come back safe. He was what they wished to be, and the little crowd now sitting on the beds in the guest house was attentive. The mason and the man with him were there, work-stained; they had finished their work for the day on Rahimullah's family house, and out of courtesy and simple fellowship were spending a little time here before going home.

Mutabar Khan talked about Karachi. He said (in Rahimullah's translation), 'I still remember with fondness the days I spent in Karachi. You could sleep safely even on the footpath. I don't think it can return to peaceful times now.' That was what Karachi was for him.

He was worried about the Pathans there. Rahimullah had told me that there were two million, that Karachi had a bigger Pathan population than Peshawar or Kabul.

Mutabar Khan said, 'They are such a huge number. They will die rather than come back.'

I asked him, 'Are there too many people here, then?'

'Too many children in the schools now. No place to sit. But it is our belief that children are God-given and cannot be prevented from being born. Allah will provide for them. When a child is conceived Allah has already decided that this child is to be born.'

8

Ali's Footprint

IN THE mornings now in the countryside around Peshawar chador-draped figures stood in front of low brick houses with kindling on the flat roofs; cooking smoke mingled with mist. In the flat chill fields there were patches of tropical sugar cane next to small orchards of temperate fruit. On the edge of some fields there grew a line or two of a spindly hybrid poplar that cast little shadow. This was also a crop; the poplar could be harvested after four years; the wood was used for matches. The crop was new here. And in that was a little history: until it seceded in 1971, Bangladesh supplied Pakistan's matches.

I took a hotel car to Rawalpindi. At Attock the muddy Kabul river met the blue Indus, in a confluence about a mile wide. It was one of the great river views of the subcontinent. It was where the frontier ended, and the Punjab began. It would have been nice to stop and look, but there could be no stopping or dawdling on the bridge. And as I went on, by car to Rawalpindi, and then by train to Lahore, the land getting flatter, the views crowded always, the Pathan ideas Rahimullah had introduced me to began to feel far away. Honour and home territory, sanctuary and revenge, the hiding away of women and the strictness of religious observance: they were ideas that needed their own setting, their own enclosed world. But the Pathans had to migrate; they needed the outside world; and then their idea of honour could become warped. Few were educated or had high skills; and the clan code, which gave them protection, could also make them predators. That was an aspect of their reputation in the outside world. It was the other side of their reputation as soldiers.

In the hotel lobby in Peshawar there had been this notice painted on a board: *HOTEL POLICY. Arms cannot be brought inside the hotel premises. Personal Guards or Gunmen are required to deposit their weapons with Hotel Security. We seek your cooperation. Management.* And when I got back to Lahore it was to news of a frontier kidnapping.

I had got to know Ahmed Rashid. He was a journalist. He also owned, with a partner, a coal mine in the Punjab hinterland. The news, from him, was that three of the mine's jeeps had been stolen, and six of the men kidnapped. The stealing and the kidnapping had occurred in stages. First a jeep and the two men in it had been taken, in the big town of Sargodha. After ten days there had come a ransom demand for two lakhs, two hundred thousand rupees, four thousand pounds. Ahmed had sent two men in a jeep to negotiate with the kidnappers. He hadn't sent any money by these two men. This had enraged the kidnappers. They had seized the two men and the second jeep. Ahmed, taking the hint, had then sent two clerks in a third jeep with the ransom money. But the kidnappers were apparently still very angry. They held on to the two clerks and the ransom money, and made a fresh demand for twenty lakhs, forty thousand pounds.

Ahmed, ever the journalist, was excited by the whole thing, this nice little story breaking on his own doorstep, as it were; and in his detached journalist's way he found the sequence of events funny, the men from the mine going in two by two into some kidnappers' pit somewhere in the frontier. He had got in touch with the army and the intelligence people; only they could help him. And he thought now – and this wasn't going to be so funny for the kidnapped men – that negotiations could go on for many months. It was important to keep the negotiations going, and in this way to prevent the kidnapped men from being taken across the border. If that happened, it was all over; the jeeps and the men could be forgotten.

Where there was no law, no institutions that men could trust, the code and the idea of honour protected men. But it also worked the other way. Where the code was strong there could be no rule of law. In the frontier, as Saleem Ranjha's Pathan guest had said at Mansoura, the modern state was withering away; it was superfluous. People were beginning to live again with the idea of clan and fiefdom; and it was good for business.

★

Three hundred miles or so to the south, where the Punjab met Sindh, in the desert, there was the old princely state of Bahawalpur. There were more than five hundred of these semi-autonomous states in the days of the British. About seventy of them were important enough for their rulers to be called Highness; Bahawalpur was one of them.

It was one of the small opportunist states or fiefdoms that came into being in the middle of the eighteenth century during the breakdown of Muslim power in the subcontinent. It was bounded for three hundred miles on the west and north by the Indus and its tributary, the Sutlej. These great rivers on one side – the Sutlej with a ravaged, meandering water course many miles wide – and the desert on the other side preserved the Bahawalpur territory against the Sikhs from the north and the Hindu Mahrattas from the south. In 1838 the British made Bahawalpur a protectorate; and then at last the Nawabs of Bahawalpur knew imperial security. They ruled until 1954, when the state was absorbed into Pakistan.

The Nawab had hoped that when the British left the subcontinent in 1947 his state would become independent. This was madness. Bahawalpur in 1941 had a population of less than a million and a half, and most of these people were agricultural serfs. But the Nawab, after an untroubled century of British protection, had developed a fantasy about the reach of his authority. It was impossible for him, when he had lost his state, to live on in it as a private citizen. In his concept of the state there were, almost certainly, no free private citizens; there could only be a ruler and the ruled. He abandoned Bahawalpur and went to England, taking much of his fortune with him. He bought a house in Surrey and lived there until his death in 1966.

He left behind in Bahawalpur many children, recognised and unrecognised, three palaces, an idle and disorientated harem, some schools and colleges, and the ambitious Sutlej Valley Project. That project, carried out by British engineers and with a loan from the British Indian government, had taken irrigation to the desert and opened up vast areas for agriculture. The land was offered for almost nothing to people who would cultivate it. The local people were too broken-backed to be interested in this gamble with the desert; more spirited settlers came in from the Punjab. The success of the project tripled the revenues of the state and made the Nawab a very rich man. This wealth, no doubt, was one of the things that encouraged him to think of independence.

The dynasty of Bahawalpur, through various accidents, of geography and history, had in the end lasted for two centuries. It had never been grand or (apart from the Sutlej Valley Project) creative; but romantic tales had begun to attach to it. It was said that it was descended from the Abbasids who had ruled gloriously in Baghdad until the Mongol invasion in the thirteenth century. One line of the Abbasids had then fled to Sindh, which was part of the Abbasid empire; and there – in this romance – they had kicked their heels for five centuries or so, before making their play for the big patch of desert that became Bahawalpur.

The recently updated *Encyclopaedia of Islam* dismisses this story: it says that the Abbas of Bahawalpur is not the Abbas of the Abbasids. In a way it doesn't matter whether the story is true or not; what matters is local belief, and the angle it puts on local history. The old Hindu kingdom of Sindh was the first territory in the subcontinent to fall to the Muslims. It was conquered by the Arabs in the eighth century. The conquest, done principally for loot, was quite a deliberate and methodical business. The first expedition was in 634, just two years after the Prophet's death, and three years before the conquest of Persia. There were eight further attempts on Sindh, before the final conquest in 710. This last assault was controlled from Syria by the caliph himself. The thirteenth-century text that celebrates this conquest, the *Chachnama*, fanciful and poetic as it is in parts, is as dreadful an account of blood and loot and enslavement as Caesar's *Gallic War*. But the conquest of Sindh can be considered in more than one way, and the Bahawalpur claim on the Abbasids is also a link to the birth of Arab and Muslim power in the subcontinent. It is like the primary neurosis of the converted.

Whatever the truth of the Abbasid story – and whatever was happening elsewhere in the world in the twentieth century – the last Nawab of Bahawalpur was fanatical about the ancestry he claimed. In Bahawalpur and Pakistan and the subcontinent he was an Arab of the Abbasids and a conqueror, a man drawing his wealth from the country, but not part of it. He wore the fez to make the point; he made his courtiers wear it to keep them in their place (and, until you had acquired the knack, it wasn't easy to keep the flower-pot-shaped hat on your head). The Nawab, driving out one day, saw one of his courtiers far off on the road without his fez. The courtier saw and began to run. The Nawab gave chase in his car. The poor courtier, forgetting dignity, fearing the Nawab and his famous stick at that moment more than anything else, ran off the road and into a sugar-cane field, with its razor-edged grass, and hid there.

The Arab faith, the Arab language, Arab names, the fez: twelve hundred years after the conquest of Sindh, this affirmation of separate-ness, of imperial and racial and religious authority: there probably has been no imperialism like that of Islam and the Arabs. The Gauls, after five hundred years of Roman rule, could recover their old gods and reverences; those beliefs hadn't died; they lay just below the Roman surface. But Islam seeks as an article of the faith to erase the past; the believers in the end honour Arabia alone; they have nothing to return to.

The Nawab saw himself as an Arab and a conqueror. With another side of himself he understood true authority. And just as he made his courtiers abase themselves before him, so he was willing to abase him-self before the paramount British power. There would have been a British Resident, generally to oversee things. The Nawab, in addition, had British people fill important official posts.

And, noticeably dark-skinned (he was called 'Brownie' at school, or so I was told), he was obsessed with white women. He, in one mode fierce about the ancestry he claimed, wished in another mode to be racially abolished. He wished passionately to have white children or hybrid children. Three of his wives were English (and a fourth was Anglo-Indian). In this he set a fashion; many people went abroad and came back with white wives. The last English wife of the Nawab was known locally as Lady O, because the British officials and the Bahawalpur gentry judged her to be common.

He sent all the sons he recognised to Aitchison College, the British-established school for the sons of princes in Lahore (where as a boy he was called 'Brownie'). But it was known that for him his hybrid chil-dren were special, magical. There is a story that he took two of his sons by local concubines to a shrine somewhere in the desert and left them there to grow up as grave-keepers. He could have done it; his power in his state was absolute. But the story may not be true. The Nawab had many wives, many concubines, many children; their jealousies and pain would have seeded many stories.

A journalist from Bahawalpur who had got to know one of the women of the Nawab's harem told me, 'In the palace he had a separate building for the English wives and their children. The Indian wives knew about the English wives, but the Englishwomen never knew about the Indian wives. When he wanted to go to the harem he would say he was going on a tour. Sometimes it would be for three days, sometimes for a week. And there would be a proper escort: the guards, the Rolls-Royce, the camel corps, who were his personal bodyguard. And all he did was to go round to the back of the palace, which was quite enormous, like an old fort, and enter the harem. The harem was at the back.'

He had had more than three hundred and ninety women. Most of them had slept only once with him; but then they could sleep with no other man. Some of these women developed a kind of hysteria; some became lesbians. Always in the harem he had sixteen or eighteen women on whom he could call.

'When he entered the harem he had a stick. The women would pounce on him and pull him, and he would keep them back with his stick, until he saw the one he wanted, and then he would tell the eunuch. After his foreign trips he would enter the harem with tin trunks, and the women would go crazy. They had asked for chemises and chiffons and feathers, and they would fight for these things. For the English wives he would shop at Tiffany's, Cartier, Garrard. The salesmen would come to him when he was in England and show the jewels. For himself he bought English country scenes, and he always had English portrait-painters come to paint him.'

One day a letter on a silver tray – the detail suggests palace intrigue and excited gossip – told the favourite English wife that the Nawab had an Indian harem. And when the poor man went to that wife he found all the harem sitting with her having tea.

'When the army took over the durbar palace they found a whole collection of dildos. About six hundred, some made of clay, some bought in England and battery-operated. The army dug a pit and buried these dildos. A lot of dirty magazines. He needed them, to use the dildos. He became impotent very early. His appetites were sated. Someone who went into the harem at the wrong time one day saw the Nawab using a dildo on a screaming woman.'

The main palace had been closed for eleven years and was now in decay. Like some other princely property in the subcontinent, it was the subject of litigation, and legally sealed; the Nawab's numerous heirs were fighting over it. The façade of the palace still looked good, but termites were eating away at its insides; the mound of their droppings over the years had forced the front door open a crack and wedged it tight. There were said to be nineteen vintage cars in the garage; five of them were custom-built Rolls-Royces from the 1930s; rust had got to them all and they were on bricks.

When I left the drive and began to go around to the back the guards shouted at me. I was able to see why. On the upper floor at the back a bedroom window had been broken, and the screen pulled away: pilferers, looters at work: the theme of the subcontinent. The gardens were overgrown: desert thorn trees, tall elephant grass, date palms growing in the pipes and guttering: like a surrealist garden now, like something designed for the decaying palace, with a surrealistically clean and well-edged drive.

Far out in the desert was the desolate enclosure – tended by families of grave-keepers – with the heavy, rhetorical tombs of the fourteen rulers of Bahawalpur and their wives. The favourite wives had marble tombs that were like gazebos, with Mogul-style marble latticework with inlay and raised floral patterns. Two of the Nawab's English wives had these marble tombs.

It was the grandson of one of those wives who took me to the tombs. The Nawab adored his grandmother, Azhar Abbasi said; she helped him, too, with certain affairs of state. Later he showed a small faded photograph; because of the laws of purdah there were almost no pictures of his grandmother. The photograph, which might have been taken professionally (or in a studio) before she married the Nawab, showed a slender woman in a calf-length dress of the 1920s or 1930s, seated, legs crossed, turned to one side; she was fine-faced, self-possessed. She was the daughter of a British army officer in India. It was strange to think of what she had chosen, this particular deal with life, so to speak, which for her had meant a kind of disappearance; and then of her tomb in the desert. She might have died from poison, because of jealousy in the court; or she might have died after an operation carried out, because of the Nawab's purdah anxieties, not in a hospital theatre, but on the palace dining table. Again, there were many stories.

The Nawab had ten sons whom he recognised. Azhar Abbasi, who had shown me the tombs, was the son of the third son, who had himself had four wives. Azhar was burdened by all the resulting family property problems. These multiple Muslim marriages, though often comic to people outside, caused untold pain to many of the people involved, and the pain could travel like disease from generation to generation, with people seemingly driven to pass on the abuse – the jealousy, the torment, the neglect – from which they had suffered.

Azhar was still Muslim, though by intermarriage down the generations he was virtually white, and Australian. I asked him what he – so
far removed racially now – thought of his background.

He said he wanted to migrate to Canada or Australia. 'My grandfather was an Indian prince. It's over. An Indian prince: that's no big
deal.'

And it all rested on serfdom. The opening up of the desert, the harem,
the more expensive English wives, the jewels from London, the house
in Surrey, the Rolls-Royces rotting in the palace garage, the pictures of
English country scenes: they represented the accumulated tribute,
penny upon penny, like the termite droppings, from the poorest of the
poor. The people in the villages belonged to their landlord, and his
power over them was almost as absolute as the Nawab's over his subjects. These people could be whipped at will; their daughters and
women abused at will. The serf knew he was not to turn his back on
his master. He backed away from him or he moved sideways past him.
Generations of servitude lay in that instinctive crab-like dance, discon-
certing at first to the visitor.

Bahawalpur had been only a British protectorate; the British had
never imposed their laws here. The *sharia* always ruled; and an antique
cruelty – hidden away in the rags and huts of the countryside, and looking only like poverty – had survived the century of the British presence.
The stories here could be like the stories from the Caribbean plantations in the late eighteenth century or from Russia in the early
nineteenth century. Even in the Nawab's time – and the Nawab was
always watchful for this kind of abuse – the wife of one of his officials
had whipped a twelve-year-old boy to death.

This was a current story:

'This woman was a Baluch. She had been a serf and had been literally bought by this feudal landlord when she was ten. She had been his
mistress, his son's mistress, and finally, when his grandson wanted to
possess her, she ran away with her lover and sought refuge on our
farm. We were also feudals. She ran from one feudal to another. There
was a lot of heat on us to return her. I knew that if we returned her
they would punish her in the most bestial manner. This feudal raped
serf women, humiliated them when they disobeyed, killed them sometimes, and destroyed their bodies. He humiliated them by tying them in

the pens like animals, having them sodomised, and making them eat excrement. He was in his sixties.

'I knew that if we returned this woman to him they would cut her nose and hamstrings. And she knew this. She begged us not to send her back. During the negotiations with the landlord, who was politically very powerful and, ironically, belonged to the liberal party, they said that she had to give up her six-year-old son. They said, "It's a matter of honour for us. If you don't give us the woman, you give us the boy."

'I had to persuade the woman to send the boy back. She started crying. She grabbed my feet and said, "You are powerful. You can get my son back. I told her I couldn't."

'She gave that boy away. It was unbelievable how she dressed this little boy. And two total strangers came for him. She dressed him up and said to him that he had to go with them, and that she would follow, and that he mustn't be afraid. Whenever he cried she said she was going to follow, she would come. She pushed him towards the men. They were tall, with their *lungis*, and with their big moustaches. She said, "Go with them. I will be right behind you. You are going to meet your father's family." The boy was scared. He kept looking back. She was impassive. No tears. She said, "Go. I'm coming." She kept saying, "I'm coming," until the boy disappeared. Then she started screaming. They weren't going to kill the boy. They would let him grow up on the farm. He would grow up as another serf.'

That had happened six years before. And, by chance, just four days before I arrived in Bahawalpur, justice of a sort was done. The landlord, the abuser of his serf women, was shot dead. Not by a serf, not by someone avenging the man's lifelong brutalities, but by a sectarian militia, a religious gang, staking out new territory for themselves: another kind of fiefdom in the making, an aspect now of the internal warfare of this area of southern Punjab and Sindh, between the sectarian militia, the Sindhi extremists, the *mohajirs*, and the long-established feudals: *jihad* upon *jihad*, holy war upon holy war.

The sectarian militia had begun to move into the landlord's area. He wished to warn them off. When they met him they fired their guns in the air, to show their disregard, and as a gesture of their power. He had one of them killed later, in revenge. And now he had been killed in return. So many bullets had been fired into him – from the Kalashnikovs, inevitably – that he had been left 'more holes than man'.

The words were used by the old woman who told me the story. Her own life had been half destroyed by the sexual obsessions of the Nawab's court. Her husband had been one of the old courtiers; he, like some of the others, kept his boys. Old hysteria showed in the old woman's face. She had a fine house; it was savourless to her. And now, talking of the feudal who had been killed, that man who had been part of the viciousness by which she felt herself surrounded, she laughed at the words she had used – 'more holes than man' – and showed her teeth.

Ibn Battuta, the fourteenth-century Muslim traveller who wanted to visit all the Muslim territories in the world, spent about seven years in Muslim India from about 1335. He passed this way (in what was then the province of Sindh) at the start of his Indian time.

As a traveller Ibn Battuta depended on the bounty of the various despots whose lands he visited. He knew the form; he knew how to give gifts to get bigger ones in return. (He gave the local governor of Sindh a white slave, a horse, some raisins and almonds.) Rulers honoured him as a religious scholar. And, like a good mullah who knew his place, he looked to them to be only defenders of the faith. He did not look beyond that, though the barbarities of Delhi – executions and tortures every day in the ruler's public audience – became too much even for him; especially when four court slaves were deputed to be with him all the time, and he thought, knowing the forms of the court, that he was himself now soon to be executed.

In India he talks constantly about slaves and slave girls; he says at one place that he can't travel without them. Slaves are part of the view. (In Aden he had seen slaves being used as draught animals; he records it only as a novelty.) But it is in almost casual sentences that we get an idea of the nature of the countryside, and the serfdom on which the glory of the sultan in Delhi and his local officials depended. For a few months, and as a courtesy to him as a visitor, Ibn Battuta was granted the revenues of a village in this Bahawalpur area by a local official. He made five thousand dinars. The dinars didn't fall out of the sky; they would have come from the fields and the serfs who worked them. They are the people never mentioned by Ibn Battuta, but always present. ('We then prepared for the journey to the capital, which is forty days' march from Multan through a continuous stretch of inhabited country.') Later, in Delhi, at the murderous court, he was to be granted the revenues of five villages. In his book there is a constant reckoning in crops; the endowment of a mausoleum, for instance, is reckoned in crops.

So in an extraordinary way in Bahawalpur and the neighbouring area – where time beyond people's memory is an unmeasured and unmeasurable flow, and where serf structures, untouched during the British time, have been reasserted with independence and the isolated Muslim polity of the poet Iqbal's dream – in Bahawalpur we can get close to the fourteenth century and perhaps even to the eighth, at the start of Muslim dominion. It was for those serf revenues, after all, that the conquest was undertaken.

Ibn Battuta knew the town of Uch. It was built around an old fertility shrine which still drew devotees. I went there one morning. The road out of the city of Bahawalpur, shaded for many miles with *shisham* (or rosewood) and wild acacia, led through rich irrigated land: cotton, sugar cane, mustard; a sugar mill; cotton-ginning factories. Before the irrigation there would have been only desert here; and occasionally, amid the flat green fields, grey-and-dun humps of sand showed what the land would have looked like. Trucks going to Karachi, five hundred miles to the south, travelled bumper to bumper, in slow convoy, because of the dacoits or bandits in the great desert of Sindh.

Uch was a mud-walled city on a big mound beside a dead river. The mound hinted at its antiquity: the debris of the centuries would have lain there, many previous Uchs. The roads went up and down. Ibn Battuta had found 'fine bazaars and buildings' in 1335; but he had his own way of seeing, his own references, and perhaps what he saw was only a version of what I was seeing: palms, donkeys, the up-and-down streets, children, rubbish, wet open gutters, and the tomb-shrines.

The first of those shrines cured bad backs, and the lower part of the outer wall, which was of brick, had been polished smooth by the scores of thousands who had rubbed their afflicted backs on it. Inside, the wooden pillars supporting the roof were like the pillars of Hindu temples: perhaps accidental, or perhaps a style now associated with the ancient magic or virtue of the site. The principal Muslim saint had a big green-covered burial mound. The lesser saints who had come after had smaller white slabs.

The second, and more important, shrine was for women who wanted children. The central feature here was Ali's footprint: fabulous:

Ali the son-in-law and cousin of the Prophet: his footprint a depression on a black granite pillar. This pillar had been brought from Baghdad, the centre of the world, by a Muslim saint who, with the help of the *djinns*, powerful spirits, had flown here to Uch on a wall. The tomb in this enclosure was of the wife of that saint. The enclosure was dark and dark-floored and with the deep smell of old oil. One part of it was like a black grotto now after the offerings of centuries, with encrustations of oil-residue from the little oil-fed lights, rolled cotton wicks in small clay vessels, that the faithful still set down. Women who made offerings here and had children came back and hung cradles or wrote their names. Women who had twins hung toy ladders. There was one that morning, of new white wood.

Anyone who had travelled in the subcontinent and looked at old Hindu temples would have recognised in the granite pillar with the depression the *lingam*, the phallic emblem of Shiva. To hear the stories about the *djinns* and Ali's footprint and the saint flying on the wall from Baghdad was like entering a still living historical moment, and witnessing the crossover from the old religion to the new.

A small mosque below a very big tree – a great trunk, many gnarled branches – was part of the shrine area. The guardians of the shrines, living easily with marvels, said that the mosque had been built by Muhamad Bin Qasim, who had conquered Sindh in 710; and that the tree was also from that time; it would have been a tree Muhamad Bin Qasim knew.

The tree might not have been as old as that; and the mosque was certainly much later. But the mosque had been given the Muhamad Bin Qasim association to celebrate the conquest – the faithful no longer saw themselves as the conquered – and also to claim the ancient site for the new faith. Just as, in Java, six or seven hundred years later, the new faith could take over the abstract Hindu-Buddhist-Jain figure of the great meditator, the *tirthankara*, the 'river-crosser', a metaphor for the achiever of higher consciousness, and spin a more literal tale for him. The river-crosser became Kali Jaga, the 'guardian of the river': obeying an order from a great teacher to sit and wait, and doing so by the river bank with unwavering fidelity until the vines grew around him, and then being released by the teacher to get up and spread the message of Islam.

The *pir* of Uch, the inheritor of the sainthood and the site, was the descendant of the saint who had been brought on the wall from Baghdad by the *djinns*, and had spread Islam in the conquered territory. The current *pir* was a man of power. He had a large religious constituency, and his sister was married to the biggest feudal landowner in the area. This was how the feudals were moving: making alliances with industrialists and with religious dynasties like the *pir*'s: religion and money and land locking together to rule.

The *pir* had gone to Sindh that day. His *murids* or followers had called him to arbitrate in a murder case. Technically there was the rule of law in Sindh, but people had little faith in the apparatus of the state, and the *pir*'s followers preferred his judgement.

So the women who had come to see the *pir* that day had to wait, and they were squatting like chickens in his courtyard in the sun. They were peasant women, serf women, chattels of their landlords and their husbands, unprotected by law or custom or religion. They lived with cruelty and their minds had half gone. The *pir* was the only kind of light for them, and they had come to see him because they were now possessed by demons. The *pir* had a reputation for dealing with demons. Demons could enter these women and for a while make them objects of dread, rolling their eyes and head and speaking filthy words in unnatural voices. The *pir* knew how to get at the demons by punishing the bodies in which they were lodged.

I was told by a journalist from Bahawalpur that there was a special ceremony every spring in the *pir*'s courtyard. His followers, who were mainly from Sindh, came to the courtyard in a kind of pilgrimage. When the time came, they lay down in the courtyard and he walked or hobbled over them. He had a club foot; it was a congenital deformity of the *pirs* of Uch; and he cured the afflicted with every heavy step.

In the big sitting room of the house, attended by contented and civil women servitors, who clearly felt themselves privileged, there was – and it was unexpected in the ragged desert town – a big Waterford chandelier. There were photographs of the *pir*'s ancestors, and photographs of the present *pir*, showing him with presidents of Pakistan, foreign ambassadors, and with the last Nawab of Bahawalpur, the Nawab seated against a bolster, dark-skinned, seemingly respectful but hard-eyed, and with his high fez.

9

War

THE TRUCKS going to Karachi on the north-south 'superhighway' travelled in convoy through the desert of Sindh. This was because of the dacoits or bandits. And, indeed, just a few days after I had seen that convoy moving slowly bumper to bumper through Bahawalpur, there was an incident on the outskirts of Karachi that made the Karachi evening newspaper: *Dacoity on Superhighway*: dacoits holding up a truck and shooting and wounding the two men in it.

But the dacoits of Sindh were not always what they appeared. A police officer I got to know had had his first posting in a dacoit area. The land was wild. On one side of the highway was marshy forest, fed by the annual river floods; on the other side was mountain and rock and desert. It was all very poor: huts of mud and thatch in the countryside, and little two-roomed brick houses in the towns, with ten or twelve people to a house, many of the people having nothing to do in the desolation, just letting the years pass.

The dacoits were almost as wretched as their victims. And then the young officer, head of a sub-division, discovered that the local feudal landlords were really running the dacoits. They protected the dacoits; the dacoits in return acted as the landlords' gunmen, without pay. It cost about fifteen hundred rupees a month, thirty pounds, to hire a gunman; to have two or three or four gunmen without paying was good business; and there would be a share in the dacoits' more important loot. The dacoits would have had serious police charges on their head, even murder charges; they could have been turned in by the

feudal at any time. And the army – 'in Sindh forever', as the police officer said, 'supposedly fighting dacoits' – was always there, to kill the
dacoit on whom the feudal 'ratted'.

The game had its formalities. The feudal, in his starched *shalwar-
kameez*, and with his gunmen with their chadors (the guns below the
chadors), might come one morning in his Nissan four-wheel drive –
emblem of feudal authority – to sub-divisional headquarters. He would
be there, together with a delegation of local people, to complain about
the dacoits. The same feudal would come at another time to say that
the dacoit the police had picked up was the wrong man. A police officer who then pressed too hard or became aggressive could be 'posted
out'.

The officer was fresh from his eighteen-month training in the civil
service and police academies. 'A British colonial throwback: a spot of
riding, a spot of shooting, a spot of academic work, very theoretical
about the world outside. In reality they knew that the officer who
would make a lot of deals and compromises, and hunt with the hounds,
would be the one who would be successful.'

Some such dislocation had befallen the *mohajirs*, the Muslim migrants
from India, who had come in great numbers after independence to the
feudal land of Sindh. They had agitated more than anyone else for the
separate Muslim state, and they came to Pakistan and to Sindh as to
their own land. They found that it belonged to someone else; and the
people to whom it belonged were not willing to let go. They, the
mohajirs, became the fifth nationality of Pakistan, after the Baluchis, the
Pathans, the Punjabis, and the Sindhis. They were a nationality without territory. And that was where, a generation or two later, the war
of Karachi began: with the *mohajir* wish for territory. They wished
Karachi to be theirs; they were a majority in Karachi. Their passion,
their sense of grievance, was like religion; it was like a replay of the
agitation by their fathers and grandfathers fifty years before for
Pakistan.

The war had lasted more than ten years; the *mohajirs* said that twenty
thousand people had died. It was not a clear-cut war, *mohajirs* against
the state. The city was too big and too varied. Governments had sought
to use the passions of various groups. The Afghanistan war had brought
guns to everyone. And now there were two militant and mutually hos-

tile *mohajir* factions; there were Sindhi nationalists and Sindhi feudals; there were sectarian groups, Sunni and Shia, both ready to kill; there were the intelligence agencies; there were drug gangs and criminal gangs and real-estate gangs. The many-sided immigrant city was at war with itself. It had been too much even for the army. They had been there for twenty-nine months; they had achieved little, and had been replaced by the Rangers, a semi-military border force.

The poet Iqbal in 1930, making the case for an all-Muslim Pakistan, said, 'The religious ideal of Islam is organically related to the social order which it has created. The rejection of the one will eventually involve the rejection of the other.' It was the convert's view: the faith was identity enough, and state enough. It was the very idea with which the *mohajirs* had come to Pakistan. In that romantic view of Iqbal's there was no intimation of the carnage and plunder and grief of partition; or of the abandonment of the more than a hundred million in India; of the war that was going to start forty years later in Karachi. And a front page like this: *Shops closed; aerial firing in protest against yesterday's killings – GULBAHAR, L'ABAD, KORANGI TENSE.*

Gulbahar, Liaquatabad and Korangi were vast *mohajir* slum areas. The war, which had begun with middle-class *mohajir* protest, had got down to the very bottom.

The editor of an Urdu-language newspaper – I met him by chance in the Press Club – said, 'Yesterday the brother of the Chief Minister here was killed. Today three thousand young men of a particular area have been picked up by the police. They will be tortured, some of them. Their families have to ransom them for twenty-five thousand rupees.' Five hundred pounds. 'So there is terror and impoverishment. You should see the city at night. The city changes at night. It's like an occupied city. Come out and see the police in action, stopping and searching. But you must have courage.'

The editor was a small and mild-mannered man of forty-two. He was sympathetic to the *mohajir* cause, though he was not strictly a *mohajir*. He was a Memon; the Memons were a Gujarati-speaking business community. The editor felt that as outsiders he and his family had suffered in Sindh. His family's businesses, in insurance and medicines, had been nationalised; nationalisation had been used to damage non-Sindhi business interests. And the editor himself, because of Sindhi nationalist 'terror' at his university, had not been able to take his M.A. degree.

The editor had changed houses four times. He had done so to protect himself not only against the police but also against the militant *mohajir* movement, the MQM. The MQM, reaching downwards through the *mohajir* community, and losing some of its middle-class support, had become as brutal as its enemies. Like other successful movements of the oppressed, it had also become authoritarian. It had a leader now who could not be questioned. The Memon editor, sympathetic though he was to the cause, could at times print things that offended the MQM leader. Once the paper was 'banned' by the leader for two weeks. The editor had then been required to write a personal letter to the leader, 'begging for forgiveness'; and after that for three days running he had had to print an apology.

Still the editor kept going. He had courage.

Abdul said, 'Please understand that when I leave home in the morning I am not sure whether I will return home.'

He was thirty-six, a family man, and also a man of the *mohajir* movement. He wasn't a fire-eater. His speech was flat, and he was dressed in white, white trousers, white shirt; on him it was like the colour of grief. He was withdrawn, expressionless, no life in his eyes; he was like a man stunned and brutalised by the long war. If Nusrat, who was a common friend, hadn't introduced us, I don't think he would have wanted to talk about Karachi or the war.

His father and grandfather were from Simla; they were catering contractors for the British army. His mother was from Meerut. They had come over in 1947 and his father had started a radio and television repair shop. The business was successful. The details had to be pulled out of him one by one; he had no vision of a life or a past that made a whole.

I asked, 'What are things like now in Karachi?'

'Very good.'

'Why?'

'The government is doing it.'

'Doing what? The murders?'

'Yes.'

'Why is that good?'

'It's the Urdu-speaking people basically who are dying, and this is the sacrifice. When you want something you have to give something.

Twenty lakhs died for the creation of Pakistan.' Twenty lakhs, two million. 'We have to make sacrifices for our rights.'

Nusrat said, 'He is talking of a *mohajir* nation. They are talking of separatism now.'

He couldn't say what had pushed him to that position. He had begun to feel ten years ago that things were not right. He had had some trouble with a Punjabi traffic policeman and had had to bribe him with fifty rupees; at the same time a Punjabi driver, who could talk Punjabi to the policeman, had been let off.

Wasn't that a very small thing?

He didn't answer directly. He said, 'Look what the police have been doing when they raid *mohajir* houses in Golimar. They break in the doors. They take the men away and abuse the women. Two months ago I saw a body in a gunny bag, and I was very upset.'

Nusrat said, 'Very common. It's a joke, in fact. If you see a gunny sack in the street invariably there's a body or parts of a body in it.'

I asked Abdul, 'What gives people courage now?'

'They are fighting for their rights and they are ready for anything.'

'Religion gives them strength?'

'What has this got to do with religion? What has Islam got to do with this? They are also Muslims.'

Nusrat asked, 'Is God on your side?'

'God is with truth and justice.'

But the mullahs in his area, though they were *mohajirs*, didn't 'touch the themes'.

I said, 'Prudence?'

'It isn't that. They don't really talk about current affairs.'

'How do you communicate with the movement?'

'We visit each other in the evening.'

'Police?'

Abdul said, 'They have spread a network of informers. Street hawkers selling popcorn and candy and ice cream. A lot of new faces on the streets in the neighbourhood. Some *mohajirs*, some not.'

He had four brothers and four sisters. All the sisters were married. One brother-in-law was dead, one was without a job, one was a draughtsman, and one worked in a paint company; the jobs were not good enough.

I said, 'I feel you are an unhappy man.'

'No. You can't call me unhappy.'

Nusrat said, 'He is in great financial distress. His wife nearly died giving birth to their seventh child. He had five sons but wanted a girl.'

Abdul said, 'Whatever Allah will do for me will be good for me.'

I asked, 'What do you talk to your friends about? Do you talk about politics?'

'We are not talking a lot these days.'

Nusrat said, 'It's true. It's not safe.'

I said, 'So what do you talk about?'

'It's the worry about how many have died today. Where the police have raided. How many have been detained.'

Nusrat said, 'People have stopped visiting one another in these localities.' The troubled areas of the city. 'Should I take the risk after eleven p.m.? Car-snatching, dacoits, police search, army as well, people in bogus uniforms. Anything. Five hundred rupees each time. Better to pay and go home. And you often wouldn't know they were bogus. They can plant a pistol in your car and say they've found it. Life has been restricted. There was a wedding yesterday which began at six p.m. instead of eleven. Even if you are making a death announcement in the papers you are hesitant to disclose your phone number and address. Because some bogus people might come to condole. They have actually come to find out the arrangements in the house. They will visit you later.'

I asked, 'How do you think it will end?'

Nusrat said, 'There is going to be a big breakdown, a big confrontation, and something will emerge out of that.'

I said to Abdul, 'Why don't you leave Karachi?'

'No. My family are here, my children are in school here, and we have to stay in Karachi in its hour of need.' Karachi now, in his eyes, a *mohajir* city, his city.

'Will you live, or will you die, you think?'

'There was firing even this morning. I take the risk of dying every day.'

'Who was firing?'

'Someone. Unknown.'

Nusrat said, 'Often we know when we say unknown.'

I asked Abdul, 'Does your father talk of the old days in Simla?'

'My father used to say that the British were better than these governments. It was not injustice in this form. My father used to say that in the British days there were little kerosene lanterns on the street. But now we have no street lights.'

Only food shops and newspaper shops, small places, were open. The bigger shops were closed; the grey steel shutters were down. A park had been turned into a rubbish dump; in another street rubbish was uncollected. There were slogans on the walls.

This was the most troubled part of the city, and Mushtaq, a teacher of English literature, lived here with his in-laws in a two-storey house. The in-laws had been in that house for twenty-five years. The 'colony' (a word of the subcontinent) was one of the first to be developed in Karachi after independence and the great migration from India. At that time, between 1949 and 1950, it was considered a middle-class and educated area, and it would have been beyond Mushtaq's family's means and style.

Mushtaq had come to Karachi in 1949. He was eight. The family was from Banaras. Mushtaq's father had been a small trader in clothes in that town, with a shop which Mushtaq thought was 'sizeable'; it was ten feet by twelve. Mushtaq's elder brother was a civil servant in Delhi; he opted for Pakistan, and the whole family migrated with him. They brought very little with them. They weren't allowed to bring jewellery and money; and they didn't sell the clothes shop; they left it to neighbours and relations. By that time migration to Pakistan was no longer a free-for-all; there were visas and permits. The family couldn't get a visa for Lahore. So they came to Karachi, and they came by rail, on a line now discontinued for strategic reasons.

Mushtaq said, 'There was a great charm and fervour in those days for being a liberated people, to be in our own country, Pakistan.'

I said, 'Why did you think it was your own country?'

'Because my family voted and worked for Pakistan. I don't know whether our elders knew the meaning of Pakistan or the two-nation theory.' The theory that the Hindus and Muslims were two separate nations. 'But emotionally they were attached to the idea of Pakistan.'

The family was supported by Mushtaq's elder brother. He had got a job with a foreign company as a salesman. The family was living in a small, rented, two-room house near the Central Jail. It was a one-storey brick house with a concrete roof. The kitchen and bathroom were in the verandah. All the other houses in the area were like that.

The plots were tiny. Some were eighty square yards and some were ninety; none was more than 120. It was more crowded than Banaras, and new people were coming all the time. But in that little house they were very happy. They thought that there were good days ahead.

The story Mushtaq now began to tell was like a story of immigrant success after early hardship. His brother, who had carried the burden of the family for some years, stopped supporting him when he was thirteen. But Mushtaq was now able to look after himself. He began to do part-time typing and clerical jobs. He got the jobs through the newspapers and employment exchanges. He found he could make eighty rupees a month, about six pounds. It was more than enough. He joined a private school, Sindh Muslim College. The fees were fourteen rupees a month, a little over a pound; the bus fare to the college was an anna, about half a penny. After those expenses, and after he had bought his books and treated himself to a little of this and a touch of that, Mushtaq found he could hand over fifty or sixty rupees to his father, who was retired and earning nothing.

He didn't mind the struggle. Karachi had a pleasant climate and it was a place of opportunity. The *mohajirs* were practising the bazaar skills they had brought and year by year they were establishing themselves. With all his hardships Mushtaq, too, began to move ahead, though at his own pace. When he was twenty he joined a teachers' training college. He got his teaching degree three years later; and while he was teaching at a secondary school he enrolled at Karachi university as a 'casual' student. He got his master's in English literature when he was twenty-seven.

It had taken time, but he had got there. There had been a special price, though. He hadn't married. He said that this was because no one in his family had assisted him. It was a real problem for people like Mushtaq. In the *mohajir* culture marriages were generally arranged. There was no one in the new country, the new set-up, to find a wife for him; and as a young man, still close to the old ways, he wouldn't have known how, he wouldn't have had the brazenness, to go about finding a wife for himself.

But he was not unhappy. He had left his brother's house now (his parents had died) and he was living in rented rooms in Central District. (This was the area where we were talking.) He had become a lecturer in a college of commerce and economics. He was getting five to six hundred rupees a month, twenty-five to thirty pounds, and he was paying only a third of that in rent. So he had money to spend and he was very happy. He loved going to coffee houses and chatting with *mohajirs* and Bengalis, who were coffee-house people.

Then things began to go wrong. In the 1960s the capital shifted in a phased way from Karachi to the new city of Islamabad. This meant that more government jobs were going to go to people in the north. Mushtaq thought that the people in the north, Punjabis, Pathans, were socially and culturally not like *mohajirs*; they were 'alien'. And then in 1971 Bangladesh seceded. That was an agony for Mushtaq; the Pakistan of 1947, for which his family had given up India, had ceased to exist.

'Many of the Bengali friends who used to sit and talk with us in the coffee houses left. A major part of our culture had been lost. The Bengalis were the pioneers in the freedom movement, and one comes to the conclusion that one is forsaken and betrayed.'

The tense had changed in that last sentence, and the language had become strange, as though spoken by another man. It was like a fracture in his story. And the success he had appeared to be speaking of became something else.

I said, 'It was too emotional, then, that idea that you were coming to a land of your own?'

'I began to feel that.'

The words undammed his grief. The Muslims who had stayed behind in India were now better off, he said; they had laws and members of parliament and ministers. I said it wasn't quite like that. I said that once the call for Pakistan had been made, partition had to come; if there had been no partition all the energy of the state would have gone into holding itself together. (And I thought, but didn't say, that if there had been no partition all the cities of the subcontinent would have been like Karachi.) He didn't listen; behind his blank, and now tremulous, face he was too deep in his own life and calamity.

I said, 'You made a career here. You couldn't have done that in the other place.'

And now, having spoken before of his career rather formally, as a series of steps up, he began to talk of the terrors he had been living with as a teacher.

'I first became aware of the MQM in 1982. In their "chalkings" on the walls of the college and the schools and buildings. It went on, chalkings and counter-chalkings. There were two groups in the college. Leaders of those groups would come to me and ask me to leave the class, so that the students could go out and take part in rallies or protests. They were about eighteen to twenty years old. They used threatening, abusive language, in Urdu. They were lower middle class. The issues were that the fees were too high, or a sympathy strike for a student killed in Punjab. I was horrified. I felt insecurity. I went to the principal. He was a man of forty-five or fifty. A tall man, a man of science. A *mohajir*. He was helpless. He said, "Let us complain to the next higher authority."'

'In 1985 a local leader of the party, a man of about thirty or thirty-five, visited the principal's office. He was well dressed, educated, a graduate perhaps. I was sitting in the principal's office. I had a chat with that gentleman. It started when he asked me to give support to his organisation. I asked him, "What do you want?" He said, "I want your help in the conduct of the examination." I understood what he meant. He wanted my connivance in the examination hall, letting the boys do what they like. He wanted freedom for the boys to copy and cheat. I said, "No. I will perform my duty." The principal was just listening. The meeting lasted fifteen minutes. Two or three days later I received a sort of threat. A boy in the verandah told me, "You have not acted well. You may be facing bad consequences."'

I asked about the boy.

'Lower-middle-class boy. Nineteen. Families residing in Orangi.' A *mohajir* slum with a population of about a million and a quarter. 'I said to him, "I will face the consequences."'

Nusrat, who had been with us all the time, and mediating when he saw the need, said in his very special innocent-brutal style, 'He is naive. He is teaching literature to students who are unreceptive, undeserving, and he doesn't know what's gone wrong in his own life. This is one way in which you can suffer without even knowing the cause of suffering.'

Mushtaq had suffered acutely at his school for the last ten years. Ironically, they were the years of his marriage. Marriage had come to him when he was forty-three.

He said, 'I leave the house mentally disturbed, remain in the college mentally disturbed, and then come back to the house with the same disturbance.'

'Something happens on the way back? The students wait for you?'

'Sometimes on the streets I come across students creating disturbance.'

'What sort of disturbance?'

'Burning buses, hijacking buses. Near the college. From 1987 to 1988 the MQM did those outrages. Groups of fifty or a hundred.'

'Have they lost interest in education?'

'Definitely.'

'A humiliation for you?'

'As a teacher I am not treated —' He didn't finish the sentence. 'Misbehaving, not attending my class. That has degraded me as a teacher. Two weeks back two students came to the college for submitting their examination. The students of a rival group gave them a good beating. With sticks. No weapon at that time. When I saw them I was scared.'

I said, 'What would you like to do now?'

'I would like to teach them.'

I was bewildered. 'You've just said they are thugs.'

But Mushtaq was only saying that he wished the world were arranged in such a way that he could actually teach his students. And when I asked again what he wanted to do now, in the world as it was, he said, 'I feel now I want to leave the profession. I am fifty-seven years old.' By my calculations he was fifty-four. 'I've been in the profession for twenty-nine years. That is the tragic aspect of my life.'

'A life in vain?'

'It may be called that, because I haven't achieved anything.'

His faith was still the one clear point in his life. He had done the pilgrimage; he had the beard of the *haji*. He was wearing *shalwar-kameez*; on him, with his white beard, it looked like a kind of sacrificial religious dress.

Nusrat had lived through hard times before. I had first met him in 1979, at the time of the Islamising terror of General Zia. Nusrat, a devout man, had tried to meet the fanatics half way, but had had little stumbles. And one careless day he got into serious trouble. He was working for the *Morning News*. It was Mohurram, the Shia mourning month. He thought it was a good idea to run a feature piece from *Arab News* about the granddaughter of Ali, the Shia hero. The piece was flattering about the woman's looks and artistic attainments. But the Shias were outraged; to them it was insulting and heretical even to say that Ali's granddaughter was good-looking. There was talk of taking out a procession of forty thousand and burning down the *Morning News*. For three days the paper was closed down. Nusrat himself was in danger; he could have been set upon at any time. Some months after this incident I passed through Karachi again. Nusrat had turned grey.

When we said goodbye he said, 'Can you arrange for me to go to a place where I can read and write and study for five years? Because in five years, if you see me again, I may have become a cement-dealer or an exporter of ready-made garments.'

That, spoken at a bad time, showed his style. And, in fact, he had become a public relations man for an oil company, and done well. The oil-drilling business was not affected by the troubles. But life in the city had been a day-to-day anxiety and Nusrat had developed a heart condition. His grey hair had gone white and short and thin; he was still under fifty. He had loved the Karachi winter and he used to like wearing a tweed jacket for it. Now he was in a loose cotton tunic that made him look frail.

He said, 'I will tell you how the ethnic infighting affected me when I was almost dying in hospital in June, 1990. I was in CCU, Coronary Care Unit. That is where you are rushed to in an emergency; that is where you live or die.

'Karachi had infighting on a bloody scale. MQM was in power in the Karachi Metropolitan Corporation. In the CCU the air-conditioner wasn't working, and this was in the middle of June. There was a shortage of medicines. The telephone exchange was blown up one night, and there was a clash between doctors and outsiders, presumably from a political party, PPP or MQM, who wanted everybody to go on strike. And I was there in that condition in the CCU. My fifth day.

'I was very close to the window lying on a cot. You want to hear about the cot? The cot had a foam mattress, and because the air-conditioner wasn't working and there was no ventilation, I asked them to remove the mattress. Of course, they were reluctant, but they finally removed it. They said the cot would be hard steel, but I said I wouldn't mind. The next morning the doctor said to me that the head of the Institute was on a surprise visit, and he wouldn't be happy to see the foam mattress removed from the cot and lying in the cubicle. I was very angry. I said, "I know the director's AC is working, and he has no health problem. I want to see the director when he comes, and deal with him suitably".'

'We asked the attendants to open the window. We were on the first floor, and the risk was – so they said – that a bullet could come and hit us. I said, "The glass is not bullet-proof?" June is suffocating in the heat.

'One day there was firing outside. I got up from my bed with all the gadgetry they had put on me, and sneaked a few steps to have a quick look at what was happening downstairs. I later realised the risk I had taken, both with regard to the bullet and having got up suddenly – which I wasn't supposed to do.

'One day I saw some attendants crying in a cubicle at about eleven p.m. I knew at this time that people were dying in this ward, and that some of the people I had seen had been taken away. In this case the attendant and the family, three people in all, were faced with the problem of taking the body from the hospital to Orangi, where there had been trouble for days on end and pitched battles were being fought. It was an area that was closed down at night by the local authorities. Then the ambulance wasn't willing to risk the journey.

'Orangi was about twenty-five kilometres away. The family was lower-middle class and had to depend on public transport. Some young men in the CCU were volunteering to help. The attendants of the deceased included a young girl. I was upset and angry, not just at the state of the city and its repeated closures, but was apprehensive about what could happen to the young girl at that time of night. I was conscious of the fact that kidnapping for ransom and kidnapping for ostensibly no reason was common at that time.

'I kept telling my attendants, who were pleading with me to rest and sleep, that please do something for the safety of the young girl. I said, "Why don't you take the body in the morning?" Someone reminded me that in the heat of June bodies decay quicker. There was little that I could do.

'I don't know what happened. I must have gone off to sleep. I can't explain this, but despite all this, I was happy in that hospital because of the friends I had made, and because the man treating me was an old school friend.'

Ehsan was part of the *mohajir* movement in the mid-1980s. It was a middle-class, intellectual movement at that time – it had developed out of an older student movement – and Ehsan knew three or four of the 'ideologues', to use his word. He thought them very intelligent. They had intense discussions in private houses, and they would get worked up in an almost religious way about the injustices done to the community and their city, Karachi. It wasn't like the charging up at the Friday prayers, Ehsan said, when I put the suggestion to him; it was more like the Shias fighting for their rights.

The movement had first to defeat the religious parties in the universities. University politics mattered in Pakistan because, with military rule, it was often the only political life that was allowed. And the defeat of the religious parties by the *mohajir* student movement was ironical; because it was the faith that had driven the *mohajirs* to Pakistan, and because it was in those religious parties that the first generation of *mohajirs* had felt most at home. But that was long ago; later generations had grown to understand what lay beyond the faith.

The war against the religious parties had been fought with guns; both sides had at different times, and for different reasons, been encouraged and armed by the government. In Ehsan's college there were four or five recognised *mohajir* fighters; people from other colleges would give support when it was needed. Ehsan was very friendly with two of the fighters. They were both from educated families, and Ehsan thought that the most important thing about them was that they were 'extremely alienated.' They took the ideological training very seriously and were ready to die for the cause.

Ehsan was studying science with one of the fighters, and every day after classes they used to go to the friend's family house. The friend, the fighter, was about five foot eight and fat, very physical, Ehsan said, with big, thick hands which Ehsan thought were the hands of an aggressive man.

The father of the family was a high-ranking government servant, and the family house was a big government house, a thousand-square-yard house. (Mushtaq's family, when they came to Pakistan in 1949, had lived in an eighty-square-yard house.) The father had built an enormous study for his five children; there were encyclopaedias and religious books and science books. They were a middle-class family that believed in education, and they were far better off than most other people in the movement. Ehsan's friend was not as good at studies as his brothers; but all the four boys were active in the MQM.

Ehsan was in the house one day, at about sunset, with the friend and one of the brothers, when there was a lot of firing outside with AK-47s and all kinds of guns. Ehsan was by now used to gunfire, but this was excessive. What surprised him, though, was when the mother of the family brought out an AK-47 and gave it to her fighter son, Ehsan's friend. He went to the roof of the house – it was a single-storey house – and took up position and returned the fire. The battle went on for five or ten minutes; to Ehsan it seemed much longer. Ehsan had seen his friend using guns at the college; the friend would make a joke of it and say that Ehsan was chicken. But Ehsan had no idea that the mother was so involved in the movement. She was a big strong lady in *shalwar-kameez*, not good-looking, but very affectionate and always ready to offer food to her sons' friends. He hadn't associated her with guns, and he didn't even know there was a gun in the house.

Ehsan saw a lot of violence ahead. He saw trouble for his friend. His attitude to the movement began to change. And then one day, at a meeting in the house of one of his ideologue friends, they were all asked to take oaths on the Koran to be loyal to the movement and the leader. The leader, of a kind created by great distress and need, was now an immense public figure, conducting six-hour rallies that ended at midnight, and moving millions, as Ehsan said.

Still, Ehsan didn't like the idea of the oath of loyalty; but he didn't have to say no. He was able at about this time to leave Pakistan, and he was away for five years. When he came back the MQM was no longer ruling the city. The army was there, and the MQM had become an underground organisation. It still obeyed its leader; he was now far away, in exile in London; but distance added to his magic. Ehsan's friend was one of those who had gone underground. On the telephone later he told Ehsan that he had been falsely accused of killing another MQM man and was on the run. And when they met – strangely, in the family house – everybody cried, Ehsan, his friend, the friend's mother.

The friend still had the thick hands, but he had lost weight. He said he was willing to swear on the Koran that he hadn't committed murder. What had happened had happened when the police were hunting him. He had had during this time to move from house to house. And then somehow he had got a job on a merchant ship. They must have had some idea of his situation, because they asked him to clean the toilets and the deck; and he had to obey. With all his *mohajir* caste sense he hated the degradation of the job and even now he complained about it to Ehsan. He said he wanted to go to London and start a new life. He had become critical of the MQM, and he knew that if he stayed in Pakistan he would be arrested or killed. He wanted Ehsan to find a lawyer for him in London, so that he could apply for political asylum.

The mother, the firebrand with the AK-47, had changed. She said that the army and the police and the government were bent on destroying her son. She said to Ehsan, 'Please do something to help him.' Her own opinions and feelings were not what they had been. She had become even a little critical of the MQM. She said they were not doing enough to help the families of boys who had been killed or were underground, like her son.

But it was to be all right for her. Her other sons had, in spite of everything, got started on reasonable professional careers. And the fighter was eventually to get to the safety of London.

What had happened in five years was that the movement, fostered in the beginning by families like hers, had changed. The movement had ceased to be a middle-class movement. It had gone down to the bottom, and there the bitterness had turned to outright rejection. The fighters and organisers came now from the poor of Orangi and Korangi, who had nothing or very little to lose. At that level – whatever had happened to the family of Ehsan's friend – the flames were unquenchable.

The army was in Karachi for nearly two and a half years. During this time the MQM was declared a terrorist organisation and its leaders absconding terrorists. Army control produced even more *mohajir* bitterness, and this bitterness grew when the semi-military border force, the Rangers, replaced the army. Whole localities continued to be sealed off and searched. Then the intelligence agencies engineered a split in the MQM, and anarchy was added to terror. No one could now be sure who was killing who.

Hasan Jafri, a journalist, himself descended of *mohajirs*, was covering the troubles at this time. He said, 'What I and other reporters saw were a lot of dead bodies. Almost every day.'

The ambulance service was the first source of information. The reporters would then check with the MQM to find out if the dead men belonged to them. If the men were theirs, the MQM would say that they had been tortured to death by the police. The police would say they had been killed in 'encounters'.

'There have been eighteen hundred people killed this year. So every day there are dead bodies on the street. One and two, two and two, three and three. When I began it was disgusting. You would see a dead body carelessly thrown in a hospital morgue. About five months back there was a shootout in Korangi. It happened in the morning. I think it was five guys who were killed. They were in the Jinnah Hospital morgue. They were lying on these concrete slabs. They were naked, all of them, and the bodies had begun to smell. The area between the heart and the shoulder of one man was completely blown off. Another one had taken a burst on his hand, and the principal bone was jutting out. One of them had an expression, as if it were frozen on his face, of shock. His eyes were wide open and his mouth was also open. Because the bodies were brought quite late to the hospital, about six hours after the incident, the expressions were very frozen. It appeared that the moment when they died was written all over them.'

Hasan Jafri said he went himself to the morgue, to get the body count, and to see what condition the bodies were in. He had, 'at a certain level', become immune to sights like this. But he felt that as a reporter he had to go and see for himself, because it was important to see 'the face of violence'.

'Another killing I remember was that of Inspector Bahadur Ali. He was ambushed, and he and about six other policemen in that vehicle were killed. Bahadur Ali had close to two dozen bullets in his body. He was a big man and his body was totally destroyed.

'The ideas and the talk – it has nothing to do with that. All there is at the end is a dead body. Someone's son, someone's brother, someone's husband.'

Fear was the biggest thing people now lived with, Hasan Jafri said. The MQM people were frightened; the police might come knocking at any time. The police were frightened; they knew they were targets. The taxi-drivers were frightened.

The police were overworked. They were brutal because they were frightened. Most of the rankers were from the Punjab and the interior of Sindh; they were far from their families. They risked their lives every day and were paid very little, 2600 rupees a month, fifty pounds.

Hasan Jafri used to do the evening rounds with the police in their APCs, armoured personnel carriers. One evening in the Liaquatabad area, a hot MQM area, a constable from the Punjab, about thirty, haggard, and clearly on duty for a long time, said to Hasan Jafri, 'Serving in District Central is worse than living in hell.' And then it became even worse. The terrorists began using rocket launchers.

When that happened Hasan Jafri stopped going on the evening police rounds.

The war had got down to the bottom, and now whenever an MQM fighter died another took his place. The authorities said there were only two thousand fighters; that was foolish, Hasan Jafri said. The names of new fighters began quite suddenly to appear in police reports; they remained names, faceless, until they were arrested or killed; then there were new names. People were recruited at first to do very little things; then the things they did became bigger, and at last they were sucked in. Hasan Jafri knew a boy or man of twenty-one who already felt that he was marked for death. He had stolen so many cars, killed so many people, robbed so many businesses; he couldn't be normal again.

'He came from a very educated family. The unlikeliest terrorist you could think of. You see, the cycle is endless. The birth and the rebirth, one after the other. My biggest fear now is that we might end up as a basket case. There are many people like myself now, educated, conscious, who are not afraid of detaching themselves from Pakistan. But I don't want to end up as a *mohajir* in another country. My parents were born in one country; I in another; I don't want my kids to be born in a third.'

The words were a fair comment, some generations later, on Mohammed Iqbal's Pakistan proposal of 1930: poets should not lead their people to hell.

Iqbal is buried in the grounds of the Shah Jehan mosque in Lahore; and soldiers watch his tomb. Rhetoric or sentimentality like that is invariably worrying; it hides things. And the tomb, with its Mogul motifs, would be a kind of artistic sacrilege if, just across the way, the great Mogul fort of Lahore (the emperor's window there recorded in some of the finest Mogul pictures) wasn't falling into dust; if, in that same city of Lahore, the Mogul Shalimar gardens and the tombs of the emperor Jehangir and his consort were not in absolute decay; if, going back four centuries, the delicately coloured tiled towers of the thirteenth-century tombs of Uch in Bahawalpur, one of the finest Islamic things in the subcontinent, were not half washed away; if, going back further still, the land just around the Buddhist city of Taxila, known to Alexander the Great, and with once fabulous remains, wasn't being literally quarried; if Pakistan, still pursuing imperialist Islamic fantasies, hadn't been responsible for the final looting of the Buddhist treasures of Afghanistan.

In its short life Iqbal's religious state, still half serf, still profoundly uneducated, mangling history in its school books as well, undoing the polity it was meant to serve, had shown itself dedicated only to the idea of the cultural desert here, with glory – of every kind – elsewhere.

IV

MALAYSIAN
POSTSCRIPT
Raising the Coconut Shell

1

Old Clothes

IN KUALA LUMPUR in 1979 I shifted for some days from hotel to hotel before settling in at the Holiday Inn. It was quietest place I could find, and I liked the setting. To the left was the race-course, with a view in the distance of the Kuala Lumpur hills. Around the race-course and in front of the hotel was the rich greenery of the wet tropics: banana fronds, flowering frangipani, the great, branching saman or rain tree of Central America: the mingled vegetation of Asia, the Pacific and the New World that spoke both of the great European explorations and the plantation colonies. It was the very vegetation I had known on the other side of the world in Trinidad.

And then what was familiar became strange. Just around the corner from the Holiday Inn was a little yellow box set in a wall or hedge. I was told it was a Chinese shrine. It had offerings; it might have been used by the Chinese taxi-drivers who did hotel work.

And the race-course wasn't really a race-course. Sometimes I saw horses being trained there in the early mornings, before the sun came up; but I never saw a race. On Saturday and Sunday afternoons Chinese people (for the most part) came in their cars and filled the grandstand. The race-course itself, green and sun-struck, with still, black shadows, remained empty. Every half-hour there was an amplified race commentary and the grandstand crowd worked itself up to a frenzy, as if at a real race. The races were real, but they were going on somewhere else. The people in the grandstand were looking at television screens; and they had come to the race-course to do so, in a strange mimicry of a day at the races, because it was the only place in Kuala Lumpur where gambling was permitted. Malaysia was racially divided: Malays, Chinese. The government was aggressively Malay and Muslim. Gambling was un-Islamic, and this weekend race-course excitement was only a humane concession to the Chinese. They were the great gamblers.

I had got to know Shafi. He was a Malay of thirty-two, originally from a village in the still pastoral and poor north-east. Though it could be said that Shafi had done well, had risen in a way his father and grandfather could not have imagined, he was full of rage as a Malay. Shafi, and Malays like him, felt they had almost lost their country. They thought the Malays had slept for too long in their villages. Things grew too easily in the warm, fertile land; the old life of river and forest was too rich and full. You could throw a seed, Shafi said one day, and it would grow; you could put a bare hook in the water and catch a fish. Used to that idea of the land, the village people hadn't seen or understood to what extent in the last hundred years they had been supplanted by Chinese and others. They had awakened now, late in the century, to find that Malays had become only half the population, and that a new way of life had developed all around them. They were not prepared for that new way.

To be a Malay like Shafi, half in and half out of the old ways, was to feel every kind of fear and frustration. It was too much for a man to bear on his own, and in 1979 Islam was being made to carry that general rage. Malays of Shafi's generation had become passionate believers; and their belief was given edge by Islamic missionaries, who were especially busy in 1979, with the revolution in Iran and the Islamising terror of General Zia in Pakistan. The missionaries were spreading stories of Islamic success in those countries, and promising similar success to people elsewhere, if only they believed. The Islamic missionary world existed in its own bubble. The extension of the faith was its principal aim; and – as for the fourteenth-century traveller Ibn Battuta – once the faith ruled, the conditions of the faithful didn't matter.

It was at the Holiday Inn that Shafi used to come to see me. He wasn't an easy guest. He said he didn't like places like the Holiday Inn, and he didn't hide his worry about the food: it might have been prepared by non-Muslims, Chinese or Indians. There were other things that would have offended him: the modest little bar, where at night 'The Old Timers' (city Malays, with an Indian or two) sang pop songs;

the lunchtime fashion show on Friday, the sabbath, when people came to see the Indian and Chinese girls see-saw their shoulders and do their walk, in the rather stale, shut-in restaurant air; and the very small Holiday Inn pool, below the coffee-shop window, where white women exposed themselves in swimsuits.

But Shafi had stopped seeing – perhaps had never seen – what he rejected. He couldn't even tell, for instance, as I found one day when I asked him, whether the sunbathing women at the poolside were attractive. When he had first come to Kuala Lumpur as a schoolboy he had been nervous; he had felt a stranger. Now he held himself aloof from it, and was strong in his self-righteousness. His ideas were sometimes confused; his Islam was being made to carry too many things. There was purity in his village in Kota Baru, for instance, purity in the life he had known there, which he had now lost; yet he wished to be like a scourge in those villages, to convert them fully, to cleanse them of what had survived of old Hindu customs. That had become part of his cause. The missionary Islam he now fed off had given him an impossible dream of Islamic purity. Out of this purity there was going to come power, and accounts would be settled with the world.

Sixteen years later, the Holiday Inn was surrounded by towers of concrete and steel. Land was precious here. The race-course view I had known could not now be reconstructed; it was half mythical, like the Roman hills before the building of Rome. And all over Kuala Lumpur there was much more building to come. At the back of the hotel where I was staying, an immense hole was being dug across the road. The hole had the area of a large city block; it dwarfed men and machines; ramps led down from level to level, from red earth to dry pale earth. The composite tropical greenery of colonial days was overshadowed now by an international style in steel and glass and stone and concrete and marble; and the very climate seemed to have altered. Air-conditioning made the big buildings cold; the weather outside was always a little surprise; it was pleasant for the visitor to play with these temperature shifts. In 1979 Malaysia had been rich; now it was extraordinarily rich.

I wondered about the effect on Shafi. I knew that, before he had begun to work full-time for the Muslim youth movement, he had worked as the managing director of a Malay construction company. He was very young for the job, but there were not many business-minded

Malays at the time. The firm hadn't done well; there were big players in the construction business in Malaysia. And then Shafi had set up on his own. He had failed. He thought this was because his Chinese workers and almost everybody else had let him down. The failure grieved him, I knew; it had got mixed up with his religious ideas. And I wondered whether, with the great new wealth of the country, and all the encouragement the government had been giving to Malays to go into business, Shafi hadn't been tempted to try again. He would now be forty-eight, in middle life. His career, whatever it was, would have been more or less marked out.

But I couldn't find out about Shafi. The people who had known him in the old days had lost touch with him. He was a preacher, I was told; he was on the move; he wasn't easy to reach.

And then one morning I was taken to an Islamic commune on the outskirts of Kuala Lumpur to meet a man who said he was Shafi and said he remembered me. The commune was a solid settlement of two-storeyed concrete houses. The houses were painted and the roads were paved, and there were gardens and cars. Whatever the commune people might say about their self-denying way of life, they were part of rich Kuala Lumpur.

We had to look for the house of the man who said he was Shafi. When we found it I found I didn't know the man. He pretended for a little, but only for a little, and only in a half-hearted way, that he remembered me.

He was in his forties and he looked happy and idle, enjoying the commune life. His house, on two floors, had a big, open, well-furnished hall downstairs. And he was playing there, in the middle of the morning, with a kind of village serenity, with a sleepy-eyed, unsteady, young child of his. It was a form of display: in this kind of commune simple things could be paraded as religious or virtuous acts that gave especial pleasure to the believer, as reward.

He said in a mechanical way that the big highway the government had built was wrong; it was opening up the country to vice. He said that the official language of the country should be Arabic; English was not the language of Muslims. But he had said these things so many times before that now – he was on the floor and trying to get the child to play with one of its many toys – he was speaking by rote, without energy.

I felt that it was out of pure idleness that he had said he was Shafi. He

wanted only to get a little attention. There was no point in being fundamentalist and dangerous and living in a commune if no one noticed.

And, in fact, Shafi, whom in the end I never met – because no one
among his former associates particularly wanted me to meet him – had
become like that idle man in their eyes. Once he had been at the
centre of the Muslim youth movement in Malaysia, the movement
using Islam to wake up the Malays. He had no other career. Now,
though he had remained true to those early beliefs, he was on the outside. It embarrassed people to be reminded of him; he was a man who
had taken the idea of the religious life to extremes.

And other ideas had changed. In 1979 Shafi, grieving for the village
of his childhood, had spoken of Malays as a pastoral, tropical people.
Once he said they were a 'timeless' people; he meant only they had
little sense of time. They were not commercially minded; they were
without the energy of the Chinese, who came from a 'four-seasoned'
country. He had worked these ideas – which were curiously colonial
ones – into his overall religious view. They were not ideas that Malays
liked now.

A young lawyer said, 'That's been laid aside. Destroyed almost. It has
been replaced by the idea of the Malays as a trading and manufacturing
and innovative people. These are all words you would not have associated with Malays in the past.'

The government had done all that it could to bring Malays into business, and over the last two generations it had succeeded. The racial
anxieties of sixteen years before had been swamped by the great new
wealth, and new men had been created on both sides. That was the
message of the steel and concrete and glass around the site of the
Holiday Inn, and the great highway through the forest that had opened
up the villages and opened up new land. A journey to the interior that
took six to eight hours, along old roads that touched many of the old
colonial towns and settlements, now took two and a half hours and
showed almost nothing of that past.

The lawyer said, 'I think it telescopes time.'

In 1979 they had all been rather young in the Muslim youth movement. The leader, Anwar Ibrahim, the man on whom they all leaned,
the man who gave them confidence, was only thirty-two, Shafi's age.

Nasar, to whom Shafi had introduced me, was only twenty-five. He was very much the junior; and physically he was even slighter than Shafi. He had just come back from Bradford in England, where he had been doing a diploma in international relations. He hadn't liked the free and easy sexual ways of England, and he didn't want those ways to infect young Malays over there.

Nasar had an ancestor who was a Malay sheikh in Mecca. A sheikh was a guide, and this sheikh guided Malays who had gone to Mecca on the pilgrimage. This kind of guiding would have become a proper paying occupation only after the 1830s, when steam replaced sail, and the journey from Malaysia became quicker and more reliable. And it is possible that Nasar's ancestor was doing this pilgrim work in the second half of the nineteenth century.

Towards the end of the nineteenth century (as I work it out) this ancestor returned to Malaysia, to a tin town, predominantly Chinese, twenty kilometres or so to the north of Kuala Lumpur. This man's son was Nasar's great-grandfather. He married when he was twelve. In 1934, when he was very old, he set up a Malay-language newspaper that preached self-help to the Malays. He was a voice in the wilderness. After him the family declined; the tradition of learning faded away. There was little money in teaching; there was more in farming.

Nasar's grandfather, who should have been a religious teacher, became a rice farmer, with seven acres. Nasar's father worked as a ranger in the forestry department. He had only the standard primary-school education, up to the sixth class; but he read the newspaper every morning before he went to work. This newspaper-reading was important: it was Nasar's greatest intellectual stimulus as a child. Nasar was one of seven sons, and the fourth of eight children. When he was eight he began to read the newspaper, like his father. It was an advanced thing for a Malay child to do.

In time, then, Nasar, the ranger's son, was able to go to Bradford to do a diploma in international relations. And now, sixteen years later, only forty-one, he was running a holding company that managed the diverse affairs of eight companies.

Nasar had a suite of offices in a skyscraper. The shadow of this skyscraper fell on the green-glassed skyscraper across the road. This made the road seem narrower; and the mid-afternoon tropical light, which would have been harsh and stinging in open fields and open streets, was softened in that narrow, protected space, so that the light and climate of Kuala Lumpur seemed perfect.

Nasar, with glasses now, and less frail-looking than in 1979, was dressed with an executive's care: belted trousers, tan shoes, matching socks, stylish wide tie, a large round watch on his slender wrist. His personal assistant was a tall and gentle young Sikh. In the main waiting room, and in the antechambers of various offices, were models, like toys, of white aeroplanes on silver sticks. Nasar's holding company had interests in aviation; they ran scheduled domestic air services.

It was an extraordinary transformation, and the man himself was welcoming and gracious, full of offers of help. It was as if good village ways had been given a kind of corporate enlargement. I had been moved in 1979 by the openness of the young men of the movement; they didn't hide things or make up things about themselves. Nasar seemed to have that kind of openness still. He remembered what he had been in 1979; he didn't put a gloss on it. And he talked without prompting of the internal demons – the phobias, the lack of confidence – that as a small-town Malay he had had to quieten before he could be what I now saw.

What they had been looking to religion to do for them in 1979, simple power, simple authority, had done for them later.

Nasar's transformation began with Anwar Ibrahim, the leader of the Muslim youth movement. It was clear in 1979 that Anwar was marked for great things. And when the time came and Anwar rose, he took Nasar with him.

Towards the end of 1981 Anwar decided he had done enough youth movement work: the lectures and consciousness-raising, the protest. He thought the time had come to move on. He decided to join the ruling Malay party. He became one of the party's candidates in the 1982 elections, and he called on Nasar – then with a master's degree from Bradford in international relations – to handle his election campaign. Nasar did so. Anwar won his election and became a deputy minister in the prime minister's department. He said to Nasar, 'Join me. Be my private secretary.' Nasar was overwhelmed. He was twenty-eight; he had been used to facing authority 'from the other side of the counter'; he had never dreamt of such a dignity, serving a minister in the government.

He was Anwar's private secretary for seven years. In those seven years Nasar shed his phobias and doubts. He met people of all sorts; he saw the workings of government from within. And Anwar never ceased to treat him as a friend, never ceased to give him confidence.

Nasar said in his boardroom, where we were talking over lunch, 'I will remember that for ever.'

After seven years he resigned as Anwar's secretary. He went to England again and did a two-year law degree. When he came back he became the senior vice-president of a Chinese conglomerate. His government experience helped him get that job. After two years there, getting knowledge of 'real business', he left, and went on his own.

I asked about the ideas of 1979, Shafi's ideas about the goodness of *kampung* or village ways, their joint ideas about religion.

Nasar said, like a man who had prepared his case, 'Shafi was a businessman. But he had failed as a businessman. Hence his romantic view of the *kampung*. In those days we talked about religion theoretically. Now we are talking about Islam as a way of life in practice. Now I confront the real world. My previous knowledge helps me – what I can do, the limit of my freedom, to what extent I can adhere to a mere capitalist philosophy. I am involved in some government contracts, and business outside the government. There is a certain kind of behaviour which I will not condone. Corruption, giving commission under the counter, taking people out, giving them ladies, condoning immoral actions to get contracts. That is the test. The test for a Muslim is when they are confronted with reality and a choice to make. Until then they are always right. Utopian.'

He might have been thinking of Shafi. I said, putting words in his mouth, 'And they can make trouble because they feel they are always right?'

'They can make trouble. When I am in the business world I am being confronted with choices, problems, people – of a kind I could not have imagined. People wanting a stake in your company – in return for a project. In the real world of business competition knows no bounds. At that juncture they contradict the values we want to create in the society.'

Nasar felt he had been educated by the Muslim youth movement; and he remained loyal to that education. Power and authority might have brought out his latent qualities and made him what he was; but it had also to be said that religion had given him the important first push.

Nasar said, 'The Malay no longer has an inferiority complex. He is no longer like the frog under the coconut shell.' That was a Malay saying: to the frog the underside of the coconut shell was the sky.

One Saturday I went by the new highway to the town of Kuala Kangsar. The famous Malay College was there. It had been founded by the British for the sons of local chieftains, on the pattern of similar schools in the Indian subcontinent. Boys of all ranks went there now. Many important careers had begun at Malay College. Anwar Ibrahim, whose grandfather had run a village restaurant in Penang, and whose father was a male nurse, went to Malay College. He had to sit an entrance examination; boys of royal family at that time didn't have to.

Kuala Kangsar was also the seat of the royal family of Perak. There was a big new palace, white and rich and rhetorical, with an air-conditioned throne room. There was also an old timber palace, really a traditional long house on pillars, narrow and dark, with much decorative fretwork, thick floor planks, and a cooling cross-breeze. It was a museum of sorts now. But one could easily in imagination strip it of its framed photographs and charts; and − dark and cool and protected inside, bush and dazzle outside − it could take one back to buried childhood fantasies about the house and safety.

On a hill overlooking the Perak river, and almost at the entrance to the royal enclave, was the house of Raja Shahriman, a sculptor and a prince, distantly related to the royal family. It was an airy house of the late 1940s, and it was furnished in the Malay style, with rattan chairs, brightly coloured fabrics, and cloth flowers.

The sculptor was small, five feet six inches, and very thin, in the pared-down Malay way. There was little expression on his face; the nature of his work didn't show there. He worked with found metal; there was a forge in the yard at the back of the house. He created martial figures of great ferocity, two to three feet high, in clean flowing lines; and the effect of the black-metal figures in that house, with the pacific, restful views, was unsettling.

The sculptor, in fact, lived in a world of spirits. He also made krises, Malay daggers; it was part of his fascination with metal. Krises found out their true possessors, the sculptor said; they rejected people who didn't truly own them. He had a spiritual adviser, and would have liked me to meet him; but there wasn't time. The world of Indonesian animism felt close again. In more ways than one we were close here to the beginning of things, before the crossover to the revealed religions.

The sculptor had a middle-aged Chinese housekeeper. She would have been given away by her family as a child, because at that time Chinese families got rid of girls whom they didn't want. Malays usually adopted those girls. The sculptor's housekeeper was the second Malay-adopted Chinese woman I had seen that day. It gave a new slant to the relationship between the two communities; and it made me think of the Chinese in a new way.

In 1979 I had been looking mainly for Islam, and I had seen the Chinese in Malaysia only from the outside, as the energetic immigrant people the Malays were reacting to. Now, considering these two gracious women, and their fairy-tale adoption into another culture, I began to have some idea how little the Chinese were protected in the last century and the early part of this, with a crumbling empire and civil wars at home and rejection outside: spilling out, trying to find a footing wherever they could, always foreign, insulated by language and culture, surviving only through blind energy. Once self-awareness had begun to come, once blindness had begun to go, they would have needed philosophical or religious certainties just as much as the Malays.

Kuala Lumpur was fabulous for the visitor: so rich, so new and glossy, so full of new public buildings and splendid new interiors, so full of energy. There was a new bank in a new building. It had been created by two Chinese brothers. They were only in their forties, and their beginnings had been quite simple. So far as vision went, one brother was all sparks, a talker; when he talked his face became flushed. The other brother was calmer, with glasses, a listener, with the manner of a physician. Yet I felt that when the time came the calm brother would be the more daring. They made great projects appear very simple, a matter only of logic. For both of them money had ceased to be simply money; business had become more an expression of energy, and vital for that reason.

It was Philip who introduced me to the brothers. Philip was the secretary of their company. He was Chinese, too, and as young as the men he worked for. He was easy of manner, humorous, quick, immensely attractive. There seemed to be an unusual depth to him; and I was to find that his serenity, which was part of his attractiveness, was something he had had to work for. It overlay great childhood unhappiness.

Philip's father had two families. Philip belonged to the second family, and he felt that his mother had been badly treated. He didn't like what he had seen as a child. He wished to put matters right for his mother, but he was adrift emotionally, until his conversion to Christianity in his fifteenth year.

It happened at his school. It was a mission school run by the Plymouth Brethren, who had been in Malaysia for about ninety years. He was at a very low point when one day, quite by chance, he went to a chapel service. He was dazzled by the teaching that God was a loving father. He felt it gave him a place in the world.

Philip said, 'It's ironical, because I would have thought I would have rebelled against that kind of religion – coming as I did from a broken family, where I didn't have a father since age eight. And the direct teaching about grace – in the parable of the prodigal son, where the father waits, and hugs and kisses the returning son. Grace: unmerited love and favour bestowed upon an undeserving person: it was something very powerful.

'I owe a lot to the faith. It gave me a certainty and belongingness, identity. It had all been confused. Who am I? Chinese, but not Chinese. In a Chinese cultural programme I would be lost. English, but not English. I've never been to England. The scriptures gave the original impetus to my love and passion for reading, which exists at this day.'

At that time, 1966 and 1967, Islam was not the proselytising force it now was. It was only one religion among others. At the time of his conversion Philip was thinking more of his future. He wanted very much to be a lawyer, a professional man.

'I remember my mother saying to me, "It's so hard to deal with lawyers." I thought one day I'll be a lawyer and give the time of day to my clients. I wanted to compensate for the family shortcomings. My father's first family had doctors. The second family, to which I belonged, hadn't done well at all. So I wanted to vindicate – to win back face for my mother.'

She was a worshipper of Chinese idols. People like her had now moved to a new form of Japanese Buddhism.

'It's quite common, the Chinese family throwing away their gods and joining this new Japanese Buddhism, which is based on strong humanistic traditions. I'm happy for them that they've liberated themselves from those kitchen gods.'

People who knew about his faith and his intellectual inclinations wondered how he could work in a bank. He told them, 'My understanding of Christianity is that we don't deny the world. We are in the world but not of the world.'

His mother's honouring of the kitchen gods was mainly a matter of habit. She would light joss sticks to them and place offerings for them; it was part of the routine of her day.

'Even as a child it had no meaning for me. When the time came to discard it we just got rid of it like old clothes. We weren't worried that the gods would come and punish us. When I was fourteen or fifteen I felt a lack. A void, an emptiness. It cannot be articulated. For me it was serendipitous that I chanced upon a chapel service. The second generation of Chinese had to anguish over the fact: Who am I, beyond my shelter, my diploma, my degree? These questions were more real to the second generation. The first generation was much too busy. For the Chinese there is inherited wealth, inherited circumstances, but also the query: Am I only my father's son?'

2

New Model

NADEZHA'S FATHER, who was born around 1940, was a *kampung* or village Malay. Nadezha never went looking for her father's village, and she was never interested in her father's background. The family would have been very ordinary, and Nadezha didn't feel she had to make inquiries. She thought the family would have been 'farmers or something like that'. She was sure they would have lived in a wooden house in a paddy field, and would have kept chickens at the back. There would have been no books in the house.

But education mattered to Nadezha's father when he was a boy. He knew – some admired older person would have told him, or he would have picked it up from conversation – that for a boy like him education was the only way out. He was a bright boy and he studied hard, and eventually he won a scholarship to the great Malay College at Kuala Kangsar.

It was in Kuala Kangsar that he saw the girl who was to be Nadezha's mother. He saw her walking out one day with a chaperone, and he was taken with her. It was easy for him to find out who she was and where she lived; the boys of the college knew about the young girls of Kuala Kangsar. Nadezha's father began a correspondence with this girl. She was corresponding with other boys at the college as well. It was the recognised way of boy-girl friendship in Kuala Kangsar; boys and girls were not free to meet.

The girl was living in Kuala Kangsar with her grandmother. Her father was in Kuala Lumpur, in the police. The girl came of an old, decayed family. At one time they had a lot of land, but they didn't use it well, and it went bit by bit. Gambling ate it up. Gambling ran in the blood. After the fasting month all the family came together, sometimes with friends, and they played poker for two days and two nights. Nadezha grew up thinking that this was usual, that it was what people everywhere did after the fasting month.

Nadezha said, 'They were decadent. They thought it would last for ever. They were not educated. That's the problem. In my time the rich didn't study.'

And what Nadezha was saying touched a chord: what she was saying about Malaysia was true of Trinidad as well, up to the 1940s, when I was growing up there. At that time rich people and local white people generally didn't study; it was part of their privilege. They didn't need to study. The colonial agricultural society required few skills. It didn't require people to be especially efficient or striving or fine.

Nadezha said, 'When I think about the colonial days, I suppose the Malays ran around and gambled and didn't do anything constructive. While the money was made by others – the Chinese tin-mining families, the rubber plantations, usually the English. I think in those days that was it. The Chinese and the English colonial masters. Malays didn't do business. The only option for them was the civil service or to become an academic. That required hard work. So they opted for the easy way out. They didn't know anything else. They were coconut shell people.'

Nadezha's father, though, had to take his studies at Malay College seriously; it was his only way out. The girl who was to be Nadezha's mother didn't have that need. Girls of her background didn't have to go to school if they didn't want to; and Nadezha's mother hardly went to school. She could read and write and that was enough. She didn't think of herself as uneducated. And, indeed, she had another, more exclusive, kind of training from her family. She was trained in loyalty and what Nadezha called old-fashioned virtues. She learned how to behave in public: she learned not to show off, not to show her feelings. At the end she was quite a finished person: Nadezha thought of her mother as someone of old-fashioned, imperious style.

Much of the family money was gone when the girl was corresponding with Nadezha's father. When the land went, and money went, there was nothing to hold once-rich people in Kuala Kangsar; they migrated, almost like the *kampung* people, to the towns. So in time, in 1958, when she was eighteen, the girl left her grandmother and two aunts in Kuala Kangsar and went to the capital to live with her father, the high police officer.

In the capital there was more freedom, and for the first time she and Nadezha's father could meet properly. They must have come to an understanding; because Nadezha's father went to Europe to study, and when he came back the girl was waiting for him, and they decided to get married. The girl's family gave their approval, but they didn't like it. They had no money, but they still had a name, and the girl's father was now very high in the police. Nadezha's father, in spite of the years at Malay College and the degree he had taken abroad, still in their eyes had the stigma of being a *kampung* boy.

Nadezha always knew as she was growing up that her father was a *kampung* boy and her mother something else. It was an unequal relationship; but Nadezha thought it balanced out in the end. Her father was a quiet man. That would have helped. Though Nadezha remembered a quarrel once, when her father told her mother that her parents had never thought him good enough. But if she had married the kind of man she was supposed to marry, he said, she would have been stuck in Perak.

Nadezha said, 'It's probably true.'

And what was strange even to Nadezha was that, when the time came for her to think of marriage, she did as her mother had done. She, too, married an ambitious *kampung* boy.

Her mother said, in warning, 'You are doing what I did.'

Nadezha was working in a stockbroking firm in Kuala Lumpur – Malaysia had been transformed – and the boy or young man worked in her office. He wasn't good-looking, but Nadezha didn't like good-looking men. Her father wasn't good-looking, and she felt that subconsciously that would have influenced her. Beauty was all right in a woman, but not in a man.

She was attracted to the young man because he was ambitious, not in a dreaming way, but in a practical and methodical way. He would say, for instance, 'This person is leaving next year. So my chances of taking over that position are good.' He would know who he would be competing against; he would work out his moves long in advance. He was quite cold about it.

Nadezha said, 'I was directionless, and I thought he would take over, and I might end up doing something.'

I asked Nadezha, 'Was there nothing else that attracted you, apart from the ambition?'

'He liked nice clothes.'

The boy's *kampung* background didn't worry Nadezha. She thought he was at ease with himself. But she didn't like his politics. He supported the government and the Malay ruling party because he thought they had done a lot for people like him. At that time the judges were under attack from the government, and Nadezha was concerned about that.

The young man said, 'I don't care about that. What people really care about is money, food in their bellies, house, shelter.'

Nadezha was repelled by his argument, but she thought she had had a comfortable upbringing, and he hadn't, and it would be wrong for her to blame him. She understood, too, that he was not interested in concepts; he was interested more in tangible things. Later all of this was to scratch at her. But she decided at the time, in spite of her misgivings, to marry him because of his directness. She saw him as a kind of new Malay man, a new model. They became engaged.

'I really think I did want to get married. All my friends were getting married, and I thought this was the way. It was my turn to get married. It was just part of life.'

One day her fiancé said quite casually that he wanted to take her to the *kampung* to meet his grandmother. His parents were also going to be there that weekend, he said. Nadezha had met the parents many times before, in Kuala Lumpur. They were pleasant enough, but Nadezha didn't especially like them. They were educated people who had lived in Kuala Lumpur for thirty years, but their conversation was quite ordinary, the idlest kind of chit-chat. They were not the in-laws Nadezha would have chosen. But Nadezha's primary need at that time was to get married. She felt it was something she had to do as a woman. She thought that as a woman she could have a future only with a husband at her side. Later, when she was divorced, her ideas changed.

The *kampung* was in Negri Sembilan. There was a highway, and then a road off the highway that became more and more of a country road, muddier and muddier. Nadezha felt she was going deep into the interior. It was much damper than Kuala Lumpur, and more humid. The houses became simpler and simpler. She saw all this, and had an idea what it meant, but she wasn't frightened enough to pull back. It was half familiar; it was like what she imagined her father had come from. As had been happening right through this relationship, she saw and felt with one side of herself, and acted and spoke with another side.

The house was in a normal *kampung* plot. There was no drive. Her fiancé's parents were already there. They, too, would have driven down from Kuala Lumpur. Their car had made marks in the grass, muddy marks. It was a normal *kampung* plot, but the house itself, though part of it was on stilts (in the traditional *kampung* style), was not the traditional *kampung* house: it had already been renovated and added to, and it didn't have woven-bamboo walls. Nadezha saw some chickens in front of the house, and then she saw more running about underneath the older part of the house. She noticed the chickens because in Kuala Lumpur she wasn't used to seeing chickens running around a house.

She said to her fiancé, 'Oh, she keeps chickens.' 'She' was the grandmother.

He said, 'She likes the eggs freshly laid. They taste better.'

The words struck a false note. They sounded defensive. She thought he had said too much: there was no need for him to talk about the taste of the eggs. For the first time she saw him uncomfortable. The moment passed; she pushed it to the back of her mind.

There were ten people at the lunch. Two unmarried aunts did the serving; they were treated like servants. They were supposed to take care of the grandmother in her old age. The grandmother was as ugly as her grandson, Nadezha thought; but the old woman was so wrinkled that no one could really see just how ugly she was. She didn't say much at the lunch; but she didn't have to. She was the matriarch; they all deferred to her. Nadezha thought it was the Negri Sembilan way: the people there had migrated from Padang in Sumatra and brought their matriarchal clan customs with them. Nadezha herself, as a fiancée, wasn't required to say very much; she just had to sit and look shy. So the actual lunch was easy for her. There were lots of little photographs on the walls: the children of the family at various stages.

There was an uncle at the lunch. He was a member of the ruling Malay party and was involved in local politics. He led a certain amount of political talk at the table; it was about some district matter. Nadezha began to get a new idea of the Malay movement. She had always taken it for granted. But now she began to understand how her fiancé saw it. She began to understand – taking everything together: the house, the renovations, the easy political talk, the general confidence – that she was among people for whom the world had changed in concrete ways.

They had seen good things happen in their village, their house, and in their own lives. They had felt themselves lifted up.

Nadezha said, 'In the old days when you went to KL you saw the club, the shops, and the only Malays who inhabited this world were the royals, the aristos. And we felt: This is our land and they have taken over.' 'They' were the Chinese. 'In the house I felt I understood why politics played such a big part in the life of the Malays. In our arguments at the office I talked about concepts. He talked about concrete things, things that had happened.'

What came over to her especially was the optimism of the people at the table. Such optimism in a family was new to her. She also saw that, for that family, her fiancé embodied the idea of success, their success, Malay success.

I asked Nadezha, 'Did they look upon you as part of his success?'

'I didn't think of it like that.'

'Did you fall in love with him a little bit then?'

'No.'

'So you were fooling yourself?'

'Maybe I felt I was having a stake in that future they were talking about. Maybe.'

After lunch something happened which she noted but suppressed, in the way she had suppressed her misgivings about the chickens in the yard and the talk about the taste of the fresh eggs.

'We went to the living room. The dining room was in the old part of the house, on stilts. The living room was the new part. Three steps down – it was part of their moving up. The grandmother motioned to my fiancé to come next to her. I thought he was going to sit on the chair next to her. But he sat on the floor at her feet. There was a carpet. It was all new there; the dining room had a reed or bamboo mat, I'm not sure which. I noticed this sitting on the floor. But then I thought it was the Negri Sembilan culture. They are known for being clannish. I didn't want to talk about it in case he thought I was upset about it. Which I wasn't. Also I thought he was confident enough to deal with all of this. Essentially all this doesn't matter if you don't care about it.'

The visit lasted about four hours, from about noon to just before four. The marriage took place two months later.

Nadezha's mother had her doubts. She said, 'You are doing what I did.' She had no personal feeling against her son-in-law; she just didn't see how Nadezha would fit in. She didn't like the man's parents. They thought that Nadezha and her family were snobs. They felt they should fight back, and just before the wedding there was something like a quarrel between the families.

The marriage customs of Malays are derived from old Hindu customs. At an early stage gifts have to be exchanged between the families. If the girl's family sends five gifts, the boy's family has to send seven; there always has to be a difference of two. Symbolic things are sent: sweets, money. Nadezha's mother wanted part of the boy's family's gift to be in gold coins rather than banknotes. This was for aesthetic reasons: the gold coins would make a more attractive display. The mother of the boy said no; she didn't have the time to go to the bank to change the notes for coins.

Nadezha said, 'Actually, this is quite rude. Because you should do what the girl's side wants, and vice versa. Everybody has to be gracious. You don't want to hurt anyone's feelings before you get married. As customs go, that is the Malay way: you give in, you have to be gracious.'

But Nadezha knew, from the experience of her friends, that there was nearly always in-law trouble at weddings. The trouble came from the rivalry between the families, and Nadezha preferred to see the awkwardness about the gold coins as part of that rivalry. Her mother was more brutal. She thought it was bad manners and a sign of low breeding.

Nadezha went to her husband's *kampung* six or seven times after they were married. She never really got to like it. *Kampung* life wasn't simple and idyllic, as some people said. It was competitive. The second or third time Nadezha was there the talk was all about the neighbour's new car or jeep: the cost, the colour that wasn't nice, and 'I bet it wasn't his own money.' The two unmarried aunts who were looking after the grandmother didn't like each other. There were few single men in the *kampung*, and the aunts had almost no chance now of getting married. One was resigned; Nadezha liked her. The other was malicious, embittered by the way things had turned out for her.

There were no cultural interests in the *kampung*. Life was shallow. There was only religion. It was important; the five-times-a-day praying marked the passage of each day. The mosque was the only kind of social centre.

Nadezha thought that it was because there was so much complaining and grumbling and comparing in the village that her husband had become so ambitious — in order to break out. It puzzled her that her husband didn't notice the pettiness as much as she did. He didn't lend himself to it, didn't sink into the gossip; but he accepted it. It was part of his *kampung*, which was part of him. And, after all, the whole business side of his life (though Nadezha didn't say this) was in his stockbroking firm in Kuala Lumpur.

They lived after their marriage with Nadezha's parents. Nadezha later thought it was a great error. Her husband, who was ambitious, and rather spoilt by his own family, felt oppressed, not in control of his own life. Very soon all the rage began coming out on both sides. Nadezha's mother never criticised her son-in-law personally; he never criticised Nadezha's parents personally. He just attacked their way of life, the things they did, the people they liked. He didn't like seeing Nadezha reading *Vogue*. He would say, 'Why do you read this rubbish?' He himself – Malay of the new model – read books about management: *Money Options, Fund Management*, things about the stockmarket.

'He went out with clients one day. He was drinking. Again I can't remember the argument. By this time we just didn't get on with each other. He hit me. I hit him back. I told him to get out. He did. And that was when we started talking about divorce. It was all done through lawyers. He never came back.'

At the time Nadezha was pregnant. So they couldn't get divorced right away. In Islam divorce is not permitted if the wife is pregnant: a baby has to be born legitimate. Still, they arrived at some kind of arrangement; but three weeks later he went back on that, and said he wasn't going to divorce Nadezha. She thought he might have been influenced by his family. They had their pride, as Nadezha knew, and they might have wanted Nadezha to have a hard time. She did. For three years she lived in an in-between way, neither married nor divorced. And it was hard for her to get custody of the child.

She thought now that she had expected too much from marriage. She had been hoping, more than she knew, to find a replacement for what she had lost. Her mother's family had been gamblers; when her mother's father died all the family money finally went. A whole way of living, everything she had taken for granted, was lost. She had told this in the beginning as half a joke. But for her it was really a calamity. And after that there were further blows. Her younger brother died; her father's business began to fail; her father and mother had marital problems.

She, the daughter of an imperious, well-born mother, began to feel a great emptiness before she was twenty. And when, later, she went to London, she found that other Malay girls there were like her. Certain girls she knew, whom she thought were well off and happy, had joined a sect; they had a great, hidden need. The leader of the sect made them give him money; the girls treated him like a god-like figure with special powers.

Nadezha said, 'Malays like these people with special powers because they believe that things don't happen because of your own actions. They think that by engaging one bomoh or shaman they will put everything right. Everyone I know is religious. They have a strong faith. They believe that as born Muslims they are secure. If you are born without religion you question your place, your role. If you are Muslim you are told from the start that you are part of a big group. In school when you have religious classes, the Malay girls would go off to their religious classes, and the Chinese girls had free time or play time. In that way you are already differentiating people.

'My father's friend is floating his company. They are involved in plastics. They began making plastic wrappers. Now they're moulding plastic chairs, and they are suddenly very rich. They've come from being comfortable to being rich beyond belief. And every year they do the *umra*' – the little pilgrimage – 'without fail, to give thanks to God. They think, "It must be luck. I am no different from the other guy. It's God who must be helping me." I am sure he realises he's not doing something substantial. That's why he can't believe his luck. In the past ten years things have been built out of air.'

This was the need she took to her own marriage; this was her faith in her husband's new-man energy and ambition. Yet she never talked about religion to her husband. He was not especially spiritually minded. He performed the rites; that was all.

She had been too hard on him; she felt that now. She had looked to him for strength; she had discovered he was insecure in his own way. She said, 'That was very frightening. I stress insecurity first, because if he wasn't insecure he wouldn't have depended on his family for everything.' He talked about his career with his mother, not with Nadezha. He didn't talk to Nadezha about his financial problems. He was all right now. He was successful. He was manager of a stockbroking firm, and he had married a girl from his own state of Negri Sembilan. He had made a new life for himself, and Nadezha thought he might still be regretting his foray into something he never knew.

She said, 'It must have been a nightmare for him. He's still under a coconut shell. He moved out of his element and didn't like what he saw.'

Something like that could be said on both sides.

3

The Bomoh's Son

THE BOMOH – healer, or shaman, or magic-man – was a year older than the century. He was of mixed Chinese and Indonesian parentage. His father had left China towards the end of the nineteenth century, part of the spilling out of the poor and unprotected from the collapsing empire; and he had fetched up in one of the islands of the Indonesian archipelago, at that time ruled by the Dutch. There he had found some kind of footing, and he had married (or as good as married) an Indonesian woman. They had nine sons.

They were very poor. They moved at some point to a northern state in what was then British-ruled Malaya. The eighth son hardly had a childhood. He went out to work when he was quite young. When he was thirteen or fourteen he was driving a truck. Life was not easy; and at about this time the mystical, Indonesian side of the boy's personality began to assert itself. He became aware of his powers, and he began to train as a bomoh. There would have been a teacher or encourager of some sort, but I didn't ask about the teacher, and wasn't told.

This training as a bomoh would have begun in 1914–1915. (While, far away, Europe was fighting the great war that indirectly weakened the British and Dutch empires in Asia; and, a little nearer home, Gandhi, after his twenty years in South Africa, was going back to India with his very special political-social-religious ideas.) The boy or young man learned very fast. He became a full bomoh when he was seventeen; and he practised for nearly seventy years. He had a big following, and he had disciples. There were certain things he couldn't do when he became physically infirm, but his powers as a bomoh never failed him.

He married twice, to two Malay Chinese sisters, with five years between the marriages. He had seventeen children altogether, and they all lived in the same house.

Rashid was the bomoh's eighth son. He was born in 1955. He was sent to good local schools from the start; and in his eighteenth year — with every kind of tenderness for his father's feelings, and every kind of respect for his father's powers as a bomoh — Rashid began to turn away from his father's magical practices, and the rituals of the house. With education and self-awareness Rashid had begun to feel the kind of philosophical and spiritual need that Philip, the Chinese Christian convert, felt; and, indeed, for some time, picking up and repeating what he had heard from some friends at school, Rashid talked and behaved as a Christian, even at home.

Then he discovered Islam and the Koran, and he stayed there. He became a Muslim in his own mind, without being formally converted, and he took the Arab name of Rashid. He had started and dropped more than one career since then. Now he was a successful corporate lawyer, close to people with power. He was only forty. He had travelled far and fast, like the country. He had lived in, or had access to, many different spiritual worlds.

People brought all kinds of problems to his father, Rashid said. Payment was often in kind, four or five chickens, fruit; and it wasn't like settling a bill. Payment, once it started, went on as a regular voluntary tribute.

People came simply to be blessed, or to be cured of pains, or to have amulets blessed. Rashid remembered that once a famous local martial arts man, an elderly man, an exponent of ju-jitsu, came and knelt before his father and asked to be granted inner strength. The bomoh was known for his great strength. He was short, five feet four and a half inches, but well built. He could bend six-inch nails between his index finger and thumb, without having to go into a trance, which was what he normally had to do when he dealt with people's problems.

When he was in this trance people who wanted to be blessed knelt before him, and he touched them on the forehead, the shoulders, the solar plexus. Then he made them turn round and he touched them on the back of the head and the shoulders. When people were in pain he touched them on the part of the body that hurt.

Every year the bomoh's followers made a special pilgrimage to the bomoh's house and brought amulets to be blessed. These followers were of all communities and all classes, rich, poor, educated, ordinary. Rashid as a child of eight remembered hearing many languages during one of these pilgrimages: English, Malay, Hokkien Chinese, Baba or Chinese Malay.

The bomoh would go into a trance and in this trance he would take off his shirt. He would start shivering, because at that moment he would be focused in his trance on the snow deity, one of the three deities from whom he drew his powers. His assistants would hand him a bundle of flaming joss sticks. He needed the flames to warm himself, and he would appear to be outlining his body with the joss sticks. He would do this for a minute or so. When he was sufficiently warmed, he passed the sticks back to his assistants. They would then dress him in his special shirt and cover him with his cloak. The shirt was important; only the bomoh could wear it; he had blessed it on the altar of the shrine.

When he sat down his assistants gave him a glass of water. He would speak some incantations, blow on the water, drink it, and spew it out. His sword would then be passed to him. This was a real sword, five feet long and double-edged. He would stick out his tongue, and use the sword to make a deep enough incision in his tongue for the blood to flow. The yellow slips of paper for the amulets would be ready. His assistants would pass him the slips one by one and he would drip blood from his tongue on each slip. He would keep on blessing slips in this way, losing blood all the time, until Rashid's mother said, 'That's enough.' By then he might have blessed a hundred slips.

When the sword was put away he would be covered up and, still in a trance, he would start giving his consultations. Women wanted to know whether they would get husbands, men whether they would get mistresses. Women who were being badly treated by their husbands wanted to know what they should do. Mothers or fathers wanted to know about those of their children who had gone astray.

The bomoh would speak in a language Rashid didn't understand. This was the special Javanese the bomoh had brought from the Indonesian island where he was born. He also spoke in Mandarin. It was only on these occasions, and in that trance, that Rashid's father spoke Mandarin.

The sword was special. It was the bomoh's own. An assistant went into a trance one day and tried to use the sword to cut his tongue. The sword wouldn't cut. When the bomoh was old, though, he allowed his tongue to be cut with the sword by one of his assistants. (But Rashid's language was ambiguous. I wasn't sure, when I looked at my notes some time later, whether the assistants cut their own tongue, or used the sword to cut the bomoh's tongue.)

The assistants were the bomoh's disciples. They didn't live in the house, but they were at the bomoh's beck and call. They came to the house every day, and they had to work. One of the things they did was to clean the altar. They were not paid. They were in no way the bomoh's employees. In fact, they had to bring offerings to the bomoh. Sometimes they even offered money – which the bomoh refused.

There were no statues on the altar. There was only a yellow cloth, with representations of the bomoh's three deities on a triangle: the snow-mountain god at the peak, with the deities of fire and sword at the base. Snow, fire, sword: the bomoh's ritual followed that sequence. He told his children on many occasions that he had masters of some kind. He had a master in China and another in Indonesia, and (just as his followers came in pilgrimage to him once a year) he regularly made his own pilgrimage to these masters. He did so by astro-travelling. Rashid never doubted what his father said; he could find no other way of explaining his father's manifest powers.

The bomoh's wives – Rashid's mother and his aunt – were Baba-Nonya, overseas Straits Chinese, people of Chinese origin who had adopted Malay culture and the Malay language. The food in the house was Baba food, Malay-Chinese food, very spicy, and they ate with their hands. They didn't use chopsticks.

Rashid's mother, Chinese though she was, worshipped a Malay ancestor, the Datuk. Many other Babas did that. Offerings to this Datuk were made on the altar by Rashid's mother. The offerings were of Malay-style food: *rendang ayam*, curried chicken, *rendang daging*, curried beef, sticky rice: food to be eaten with the hands.

Once a month everybody in the house would have his cheeks pierced with a steel needle by the bomoh. This cheek-piercing was done as a form of purification. There was a different needle for every-one; the older the child, the longer and thicker the needle. The child whose cheek was pierced first would have to endure it the longest: the needle would stay in until everyone's cheeks were done. Sometimes, on special occasions, photographs were taken of the family, the seventeen children and the mothers, all with needles in their cheeks.

Up to the end of the second world war the bomoh and his family lived in a *kampung* in a *kampung*-style house. Afterwards they moved to a resettled area, to a two-storey terrace house. This was the house that Rashid had grown up in. There were three bedrooms upstairs and one bedroom downstairs. Rashid's mother and one or two of his sisters were in the room downstairs. Rashid's grandmother was in one room upstairs, with all the other girls. An uncle and his whole family lived in one room. All the boys slept on the landing. At any one time twenty people could be found living in the tiny house. And, with all of that, the bomoh practised his profession downstairs, in the living room, which was also the temple.

The bomoh's powers were known in the neighbourhood, and people were careful not to cross the family. As an aspect of his success, the bomoh also had a certain social standing in the community, and he was concerned to live up to it. He was particular about his dress when, relaxing from his bomoh work, he went out, as he sometimes did, to his Chinese clan clubs in the town. He dressed in the colonial way then, in a suit and with a bow tie. He would have a game of cards, and an occasional pipe of opium. One of the bomoh's brothers was an opium addict, and died from his addiction. But the bomoh was not an addict.

The bomoh had never gone to school. He alone knew how much he had suffered because of that as a child and young man, in that far-off time before and during the first world war. And now, in a changed world, he wanted all his children, daughters as well as sons, to be properly educated. He did the best he could for all of them.

Rashid was sent to a local primary school, and then to one of the most reputed colonial secondary schools in the district. Rashid didn't say it, but he would have known when he got to the secondary school that he was in another sphere. At home Rashid was proud of his father's powers, and liked them to be talked about locally; but he never talked about them at the secondary school. He never thought to 'brag' – he used the schoolboy word – about his father there.

It was at this school that Rashid became aware of other religions. A friendly Tamil boy engaged him one day in 'a very basic discussion' about big issues. The Tamil boy said, 'Look at Hitler. Look at all those brutalities. You think these people are going to go scot free when they die? And who do you think will punish them? God will punish them. You think all of us are here without any purpose?'

The Tamil boy was a Christian. He didn't push his faith too hard at Rashid. He was just very friendly, and it was because of this boy that Rashid joined a school Bible class. At the same time Rashid began reading the King James Bible. He liked the language, the pace of the stories, the movement. Other Chinese boys were doing the same thing. The Chinese boys were Buddhists, like Rashid; but they wanted more than they got from the Buddhism of their parents.

Rashid's little terrace house was full of rituals, with his father's temple downstairs, its festivities, the annual pilgrimage, and his mother's daily worship of her Malay Datuk. But these rituals couldn't give answers to the bigger questions that Rashid was now beginning to have. His father's three deities didn't offer anything like 'the ecumenical love' (the words were Rashid's) he was discovering in Christianity. 'Ecumenical love': it was like the idea of grace that had overwhelmed Philip, the Chinese Christian convert. The deities of snow, fire and sword, and the temple rituals, offered Rashid no comparable philosophy, no 'big picture'. What happened in his father's temple was private. People just came there day after day to his father's temple with their practical problems.

And Rashid couldn't question his father about what he did. It was inconceivable, for instance, that he should ask his father whether God existed. His father was a bomoh; he had mystical powers. To question him about religion, to express doubt, would be to show disrespect, and that was the last thing Rashid wanted to do.

One of Rashid's brothers was more than half way to being a Christian. He was going to church regularly. And Rashid was going to the school Bible class. Sometimes at home, in the living room of the terrace house, where the temple altar was, they sang hymns together in the evenings. The bomoh might then be relaxing, watching television. The hymn-singing in his temple didn't worry him; he paid no attention.

At school Rashid and the Tamil boy had many talks about Jesus and the Trinity. Rashid wasn't actually converted, but he went around saying to people, 'Why don't you start reading the Bible?' He preached at them the way the Tamil boy had preached at him. He talked to them about the purpose of life.

He did this to one of the bright girls at the school. The girl was a Pathan; Rashid was attracted to her. She said to him, 'Have you ever read the Koran?'

He was prejudiced against Islam at that time. He thought of it as a backward religion; he associated it with Malays, whom at that time he considered a backward people. But he wanted to have something to talk to the girl about. So he began reading the Koran, in the Marmaduke Pickthall translation. He was fascinated by the introduction to the opening chapter; he thought it the equivalent of the Lord's Prayer. He liked, too, the constant reference to God as the Most Beneficent and the Most Merciful. This went against the idea he had of Islam and the sword.

But he had doubts. He didn't like the idea of polygamy and what he could gather from his reading about the position of women in Islam. He asked the Pathan girl why the Prophet had married more than four wives, and the Pathan girl couldn't answer. Still, he kept on reading the Koran, and it began to appeal to his heart. He felt humbled by it. He liked the repeated references to God's guidance and man's need of it. 'Show me the straight path': that, the fifth line of the opening chapter, went deep into him.

He began thinking of himself as a Muslim. To be a Muslim was to bear witness that there was no God but God, and the Prophet was his messenger. This should have created problems in his own mind about his father's practices as a bomoh. But it didn't. Rashid never associated religion with what his father did.

He was still seeing the Pathan girl. To him she was a living Muslim, an exemplar, and he began to follow her dietary habits. He was able now to recite Koranic verses. He didn't think it was enough for him; he thought he should read the Koran properly, in Arabic. He set himself to learn the Malay Arabic script; it took him two years to do sight reading.

By this time there was worry about him at home. Rashid's parents didn't like it when he refused to touch pork and refused to hold the joss sticks and perform rituals before the altar. He refused to eat cooked food and even fruit that had been offered up on the altar. To avoid trouble he made himself scarce when the rituals began. His parents knew now that one day he would take a Muslim name. That upset them a great deal. They were Taoist-Buddhists, and as a bomoh Rashid's father had a position in the community. Rashid was as conciliatory as he could be; he didn't argue. He never wanted to hurt their feelings.

All this was in 1973. Rashid was in his eighteenth year.

It occurred to me, hearing his story, that four years before, in 1969, there had been terrible racial riots in Malaysia between Chinese and Malays. I asked Rashid about that time.

He said, 'All of us were affected. I was in form two. The riots started on 13 May. I was thirteen plus. Thirteen years, six months. I remember cycling to school and finding the place deserted, the streets deserted. And then we saw some people coming back this way, and they all called out to me, "Go back! Go back!" This was very early in the morning. By eight or nine everybody knew what was going on.'

The family had to survive for some months on what they had at home. Rice, salted fish, salted black beans. They had no fresh food. Rashid's father had no savings. Because of the curfew people couldn't come to him. So he had no income, no tribute. It was a time of great hardship for the family. After a few weeks the curfew was lifted, but the fear was so great that for three months people didn't leave their houses. There were stories of Malays rounding up Chinese people, loading them on to trucks, executing them, and then dumping the bodies. There were stories, too, of Malays being hacked to death by Chinese gangsters.

Gradually things calmed down. Classes started up again at the schools. The bomoh, born on an Indonesian island in the last century to a Chinese father and a Malay mother, would have always known about Malay hate, Malay racial rage. Yet, perhaps because of his work, which brought sufferers and suppliants of all sorts to him, he felt that people were people. He refused to believe that human beings could cease being human, and he told his children so. He refused to believe the stories that were brought to him of Malay soldiers going round the country shooting Chinese people. He was never vengeful or bitter.

But it could not have been easy for him when, four years after that terror, his son became a Muslim and took the name of Rashid and stayed away from the old rituals of the house. He hadn't minded when his two sons sang hymns about Jesus in the temple. But becoming a Muslim was something else. It would have seemed like a turning away from the family. The bomoh could be philosophical about the riots; but the antagonism between Malay and Chinese went deep; it couldn't be wished away. Officially in Malaysia to be a Malay was to be Muslim.

And, though Rashid didn't say so, it was the race riots of 1969 that had given a push to the Malay movement and the new Islam among the young.

There were twenty people in the house, and Rashid (when he got to the higher forms of the secondary school) could begin to study only at about midnight, when the television was turned off and people went to sleep. He would sit on his father's bomoh chair in the living room, the chair on which his father sat when, sometimes in a trance, he received people and gave his consultations, and he would study or read or write for three or four hours. That was where, below the deities of snow and fire and sword, he read Shakespeare and Jane Austen and Dickens, and wrote his essays, and studied for his examinations. He never thought he was suffering hardship; that idea came to him much later, when life was easier.

His time in the family house came to an end when he finished at the secondary school and went on to the university in Kuala Lumpur. He did English. It was an insubstantial thing to do, but – from the account he gave – he was going to the university really to be free. He was able to support himself. The tuition fees were low. And he was able to earn enough in the long vacation doing various jobs to pay for his lodging in the college. He taught; he did little jobs in the media and advertising.

He didn't take his studies seriously. He spent so little time at lectures that in his second year the university authorities gave him an ultimatum. A fatherly Indian tutor helped him to pull himself together, and in the end he was able to get a reasonable second-class degree. In the three years he spent at the university he went home only once, for a week. That was in his second year. After he got his degree, at the end of his third year, he began to work full-time in Kuala Lumpur; and he couldn't even think of going home.

The insubstantial English degree didn't help him get a job, and he began to do full-time what he had done in the vacations. What had been exciting in the beginning, part of his freedom, soon became tedious. He could make a living, but his life was unfocused and disordered. Without Islam – which mattered more and more, and had mattered even at the university – his life would have been without point.

He was driving to work one day when a traffic policeman signalled to him to stop. He rolled down the window and said, 'What's wrong?' There was something in Rashid's manner that enraged the policeman. He said to Rashid, 'What do you mean, "What's wrong?" It's "What's wrong, *sir*?"' And he began to write out a ticket.

The policeman was Indian. It was well known in Kuala Lumpur – so Rashid said – that Indians became arrogant in power. And, though Rashid didn't say, the Indian policeman might have been especially rough with Rashid because he was a Chinese. Rashid said in his heart, 'I will fix you up. I will get even. You just wait.'

Rashid decided at that moment that he was going to join the police, to 'invest in power'. The decision was sudden, but he had been thinking about it for some time. For some time he had been dreaming of wearing a police uniform, to win respect from people, and to protect himself from people like the Indian policeman and from security guards who chased him away from parking spaces reserved for dignitaries.

What came out now was that Rashid's eldest brother was high in the police. This brother was a full twenty years older than Rashid, and Rashid would not have seen much of him. He had joined the police force as a constable and – he was another son with the bomoh's energy and drive – he had risen through the ranks, becoming first an inspector, and then a gazetted officer. Rashid had a childhood memory of this brother coming to the family house in his inspector's uniform. At some point the local police station needed to contact the inspector – no telephone in the bomoh's house at that time – and a police sergeant came to the house and saluted the inspector in front of the whole family. This excited the children. Rashid also remembered the inspector's handgun.

Rashid said, 'The whole idea of putting on this uniform with the three pips on the shoulder gets the adrenalin pumping. On reflection it all seems silly, but it was real then. Once you had the power' – and Rashid was telling the story from his later position of ease and security and influence – 'it was very different altogether.'

Rashid also felt that, after his too-liberated time at the university, and his unfocused freelance career afterwards, he needed order and discipline, even regimentation, in his life again. He thought the police force would do that for him. And though his insecurity and aggressiveness and drive to power (as he thought) were real enough at the time, he recognised with a part of his mind that his approach was contrary to his upbringing.

He said, 'My father and my brother had different kinds of power. My brother had authority. My father had the respect due to his gifts, and also because he was a very generous man. Which was why, when the riots came, we had a very tough time. We had no savings. My father would buy four or five loaves of bread from the bread-man because he didn't have the heart to tell him no – it didn't matter how much bread we had. And I still do that today when the bread-man comes. And the policy was to give more than the price of the bread. He never took change. He said, "With these people you must not be calculating." '

It was a year before Rashid could join the police. Five hundred applications were processed; many more had been received. After physical and classroom tests 250 were called in for the first induction. One hundred got through the formal interviews; that took some months. Examinations and intelligence tests then sifted out half of those. At the end twenty were chosen and sent to the police training school; Rashid was one of them.

He gave himself a new haircut for the training school. The first thing he and the others had to do was to get their heads shaved by the training-school barber. He had joined the police for the sake of power. His first experience as a trainee officer was this ritual humiliation.

And for the next two months he and the others were at the mercy of sergeants and constables. The police training rules hadn't changed since the British time. Small misdemeanours – like talking on parade – could be severely punished, with an hour's double-time marching in full uniform in the heat, with an M-16 rifle held in a position that after a while caused fine, excruciating pain in the triceps and elbow.

At the end of his two months he had, indeed, become disciplined. The urge to power, the constant little urges to get even when the time came with the sergeants and constables who were roughing him up, had been burnt away. He even felt regard for the men who had trained him.

When he had graduated and been commissioned he went to see his father. He hadn't seen him for some years. Rashid knew now that the bomoh would be proud of him; and the bomoh was very proud of him.

Rashid said, 'He was very happy to receive me. In his eyes his son had been transformed. My Muslim conversion wasn't brought up any more. I had sent him a photograph of me in uniform, with my name tag, with my Muslim name, RASHID. And he had it hanging on the wall of the living room.'

To be a police officer was to do more than wear the uniform and receive salutes. It was constantly to see, in the rough area where he had been posted, dead men, mutilated corpses, cruelty. Rashid soon couldn't take any more. He joined the Intelligence service. It had not figured in his fantasy of power; but he understood now that in the police that was where the real power lay. But he didn't like it. He had lost his taste for police work.

He thought of the law. He had been told by one of his police instructors, while he was training, that he reasoned like a good lawyer. That had stayed with him; and after less than four years in the police he resigned, did a business job for a while for the money, and enrolled in the law course at the university. It was what he was born for; the law engaged all his instincts; he was successful from the start. The Malaysian boom had made it possible for him to chop and change as he had done; in an earlier time he would have had to be more cautious, to stay with what he had found.

He said, 'Though now I am in touch with sources of power, all that excitement that consumed me in those days is not there now. Looking back, I feel that all the stages I had to go through were necessary. The stages of my childhood, the conditions I was brought up in, the opportunities, helped me to be self-sustaining.'

His background had made him a very positive sort of person. He didn't moan and groan. He didn't think that was because he was Chinese; he had Chinese friends who moaned and groaned. He thought it was something he got from his father. He never knew his father to complain. He suffered much pain from a hernia, but he told no one about it. He had a problem with his spine that kept him in constant pain.

Rashid went to see him a few months before he died. He was eighty-eight, and was bedridden. His body had wasted away. He had lost about thirty or forty pounds. He had shrunk.

Rashid said, 'Father, you have grown so thin.'

The bomoh said, 'Everything is okay. I am fine.' But there were tears in his eyes.

Rashid, seeing his father so close to death, thought of his hard child-hood, and of all that he had managed to do. All his children, so many of them born at an unpromising time, were now well placed.

Rashid said, 'When I was having fantasies of power, even before I was a policeman, he was exercising real power.' As a bomoh. 'Compared to him, I was, year to year, infantile. I will not tolerate any kind of criticism of him, not even from members of the family. What he did we saw with our own eyes. He did not have to make a proclamation of his power. It may be that I have a direct affinity with my father. He was an eighth son. I was an eighth son. I was told by my mother that I look exactly like my father. My mother is not very good with words. She doesn't go around flattering people.'

Rashid's father didn't want anyone to follow his calling as a bomoh, or to profess his faith. He just wanted his children to go through the rituals. Rashid couldn't do that when he became a Muslim. But it pleased Rashid that his mother did the rituals, and that when she died, other members of the family would be carrying on her worship of her Malay Datuk spirit in her kitchen, and doing the rituals on the family altar.

4

The Other World

SYED ALWI, the playwright, had sat out the Malaysian boom. People who write Malay plays do not make a great deal of money; and Syed Alwi had made that kind of writing his vocation. Still, with a fee here and a fee there, he had over the years managed to put a little sum by; and when he was in his early sixties he thought he should build a little house to see him through the evening of his days.

By birth and instinct he was a country boy; he had the Malay love of trees and rivers. He found a plot in a development in a *kampung* far out of Kuala Lumpur. In his stuttering little red car it was about half an hour's drive from Kuala Lumpur, even with the fast new highways through the raw, opened-up hills. When you left the highway you drove for a while down a winding road through pleasant sun-spotted woodland, and then you came to the rich green *kampung*. At the foot of Syed Alwi's little plot was a small stream, just a few feet wide and a few inches deep.

The Malay instinct that had led him to this spot made him entrust the building of his house to a young man who was a relation and had set up as a builder. It was a calamity. The money was consumed and the house was unfinished and the builder had gone away. Syed Alwi, in his ambition, had dreamed of a studio section of his house where he might rehearse his plays. But the greater part of what had been put up was a mere dangerous outline, wall-less and floor-less (and ambition had led him to ask for a house partly over the stream), an uneven see-through frame of leaning and sagging timbers too slender to bear any weight.

Syed Alwi, going against his Malay instinct, had complained to the builder's father. And his instinct was right. The father had become enraged, had said he was in no way responsible for his son's competence or otherwise as a builder. That was something for Syed Alwi (whatever his feelings about family solidarity or Malay solidarity) to assess for himself.

And so there Syed Alwi and his wife were, living in a corner of this strange structure (without a telephone), and receiving people and working on plays and trying to get on with things. The hilly land above the little stream had been cut into and levelled for the building. Snakes (attracted by the stream) had made big holes in the dry earth wall at one side of the structure. Syed Alwi and his wife sometimes saw the snakes; neither of them minded. She was a beautiful and serene woman. She liked those things about the site that were nonetheless beautiful: the stream, the trees, the green.

Something like this had happened to Syed Alwi's father in 1930. He was distantly related to the royal family of Perak. For some reason it was not a good relationship, and he had suffered as a child because of it. He had then, however, while still very young, become a successful civil servant. The strains – social, academic, colonial – might have been too great. When he was twenty-two he became schizophrenic. In the other world, or in his other personality, he had religious obsessions and could be violent. But he also had his lucid periods. In 1930, in the eighth year of his schizophrenia, during one of his lucid periods, he began to build a two-storey house for his family in the *kampung*. He was too ambitious. He had only his civil service pension and he didn't have the money to complete the house. It remained without its upper storey.

Syed Alwi was born about this time. He might have been born in the unfinished house; he certainly grew up in it. It was the house in which the family lived out the deprivations and horrors of the Japanese occupation from early 1942 to 1945. And it was the house where, days after the end of the war in the Pacific, Syed Alwi's father died.

Unimaginable experience: it could be said it made Syed Alwi a playwright. But it isn't always easy for a writer to see his material when he is starting out. Sometimes distance is required; and sometimes an experience is so bad it cannot be written about directly. Syed Alwi's first approach to what he had lived through was oblique, symbolical. It is one way in which the creative imagination can deal with extraordinary pain. His first play developed slowly, over four years.

It began with something he wrote in his twentieth year, when he was studying at the Clifford School in Kuala Kangsar. (He had missed four years of school because of the war.) In Kuala Kangsar at that time there was a local man of religion called Sheikh Tahir. He was a learned man who had travelled, and he knew enough astronomy to work out the beginning of the fasting month on his own. He was a local legend. He used to come to town on his bicycle and people would stop him and talk to him. Syed Alwi admired Sheikh Tahir, wanted to be like him. He did a piece about the Sheikh for the Clifford School magazine. It was curiously angled: he wrote of an imaginary encounter on a train between the Sheikh and a boy like himself. The boy boasts and boasts; the old man hardly speaks; and the boy realises later, with bitterness and shame, that he has been in the presence of the great man without really seeing him.

The idea of the meeting on the train stayed with Syed Alwi. He added to it. The boy became a university student; the father-figure of the Sheikh became a ghost, seen and not there. The background was developed: it was the Emergency, a time of breakdown and general decay and sudden death in familiar surroundings.

Four years later Syed Alwi went to Minnesota on a Fulbright fellowship to study journalism. After a long period of idleness he began to write one day, and the play, his first, was done in less than two weeks.

There is the meeting on the train. The university student thinks the older man is a farmer, talks philosophy at him, and tries to make fun of him intellectually. The older man at last puts a question to the student: 'If you knew somebody was going to die, would you tell him?' The student begins to babble; he knows now he is not dealing with a farmer. He can give no answer. The old man says, as if to calm the student, 'I have that problem. My daughter is going to die.' And then he isn't there. He is a ghost; he might have existed only in the student's head. The train gets to the railway station – it is the time of the communist insurgency after the war, when railway stations were attacked – and an unlikely, random death occurs there. It links the young man and the ghost he had seen.

The play might have seemed fanciful in Minnesota, but everything in it – the death of the child, the universal decay, even the religious ghost – referred to something in Syed Alwi's experience. A writer's earliest imaginative work, even when unachieved or artificial-seeming, can hold, sometimes in coded ways, the impulses and emotions that will always rule him.

Syed Alwi, talking of his ancestry, said, 'Legends are more real than history.' The legend in his family was that his father's father was a 'Syed', a descendant of the Prophet. This meant, in Malaysia, that an ancestor would have been an Arab or Indian merchant; and Alwi was an Arab clan name. But Syed Alwi, with all his Malay instincts and passions, looked more European than Arab or Malay; and he said that the doctors had told him that the skin inflammation on the tip of his nose was a European and not an Arab affliction. So, as he said, there was a mystery.

But the legend was the legend. A Syed was a Syed, and an Alwi an Alwi. And the legend was that Syed Alwi's grandfather, who was distantly related to the Perak royal family, had rebelled in some way, had rejected the life of the royal enclave and crossed the river and married a commoner on the other side. There were no dates to the legend; but that rebellion might have been in the 1880s. At that time people would have been locked into ritual and clan ways; and there would have had to be a very good reason – Syed Alwi's grandfather was not an educated person – for something as desperate as rebellion and running away. Syed Alwi could find out nothing beyond the legend.

The rebel's son, Syed Alwi's father, was made to suffer. He was born in 1900. He was adopted by the royal community and sent to the Malay College at Kuala Kangsar, the college for the sons of ruling families. That was the family's public obligation; the boy was of royal blood. In private, though, he was badly treated by the royal family. They didn't allow him to eat with them. He was made to do housework and treated as a servant.

In spite of everything, the boy did well at Malay College. When he was sixteen he got a job with the land office as a settlement officer. A settlement officer helped *kampung* people claim lands in a new settlement; the officer made recommendations to the land office. This would have been quite a high job for a Malay in the colonial set-up of 1916, and remarkable for someone so young.

The royal community then chose a bride for the settlement officer. The story was that she was a *sharifa*, a female Syed, and rich. That was all that the legend said, and the legend must have left out a lot. Because the boy or young man didn't want to get married to the girl who had been chosen for him, and on the eve of his wedding he – like his father before him – ran away. This would have angered many people. They would have felt that their honour had been violated. The young man knew he was going to be pursued. He had to find protection.

He had been working as a settlement officer in the north of Perak, and that was where he thought he would go. He went to a *kampung* he knew very well. He said to the headman there, 'Find a wife for me.' This was acceptable Malay custom. You normally asked a relation to find a wife for you; you could, in an extension of that practice, ask the headman.

There were *rajas* in the *kampung*, people of princely lineage; so there were suitable families. The headman chose two girls. The first girl was not a *raja* and was divorced. It was her privilege as a divorced woman to refuse; and she refused the seventeen-year-old settlement officer. The second girl had to accept.

She was a *raja*. Her ancestors had founded the *kampung*. They were of Bugis descent. They were people from Sulawesi (the Celebes in colonial days), and at some unknown date they had migrated to the northern Malaysian state of Kedah. There they had intermarried with the local Malays and had in time acquired their status as *rajas*. The archipelago in the nineteenth century was full of this kind of move-ment; Europeans and Chinese were not the only people intruding into the territory of others. At some stage the neighbouring Siamese attacked Kedah, and the Kedah *rajas* ran down south to the state of Perak. They settled on a promontory on a bend in the river. They cul-tivated the land there and the place developed into a *kampung* called Pondoktanjung, which meant 'a hut on the promontory'.

The *raja* bride from Pondoktanjung was thirteen, four years younger than her husband. It was the duty of a wife to follow her husband; it was what girls held themselves ready for. But the life of this girl was to change more than anyone knew. Sacrifice and pain and passages of pure darkness awaited her.

In the beginning, though, perhaps for as much as four years, every-thing went well. The bride had her first child, a boy, the year after her marriage; it was the first of fifteen conceptions. She had two more chil-dren in the next four years, the good years, and in that time her husband also rose fast in the civil service. The people of Pandoktanjung grew to accept him as one of themselves; so he was no longer a man without a clan.

In 1921, when he was twenty-one, he became a magistrate. To rise to that position he would have needed a fair amount of legal knowledge. He would have had to study a lot; this would have been in addition to the travelling and the work he was doing as a settlement officer. His life would have been like a continuation of his time at Malay College: classes during the day, homework in the evenings. With that study there came an increasing restlessness of mind. And even while he was becoming more secure in the world he was turning away from it. He was becoming fascinated by philosophy, religion, the nature of God.

He used to discuss these matters with a friend, a teacher at the teachers' training college. The story was that they met every evening. No one else knew about the turbulence in the magistrate's mind. To the people in the *kampung* and to his wife's family he was simply living in the Muslim way, like everybody else, and doing the rituals. He was careful, it would seem, not to worry or offend people; he kept his agitation to himself. He didn't talk to the British officers either. It would have been awkward for him. He didn't like speaking English, and he made a point of not living in the colonial style. So he was quite alone.

In 1922, when he was twenty-two, he broke down. This seemed to have happened almost in a physical way, and at a particular moment. He was in Perak, in a town called Tapah, when it happened. He was able somehow to go back, or was taken back, to Pondoktanjung. He never recovered. For the remaining twenty-three years of his life he moved in and out of his two worlds. His wife was eighteen when he broke down. She stayed his wife in every way until the end.

He was medically boarded out from the civil service. He was given a pension of seventy-five Malay dollars a month, worth in strict exchange terms about eighteen pounds today, but in 1922 quite a fair sum. The pension was paid until the Japanese occupation. Then there was nothing.

He lived two distinct lives, one in this world, the other in his private world.

In his normal life, if the words can be used, he didn't like speaking English; he spoke it only when he had to. In his other life he spoke nothing but English. In his normal life he wasn't much of a writer; in his other life he spent much of his time writing. The family bought him lots of exercise books and pencils, and he wrote and wrote. When he came out of that world everything he had written was burnt. Syed Alwi wasn't sure whether, in his normal personality, he wanted it burnt; or whether the family wanted it burnt.

In the normal world he was not a smoker. In the other world he smoked four or five cigarettes at the same time, holding them between his fingers.

In the normal world he couldn't bear to see anyone suffering physical pain. If his wife beat any of the children, he would run away from the house. He might stay away for weeks; sometimes the family couldn't find out where he had run to. But in the other world he was violent. Though in the other world he didn't recognise his family as his family, he was never violent with them. The violence was for others. His wife's brother might be taking him to get his pension. On the way he might meet someone and for no reason he would slap that person. There was a time when he was so violent that a cage had to be built for him in the house. In the eighth year of his breakdown his violence began to lessen. When Syed Alwi was born, in 1930, the violence had practically stopped.

In the normal world he liked to cook and he liked to eat. In the other world he didn't care about food. He had two passions only, writing and talking.

In 1953, by an extraordinary chance, Syed Alwi met the friend, the teacher at the teachers' training college, with whom his father had been having nightly discussions just before his breakdown, thirty-one years before.

Syed Alwi was going to the United States, to Minnesota, to take up his Fulbright fellowship. The friend came on the aeroplane at Manila, for the Manila-Hawaii sector of the journey; and by a further chance he was given, or took, the seat next to Syed Alwi. During the long flight he told Syed Alwi what he remembered about his father's mental restlessness and breakdown. And for the first time Syed Alwi understood that while his father was doing his magistrate's work as assistant district officer in the land office, and working very hard, he was facing a spiritual horror. It was undoing his world. He couldn't accept the Islamic

God. He wanted to know God more personally, more intimately. He was reading the books of other religions in his search for a God he could accept.

It was Syed Alwi's idea that at some stage his father might have had to compromise, or might have had to accept that he couldn't find the God he was looking for. But this was only conjecture, and for Syed Alwi painful conjecture. I felt, from what he said, that fifty years after his father's death – out of grief, love, and a wish to share the pain – he still very much wanted to have a glimpse of his father's internal life, still wanted to understand his father's other world. That world was lost, and for that reason always a cause for grief. He had only scattered clues, to cherish and examine, like the memories of the friend from 1921.

(And this meeting with his father's friend, just at that moment, when his thoughts were of the United States and writing, might have been one of the critical things in Syed Alwi's own career. It might have driven him, some months later, to that creative burst in which he wrote his first play, with its coded references to the mystery of his father.)

Syed Alwi said of his father, 'To me he was not strictly looking for God. He was searching for the meaning of life. That was translated into the search for God because of his Islamic upbringing, where Allah is the ultimate. The search for Allah or God was the constant in both worlds, and probably the only thing that could exist in both worlds for him. Although it does not explain why he was violent, or explain such diametrically opposed behaviour. I often ask myself: What was his real world? The world that was created for him, or the world he created for himself?'

And it was possible, as Syed Alwi was suggesting, that the world his father had found had been too much for him. In what Syed Alwi had said of his father's behaviour in his other world there were hints and echoes of torment in this world. He had suffered, and perhaps even been maltreated, as a child. In his normal self he couldn't bear pain; in his other world he inflicted it; he slapped people for no reason. As a kind of social outcast, he would have had to prove himself at Malay College; and in the colonial world he would have had to prove himself as a Malay. So, in his other world, in a parody of school and the civil service, he wrote all the time, and in English; and, in colonial style, he smoked cigarettes (the best cigarettes) four and five at a time.

Syed Alwi said, 'The Malays have been under pressure to prove themselves. And one of the things the Malays were not supposed to be

capable of was to be people of the mind. They were conceived as crea-
tures of habit, or subjects of the sultans or the British. They had to have
other people think for them, and lead them, and they would be loyal –
to the sultans, and to the British, who in return protected them by laws
that said that non-Malays could not interfere with their customs and
ways of life.'

When it was understood in the family that something was very wrong
with their son-in-law, they took him to the sanatorium. The place was
little more than a madhouse, and the people in charge weren't going to
cure anyone. They had certain tests for lunacy. One test was for the
patient to be shot at with water from a fire-brigade hose. The other was
for the patient to be fed rice mixed with sand. If the patient didn't complain about the water-hose or the rice, he was mad. Those things were
done to Syed Alwi's father. Worse things, Syed Alwi said, were done to
other people.

Then the family took him to bomohs, one after the other; and again
there were tests and treatments. A bomoh would look into a bowl of
water and see why the man before him had become what he was; he
would see heredity, or ghosts, or upbringing.

Once Syed Alwi's father and uncle sat side by side in front of a
bomoh. Incense was smoking away and filling the room – Syed Alwi
had the story from his uncle – and at last the bomoh said that there was
someone trying to destroy Syed Alwi's father. This wicked person had
buried evil things around the house, and for Syed Alwi's father to break
out of his spell, those things had to be removed. The bomoh said that
was what he was going to do, right then, and sitting right there, in his
room. He began to go through his bomoh's act, making big, mystical
gestures in the incense smoke, and talking all the time, explaining what
he was doing. The smoke wasn't thick enough, though. Syed Alwi's
uncle saw the bomoh take a little packet from below his knee, something wrapped in yellow cloth, and throw it to one side. The bomoh
then said, 'The man is now cured.' And, in spite of what his uncle had
seen, money was paid.

There were other cures like that. The family went to bomohs for
years. Then they ceased to hope for a cure, and they let the invalid be.

At one time he ran away from the house. Again there was no date;
people didn't want to talk about this episode too much. He went to the

state of Kelantan, and there he had a breakdown within his breakdown. When the family went to bring him back, they found that he
had been translating the Koran, from English into Malay. They burned
what he had written.

Syed Alwi said, 'The translation is important, because it shows that
even in the other world he was still trying to find God. But I am not
sure whether this translation was done in the other world, in this world,
or in both. He accepted the burning as a natural thing to have happened, because it was in accordance with their beliefs. As he accepted
the way of life of the *kampung*.'

So all the writing of his father, from the time before he was born,
was lost to Syed Alwi. Many years later he saw some of his father's exercise books.

'The handwriting was bad. I couldn't read it very well. Hardly at all.
But practically at the end of every other sentence was the word
"always".'

For Syed Alwi it would have been a haunting word.

There were lucid periods. In one of those, some time before 1930, he
began to build a new house in the *kampung*, but the money ran out and
he couldn't put up the first floor. Syed Alwi, telling the story in his own
unfinished house, between the snake holes in the hillside cutting on one
side and the little stream on the other side, said, 'So when this thing
happened to me in my house, the image of my father's unfinished
house came to my mind.'

When Syed Alwi's father broke down in 1922 there were three children. After that six more children were born, and there were six
miscarriages. Out of the six born, two were stillborn.

Syed Alwi said, 'So my mother had fifteen conceptions.'

Twelve of those were after the breakdown.

I said, 'It sounds murderous.' It was the word that came.

He looked very worried. He said then, with melancholy, 'I don't
know.' Tears came to his eyes.

His father wanted his children to be educated. He had only his pension, but there was an Indian woman in the *kampung* who helped. She
had a great regard for the family, and she loved the children. She had a
certain amount of jewellery in solid gold, and whenever money was
needed for the children's education or for their books she lent all her

jewellery to Syed Alwi's father for him to pawn. She lent her jewellery in this way only for the education of the children. When one of the sons came back from Singapore in the uniform of Raffles College, a famous colonial college, she was as proud of him as if he were her own son. Her own son – she had only one – worked as a labourer on the railway.

She was a Tamil. She was not rich. Apart from her jewellery she had nothing. She made a living preparing small snacks and savouries for the government-run toddy shop in the *kampung*. Her father would have come from South India to work as a contract labourer on the estates. Her husband would also have been a labourer on an estate. When he died, she left the estate and the estate life and struck out on her own. She came to the *kampung* and built a house not far from the Alwis' house.

This woman became Syed Alwi's fairy godmother when he began to go to the Malay primary school in 1936. He remembered her as a woman in her late thirties, wiry, not kindly-looking, off-putting but not ugly. Every morning on his way to school he stopped at her house. She had a jug of hot milk waiting for him on her earthen fireplace. Milk was seldom drunk in the Alwi house. Malays didn't drink milk; they used condensed milk in coffee, but that was all. The milk used in cakes and curries and meat was always coconut milk, made from the white kernel of the ripe nut.

In 1940, after four years at the Malay primary school, where they mainly studied geography and literature, Syed Alwi and an elder brother were sent to the King Edward VII secondary school in the town of Taiping. Syed Alwi's father, at great sacrifice, and again with the help of the Indian woman, rented a house there for his sons. Syed Alwi understood later that his father, through all his darkness, was educating him to be a high civil servant, as he himself had once been.

Everyone in the *kampung* knew about the condition of the father; and people knew about it at the school in Taiping as well. There was no stigma. In fact, there was a little awe. Malays felt that great minds cracked when they were over-extended; and Syed Alwi's father, known to have been quite brilliant when very young, was considered such a great mind. There was a word in Malay for that kind of crack-up: *gila-isin*, becoming mad through over-application, studying too hard, believing too hard.

Syed Alwi said, 'My father was considered *gila-isin* because he was pursuing God or something like that. Though the idea of pursuing God was something that only some relatives knew. It was not spread out, just in case people might misinterpret it, and think that this *gila-isin* was a kind of punishment.'

In 1941 Syed Alwi's brother ran away and joined the Royal Navy in Singapore. He was a *kampung* boy, really; he liked the *kampung* life, the *kampung* fellowship. He liked going out to work in the rice-fields with relatives. He didn't like being at the college in Taiping; that was his father's idea. So – with the help of people in the *kampung*: there was a kind of *kampung* conspiracy – he ran away to Singapore and said he was older than he was and joined the Royal Navy. Syed Alwi's father, apart from wanting his son to finish his secondary education, was a pacifist; he hated the idea of pain and killing. He went to see the British Resident in Perak; and in the end, after a lot of trouble, he paid seventy-five dollars, a month's pension, to buy his son out of the navy. Just then the war started. On 7 December 1941 the Japanese bombed the Singapore naval base, and no one in the family ever got to know what happened to that brother.

Syed Alwi said, 'The Japanese came at the end of December 1941. In January I was thinking of going back to school. It was the end of the school holiday. But then I was told there was no English school any more.'

There was also a rumour that the Japanese would punish people who had English books in their houses. There were many English books in the Alwi house, brought back by the two boys who had studied at Raffles College in Singapore. Nearly all these books were destroyed. Some were buried; some were burnt, as Syed Alwi's father's writings were burnt. The one important book that was kept back was a dictionary. Syed Alwi was hoping one day to read his father's writings, and he thought he would need the dictionary to help with the big words. That day did come; but he couldn't decipher the writing in his father's exercise books. He could only make out the word 'always'.

The British had blown up a road bridge outside the *kampung*, and the Japanese spent some weeks putting up a new bridge. So Japanese soldiers were about, foraging. One afternoon a Japanese soldier came with a drawn sword to the Alwi house. The children ran away. The father stayed, and after half an hour he began shouting to them to come back. When they went to the house they saw the Japanese soldier leaving with a chicken and a pineapple. Nobody knew what had passed between the two men, and the father never said.

Syed Alwi said, 'He was not afraid. He was not a brave man, but he wasn't afraid.'

The Japanese were in Malaysia for three years and eight months. Until they came, Syed Alwi had not seen violent death. Now, near the market in Taiping, where his old English-language school was, he would see staked heads. He was told that they were the heads of Chinese people.

Syed Alwi said, 'After the first year things became bad. Food became very short – the basic necessities, rice, sugar. The life in the *kampung* began to go very bad when disease became rampant. We didn't have much nourishment. So you got ulcers, skin diseases. We had lost our knowledge of local herbs. We had grown used to hospitals and Western medicine. We couldn't cope with the breakdown of society.

'Besides, the Japanese had promised that everything was going to be all right, and that there would be abundance of everything. They specifically mentioned that a lot of rice would be coming, because in Japan they grew a lot of rice. Whenever they took anything from us they would say it would be repaid many times over. They would say, "I take your bicycle now. I will repay it with five bicycles or more." And they would add, "Not only bicycles, but other things as well." They mentioned silk. And for months and months the community waited. The Japanese kept that promise alive by circulating rumours that shipments of rice had arrived and people in certain *kampungs* had already received theirs.

'At the beginning of newsreels, in the mobile cinemas and the theatres, they would say in Japanese, Malay, and English, 'Thank God Asia has been given back to Asians.' What followed were images of the greatness of Japan: bundles and bundles of silk and other luxury goods. This had an effect. The first Hari Raya – the festival after the fasting month – we were talking about how everybody would be dressed in Japanese silk.'

But things just went from bad to worse. At about this time Syed Alwi's uncle died. He was the uncle who had figured in many of Syed Alwi's stories about his father. He was the uncle who used to go with Syed Alwi's father to get his pension; he sat with him before bomohs, in the days when they went to bomohs. Syed Alwi was full of grief. He and his father were chopping wood one day. With all the grief, it was a precious moment of companionship; Syed Alwi remembered it. He talked about the uncle, and his father said, 'Your uncle didn't die.'

Syed Alwi said, 'What do you mean?'

His father said, 'Later you will understand what I mean.'

The words made an impression on Syed Alwi. He thought he should talk more to his father about what he had said. But he didn't; the occasion never came again, the moment of companionship. Because his father then entered his other world and stayed there for almost three years, until the end of the war. When he came out of the other world it was only to die.

It was Syed Alwi's idea that this going into the other world had always been deliberate or willed, a form of cutting out. And in the normal world, or the outer world, things had now broken down.

Syed Alwi said, 'A new way of life, a decayed way of life, began to develop. Right and wrong began to be decided not by any moral or religious or spiritual standard, but by what was good for the self and survival. If moral values were applied you couldn't survive. What was normal life then? Pain and suffering and starvation and deprivation and disease. If those were things of normal life, why should morality be the deciding factor? What was of value would be what could alleviate your pain. Or what you could find to keep yourself some self-esteem. What was normal was that you saw Japanese soldiers beating up people. You saw people being snatched in all kinds of ways. You saw people being destroyed by torture, or escaping torture or worse by jumping in the river.'

Young men – of all races, Malay, Chinese, Indian – abused young girls, and never felt they were behaving abnormally.

'I always think of this beautiful Indian woman, probably in her twenties or early thirties. She was from another estate, where her husband was a tapper. He had disappeared, and she was looking for him, going from estate to estate. She passed through my *kampung*. There were a number of young people doing hardly anything, being just there, and they saw this woman and they looked at one another, and I knew – I was with them – that they were going to have fun with her.

'They followed her some distance beyond the shopping area, and they raped her. When it was supposed to be my turn, they said no – I was under age. I was then about twelve. So there was still some kind of morality. There were two of us who were considered under age. If not for this, some kind of morality, I would have been one of the rapists.

'And then they left her, and she continued her journey. We saw her again as she passed through the village centre again, on her way to another *kampung*. She looked none the worse for wear. Maybe she had been raped before. It was something that had happened. It didn't stop her searching for her husband. For the young men it was just another activity. They never mentioned the girl again. Yes. They mentioned how beautiful she was.'

It was during this time that Syed Alwi, in his own eyes, became a man. He began to work, and was at last able to help with the upkeep of the family.

The Japanese set up a charcoal factory. They came to the *kampung* and announced that they wanted people; and Syed Alwi, in his fourteenth year, became one of the workers. The factory was two and a half miles away, a longish walk morning and afternoon through a rubber estate and jungle. He was paid eight dollars and a tin of rice a day; the big attraction was the rice. Later, cigarettes were also given. The job was easy, to see that cracks in the kiln were patched up. He did it for a year or so.

There was double pay for heavier work: breaking open the kiln door when the charcoal was ready, and pulling out the charcoal. Syed Alwi tried it once. The heat was scarcely to be borne, and the hot charcoal dust got into his lungs. When he went to bathe he coughed up black phlegm. He kept on coughing black, and that so frightened him he never did that job again.

Late in 1944 he became a junior lumberjack for the charcoal factory. It paid more: twenty dollars a day, a bigger tin of rice, cigarettes. The cigarettes were usually local, and quite ordinary; but sometimes now there were Japanese cigarettes – he still remembered the brand name: it was 'Koa' – which were much nicer.

Cigarettes were important, because in the other world, where he was, his father was a smoker. There was a kind of country or *kampung* cigarette with a wrapper made from the nipah palm leaf; but Syed Alwi's father wanted none of those. He insisted on 'real cigarettes', and when they had none to give him, he became angry and violent, not hitting anyone, just knocking things about.

But he was now fading. There was little food to give him; and he was bedridden. He seemed gradually to understand that there had been a calamity outside, and that cigarettes were scarce. And, anyway, he was weak; he would manage only one cigarette a day. There was no shortage of exercise books, but he was writing less and less. In the last six months of his life he hardly wrote. But – and it was like a remnant of his writing passion – he became very particular about his pencils. He had used them down to the stump, but he never threw them away, and he didn't want anyone to touch them.

One day, when Syed Alwi and the lumberjack gang had gone to the jungle to cut wood for the charcoal factory, they found – about a mile and a half in from the road – an unexpected clearing: a rice-field, five or six acres.

It was in this way that Syed Alwi got to know about the communists – mainly Chinese – of the Malayan People's Anti-Japanese Army, the MPAJA. The rice-field was theirs; and the *kampung* was to some extent already under their protection.

The men didn't want to drag the logs through the rice-field. But the boss of the gang – not a Japanese: there were no Japanese bosses in the *kampung* – had to do his job. Syed Alwi remembered him saying, 'Go on, drag the logs through the rice.' Some of the men said, 'But it's sinful to destroy rice.' And Syed Alwi understood that some of the lumberjacks would have known the people in the *kampung* who were looking after the rice-field.

So, as a man, earning money and entering the world, he became aware of things in the *kampung* that had so far been hidden from him. He even had a kind of explanation for the staked Chinese heads near the market in Taiping.

The work was hard; he had little food; there were no medicines. He had fourteen ulcers. And then one day a log fell on his ankle. The scratch didn't heal; it developed into a big ulcer. It hurt him night and day. It was hard for him to sleep. He would shake the ulcerous leg to deaden the pain, and then he might sleep for an hour or so. From time to time he drained the ulcer, collecting about half a cupful of pus. The flesh was rotting away inside; after he drained the ulcer his calf was slack. He walked or hobbled on one foot.

Other people in the *kampung* were worse off. A woman in her forties had ulcers all over her body. These ulcers spread, and her body became one big ulcer. Worms, maggots and flies lived in her flesh. The smell – even from yards away, even from outside her house – was very bad. In the last weeks of her life she was a mass of rotting blood. She wailed and shrieked. There was no painkiller. People wouldn't go near her. She was abandoned. This added to her pain and gave a special quality to her cries.

A few days after the Japanese surrender – some food had already begun to come to the *kampung* from outside – Syed Alwi's father came out of his other world. He had been there for nearly three years. In the family they knew he had come out of the other world because he had stopped talking to himself and was no longer asking for cigarettes. He had been bedridden for a long time. Now he was badly undernourished, and weak and ill.

He wanted to see outside. Syed Alwi and his mother together helped him up and brought him near a window. He looked for a couple of minutes and didn't say anything. Then – Syed Alwi hobbling on his good leg – they took him back to his bed.

The world he had looked out at was a little more decayed than it had been during the Japanese time. In the two weeks between the Japanese surrender and the arrival of British troops, the communist MPAJA ruled. They had many scores to settle and they were going about punishing people, betrayers, deserters, collaborators.

The real world had fallen to pieces, but Syed Alwi and his mother were glad that the father had come out of his other world. He had never been so long there; and Syed Alwi, and his mother, felt that he might have had enough of that world and wouldn't want to go back there; and that now, with food and medicine, he might become well again. Syed Alwi was hoping – as an adult now – to talk to his father about his writing; to ask him what he had meant three years before when they were chopping wood together and he had said that there was no such thing as death; and to find out about the world he used to go to.

None of this was to be. About a week after they had taken him to the window he died. It was as if, at the very end, he hadn't wanted to die alone in the other world.

Syed Alwi said of his mother, once the thirteen-year-old bride of the seventeen-year-old settlement officer, 'She was the community. From her Malay upbringing, her Islamic upbringing, she provided him with the support that enabled him to have his two worlds. Without her he would have been thrown into the madhouse' – the place of water-hoses and rice mixed with sand – 'and he wouldn't have lasted two years. As it was, he lived in his two worlds for twenty-three years.'

July 1995–May 1997

Acknowledgements

In Indonesia: John H. McGlynn; Navrekha Sharma; Eugene Galbraith. In Pakistan: Ahmed Rashid. In Malaysia: Karim Raslan.